EXPERIENCING
WORLD HISTORY

EXPERIENCING
WORLD HISTORY

·

Paul V. Adams, Erick D. Langer, Lily Hwa,
Peter N. Stearns, and Merry E. Wiesner-Hanks

NEW YORK UNIVERSITY PRESS
NEW YORK AND LONDON

NEW YORK UNIVERSITY PRESS
New York and London

Library of Congress Cataloging-in-Publication Data
Experiencing world history / Paul V. Adams . . . [et al.].
p.   cm.
Includes bibliographical references and index.
ISBN 0-8147-0690-8 (alk. paper) — ISBN 0-8147-0691-6
(pbk. : alk. paper)
1. World history.   I. Adams, Paul Vauthier.
D20 .E975 2000   00-008518

New York University Press books are printed on acid-free paper,
and their binding materials are chosen for strength and durability.

Manufactured in the United States of America

10 9 8 7 6 5 4 3 2 1

CONTENTS

PREFACE

This book offers a distinctive approach to aspects of world history, focusing on how ordinary people experienced some of the big changes that resulted from the formation and evolution of civilizations and from larger global processes such as the spread of agriculture and the rise of missionary religions. A number of excellent world history textbooks already exist. Each has its own flavor, but it is fair to say that most cover some fairly standard territory. This book attends to that standard territory—it briefly sums up conventional developments and can certainly be used in conjunction with other treatments—but concentrates primarily on a different domain, the domain of social history on a world scale. How people worked and played, how they reacted to the physical and biological environment, how they organized relations between men and women—this is the stuff of the treatment that follows. The result brings world history to a different level, combining a sense of some of the big shifts in global framework with an interest in the ways in which people lived.

This is a genuine world history in the sense of focusing on a global geography and a wide range of societies. It uses a familiar chronological framework, highlighting periods such as the classical age or the centuries of industrialization and imperialism. As world history with a difference, however, it joins with the other new discovery field in history—the field that has opened new understandings of issues such as male-female relationships and the role of sports in leisure or as an expression of popular cultural values. This is an area that has been hard to fit into world history previously because of a predominant focus on leading political systems, wars, and formal intellectual life. Bringing this area front and center inevitably recasts the way in which even standard world history features, such as the role of governments, can be understood.

The authors thank a number of individuals who have helped the book along. Craig Lockard offered a useful critical reading of an earlier draft.

The staff at New York University Press and its editor, Niko Pfund, provided vital encouragement and a host of practical supports. Joanne Ursenbach assisted with manuscript preparation. Each author wishes also to thank her or his students in world history courses, who have provided guidance and (usually) enthusiasm as some of the newer approaches to world history have been worked out.

CHAPTER 1

SEEING WORLD HISTORY AS HUMAN EXPERIENCE

How did the major passages in world history affect the experiences by which most people—the privileged and the ordinary alike—measure their lives? What did European contact with the Americas or the rise of Islam mean for men and women in distant areas, many of whom would never see an ocean or hear a muezzin's call to prayer but would nevertheless be touched by these new forces? This book presents the framework of world history in terms of its impact on key facets of social behavior—the patterns of birth and death, the basic value systems by which people explain the world around them, relationships with government, interactions between men and women, and how people work and play. This focus captures two of the most exciting expansions of knowledge about the past in recent decades: the opening of world history itself and the rise of a social history aimed at exploring a range of behaviors and beliefs on the part of people at all levels of society.

Introducing World History

World history has gained ground for two basic reasons. First, we live in an increasingly interconnected world, in which knowledge about the ways in which other major societies have developed and about the evolution of international processes becomes increasingly vital simply to situate ourselves. Purely national history or even the history of a broader Western tradition is no longer sufficient. Second, improvements in available knowledge about other societies and about the rise of patterns such as international trade, cultural linkages, and even the spread of diseases make it possible to tell the world story.

The story is immense, and every world history account must be highly selective in what it emphasizes. World historians agree, however, on a number of points that help make the task manageable. They emphasize the importance of human origins and early patterns of culture and migration, but they cover this framework usually in fairly sweeping terms. The first great change in the economic structure of the human species—the development of agriculture—provides an early landmark, followed by the establishment of civilization as a form of human organization. While groups that lived in different kinds of communities require attention, world history increasingly focuses on the nature of the most populous civilizations and the ways in which they interacted.

In exploring world history and its main chronological periods, historians are pursuing three overlapping stories. The first story involves the gradual development of some similar human patterns, as people come to terms with changing environments. Every society, for example, has a language; every society has some kind of family structure to help organize reproduction and the raising of children. Every civilization has some kind of government. Every government, at some point, develops the idea of providing specific training for its officials and administering tests to try to make sure that talented officials are selected; when this happens varies greatly—China began the process over two thousand years ago, for example, whereas Western societies introduced their system over the past four centuries. But, despite differences in timing, there are many common features to the human record, and these must be conveyed.

The second story involves the particular ways in which major civilizations developed, the special twists they put on basic institutions of government, beliefs systems, social structures, even family arrangements. Because of distinctive environments and historical experiences, every civilization (indeed, every society, whether civilization or not) is unique in some ways, and the patterns of the largest societies, at least, must be conveyed. World historians acknowledge that they must omit detailed consideration of many interesting societies in order to focus on a manageable number. But they insist on the importance of civilizations as they emerged in every major inhabited area—various sites in Asia, Africa, Europe, and the Americas. They work on defining what the special flavor of each major civilization was, how it compared to the features of its counterparts elsewhere, and how it changed over time.

The third story focuses on the ways in which different societies interacted with each other, through trade, migration, cultural diffusion, deliberate imitation, war, or explicit aversion. Certain kinds of interaction began very early in world history. Gradual contacts help explain, for example, how agriculture spread, for it was newly invented only in a few places around the world. Interactions have helped shape the first story—that of similar human patterns—by letting societies know what other societies had already developed. They have modified the second story by forcing distinctive values and institutions to adapt to the results of contact and outside pressure. Obviously, the third story becomes steadily more important as world history moves from past toward present, for the intensity of contacts has, on the whole, accelerated.

Social History

This book, dealing with all three of the story lines in world history, in all the major chronological periods, focuses particularly on key facets of the human experience. After sketching the leading features of world history in terms of the development of the major civilizations and key changes in global connections in each basic chronological period, it turns to fundamental biological experiences of the human species, including population trends and movements, foods and diseases; to patterns of belief and expression; to the organization and functions of governments; to men and women in their roles and cultural definitions; and to systems of work and leisure. These five categories have been central in the efforts of social historians over the past generation to gain a better understanding of what human life was like in the past, how and why it has changed, and how it has led to the patterns of today. Social historians have not been content with a focus on the doings of major political and military leaders or intellectuals and artists, though they incorporate the impact of these people on broader societies. They want to know how the key processes of social life—the same processes people participate in today—have evolved over time. This means paying attention to the ways in which ordinary people have been affected by the ideas of intellectuals or by the institutions that kings and generals have created but also attending to how ordinary people have contributed directly to the shape of their societies.

This book paints this social history canvas on a world scale, by looking at five major categories of human activity in terms of the key world history periods and in light of the three overlapping stories of which world history is composed. Having introduced the components of world history, we turn to a similar introduction of the five facets of society that this book explores.

Introducing History at the Biological Level

For nearly all of human existence, through countless millennia, biological and environmental realities determined the limits of thought and action. Over vast stretches of time, human biology and how humans interacted with their environment changed profoundly. Those realities and how they changed constitute the biological foundations of history.

Conventional narrative history first took shape in the latter half of the 19th century, before the full development of modern science. It customarily began with the rise of the great civilizations in Mesopotamia and Egypt and was chiefly interested in religious and political institutions, as revealed in written records or artistic and architectural monuments. Today our understanding of history is quite different. Recent dramatic advances in the sciences of paleoanthropology and prehistoric archaeology have extended the chronological range of history by hundreds of thousands of years. Archaeology also has extended the geographic range to cultures and peoples who, although they lived in the era of civilization (i.e., post–3500 B.C.E.), left hardly a trace in written records but nonetheless affected the development of world societies.

By vastly extending their scope, historians have come to understand the critical importance of the biological foundations. At first, conventional narrative history could not accommodate the new scientific information on human developments before the first civilizations, consigning it instead to "prehistory," that is, not history, not the proper subject of genuine historians. It lumped together all of life before civilization into an amorphous "early man" or "before civilization," thereby neglecting several hundred thousand years of human growth. Crucial changes that occurred in this time frame were the biological development of humans, including evolution of modern intelligence; advances in the technologies of hunting-gathering or foraging societies, then in agricultural technologies and societies; and the massive colonization and populating of the entire habitable earth. Without these dramatic changes, the development of civilization would have been quite impossible.

The long-term trends in population growth describe patterns of population growth observed also in insect and animal populations. The logic goes like this: Species ensure their survival by having strong capacities to reproduce their kind. In mammalian species, this means a strong urge to sexuality and a strong desire to live. The former promotes births; the latter avoids deaths. Species who succeed at these instinctive goals have birth rates substantially higher than death rates and therefore experience population growth. In a sense, population is like a coiled spring: As pressure on it is reduced, it uncoils or expands. The pressure holding down population growth is imposed by the environment, not the species itself. One set of limits includes supplies of food, water, and a suitable temperature range. While these are adequate, a species will reproduce endlessly. Another set of limits is set by parasitic macro- and microorganisms, that is, those species for whom other species are food. Macroparasites are the large predatory creatures, which for humans and herbivorous vertebrates would include lions, tigers, some bears, killer whales, and the like. Microparasites would include the tiny creatures—fleas, lice, ticks, intestinal worms, mosquitoes, and such—as well as invisible ones such as amoebas, bacteria, and viruses. Parasites cannot themselves survive if they so rapidly consume their prey or hosts as to exterminate them, in effect wiping out their food supply. So species are linked together in webs of interdependence that keep one another's populations in rough equilibrium. A pattern of rapid population growth therefore occurs only in situations where food and water are abundant and parasitic organisms scarce, typically situations in which a species is introduced into a new environment, a kind of colonial frontier.

For the human species, the world beyond its original home in South and East Africa was a vast frontier into which it expanded and multiplied over thousands of years. But humans also changed their behavior. They developed technology and cooperative social systems to coax more of what they needed from the environment, first by more effective hunting and gathering, then by more systematic environmental management, namely, agriculture, to encourage production of the things humans wanted and to discourage production of those things they did not. Humans uprooted weeds, cleared away forests, and drove away or exterminated predatory animals. Microorganisms proved more intractable, but eventually, through their immunological systems, by behavioral changes, and, only in the last century and a half, through the development of medical science, humans overcame nearly all the major diseases.

A general picture of rapid growth trends conceals how the population changed in composition and geographic distribution, and how behavior changed, too. These changes might be imagined as three great population waves that preceded civilization and set it afloat. The first wave, beginning about 1.7 million years ago, saw protohumans expand across all of Africa and Eurasia in the warmer latitudes below 50 degrees north. The second wave represents anatomically modern humans, or *homo sapiens sapiens*, evolving out of and replacing all other human species, then expanding to the as-yet-uninhabited continents of the Americas and Australia. Wave three represents agricultural societies (all humans now, all others extinct) replacing hunting and gathering societies. With each wave, populations increased dramatically and societies became more complex.

Introducing Cultural Analysis

A society's culture involves its basic beliefs and values and the styles and methods it uses to express those beliefs and values. Complex societies may have several cultures in operation, though usually there is some effort to clarify what culture is officially most approved. But subcultures, held by particular regions, social classes, or racial groups, can be very powerful as well, and this means that in addition to asking about the culture of a major society, it is necessary to investigate its cohesion. Many conservatives in the United States at the end of the 20th century and beginning of the 21st believe that mainstream culture is being undermined by too many separate cultural systems, and that the United States must reemphasize a dominant set of values if it is to hold together as a society.

Studying culture historically involves defining what a society's basic beliefs are and whether or not it has strong competing subcultures (degree of cohesion). To determine distinctive features, cultures of two or more societies must be compared. The extent and causes of cultural change over time, as well as efforts to preserve cultural traditions, must be probed. How cultures relate to innate human features and what kinds of different behaviors and institutions different cultures cause *(cultural construction)* round out the basic analytical targets.

Human beings are unique in having elaborate cultures. People have fewer instincts at birth than do most other animals, which is one of the reasons it takes so long to learn enough to be counted as an adult. Absent instinct, education—whether formal or informal—must do the job of teaching people what nature is all about, how to deal with knowledge of death, how to define family relationships, how to define appropriate economic behavior, even what is beautiful. Of course, not everything is culture rather than instinct. For instance, while different societies have quite different ideas about how disgusting human feces is, none has ever claimed it should be touted as an object of beauty; humans thus demonstrate some instinctive aversion. Instinct, including in this case a sense of smell, constrains culture. Nevertheless, much of what any society values is a product of the culture it has developed, not some inevitable result of human nature.

Culture also has unique human features because of the capacity of the species to transmit information. Knowledge does not have to be entirely reinvented in each generation. The power of language, developed during the hunting-and-gathering phase of human history, is that it allows culture to be defined, expressed, and passed on. Specific features of culture are, indeed, intimately related to language, for the values available to a society depend on the words that can express them and vice versa. Most people through history have depended on oral transmission of cultures, and illiterate groups have extraordinarily powerful memories for stories and other information passed by word of mouth. Writing further enhances the ability to store and disseminate culture across the generations.

While societies use culture to deal with many of the same issues—for instance, what nature is all about, what makes governments legitimate or not—each society has its own culture. This reflects the extent to which societies developed key ideas and styles in isolation, during the early phases of human history when contact among regions was limited. Many anthropologists see culture as the means by which groups of humans adapt to their environment, and since environments vary, cultures must too. Cultural values of desert peoples obviously differ from those of groups depending heavily on fishing, and so on. Each group will have distinctive views of nature and work but also distinctive attitudes about family relationships or about fate and accident. Cultural diversity, in other words, initially results from different kinds of specific problems that different human groups had to address, in addition to the fact that cultural systems often were set up separately and so, by sheer accident, might decide on distinctive emphases. This is why comparison is so important in understanding cultural dynamics.

Diversity also expresses yet another function of culture: to provide identity and define membership in a given group and to allow the group to label outsiders, partly because they lack the common culture. Cultures can be profoundly divisive, as the daily headlines regularly demonstrate.

Yet culture is important for more than group identity. Nor does culture simply set the basis for formal movements in art, literature, and philosophy. Culture causes a wide range of human and group behaviors, even key emotions. (This causation is what cultural construction is all about.) In 1870, in the United States, members of the middle class were imbued with a culture that highly valued grief. Signs of grief were abundant on the death of a family member, from black-draped houses to the coffins and mourning paraphernalia that girls could buy for their dolls. Just fifty years later the culture of grief had changed, with people told that excessive grief was annoying to others and, probably, a sign of mental illness. Mourning was cut back, and people who did still feel serious grief groped for new mechanisms to handle the emotion. Grief, in other words, was reconstructed. The new emotional culture really counted in shaping human lives. By the same token, cultural differences show up in constructing different behaviors. Chinese culture was long suspicious of merchants, believing that making money was crass and unsuitable to the life of a gentleman. Middle Eastern culture, in contrast, valued merchants, particularly under the religion of Islam. With this difference, it was small wonder that Islamic governments encouraged trade more than their Chinese counterparts, or that China at key points cut off commercial initiatives that threatened to give merchants a greater role.

An obvious cultural variable, of great importance in world history, is the reaction to other value systems when cultural contact occurs. No culture is so porous or tolerant that all features of another set of beliefs and artistic styles are embraced with full enthusiasm; almost always, people seek to retain some of their previous culture, if only because it was so deeply ingrained in their own childhoods. But some cultures encourage a certain amount of imitation, whereas others emphasize proud isolation. Noncultural factors may force culture contact even on reluctant societies; wars, trade that cannot be resisted, or, more recently, ubiquitous technologies such as satellite transmissions and E-mail may require adjustment. Yet possible patterns of interaction are numerous and varied, and much of the stuff of world history involves looking at how societies deal with new cultural opportunities—whether they seek them, adjust if compelled, or actively resist. Is the culture of the contemporary United States particularly open to influences from other societies? Has effective tolerance increased or decreased during the past hundred years?

Introducing the State in Society

Human beings, said the Greek philosopher Aristotle, are political animals. Most humans have always lived in groups, and living together involves needs for defining relationships, regulating interactions, and maintaining order. Through leadership or joint decision making, people have to figure out what the rules are, how to make choices for the group, and how to preserve and defend the shared community. While these vital activities are part of human history at all times, as far as we know they do not necessarily involve a formal state, defined as an institution with some specialized leadership and assigned powers. Hunting-and-gathering groups and many agricultural societies have been stateless.

Civilizations, however, have states, and many historians argue that the advent of states is one of the watersheds of the human experience. The rise of states reflected growing complexity, as people needed more formal institutions to define property, protect against outside attack, and provide some economic policies. It also reflected growing prosperity in communities with enough surplus to afford formal rulers (often living in considerable luxury) and officials, including some paid military groups. With states, new divisions separated those who had some direct voice in policies from those who did not; states involved more elaborate definitions of power relationships.

A great deal of history has always been about states and politics. Rulers early on found that they enjoyed accounts of their glories and those of their ancestors, so much early history involved chronicles of the great deeds of kings. More recently, the growing power of nation-states encouraged history lessons to focus on the development of the nation and its political institutions, seen as the central point of human activity and providing examples of loyalty and good citizenship.

The rise of social history has de-emphasized the state to some extent. Political rulers and institutions are now seen as one of several factors that shape the way a society operates and as products as well as guides of basic social change. The power and impact of states vary. States' policies clearly affect the course of civilizations, but the crucial point is to analyze how states function, what kinds of actual contacts they have with other facets of society and with key social groups, from elites to ordinary people. This approach, emphasizing political developments as interactions, looks at states in the context of societies.

The state-and-society approach is complicated for any period in world history since the advent of civilization by the fact that states almost always claim far more power and authority than they actually have. This may be particularly true in early states, when rulers claimed to be gods or directly inspired by gods and spoke as if their policies and laws would be automatically carried out throughout their realms. But it applies in some ways to modern states as well. Modern states may prohibit crime, but they have varying success in fact. Some may try to regulate birth rates and family life, but they do not necessarily have much influence; governments in Europe and the United States, for example, hoped during the later 19th century to encourage population growth, in order to spur the economy and provide soldiers, exactly at the point when ordinary people were deciding to have fewer children. The state assertions of power are an important part of history, but they must be evaluated and not merely chronicled. Different societies develop different beliefs about what states can and cannot do, about what constitutes legitimate uses of power and what does not. Looking at the impact of the state on society requires particular attention to government *functions* and their effectiveness, and not just to formal structures such as monarchies or democracies.

States vary from one another for a number of reasons. Technology and economic levels provide crucial contexts in which to evaluate states. The effective power of states, particularly those that rule over sizable regions, depends heavily on available communication and transportation technologies. Record keeping is another crucial technology, which is why the Chinese invention of paper so interestingly reflected and furthered an unusually bureaucratic state tradition. Economic performance sets resource constraints and opportunities. Both technologies and economies characteristically differ from one society to the next—in the past and still today—which is one key reason that state impact on ordinary people varies so much.

States vary also because of different cultural values. While all states seek to preserve order, if only to protect their own existence, some cultures emphasize order more than others and define order more rigorously. Certain value systems argue that devotion to political life and governance is the highest human good, whereas others contend that, though states may be necessary, religious goals should come first, even limiting the degree of allegiance owed to rules and rulers in this world.

The same factors that cause states to vary from one civilization to the next also cause change. It is important to balance the momentum of certain political traditions with the recurrent possibility of major shifts. New ideas, technologies, and resources have helped states grow in most civilizations in the modern world, causing new tensions between state activity and private organizations or individual rights. While some disputes continue, preferred political structures have tended to move away from monarchies toward alternative forms and have tended to downplay explicit religious functions in favor either of greater tolerance or of different kinds of cultural control. Most states have also downplayed emphasis on control by a traditional privileged class, installing at least superficial mass participation. But some common directions of change have not created uniformities, and comparison of differences and the reasons for them remains essential. The Chinese state, for example, still assumes it has certain powers over individuals that the American and Indian states do not.

Introducing Gender History

The vast majority of human beings are born with external genitalia that cause them to be quickly labeled "male" or "female" at birth, assigned to one of two sexes. Most of the world's cultures have added enormous numbers of other distinctions to these physical sex differences, such as distinctions in dress, in educational opportunities, in types of work performed, and in political and familial roles, creating great differences between what it means to be a man and what it means to be a woman. These cultural distinctions based on initial sex assignment are now labeled "gender," and they are widely variable across time and space, although no culture, past or present, has yet been discovered that made no distinction between the roles of women and those of men.

Most people may be accurately assigned to one sex or the other, so most of the world's cultures conceptualize two genders, men and women, either as two ends of a continuum or as two distinct groups. This conceptualization is so strong that infants born with ambiguous external genitalia—a condition known as *hermaphroditism*, which happens occasionally—or with chromosomes that differ from the most common patterns are usually simply assigned to one sex or the other, sometimes with surgical procedures performed to reinforce this assignment. There are also individuals whose physical characteristics mark them as one sex but who mentally regard themselves as the other or choose to live and dress as the other. In the 20th century, some of these individuals choose to undergo sex-change operations and become *transsexuals*, though in earlier centuries this was not possible, and we have very little record of what might have happened to them, other than occasional legends and folk songs about women who did heroic deeds while dressed as men.

The situation of individuals such as hermaphrodites and transsexuals indicates that gender identity and physical characteristics may be at odds and that, in fact, cultural structures may be more important than biological differences in determining whether individuals regard themselves or are regarded as men or as women. The preeminence of culture is very clear in certain areas of the world—including Alaska, the Amazon region, North America, Australia, Siberia, Central and South Asia, Oceania, and the Sudan—where some individuals who were originally viewed as male or female assumed the gender identity of the other sex, altering their clothing, work, and ritual activities. In some cultures, such individuals were regarded as a third sex and treated differently than either men or women. Gender is further complicated by the issue of sexuality, for persons of either sex may be sexually attracted to persons of the other sex, persons of their own, or both. Just as there is great variation in gender structures, there is also great cultural variety in how sexual attraction and sexual activity have been viewed and shaped and in how gender and sexuality have interrelated.

Despite the complications in gender systems created by people who are physically or culturally neither clearly male nor clearly female or by ambiguities created by the interaction of gender and sexuality, the two-gender system is the most common among the world's cultures. Its dichotomous, or dualistic, nature has caused it to be often identified with other cultural dichotomies, such as nature/culture, body/spirit, public/private, and sometimes with physical dichotomies, such as sun/moon, light/dark, wet/dry. The strength of these identifications then plays back on the gender structure, leading what are culturally created differences to be labeled "natural" or "divinely created." This may be one of the reasons that gender structures are often the slowest to change in any culture; political systems may be overthrown in a revolution, but what men and women do remains the same.

Gender structures are also related to other social inequalities. In most of the world's societies, one group of people has asserted that it is somehow better than the rest of the population and so has the right to political authority and economic power; for many of the world's cultures, until very recently, this group was a hereditary aristocracy. No matter what the source of the original distinction between this group and everyone else—military might, religious authority, intellectual interests—this distinction has to be maintained through a regulation of sexual behavior. If there were no regulation of sexual behavior, the dominant group would mix with everyone else, and there would be no basis for its claim to superiority. Thus all hierarchies—whether of race, caste, class, ethnicity, religious allegiance, family of origin—are maintained through a hierarchy of gender, which has generally meant a notion that men are superior and that it is *women's* sexual behavior that must be controlled.

Worries about too much contact between groups have led at times to the seclusion or veiling of women or to laws against "mixed marriages" and *miscegenation*—sexual relations between persons of different groups. Even in the contemporary United States, some extremist groups advocate a return to the laws against miscegenation, or "racial mixing," that were in place in some states until the U.S. Supreme Court declared them illegal in 1967. Though restrictions on miscegenation are generally couched in gender-neutral terms, most cultures regard only sexual relations between a woman of the dominant group and a man from a subordinate group as a serious matter; men from dominant groups—such as southern slaveholders in the United States and nobles in medieval Japan or England—were permitted, even expected, to engage in sexual relations with women from subordinate groups, though the children that might result from these unions were generally legally disadvantaged.

Gender structures are thus not a separate system in any culture but intimately related to every aspect of culture. Until very recently, most of the world's cultures were structured around some sort of family group, an institution built on the relationship between a man (or men) and a woman (or women). Family structures and functions vary widely within a single culture, from culture to culture, and across time, but almost no culture fails to distinguish between men's and women's (and usually girls' and boys') roles within the family. It is within the family that children get their first lessons about gender structures and develop their own gender identities, though most cultures regard gender structures as so important that their inculcation is not left to the family alone.

Tracing the patterns of gender in world history involves two major tasks. First, while recognizing some common aspects of gender in all societies—including the importance of gender designations themselves—different, specific gender cultures must be identified and compared. Why major societies defined gender relations differently and what impact this had on individual men and women and on other aspects of history form important aspects of this inquiry. Second, change over time must be described and assessed. Gender may change more slowly than other aspects of history, but precisely because it is a culturally constructed category, it does change. Sometimes, in fact, as with the return of women to the labor force in many countries during World Wars I and II, change can be quite abrupt. Relating gender change to other developments in culture and economy and to new contacts among societies with different gender systems forms a vital part of world history.

Introducing Work and Leisure as History

Work and leisure are among the most basic human activities throughout history. Human beings have needed to labor to provide shelter, food, and clothing for themselves, as well as for dependent family members and other members of society. Closely related to work is leisure. More is known about labor systems than about leisure. Rather than the opposite of work, it is better to conceive of leisure as an integral part of everyday existence, often calling for considerable effort to accomplish it. Indeed, leisure activities serve important functions beyond just relaxation. Community festivals, for example, or drinking in taverns often create a more cohesive community and, depending on who sponsors these activities, reinforce social hierarchies.

Work and leisure are vital historical topics not just because of the central role they play in people's lives but because they have changed in important ways over time. Both activities reflect significant shifts in how societies function, since the many ways in which people make a living show, on a human level, the underlying economic and social structures of each major historical period. Three large-scale changes have occurred over time in work patterns, all of them closely related to changes in technology. The first change occurred when hunters and gatherers became farmers and cultivated crops for their livelihood. This entailed adjusting to the rhythms of growing crops, involving periods of intense activity, such as sowing and harvest, at certain times of the year. The second change occurred when towns and cities emerged, making possible an increasing specialization of labor (though based mainly on the labor of agriculturists in the countryside). The third occurred only a few centuries ago, when industrialization swiftly transformed labor relations and leisure. The transformation of agricultural societies to industrial ones created a whole new type of work—factory labor—in which gender roles, specialization, rhythms of time, the ownership of tools and other materials for production, as well as many other factors all changed, altering the basic human experience for a large segment of the population. As we will see, leisure activities also changed significantly as a result of industrialization, moving from festivals in which the whole community was involved to more individual and family-oriented activities.

Work and leisure have varied not just across time but also among social groups. Organizing work in order to establish different functions was a key ingredient informing social and gender hierarchies, and though work stratifications have changed many times, the historical connections are vital even in our own society. Work differentiations became especially marked with the rise of agriculture, for only then did people begin to produce a sufficient surplus to make possible the creation of groups such as priests, soldiers, and government officials, who were not directly involved in producing food. Moreover, people achieved different levels of ownership over land and different degrees of freedom to dispose of their labor as they wished. For the purposes of this book, it is useful to distinguish among several basic types of work. First and foremost were the agriculturists, who constituted the vast majority of the laboring population up until very recently in human history. Indeed, in most agricultural societies, those working the land composed more than 80% of the total population and sometimes (especially in earliest times) even more than 90%. This was the most important population segment numerically, and the various means of working the land define much of the experience of work and leisure. Other categories include military specialists and urban professions such as artisan (skilled craftspeople), scribe, government official, merchant. Another important category was that of domestic servant.

Gender describes another important dimension of work and leisure patterns. Since the advent of humankind, men and women have, to a large extent, divided up tasks according to gender. Thus, in hunting-and-gathering societies, men hunted and women gathered (often collecting foods of more value than men were able to generate). Only extremely recently (and at best partially and only in some societies) have the distinctions between the sexes in labor roles diminished. Divisions have partly resulted from the biological fact that women bear children, whereas men do not. There are also other physiological characteristics that distinguish men from women. Interestingly, particular cultures have interpreted these differences in various ways and have acted on them differently. For example, among many

Amerindian groups, women were seen as more adept than men at agricultural labor, such as cultivating corn, whereas in European societies, heavy farm labor is more closely (though not exclusively) associated with male labor. Other types of work, such as domestic labor, military service, and slavery, were often associated with certain genders, though this varies across time and across different cultures. Similarly, certain leisure activities, such as watching professional sports events in modern times, have been closely tied to one gender or another.

The different categories of workers in all complex societies—slave and free, women and men—are not simply items on an occupational chart. They reflect more than degrees of freedom, though the power to determine how one works (and, sometimes, how one plays) varies greatly and forms a vital factor in human life. Different labor categories often have maintained distinctive work experiences, varying, for example, in pace and intensity. In some cases, women have defined the working day differently from men. Workers in lower social categories might work harder than their "superiors"—or in some cases, they might work less hard. The history of work deals with these basic patterns and how they have varied from one group to another, from one large society to the next—and with how they have changed over time. Do people work harder in modern societies than their ancestors did? The answer is complex, perhaps surprising, and it provides a vital measurement of the human experience from past to present.

The analysis of leisure relates closely to that of work. Different social groups, as well as men and women, often have different leisure styles. Indeed, aristocracies frequently define themselves by elaborate leisure activities such as banquets, gambling, and hunting. But leisure in some societies also connects groups, providing some nonwork occasions, such as festivals, where elites and commoners are supposed to celebrate together. It is important, then, to interpret leisure patterns in terms of both differentiations and community building. Leisure can also serve particular social purposes, such as keeping young people occupied and preventing them from disrupting the rest of the community unduly. Leisure's relationship to work is often complex: Sometimes leisure seems designed simply as an alternative to work—an escape. Most societies embellish leisure with habits like drinking that are intended to dilute reality (among other purposes, including communal bonding). But much leisure, including children's play, actually mimics work habits and helps train for work life; in modern sports, team play is often touted as an admirable preparation for the qualities needed in corporate management. Finally, societies and groups within society have explicit or implicit leisure ethics, closely related to attitudes toward work. Some societies officially frown on leisure as frivolous, whereas others tout leisure as essential to a well-rounded person. The meaning of leisure, and not just a catalog of specific activities such as games and dances, is the key analytical target. As with work, meanings can be compared from one society to the next, and key changes and their causes (including shifts in the leisure needs created by work) must be traced over time.

Conclusion

Looking at people and societies in terms of biological, cultural, political, gender, and work experiences provides a real sense of how human beings have been shaped by major civilizations and by the evolution of international contacts. Of course, just as world history, in focusing on some of the most populous civilizations, leaves out other important communities, so a selection of five major social history topics does not fully cover every important aspect of human behavior. Crime, for example, has an important social history, related to governments, work, even gender, but ultimately worth attention in its own right. Age groupings, along with the two genders and with social classes defined in part by work roles, help organize our understanding of how societies function.

The five aspects of human experience that are directly treated in every section of this book obviously interrelate. Population patterns have a crucial impact on gender and vice versa. Religious values are part of culture, but they also help shape or reflect work systems and gender relations. Priorities can change. New organizations of work or gender have more sweeping consequences in some periods than in others. Cultural construction or new state initiatives vary in their importance in shaping other social activities. Keeping track of the interconnections—aided by epilogues at the end of each chronological segment—helps orient the reader in using this book.

The five topics not only describe major facets of the human experience; they are also subject to change and variation, which means that they can be understood only historically. We live in a time of great debate over gender definitions, for example—which means that we must try to see what past formulations have been and why they are under new pressure. Gender, work, and demography have a few constant features, deriving from the nature of our species, but they are in large measure shaped by particular historical conditions—and they help shape these conditions in turn.

One final point: World history is a challenging subject. It requires learning about a number of past periods and a number of different societies. At the same time, it must involve active use of historical thinking— what historians often call the key habits of mind of their discipline. This book includes active invitations to develop further skills in dealing with historical debates and issues of historical process over time. It includes summaries of differing interpretations and methodologies that require consideration beyond standard textbook reading. Precisely because social history and world history have recently advanced, they have provoked important disagreements. The book also invites careful attention to change and continuity and the causes of each—the analytical area most central to historical understanding. Throughout, the book encourages comparison among major human societies and consideration of some of the larger perspectives of world history over time. Ultimately, it invites an active juxtaposition of present and past, an assessment of what past patterns are still active in human affairs and why, and a consideration of where and why decisive change seems most appropriate in describing the human condition as a new century begins.

PART I

Human History from Origins through the Early Civilizations

Highlights.   From the origins of the human species to the rise of early civilizations, people went through a variety of phases of biological evolution. They also spread over most of the inhabitable parts of the world. Toward the end of the long early period, they introduced agriculture, a decisive change of basic economic framework. Most agricultural societies then added other innovations, including the forms associated with civilization as a system of social organization. During these key phases, basic patterns of culture were introduced and, a bit later, political structures as well. Agriculture and civilization massively reshaped patterns of gender and work. By the end of the first civilization period, around 1000 B.C.E., systems were in place, from biological contacts to common leisure, that would prove extremely durable, though not immune to change or variety.

Key Developments.   The human species began to emerge between 2.5 and 4 million years ago, in East Africa. Various human species succeeded one another, sometimes coexisting, until the emergence of *homo sapiens sapiens* about 120,000 years ago, again in East Africa. This species spread rapidly and ultimately overcame other remaining human species. Both before and after this point in evolution, humans operated hunting-and-gathering societies, using stone tools that they gradually learned to improve. Tool use aided adaptability, while the considerable territory hunters and gatherers required—an average of about two and a half square miles per person— forced steady geographic dispersal, from Africa to Europe and Asia, and from there to the Americas, Australia, and various island groups. Dispersal, in turn, encouraged the development of considerable differentiation in the practices and institutions of key groups, which often existed in considerable isolation.

The pace of change accelerated after the end of the last great Ice Age, about 15,000 years ago. Improvements in tools, including wood and bone as well as stone, gave rise to the final Stone Age period, the Neolithic. At the same time, growing populations and the retreat of some big game forced economic adjustments in key areas, such as the northern Middle East, around the Black Sea. Between 9000 and 7000 B.C.E., agriculture was introduced into this area and gradually took over as the primary economic system. Very slowly, diffusion spread agriculture to other regions, such as North Africa and western India, while several societies invented agriculture separately. By 1000 B.C.E. agriculture was widely known in Asia, southern Europe, Africa both above and below the Sahara desert, and parts of the Americas. Agriculture's great advantage—amid several drawbacks—was its capacity to support larger populations, because of improvements in total food supply.

Agriculture also generated both capabilities and needs for further change in many regions. The system could produce economic surpluses—farmers could grow more food than they needed themselves, sometimes as much as 20% more (a noticeable margin, though very modest by contemporary standards). Agriculture often required increased group collaboration, for example, to build and manage complex irrigation systems. It usually demanded some concepts of property as a means of assuring families or communities of rights over improvements they introduced. It also required new technologies, for example, in producing goods such as pots and baskets that could store food and seed. Around 6000 B.C.E. the first potter's wheel was introduced in the Middle East, and soon thereafter bread was invented as a tastier way to use grain. Small amounts of trade with neighboring populations usually accompanied agriculture, and this, in turn, helped generate the first small cities.

An important series of innovations around 4000 B.C.E. took shape, again initially in the Middle East but with opportunities to spread to other societies. The wheel was introduced, with implications for farming, transportation, and war. People discovered the use of metals, particularly the mixture of copper and tin called bronze, and Stone Age technology began to be replaced in some, though not all, parts of the world.

Where metal tools were used, the period 4000–1500 B.C.E. is often called the Bronze Age. People in the Tigris-Euphrates valley developed the first writing system around 3500 B.C.E., which facilitated communicating and storing knowledge.

These developments, in turn, undergirded the emergence of the form of human organization called civilization, first in Mesopotamia, with the Sumerians in the northeastern Middle East, then in several other key centers. Civilizations depended on a relatively high level of agricultural surplus, which could free a minority of the population for other activities, including manufacturing, politics, and religious leadership. Cities emerged more fully as centers of political activity and trade—though the vast majority of the population remained rural. Resources and cities alike normally encouraged cultural innovations such as large monuments, usually with religious purposes. Explicit governments arose, replacing the more informal regulations of earlier, stateless societies. Civilizations, like agriculture, had a host of drawbacks, including increasing inequality, which helps explain why they did not spread everywhere; but because they generated more effective power arrangements, they did tend to expand and proliferate, while also producing beliefs in superiority over herding or hunting peoples (often called barbarians).

Between 3500 and 1500 B.C.E., four early civilization centers emerged, all in river valleys well suited to irrigation. Soon thereafter a fifth center developed in Central America, with the Olmecs. Along with Mesopotamia, Egypt, the Indus River valley in northwestern India, and China along the Yellow River hosted the key centers. Each developed a standard apparatus: a writing system; a formal government that usually claimed backing from the gods; expanding trade; significant urban centers; pronounced social inequality, including slavery; some formal science. Each also, however, had a distinctive flavor; because early civilizations developed for the most part separately, they established different traditions. Writing systems varied. Cultural tone varied. Mesopotamian religion and literature were rather gloomy, dwelling on the misfortunes of mankind; Egypt was more upbeat, believing in an agreeable afterlife. Egypt was orderly in politics, with emphasis on the rule of the pharaoh; Mesopotamia was more marked by invasions and change. Indus River cities had elaborate public works and, apparently, a fairly decentralized political system. China, developing a bit

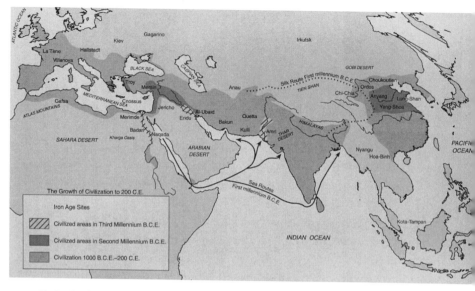

Early Civilizations in Afro-Eurasia. Patterns of Expansion and Contact. From Peter N. Stearns, *World History in Brief: Major Patterns of Change and Continuity*, 3rd ed. Copyright 1999 by Addison-Wesley Educational Publishers Inc. Reprinted by permission.

later, was unusually isolated. Egypt had important contacts with other parts of the Mediterranean and also with areas of sub-Saharan Africa along the Nile, where a partially separate civilization developed in Kush toward the end of the early period. Mesopotamia influenced smaller societies along the eastern Mediterranean: One, Phoenicia, developed unusually far-flung trade and also simplified the cuneiform alphabet. Another, Palestine, saw the emergence of a distinctive monotheistic religion, Judaism, that contrasted markedly with the more common patterns of polytheism.

The river-valley civilizations all declined or changed around 1000 B.C.E., drawing this first civilization period to a close. A wave of invasions contributed to the destruction of the cities of the Indus valley. Political units in Mesopotamia and Egypt wavered, again partly because of invasions. The introduction of iron weapons from Central Asia helps explain why new attacks gained particular force. Changes in China were more subtle, but the advent of an expansionist dynasty, the Zhou, and the advent of iron use marked a break here as well. Here, and to an important extent in Africa and the eastern Mediterranean/Middle East, significant continuities would extend into the next world history period even as civilizations began to take on additional, novel features.

The chapter that follows deals with human biology: the emergence of the species, its migrations, its experience of birth and death. Later chapters move more fully to the early civilization period in discussing culture and politics. Finally, attention to gender patterns and work experience involves consideration of traditions first formed when people foraged for food and then the extent of changes when agriculture and, subsequently, organized states entered the picture.

TIMELINE

I. Origins–1000 B.C.E.

1.7 million years ago	Emergence and spread of *homo erectus*
500,000 years ago	Use of fire
200,000–120,000 years ago	*Homo sapiens sapiens*
18,000–12,000 years ago	Passage of people to Americas
9000 B.C.E.	Neolithic revolution (New Stone Age)
8000	Development of agriculture
5000	Agriculture in Central America
4000	Bronze tools, other inventions (Bronze Age)
3500–2600	Urban centers emerge in Mesopotamia (Sumer), development of cuneiform writing
3200–2780	Unification of Egypt under one pharaoh
3000–1300	Indus River cities
2600–2420	Akkadian invasions and empire
2100–1788	Expansion of Egypt to Sudan, Palestine
2050–1750	Kingdom of Babylon
ca. 2000	Hwang Ho civilization; myths of Hsia dynasty; golden-age writing of *Gilgamesh,* world's first known heroic epic
1700	Hammurabic Code
1500	New Kingdom in Egypt; increase in use of slaves; use of iron in Asian civilizations; Shang dynasty in China
1400–1150	Phoenician cities and colonies in eastern Mediterranean; formation of Jewish religion

1300–900   Aryan invasions in India; intense invasions in Middle East

1200   First Olmec center in Central America, San Lorenzo

1150–130   Writing of books of Old Testament

1050–800   Decline of pharaohs; rise of Kush

1029–258   Zhou dynasty in China—feudal period, with manorialism

1000   Olympic Festival first held in Greece

CHAPTER 2

HUMAN POPULATION AND MIGRATION PATTERNS

Wave One, Populating Afro-Eurasia: Homo Habilis
and Homo Erectus

The first great changes in humanity were mainly biological. They were adaptations driven by sharp changes in the global climate during what geologists term the Pleistocene, or last great Ice Age, which began about 2 million years ago. It had long cold intervals of about 100,000 years; between them were warming intervals of 10,000 to 30,000 years, of which the last, known as the Holocene, began about 13,000 years ago and continues to the present. These climatic shifts stressed plant and animal species, causing extinction in some, evolutionary changes in others. Humanity adapted by becoming larger, walking erect (bipedalism), and developing larger brains. These adaptations together allowed development of fine motor coordination of muscles in the hands, mouth, and face and eventually led to tool making (technology) and language.

The first humanoids appeared in South and East Africa nearly 4 million years ago with *australopithecus afarensis.* From them descended four other types of australopithecines: *africanus, aethiopicus, robustus,* and *boisei.* These all became extinct, leaving only one line of their descendants, whom paleoanthropologists designate *homo habilis* (human and maker of tools). First appearing about 2.5 million years ago, *homo habilis* increased brain capacity to about 650 to 750 cubic centimeters, more than australopithecines at about 530 cubic centimeters (cm^3) but considerably less than modern humans, which average 1,400 to 1,500 cm^3. Their legs developed for erect walking and running, freeing their hands for tools. Their greater intelligence made them more effective at finding a greater variety of and more nutritious foods than had the australopithecines. These foods included tubers, fruit, nuts, bud ends, tender leaves of certain bushes and trees, grass seeds, and a variety of insects, such as grubs, grasshoppers, ants. They relished reptiles, birds, eggs, and small animals. They also scavenged carcasses of large animals killed by the big carnivores. Hardly "man the hunter," these early men and women were instead omnivorous opportunists, probably more often prey than predators. Both australopithecines and *homo habilis* were relatively scarce species, probably never numbering more than a few hundred thousand.

The First Great Colonizing Wave: Homo Erectus *and* Afro-Eurasia

Homo habilis were long transitional ancestors to *homo erectus,* who developed about 1 million years ago (some estimates defend an earlier date). The longest enduring of human species, *homo erectus* differed from its predecessors in two important ways. First, members of the species became physically larger, with increased intelligence. Second, from about 1 million to 400,000 years ago, they spread out across all of tropical and temperate Afro-Eurasia and, in doing so, increased their populations.

At 833 to 1,043 cm^3 their brain size reached the lower range of modern humans and apparently increased over time. Humans henceforth were genetically programmed to be inventive, not instinctive. High intelligence produced techniques for coping with the environment that were learned and passed from generation to generation; this is known as culture, the human survival mechanism (see chapter 1, on culture).

Homo erectus were not vastly inventive. Wherever they went, and for over a million years, their stone tools followed the same characteristic design. Termed Acheulean, it varied only in use of locally available stone, for instance, quartz, limestone, basalt, or flint. They constructed crude shelters or windbreaks. Charred bones and hearths at widely distant points in northeastern Asia and southern Europe prove they used fire by 500,000 years ago for warmth, light, and possibly cooking.

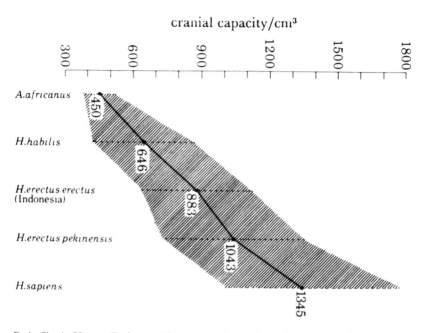

Brain Size in Human Evolution. The pattern of cranial capacity increase in human evolution over the past 3 million years (shading indicates 95 percent population limits). From Peter C. Bellwood, *Prehistory of the Indo-Malaysian Archipelago* (Honolulu: University of Hawaii Press, 1997). Reprinted by permission.

These innovations enabled *homo erectus* to utilize a vast range of terrain and resources.

Just how they expanded is not known. Based on analogies with later foraging societies, they almost certainly lived in small bands of 20 to 50 persons, each band occupying a home territory of perhaps 30 to 100 square miles. As a band grew, it had to expand its range, often by splitting to form a second group. As groups increased, violent conflict over home foraging ranges increased. Evidence from skull fragments reveals a good bit of head bashing and even cannibalism, particularly in South Asia, which had evidently become crowded. On the frontiers, however, as they moved out across Eurasia, bands multiplied quickly, finding a treasure trove of animals never before hunted. Their numbers grew proportionate to their increased habitat, totaling possibly 1.5 million. They became the base population of the modern world's people.

Wave Two: Population Replacement by Neandertals and Homo Sapiens

Where did modern humans come from? And how did the physical variations in Asian, African, European, and Australian populations develop? Experts disagree sharply despite remarkable recent advances in scientific techniques—for example, genetic tracing of mitochondrial DNA—and new archaeological findings. There are two conflicting hypotheses: multiregional evolution and the out-of-Africa replacement model. The multiregionalists cite evidence that widely across Afro-Eurasia about 400,000 to 200,000 years ago, new types grew out of the *homo erectus* stock. Called *archaic homo sapiens*, they retained some features of *erectus*, such as thick craniums and heavy brow ridges, but the forehead rose vertically, the jaws were less robust, and the brain capacity was larger, about 1,200 to 1,500 cm^3. Already they showed regional characteristics that persist in present indigenous populations. For example, in China, at Zhoukoudian and Dali caves, fossil remains dating back more than 250,000 years show distinctly Northeast Asian features: small, delicately boned faces; high horizontal cheekbones, with a notch in the cheekbone (called the *incisura malaris*); and shovel-shaped incisor teeth. These characteristics persist through the archaeological record and are evident still in Asians and American Indians. Similarly, skull remains in Java, an island in Southeast Asia, show facial features that continue for several hundred thousand years, reappearing in aboriginal Australian populations, with brain capacity increasing over time. According to the multiregional hypothesis, these regionally differentiated populations crossbred sufficiently to remain the same species and to spread advantageous genetic mutations, mostly toward greater intelligence, the human adaptive mechanism par excellence.

An extreme regional variation of *homo sapiens*, the Neandertals, appeared in southern Europe 200,000 years ago during a cold interval. They flourished, expanding their range from the European Atlantic coast to southwestern Asia. Some artistic re-creations of Neandertals make them appear squat and brutish. But they walked fully erect; had brain capacity slightly larger than modern humans; made clothing and footwear; produced hafted stone axes and spears; dwelt in cave shelters through nine-month-long winters; buried their dead; had incredible physical strength, exceeding that of the strongest modern humans; and were marvelously well adapted to their environment.

The out-of-Africa hypothesis contends that modern *homo sapiens sapiens* evolved once, in Africa, sometime after 200,000 years ago. Fully developed, their populations began growing rapidly about 80,000 years ago, spreading across Eurasia, multiplying all the while, and replacing all other human types. Geographic variations in superficial characteristics such as skin color, hair color, and physique developed recently, possibly after 40,000 years ago. These new model humans abruptly drove all other human types into extinction, either violently or by foraging more effectively and increasing their populations more rapidly.

These two hypotheses are not totally contradictory. As we will see, later history provides multiple examples of confrontations between populations different in culture, technology, and physical appearance. Perhaps the most dramatic example was the meeting of Native Americans and Europeans in the age of Columbus, but there were many others. These suggest one population could replace another by a mixture of assimilation and removal that varied according to regional circumstances. Assimilation could be by a mixture of crossbreeding, cultural borrowing, conquest, and alliances. Removal could be by diseases, warfare, migratory retreat, or simply by one population reproducing more rapidly than another.

Researchers suggest several possible explanations for the disappearance of Neandertals, who coexisted with *homo sapiens sapiens* for thousands of years. Some believe Neandertals became modern humans by mixing with *homo sapiens sapiens*. Others believe *homo sapiens sapiens* simply replaced them. Either way, the Neandertals dwindled, and by 18,000 B.C.E. the last traces of them—in southern Spain—vanished. *Homo sapiens sapiens* alone remained, by replacement, assimilation, or both. Their distinctive advantage was their culture, here defined as group-learned behaviors.

Wave Two, Continued: Population and Cultural Explosion

In the late Paleolithic age, 45,000 to 10,000 B.C.E., populations increased; humans expanded their geographical range and achieved dramatic technological, economic, and cultural advances. Modern humans moved into the

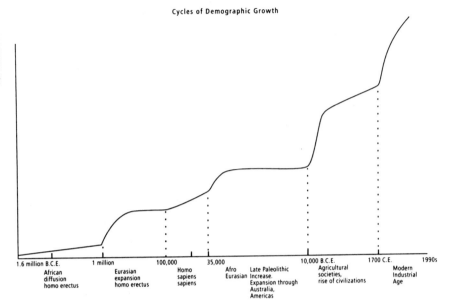

Cycles of Demographic Growth.

northern latitudes of Eurasia and for the first time inhabited the Americas and Australia. This global migration was accomplished by a set of technological innovations: improved hunting and foraging tools, sewn clothing, constructed housing. Innovations also included social adaptations: hunting together in large cooperative bands, long-distance trade, formation of regional or tribal associations. Populations grew dramatically because of the increase in occupied territories and because improved technologies sustained higher densities.

About 45,000 years ago, anatomically modern people in the Near East, after millennia of technological inertia, developed a new stone technology termed *Aurignacian*. A version of it had been invented but forgotten some 15,000 years earlier, far in the south of Africa; this time, people retained it and took it with them across the Near East and India and northwestward into Europe. Aurignacian tools are an archaeological signal, permanently associated with not only anatomically but also culturally modern humans.

In Europe and most of Asia the climate was bitterly cold, the hardest between 20,000 and 18,000 years ago. Plants, animals, and people adjusted to these cycles by moving southward into sheltered valleys in the harshest centuries, and people adapted by developing improved clothing and housing.

The critical technology involved highly crafted stone tools and creative uses of reindeer bone and antler and ivory. Stone implements now were made of fine-grained flint, often obtained at distant quarries. The basic technique was to make a rectilinear "core" from which blades—long, smooth fragments—would be struck and worked to make spear points, knives, or other tools. Reindeer antler was a malleable material from which to carve barbed harpoons, spear tips, and needles. An important new hunting tool was the spear-thrower, which, when attached to the shaft end of a light spear, provided powerful leverage for long, lightning-fast throws.

Despite biting cold and a hazardous life, late Paleolithic peoples had a highly creative culture, and their populations increased, rapidly by Paleolithic standards. The subarctic grasslands sustained vast herds of animals, which excellent tools and techniques captured handily. Winters certainly took their toll, but the cold also had its advantages: It kept meat caches fresh frozen, prevented infectious diseases, and forced people to live close together for months at a time.

Group harmony had to be maintained, especially as populations grew and competition for resources became sharper between groups. Skeletal remains of the late Paleolithic show many fractures of skulls and forearms, mostly on the left side, suggesting someone right-handed delivered the blows. Modern travelers' accounts of the last two or three centuries are filled with stories of Stone Age peoples at war with each other, across Inner Asia, the Americas, the Pacific Islands. Intertribal violence seems to have acted as a restraint on population growth, and its threat provided incentive for creating associations that bound regional groups together.

By tracing the spread of Aurignacian tools and other artifacts, researchers can follow the spread of modern humans. In Europe known as Cro-Magnons, they spread rapidly—first across the east, with large numbers settling in the Danube valley, and then to the Atlantic edge of western Europe by 40,000 years ago. Some groups fanned out from the Middle East to India south of the Himalayas, beginning about 45,000 years ago.

Populations increased in the Malay Peninsula and adjacent islands, forming a culture dependent on canoes and rafts. Perhaps as early as 60,000 years ago, some groups with archaic Southeast Asian physical traits managed to cross from the archipelago of Southeast Asia to New Guinea and Australia. Another group with East Asian physical traits followed about 30,000 years later. People arrived in Northeast Asia in another migratory surge sometime after 40,000 B.C.E. From there they spread through Siberia, the islands of Japan, and the long-isolated island of Okinawa after 32,000 B.C.E.

Although dubious claims are made for earlier dates, certainly sometime between 18,000 and 12,000 years ago, bands of Northeast Asians migrated across the broad Beringian plain to North America. Before them were two continents teeming with animals and plants, some of them familiar, some not. Because they came in small numbers, passing through a frozen landscape on migratory trajectories that took hundreds of years, they left most diseases of Afro-Eurasia behind. With limitless food, disease free, and undeterred by hostile inhabitants, these first Americans scattered across a widening frontier. They multiplied rapidly and became accomplished big-game hunters. By 9000 B.C.E., many American grazing species became extinct: horses, camels, the giant bison. Hunting shifted to smaller species—for instance, deer, caribou, the smaller species of bison—and to fish and sea mammals on coastal areas and in lakes and rivers. In a few thousand years, people filled both continents, north to south. The potential for quick population growth in these optimum conditions was obviously enormous.

Demography of Foraging Societies: Holding Population Down

Throughout the Paleolithic ages population sizes were very small, but there are no data to allow real estimates. Some guesses calculate how many persons per square mile hunting and gathering might support, then multiply by the number of habitable square miles. For around 10,000 B.C.E., guesses range from 3 to 13 million, most hovering around 6 to 8 million. Very slow growth over a very long time had a large cumulative effect. For example, if we begin with a population of 10,000 persons, propose a growth rate of .01

percent per year (modern growth rates since around 1750 range from 2 to 4 percent per year), and allow for one person per square mile, the population increases to 10 million in 169,000 years; and at about 1.8 million years, the Paleolithic age was much longer.

When *homo sapiens sapiens* first appeared, less than 200,000 years ago, populations initially remained very small. But when they expanded out of Africa, somehow joining or replacing other human groups, and when, after around 45,000 B.C.E., they developed the new Aurignacian technologies, the world experienced its first major population surge, increasing to a new plateau.

Certainly, human colonization of Australia and the Americas added people. But Afro-Eurasia itself experienced a thickening of people over the landscape. Evidence of this includes the great cultural flowering and technological advances of 40,000 to 30,000 years ago. Archaeologists also find a substantial increase in skeletons, campsites, lodgings, and the paraphernalia of households. Only larger populations and new gregariousness could account for great seasonal clan meeting places and even quasi towns.

Populations grew for two reasons. First, anatomically modern humans produced more food. They had become efficient hunters of the great herds of the Eurasian northern plains and sheltered valleys of the south, by development of improved hunting equipment and well-organized cooperative routines. In South Asia and Africa, they collected vegetation with new intensity, developed new implements for harvesting and grinding, and even encouraged growth of favored plants. They became adept fishers in rivers, lakes, and seas. Second, as modern humans expanded north of the Sahara, they left behind a dense aggregation of microparasitic organisms that had evolved in tandem with humans over millennia and had kept population growth in check through disease. These new environments inhibited growth of pathogenetic microorganisms, so people and animals flourished.

By about 25,000 years ago, however population growth leveled off, perhaps having reached the limits set by the low productivity of hunting-gathering economies. Limits mostly were enforced by powerful demographic and cultural mechanisms that kept growth nearly at zero. Researchers infer how Paleolithic peoples restricted growth by making analogies with modern foraging cultures. Some researchers also study skeletal and dental evidence for clues to nutrition, disease, and life expectancy. Together these provide a fairly coherent picture. Communities numbering about 25 to 50 persons typically migrated seasonally, pursuing animal herds or moving where favorite plant foods ripened. Need for mobility and their physically stressful lives kept birthrates low and life expectancies short. A woman who reached physiological maturity at age 16 to 18 would have her first birth about a year later. Before dying at 30 or 40, a woman on average bore not more than 4 or 5 babies. Of those, half died before age 5, leaving 2.25 surviving. The bare replacement level for a couple, man and woman, required a minimum of two, not allowing for incidental catastrophes of war, accident, famine, or epidemic. A band of 40 persons might have 8 or 9 women of childbearing age. With unrestrained fertility, each might have two or more children under age 7, making the total number of children for the group 16 to 18, a whole nursery school, which a fast-moving band could hardly fetch along! Consequently, migratory groups applied rigid rules restraining births. Extended suckling periods of 3 or 4 years constituted one technique of restraint. Protracted breast-feeding induced partial infertility for many months. Partial abstinence from intercourse and deliberate efforts to prevent conception, such as coitus interruptus, were others. Infanticide also was commonplace.

Diets were certainly adequate. Lean game meats combined with foraged carbohydrates made Paleolithic peoples tall and healthy, attaining heights not approached in all of history until the mid–20th century, and then only in affluent societies. Dental and ossuary remains show little sign of malnutrition, starvation, or chronic diseases. Short life expectancy therefore resulted from the stress and dangers of hunting-gathering existence. Many died from violent blows or wounds received in battles—as many as 40 percent of adult male skeletons at some sites. Women had even shorter lives, due to the stresses of multiple childbirths and hauling household goods and infants from camp to camp.

The grim realities of demography were partly counterbalanced by the pleasant tone of life that many anthropological studies present. Hunting men occasionally ranged far from camp, but their searches did not take much time. Even in foraging societies that today occupy arid, remote places, men hunt only every third day or so, sometimes only for five or six hours. Women breast-feeding infants, caring for toddlers, or in late pregnancy remained close by camp, as did old or crippled persons. So mostly women and children foraged vegetative foods nearby. Studies of today's foraging societies find that women gather more calories than men produce by hunting, and Paleolithic diets show the same, although less so in the vegetation-scarce subpolar regions. Women did not work much either, gathering perhaps five hours per day, although over more days than men hunted.

Migrations were purposeful travel to familiar destinations. Campsites, some even with houses, were visited at seasonally determined intervals. Home was where the hearth was. Fires were for cooking, to ward off predatory animals, for warmth and light; in warm seasons or climates, smoke drove off maddening swarms of mosquitoes. People gathered around fires to eat, sleep, talk, tell stories, for rituals, or to make tools, jewelry, and clothing. Some anthropologists describe Paleolithic culture as "the original affluent society." They needed little and provided it readily, with little labor. Yet life was short and precarious, and population growth hung at nearly zero.

A profound climatic change reshaped the Paleolithic world, starting about 15,000 years ago. Temperatures rose; ice sheets gradually melted and receded; sea levels slowly rose, eventually by 100 meters or more. North America, Australia, and New Guinea became separated from Asia; for the next 11,000 years, they developed in isolation from the rest of the world. Climatic warming and increasing settlement along waterways seem to have caused deteriorating health conditions. Life expectancies fell; stature shortened; and by some estimates, populations may have declined in Eurasia. Somehow these climatic shifts burdened foraging peoples. Evidently, food became scarcer in some regions, and at least some peoples began practicing agriculture.

Wave Three: The Transition to Agriculture

Agriculture is customarily regarded as the most important human development and as the critical determinant of the later rise of civilization. But it was not a single or a sudden discovery. Rather, agriculture's development involved a slow transition from foraging, which took several thousand years, occurred independently several different times, and involved considerably more than learning simply that seeds germinate when planted. Late Paleolithic peoples knew intimately the ways and life cycles of the animals and plants on which they depended. They accumulated and transmitted through many generations an oral tradition rich in botanical and zoological lore. Researchers describe some ancient societies around the world as having had "incipient agriculture," beginning but not quite committed to food production. Certainly, those who burned off dry grass or brush to encourage succulent new growth to attract animals were at least managing their environment, and capturing but not immediately killing wild animals was a step toward domestication. Cultures in West Africa and Southeast Asia and other places cultivated tubers and tended fruiting trees in the environs of seasonal camps or fishing villages, but their main modes of existence remained hunting and gathering.

Archaeological techniques until recently could definitely identify and date only domestic cereal grains, but new scientific techniques that can analyze softer vegetative matter, for example, root crops, are turning up evidence at many locations that at least partial dependence on farming had developed. These areas include the Andes Mountains, with potatoes and llamas, and the Amazon lowlands, with manioc, guinea pigs, and forest crops, both by 3500 B.C.E. Northeastern America developed sunflowers and goosefoot by 2500 B.C.E. The Sahel (desert's edge) in western Africa developed sorghum and African rice by around 5000 B.C.E. The Ethiopian highlands developed teff (a grain) and coffee (date uncertain but ancient). New Guinea developed bananas and sugarcane, certainly by 5000 B.C.E. and possibly much earlier.

The deliberate growing of grain in combination with animal husbandry provided the foundation for the definitive transition to sedentary village-based cultures. Large populations of grain-based agricultural societies emerged in at least four specific settings where geographic and climatic circumstances were ideal, where native grains grew wild, and where communities who had gathered them had come to depend on them for hundreds of years. These were the highlands of southwestern Asia (the Middle East), relying on wheat and barley; Northeast Asia, dependent on millet; Southeast Asia (meaning here from the Yangtze River valley southward), dependent on rice; and Meso-America, relying on maize. A fifth area, in West Africa, made a transition that began as vegeculture, dependent on gardening and tree crops, then eventually acquired grain. These five produced remarkable population surges that resulted in colonization, or expansion outward from the agricultural homeland.

Mostly, as we will see, each system not only developed but also spread independently. But China and sub-Saharan Africa experienced encounters between two (China) or three (Africa) of the agricultural systems, which produced unusual complexity.

For five independent hunting-and-gathering cultures to have made separate transitions to agriculture required compelling forces. Most experts today favor a carrot-and-stick explanation: The cultures were driven into transition by population growth and environmental overload and attracted by social advantages. Hunter-gatherers did not switch readily to food production simply because the concept occurred to them as a flash of discovery. Agriculture involved more than simply the domestication of plants and animals; it involved an entire mental and even physical transformation. Agricultural systems required vast investments of labor and a commitment to long-term residence. Tillage, planting, and harvesting were only part of the work. Agricultural terrain literally had to be made from raw land—removing rocks, brush trees, and competing weed species. Sods had to be broken up, turned under, and prevented from regrowing. Water had to be controlled by building drainage channels in wet areas or irrigation canals in dry climates. A variety of hand tools, wagons and plows, containers such as baskets and pottery, grindstones, fences and shelters for livestock, grain storage facilities, houses, and protective walls or fortifications all had to be manufactured, built, and maintained. Hunter-gatherers, by contrast, had few tools or implements, and their temporary shelters were quickly built and abandoned; they neither tilled nor planted, but they did harvest, enjoyed ample diets, had greater variety in their life, and were healthier.

Yet the first peoples to embrace agriculture were hunter-gatherers. They gradually were captured by relentless economic, demographic, and social bonds. Where communities gathered certain widely abundant wild grains or tubers, they became dependent on them. Eventually, as their populations grew, harvests became inadequate, maybe even dwindling as avidly collected grains could not seed themselves for the next harvest. The solution was to plant crops deliberately and encourage their growth by tillage and weed control. Meanwhile, communities found social advantages to a sedentary life. Fields, homes, and material possessions could not be moved readily, so there were incentives to increase food production at a given site, by modifying existing crops and by developing additional ones.

In the Middle East, wild varieties of wheat—mainly emmer and einkorn—and barley grew wild in highland areas stretching northward from present-day Israel and Lebanon to Turkey and eastward to the Zagros Mountains, which rim the Mesopotamian Basin. Since 17,000 B.C.E., people had been gathering these grains and hunting sheep, gazelles, goats, and onagers. By 13,000 B.C.E. their descendants, some called Natufians (after the site Wadi en-Natuf in Israel), had established relatively permanent villages, becoming sedentary hunter-gatherers.

They did not abruptly shift to agriculture. For example, discoveries at an archaeological site in Khuzistan villages in southwestern Iran from around 7500 to 6900 B.C.E. reveal that some 90 percent of seed consisted of wild legumes—alfalfa, spiny vetch, and others of the pea family—and wild grasses. Cultivated wheat and barley made up but 10 percent. By 6500 B.C.E., however, cultivated grain had become 40 percent of the total. For meat, these peoples mostly hunted wild goats, then gradually shifted to domesticated sheep. From about 9000 to 6000 B.C.E., agricultural villages came to prevail and replicated themselves all across the region. By the 6000s the people moved onto the dry plains of Mesopotamia, where they developed techniques for irrigating the fertile alluvial soils. Date-palm trees became an important resource for their fruit and for building materials. A few villages situated in the steppe grasslands near forests became substantial towns, among them Jericho, Jarmo, and Çatal-Huyuk, each of which held 1000 or more residents. By the Ubaid period, 5900–4300 B.C.E. (named after Tel al-Ubaid in southern Mesopotamia), irrigation techniques had become advanced; villages became larger, and a few advanced to become market towns.

Meanwhile, farming villages and peoples radiated outward in all directions. By 6000 they had spread to various parts of India. By 5000 B.C.E., agricultural communities spread along the Mediterranean coast of North Africa and down the Nile. Agricultural peoples moved into the Balkan Peninsula of Europe by 6500 B.C.E. and from there along the Mediterranean coast to the Iberian Peninsula and up the Danube to North and Central Europe.

Northeast Asian agriculture developed on loess soils with the growth of millet. Loess are deep deposits of windblown soil particles, built up by winds blowing eastward from Inner Asia during the arid ice ages. Millet agriculture originated in the arid uplands of the Wei tributary and western Hwang-he valley. Soils supported a light grass cover, easily tilled with simple implements. Here, beginning about 5500 B.C.E., the first farmers, known as the Yang-shao culture, cleared grasses by burning, then worked the soil with stone hoes, spades, and digging sticks. They planted millet for two or three years in a given field, then moved to another. Soils remained perpetually fertile, and villages multiplied. Settlements shifted every few years, but people returned to favorable sites repeatedly. They continued to gather wild crops and hunt. Their principal domesticated animals were pigs and dogs, along with some cattle, sheep, and goats. Hemp for rope was cultivated, and already mulberry trees were tended and silkworms raised.

By 2300 B.C.E., Yang-shao culture gave way to the more highly developed Lung-shan. Crafts became more refined, for example, specialized carpenters' tools and potters' wheels. Villages became walled, suggesting that conflicts had increased as populations thickened across North China. Villages and their agricultural system expanded into the eastern plains, northward into Manchuria and into the Ordos grasslands at the bend of the Hwang-he, and southward into Central and South China, where they met and mixed with southern rice growers.

The wild ancestor of rice, *oriza nivara*, was harvested wild in its indigenous habitat, reaching from northeastern India in the upper Brahamaputra and Irrawady River watersheds and across mainland Southeast Asia. Several culture groups began cultivating rice, and as cultivation moved northward into the Yangtze valley by 5000 B.C.E., rice was selected for shorter dormancy, larger grains, synchronous ripening, and resistance to shattering. It joined pigs, chickens, tropical fruits, and vegetables to comprise a mixture of agricultural products (we might call it an agricultural package) different from those of North China and developed by culturally different people—a separate agricultural transformation, spreading out from a different center.

As this agricultural system moved northward to the lower Yangtze valley and South China coast by 5000 B.C.E., it met the Hwang-he millet-based system, moving southward. As rice-growing populations increased, some expanded southward. Speaking languages that linguists call Austronesian, they formed one of the greatest migrations in world history. From the South Chinese coast settlers moved into Taiwan and then, by about 3500, to Luzon, where they became linked with seafaring and fishing peoples. As settlements continued southward, their agricultural package added breadfruit, bananas, taro, and sugarcane.

What happened in New Guinea helps explain expansion of agricultural societies. Its indigenous residents had already developed their own agricultural crops, including taro, sugarcane, and bananas. New Guineans themselves did not migrate, but their agriculturally enlarged populations made New Guinea largely impervious to Austronesian seafaring farmers. Austronesians established some scattered villages along the northern coast of New Guinea but mostly continued eastward, eventually finding and populating hundreds of uninhabited islands, including Samoa, Tahiti, and the Cook Islands. After 1000 B.C.E., one key group became Polynesians, their languages, agriculture, and genetic traits all linking them to ancient South Chinese and Taiwanese ancestry. Thereafter they found every habitable island in the Pacific, arriving finally in New Zealand about 1000 C.E., the last significant place on earth to acquire humans.

Middle Eastern agriculture, which had spread across the North African coast and up the Nile, met and combined with Africa's indigenous agricultural revolution at the southern edge of the Sahara. In West Africa, sometime early in the fourth millennium B.C.E., a group speaking early versions of Bantu languages cultivated yams, gourds, beans, and weedy vegetables in forest clearings. They tended naturally growing oil palms and fruit trees and herded goats. They also trapped wild animals—for instance, antelopes and pigs—attracted by their crops, and they fished in rivers and ponds. Gradually, as they added crops and animals, their agricultural dependency increased. A vital impetus came from acquisition of iron metallurgy sometime between 800 and 300 B.C.E. This, in turn, launched a long but vital process of Bantu migration. Gradually, Bantu-related tongues came to make up more than 90 percent of the languages spoken south of a line between the Bight of Benin and Somalia, spoken even by non-Bantu groups. Hunters and gatherers retreated—pygmies to the deep forests, bushmen to the arid wastelands of the southwest.

But people in the north held their ground. Africans at the Saharan fringe, the Sahel, and the savanna of Ethiopia and northern Nigeria had domesticated millet and sorghum where wheat and barley would not grow. Some had been specialists in grazing cattle. As the Sahara had gradually become desert in the second millennium B.C.E., its pastoral peoples and farmers moved north toward the coast or south into the Sahel. In the Sahel, the migrants became a demographic counterweight, not unlike the meeting of agricultural peoples at the Yangtze valley in China, and with similar effects: a massive migration and language diffusion southward, much like that of the Austronesians.

Finally, the Austronesians turned up in Madagascar, the island off the southeastern African coast. They had crossed the entire Indian Ocean sometime in the last centuries B.C.E., having become expert seafarers and traders. They brought Asian yams, bananas, sugarcane, and coconuts. So, in the incredible climatic and topographical diversity of Africa, no fewer than three agricultural systems met and melded, one indigenous (the Central African Bantu) and two imported (the North African/Sahel and the Indian Ocean).

A completely separate agricultural transition occurred in Meso-America, centered on the domestication of maize, probably a descendant of teosinte, a wild grass. The cultivation of maize began some time after 5000 B.C.E. in the upper reaches of the Balsas River in the Mexican highlands. About a thousand years later it had spread to Peru, and by 2000 B.C.E., northward to New Mexico. Many productive varieties developed, which, combined with beans, squash, and chilies, provided a diet that sustained large populations, requiring hoe cultivation only. As maize strains improved—with cobs becoming larger and longer—it far outyielded Old World cereals. Other Meso-American foods included avocados, cocoa, sweet potatoes, runner beans, and tomatoes and, by 700 C.E., sunflowers and turkeys. From the Peruvian highlands came also lima beans, peanuts, peppers, potatoes, and domesticated animals that included guinea pigs, alpaca, and llamas; from the southeastern lowlands came pineapples and yams. Although rich in agricultural foods, especially maize and potatoes, the Americas were impoverished of large domesticated animals by the Pleistocene extinctions, leaving the New World with no substitutes for horses, cattle, or pigs. Draft animals therefore were limited to sled dogs in the Arctic north and left later American civilization quite without wheeled transportation.

Agriculture and Human Biology: Dramatic New Population Patterns

These five quite independent agricultural revolutions and their peoples spread slowly and relentlessly across steadily advancing frontiers, a process that continued into modern times, with, for example, agriculture arriving in Australia at the end of the 18th century. In all, the process took about 11,000 years (from ca. 9000 B.C.E. to 1800 C.E.) but was sudden, almost abrupt, by comparison with the Paleolithic colonization waves. Moreover *homo sapiens sapiens* and agricultural peoples both expanded into a world already occupied, except for Australia and the Americas, raising questions about relationships between colonists and earlier inhabitants, for instance, with regard to population replacement and genetic and cultural mixing.

The spread of agricultural peoples was a great demographic takeover. Not a biological evolution, like the appearance and spread of *homo erectus* and *homo sapiens sapiens*, it was a cultural adaptation, humans applying their intelligence as a survival mechanism. Agriculture, however, created a new kind of relationship with the ecosystem, a cultural adaptation almost equivalent to biological evolution. It created a disequilibrium that resulted in a demographic explosion, a plague of people. A sharp upward surge of population occurred after about 8000 B.C.E., which continues into the modern age, driven almost entirely by the increase of agricultural peoples.

Populations did not grow because agricultural peoples were better nourished or healthier or somehow lived easier. Disease actually increased, in part because population densities rose and because many diseases of livestock transferred to humans. Living together, people and animals thickened the web of infectious connections. Agricultural villages were ten or twenty times larger than foraging camps. They multiplied and formed clusters over the landscape, interacting through trade and social contacts. Rivers, streams, and wells became contaminated. Dysentery and other intestinal disorders were especially debilitating for young children and contributed to their malnutrition. In warmer climates, agriculturally rich river valleys and estuaries developed malaria and schistosomiasis, caused by a blood fluke transmitted in water. In short, mortality and malnutrition increased, and life expectancies fell.

But agricultural populations increased because birthrates rose. The settled life permitted women to have more children during their reproductive age by shortening the intervals between births. Given the natural urge to sexuality, a sedentary living pattern meant that cultural restraints against multiple children relaxed. The duration of breast-feeding periods shortened for each infant; porridges of grain that served as milk substitutes caused malnutrition but also a rise in birthrates. Large families meant that siblings and old people could care for young children. Older children gardened and herded livestock and farmyard animals. More labor readily produced more food, particularly where cultivation could be extended to more land.

Agricultural populations expanded into their frontiers by creating new villages, usually in terrains and soils like those of the homeland. So agricultural colonization in its early stages chose favorable locations first, bypassing vast tracts, for instance, densely forested areas or stony, infertile soils. Foragers continued to occupy these areas, and agriculturists had contacts with them. These contacts could be friendly or hostile, or even alternately so, depending on circumstances. Trading relationships developed, such as exchanges of manufactured wares for forest products and game meats for cereals.

Agriculturists enjoyed numerical superiority in occasional skirmishes with foragers, but social and economic interaction proved more subversive to hunting-gathering cultures. Trading relationships led to overhunting as agricultural populations transferred some of their food demands to hunting, and possibly also because hunting-gathering populations increased, too. Eventually, foragers felt pressured or saw advantages in adopting a few agricultural practices, perhaps only tending a small herd of goats at first or wishing to stay put and accumulate more personal possessions. Agriculturists' numerical superiority resulted in their languages gradually replacing those of foragers. So, even where foraging and agricultural cultures coresided for hundreds of years, foraging technologies and languages were greatly altered.

Meanwhile, agricultural societies themselves were biologically and culturally transformed. They grew to a size and developed mentalities that made returning to hunting and gathering unthinkable. Expectations about housing, family life, and personal possessions became established. Knowledge of farming became respected wisdom while foraging knowledge shrank. Tastes for certain foods and the rhythm of the seasons became entrenched habits. Even the crops had become domesticates that could not propagate without human help. Peoples' lives had become linked biologically with their plants and animals. Culture and agriculture evolved together. Caught in the momentum of growth, agricultural societies expanded, absorbing and obliterating other peoples and cultures in their path.

Eventually, agricultural peoples descended into the great, fertile river valleys, where by the fourth millennium B.C.E. the first civilizations emerged. These were difficult environments to convert to cropland with simple stone implements, thick as they were with trees, brush, river grasses, and marshlands. But once brought into cultivation, the valleys of the Nile, Tigris-Euphrates, and Indus-Hakra and Hwang-he river systems became vastly more productive than the semi-arid highlands above them. Villages and towns became larger and situated closely together. A new, higher threshold of population density resulted in increasing conflict over resources, for instance, water, wood, building stone, and trade routes. Agricultural production now attained a level at which surpluses were possible, which could support classes of nonagricultural specialists. Somehow out of this mix of new forces, social stratification, fortified urban centers, and political systems arose.

These bound together vast interactive human groups, properly termed agrarian civilizations. The peoples remained predominantly village-centered agriculturists but in a new, dense sociobiological environment wherein human groups and diseases interacted differently and more intensively. The consequences, to be discussed in chapter 6, were to increase mortality and reduce rates of population growth. These agrarian civilizations grew very slowly, expanding down- or upriver mostly but remaining largely confined to the river-valley environments for about two thousand years. About the only exception were towns along the coastal areas of the eastern Mediterranean and Aegean. Constant cropping, irrigation, and woodcutting in the upriver regions resulted in environmental deterioration, which for the Sumerians and the Indus valley inhabitants, at least, compelled population stagnation, relocation upriver, and even decline of urban centers.

Not until the early first millennium B.C.E. could agrarian civilizations expand out across the rain-watered lands around them. As with the Bantu, the vital element was probably iron metallurgy, which, applied to agricultural uses, permitted forest clearance, plowing, and hoeing with new efficiency that raised productivity to generate surpluses. Sometime between 800 and 500 B.C.E., agricultural communities ruled by urban-centered military elites spread southward in China, eastward across northern India, and along the coastal Mediterranean. Their populations grew rapidly again as the environmental constraints of the alluvial valleys were transcended.

CHAPTER 3

CULTURE AND POLITICS IN EARLY SOCIETIES

Innovations in early human history were vital in creating basic beliefs about how the world works, as well as artistic styles to represent these beliefs. Innovation was also crucial in generating organized governments. The development of cultural systems clearly preceded formal statecraft in human history, though both would produce important structures by the end of the river-valley period around 1000 B.C.E. Human beings needed culture early, as part of communication and to explain the world around them. Absent elaborate instincts, as the species evolved learning was vital for adaptation, and learning involved generating as well as transmitting the beliefs and values central to culture.

Although crucial developments in culture occurred relatively early in the human experience, focus on known cultures, and certainly on politics, draws attention to the advent of civilizations. Whereas the previous chapter, on the biological underpinnings of human history, emphasized changes from the advent of the species stretching over long spans of time, this chapter stresses later additions to the framework for human experience.

From Early Culture to Full Cultural Systems

Evidence for early culture is sketchy. Spoken language surely emerged between 1,500,000 and 500,000 B.C.E. Ideas and practices about death developed fairly early. Several human groups began to bury their dead, suggesting some belief in an afterlife—particularly when tools were included with the body. Formal art, in cave paintings relating to the hunt, was introduced by 16,000 B.C.E., in Europe and elsewhere. This art was both decorative and symbolic, designed to conciliate the fierce spirits of the mammals being killed. All this suggests some early religious ideas relating to beliefs about divine forces manifest in nature, including powerful animals such as the wild bull, that needed to be conciliated through rituals and magic—the origin of polytheistic religions and of religious art.

We do not know if further cultural changes helped bring about agriculture; quite possibly, only new survival needs and discoveries caused this huge development. Unquestionably, however, the rise of agriculture had a powerful impact on human culture. Monuments became more elaborate, and the leaders of kinship groups began to generate the fanciest tombs—a cultural acknowledgment of growing inequality, even the attribution of divine status to powerful figures. Specialized artists also emerged, providing new kinds of designs for pottery and other artifacts. Emphasis on agriculture shifted religion toward greater stress on gods and goddesses relevant to fertility and the harvest; along with these abstractions, often involving emphasis on female principles of generation, many agricultural societies developed the idea of a male creator god.

Cultures in agriculture and in hunting-and-gathering societies shared many features, despite the wide dispersal of the groups involved. Varied languages had common features—40 percent of languages today, for example, organize sentences in terms of subject first, then verb, then object; another 35 percent put object first, then verb, and then subject. All recognize action agents, actions, and objects of actions, reflecting ways in which the human brain is programmed. Many specific languages also derived from common earlier cores. A spoken language scholars call Proto-Indo-European developed in nomadic Central Asia at least 5,000 years ago: From this would come Sanskrit, Iranian, Celtic, Greek, and all the major languages of contemporary Western and Central Europe. Some scholars even argue for a still more general common language earlier, which may provide links among languages seemingly as different as the European languages, Arabic, Dravidian (South India), even Japanese. Thus a connection between the word for fist and the word for five is clear in a host of otherwise very different languages (including English, of course). Diverse peoples may also have spread common stories. An Italian historian, Carlo Ginzburg, claims to have found similar magical beliefs and related fairy stories from Siberia to ancient India to Europe, which he thinks were spread by nomadic peoples. One common story of this sort involves a lost shoe leading to a hero conquering forces of evil—the tale that ultimately ended up in Europe as the story of Cinderella. Unknown but powerful early contacts as well as the common capacities of the human brain clearly have shaped cultures in many similar directions.

But cultures also vary widely as they reflect different environments and experiences. Comparison, from the early stages onward, must involve a balance between similarities and contrasts. Some hunting-and-gathering cultures honored older people, assuring them the best food, whereas others were extremely harsh, forcing older parents to turn over property to the young. Differences of this sort initially reflected different resource availability, but they could continue to shape distinctive experiences even after the physical environment changed. Some cultures to this day emphasize veneration for the elderly more than others, in societies with otherwise similar basic economies.

During the early civilization period, the elaboration of cultures, including writing and specific artistic styles, tended to highlight a differentiation process. Egypt and Mesopotamia provide a prime example. Mesopotamian culture emphasized human frailty and the difficulty of achieving anything against a difficult environment and frequently hostile gods. As the epic *Gilgamesh* (ca. 2000 B.C.E.) put it: "As for mankind, numbered are their days. Whatever they achieve is but the wind." Egypt, in contrast, valued people's ability to triumph over nature and achieve a stability that would bridge the transition from life to after death. Aided by the gods, some of whom, as pharaohs, directly led humankind, people could count on a secure order.

Mesopotamian gods, though powerful, embodied selfish and quarrelsome characteristics, which made for interesting stories but created a fear that the gods might be difficult to control. In a region where natural disasters were frequent, the gods were seen as agents who unpredictably sent floods and other undeserved torments. Sumerian temples and priests were meant more as offerings to please angry deities than as celebrations of divine power. Egyptian culture, in contrast, was considerably more cheerful. Egyptian modes of expression were less literary than Mesopotamian modes (though writing was widely used to keep official records) and more artistic—beginning with the fact that the writing itself was more pictorial than was Sumerian cuneiform. And the art involved colorful and lively pictures. Egypt's multiple gods required careful attention, and some were capable of harm if not properly conciliated, but there was far less emphasis on whimsical disruptions than among the Sumerians. Because the pharaohs themselves were regarded as gods, artistic production highlighted portrayals of majesty, spiced with varied scenes of everyday human life. The vivid art was also highly stylized, with figures presented stiffly, perhaps reflecting a belief that basic characteristics could be abstracted from the varieties of actual human experience.

These general distinctions carried over into beliefs about life after death. Mesopotamian religious ideas included an afterlife of suffering—the origins of the concept of hell, though in the Mesopotamian rendering this a time more of sorrow than of active punishment. But primary emphasis rested on the interaction between humans and gods in this world, not preparations for the next, which could not be controlled. Egyptian culture focused strongly on a concern with death and the belief that in an afterlife, a changeless, happy well-being could be achieved; though the religion emphasized the need for a favorable judgment by the powerful god Osiris. The famous hallmarks of Egyptian society all pointed in this direction: The care shown in mummifying bodies and preparing tombs, along with elaborate funeral rituals, particularly for the rulers and bureaucrats, all emphasized the hope of assuring a satisfactory afterlife. The great pyramids enshrined the leading pharaohs, stocked with all sorts of daily artifacts available for use after death. Mesopotamian art and ritual, in contrast, reflected far less sense that death could be transcended, and they were far less elaborate.

Sharp distinctions of this sort reflected the separate cultural paths even of neighboring civilizations. Though Egypt and Mesopotamia traded and occasionally warred, there was little mutual cultural influence. This left the religions of the two societies free to reflect differences in geography and human experience. Egypt was a more stable society than Mesopotamia. It experienced fewer natural disasters, though Egyptian religion abundantly recorded the need to celebrate the greatness of the Nile, on which agriculture depended. Egypt was also more protected than Mesopotamia from outside invasion. The dynasties of the pharaohs occasionally collapsed, and later in Egypt's history conquest occurred from Kush, to the south, and then from Rome. But the region underwent nothing like the Mesopotamian experience of fluctuating empires and recurrent waves of invasion

Egyptian Preparations for the Afterlife. Tomb walls were often covered with scenes of the deceased both in earthly life and afterlife. In this tomb portrait, dated 700 B.C.E., a couple from Thebes face the gods of the underworld. What kind of ideas about death are implied? From Deir-el Medine, Thebes. Reprinted by permission of Hirmer Verlag, Munich.

from the north. These differences in natural and historical patterns surely helped form Mesopotamia's cultural need to deal with unpredictability and a sense of lack of control. Egypt's preference for ordered stability even sought to carry the political emphasis on authority and continuity into the afterlife, where the chance of change would be even more remote.

Yet, while cultural differences mirrored the need to cope with distinctive environments, they also shaped the human context. Egypt's emphases ultimately helped perpetuate not only the monumental artistic styles but the authority of the pharaohs, which explains why the system was recurrently revived during a span of almost 2,000 years. Cultural assumptions in this sense could become self-fulfilling, helping to account for political differences as well as distinctive religions and representations, all of which would help confirm the special features of the culture itself. Mesopotamian culture played a more subordinate role in the fortunes of the region—in no sense did it cause the invasions and the rise and fall of diverse empires. Yet it helped people accommodate to these changes, preserving cultural emphases even amid political shifts.

One result is quite clear: Two quite different cultural models were available for consultation in northern Africa and the eastern Mediterranean, not only during the early civilization period but well beyond. There is no question that Egyptian culture produced the most durable structures, its pyramids and mummy cases lasting to the present day, in contrast to the smaller, more fragile temples of Mesopotamia. But for succeeding groups in the region—the Greeks and Romans and, soon, Christians and Muslims—both cultures might be sampled, and at points the Mesopotamian version would clearly seem more useful.

Religious and artistic differentiations and their legacy were not the only fruit of this formative cultural period, for the advent of early civilizations also created new possibilities for persuading regional societies or invading peoples that they should adopt important features of a dominant cultural mode. Early civilizations could cut into local cultures, sometimes displacing them altogether. Their splendor and their frequent association with political power and commercial success gave them particular persuasiveness, as well as unusual geographical range. Even invading peoples, bringing in very different languages and cultures, frequently merged their beliefs with the more settled cultural systems they overran. Rare was the case, as with the collapse of the Indus River valley cities, in which a prior culture was largely eclipsed. Thus all sorts of groups in Mesopotamia came to adopt Sumerian cuneiform, applying it to their spoken languages; even the Indo-European Hittite invaders followed this path. Artistic forms, stories, even the existing range of gods were appropriated. The culture of

Mesopotamia, in other words, was far more stable than its politics because of its absorbing power.

Further, the culture showed the capacity to spread from initial centers near the Tigris-Euphrates. The *Gilgamesh* epic, for example, fanned out from the Persian Gulf to the Mediterranean coast. Artistic motifs drawn from it, such as a statue of Gilgamesh strangling a lion, won wide favor— and they were preserved, used (without knowledge of the source) even on European cathedral doors three thousand years later. Sumerian deities also won converts. Ishtar, the goddess of human fertility, was worshiped as Astarte in Semitic lands in southern Arabia and later as Aphrodite, goddess of beauty, in Greece.

A dramatic indication of the power of a civilization's culture to spread, along with its trade and (occasionally) government structures, involves the story of the great flood, based initially, in all probability, on a mythical exaggeration of the real flood problem in parts of the Middle East. A Babylonian story involved gods who grew angry at obstreperous humans: "By their uproar they prevent sleep." They vowed to punish by a damaging flood, but first they asked Atrahasis ("the exceedingly wise") to build a great ship and to house on it samples of all the beasts of the field. In the *Gilgamesh* story the hero was Utnapishtim, who constructed an ark that survived seven days of flooding; after the rains stopped, he landed on a mountaintop and sent a dove, a swallow, and a raven to investigate, until land finally appeared. The flood story, in various, specific versions, spread throughout the Middle East, and it was picked up as part of Jewish lore and incorporated, with Noah as the ark builder and a single God as the source of wrath and salvation, in the Old Testament, as this collection of scriptures began to be assembled after 1000 B.C.E. Sharing the story did not, of course, mean sharing the whole culture; Jewish religion as a whole represented a major innovation compared to Mesopotamian cults. Similarity, including the result of contact, must still be balanced with differentiation.

By 1000 B.C.E., in fact, many of the key analytical themes of culture and civilization were clearly established. As individual civilizations built up, they gained identity by emphasizing some distinctive cultural features; this ensured that contrasts among major cultures would long persist. At the same time, the well-established cultures could integrate newcomers and could radiate into adjacent regions, creating new possibilities for at least partial cultural integration.

Civilizations also, thanks to their elaborate cultural apparatus, left legacies of beliefs and styles. Egypt's monumental architecture clearly influenced later Mediterranean societies. Specific building blocks, such as the Chinese writing system, were obviously passed on to later periods. For the river-valley societies, limited evidence inevitably creates debate about the ongoing power of basic ideas. Later Chinese civilizations liked to point to the river-valley period as the source of basic concepts of balance in nature, vital in Chinese philosophy and public belief. They believed that their civilization's identity was formed in this semimythical past, and they insisted that educated people study the history and stories presumably derived from this period. The great philosopher Confucius argued that he was merely codifying ideas and literature derived from ancient China. We have no way of knowing how much truth there was in these undoubtedly sincere claims. It is certainly possible that the core of what became a very durable cultural approach in China was shaped along with initial civilization itself.

A similar debate about cultural origins has been applied to Egypt and Mesopotamia. As we have seen, key artistic styles and stories were passed on to later cultures, such as the Jewish religion. The same holds for basic advances in numbering systems and in science, which were utilized by Greek and other Mediterranean thinkers. Recent discussion focuses on the extent to which basic religious concepts and stories also were simply copied by the Greeks from the two river-valley civilizations of the eastern Mediterranean, along with fundamental standards of beauty and an understanding of human nature. How original did the Greeks have to be? How much did they utilize Indo-European mythologies, brought by the invaders who coursed through the region after about 1200 B.C.E., and how much could they simply revive established culture?

Debate here has sharpened since the 1987 publication of Martin Bernals's *Black Athena: The Africanistic Roots of Classical Civilizations.* Bernals argues that Greece not only adapted earlier alphabets and architectural styles but took over basic philosophical and scientific concepts from earlier African and Middle Eastern cultures. He contends that this borrowing has been neglected because scholars were so bent on highlighting

Greek genius, and this because the Greeks were recognizably European in contrast to Africans and Middle Eastern peoples, like the Jews, who have encountered intense racial prejudice in modern times. Bernals's arguments have been rejected, however, by another set of scholars, who find his attempts to trace Greek ideas far-fetched and unsupported by evidence and who also resent his implicit accusations of scholarly racism. The debate continues, as Bernals proceeds to lay out his case.

The issue of cultural legacies of prior civilization surviving amid great change is not unique to this case. Today, American intellectuals continue to debate how much their civilization owes to Greek and Roman origins and how much was more recently invented or combined from a greater variety of cultural sources.

One cultural issue was not directly confronted in the period of the river-valley civilizations, though it was prepared: The cultures of established civilizations had yet to confront one another directly. As we have seen, Egyptian and Mesopotamian contacts had little cultural significance. Mesopotamia may have influenced developments along the Indus River, but the extent of such influence is unknown. Indus River cities traded with Sumeria, but we lack evidence that ideas were exchanged in the process. Given the capacity of civilizations to insist on sharp cultural identities and to develop elaborate apparatuses to express and maintain these identities, what would happen when more elaborate and significant encounters occurred? It was only in the next period of world history, when civilizations developed even larger powers of regional integration, that this issue could be tested.

Creating States

The emergence of formal governments as a factor in human history was a much later development than the creation of discernible cultures. Small hunting-and-gathering groups and even early agricultural societies did not require political specialization. Kinship chiefs, rather than explicit government officials, helped organize power, usually in consultation with other leading warriors. Even nomadic groups in Central Asia long operated without clear government institutions, often building kinship groups into interlocking chiefdoms that sometimes generated a military leader at the top.

Rules were produced by group decisions and enforced through rituals and religious taboos. But the river-valley civilizations all created governments, justifying them by religion and enforcing their existence through laws, punishments, and military force. Thus the Shang dynasty in early China claimed appointment by the gods and also led the military force, controlling much of the production of weaponry. Civilization, among other things, always meant formal states, and this was a major innovation.

The first states arose in Mesopotamia and Egypt up to five thousand years after the agricultural revolution. Once invented, they usually proved so useful (or self-protective) that they were rarely dislodged, save by temporary catastrophes such as invasions; and they were often copied by other societies, whose leaders saw the advantages in a more formal apparatus of power.

States arose in societies whose economies were operating on a relatively large scale, with many people and over a sizable region (though by modern standards, population and region might still seem very small). Intensive farming, often involving irrigation, provided a food surplus, which could support a small, powerful elite class that gained control over much of the land and used force and religious power to back their authority. Many archaeologists theorize that states emerged because they were helpful as a way of organizing both increased food supplies— through intensified, coordinated agriculture and trade—and external relations with sometimes-hostile neighbors (including hunting groups who resisted agriculture but liked to prey on settled populations). Effective, centralized management of trade and of food production, through state-organized irrigation systems and other methods, could be the only means of maintaining agriculture in arid climates. On major rivers such as the Nile and the Tigris-Euphrates, purely individual attempts at irrigation could divert so much water that the populations downstream could not survive. A formal state, making decisions about where to build irrigation systems and when to release water flow, was the only way to avoid incessant conflict and ecological imbalance. The same state could undertake formal negotiations with warlike neighbors, offering desirable goods (such as the volcanic glass, obsidian, widely used as a token in Mesopotamia) as peace offerings. This whole process, emphasizing the economic advantages of states in certain environments, helps explain why many early states, like those of the Egyptians or the Aztecs in Central America, developed such an important role in regulating labor.

The world's first state arose in Mesopotamia, though Egypt was not far behind. The political and social conditions of Mesopotamia provide another example of the challenges involved in studying early states. On the whole, earlier ideas about the power of Mesopotamian rulers have been modified by findings that suggest a gap between their claims and their effective functions. Yet there is no question that the Sumerian founders of Mesopotamian civilization introduced the state as a new kind of policy-making, power-implementing device. The Sumerians themselves had invaded the region around 4000 B.C.E. Their tribal chieftains, settling down to agriculture, doubtless appropriated large landed estates. At the same time, new political structure were needed to improve control of complex irrigation systems and supply the needs of a city economy. Economic and irrigation needs may also have involved the early state in intervention in property disputes. Hence a principal leader—a king—emerged, who nevertheless continued to consult other residents, just as chieftains long had done. Strong local religion quickly began to provide additional justifications for the state, as priests participated in the early officialdom. The small size of the Sumerian city-states, with no more than 10,000 residents, did not support a strong political authority. But political power tended to increase with the size of the state, especially in early civilizations.

Enhanced state power and new military and religious claims resulted in part from invasions, which generated larger empires in the region, new defense needs, and new resources for the war chiefs. The Mesopotamian kings were military leaders. The flat but fertile land, with no natural protective barriers, opened Mesopotamia to nomadic invaders whose recurrent incursions made it imperative for the rise of military men as state leaders to defend the land. As wars, defense, and conquests won them power, recognition, and gratitude, their positions, which initially might have been elected by kinship groups, became hereditary. Because military forces were essential for survival, advanced military organization and war techniques developed early in this region. Military defense easily extended into aggressive expansion. It was not accidental that in this region the Akkadian king Sargon I created the world's first empire, or that the later Assyrians established a formidable military empire. While bronze weapons greatly enhanced the fighting capacities of these peoples, their superior military organization and skills, nourished by the constant need for superior military might, were the underlying factors in their success. In time, military power combined with the strongest cultural feature of the region, religion. And the growth of military activity increased the resource demands of the state; some kind of enhanced taxation was essential. If elements of religion could be used to make the state's new power and demands seem legitimate, the combination was virtually inevitable.

The strong religious tradition of the region provided the basis for the later kings' claims of divine appointment to legitimate their positions. A royal inscription of the king Esarhaddon (680–669 B.C.E.), for example, tells that deities Shamash and Adad confirmed a positive yes to his succession to the throne. While we do not know if the Mesopotamian kings took on direct responsibility for enforcing people's religious obligation, we do know that they assumed the state should not only utilize the protection of the gods but enhance their worship. Hence a key cultural and public-works function of the Mesopotamian state was to organize the design and labor for building magnificent new ziggurats, an act that was supposed to enhance the well-being of the ruler and the people alike. In this way, political power received religious sanction and the state promoted the faith. Religion was powerful influence, and the state wanted to assure that it operated under its direction and for its benefit. Very often, the state tried to control the priests and the temples, the powerful rival forces of influence, to consolidate its political power.

Besides military and religious functions, and of course, the organization of irrigation systems and public works, the state undertook other activities. It collected taxes to support its very existence, a process that yielded many complaints. The government also claimed to regulate and control different aspects of people's lives. The best sources on these interactions are the contemporary law codes, such as the code of emperor Hammurabi, which offer a vivid picture of state in society.

For all the magnificent temples and proclamations, however, this was a small state. It had very few full-time officials, including soldiers—well under 1 percent of the total population. To be sure, Mesopotamian civilization had a definite bureaucracy. The state appointed and paid judges and some other officials. It set up schools to train priests and scriptwriters in cuneiform writing, which was essential for record keeping and administration. But the result was a vital yet very small set of top officials. Even taxes were not directly collected by state agents but were contracted out to private entrepreneurs who were supposed to give the government a percentage of their take; this was a common procedure for governments in agricultural civilizations throughout much of later world history (China was the lone exception), but it both reflected and confirmed the limits to effective state control.

In this situation, the government depended heavily on its ability to require help from its subjects. It was most effective in demanding labor service from dependent workers, during portions of the year when they were not needed on the farms. This was the source of public works, temples, defensive walls, and a rudimentary roads system. Even here, the bulk of attention focused on the scattered cities, except for the vital irrigation networks that had to be kept in careful repair. On other matters, reliance on private cooperation might be less effective, and the law codes reflect this vulnerability as well. The state depended largely on private individuals to identify and catch criminals, for example. Finally, certain kinds of functions were not undertaken at all. Except for training a few officials, the state maintained no educational system. It had no police force, though it did claim a responsibility for punishing crime. It had no formal welfare functions as far as can be determined. This was a state that could work very well—though defense was constant problem—but its functions were circumscribed. At the same time, however, the Mesopotamian state recognized no clear boundary between its sphere and private life. Property ownership was acknowledged—the state did not claim to own everything—but the government asserted a major responsibility in family relations. It also claimed sweeping responsibilities for maintaining order and for avoiding private vendettas, and minor criminal offenses received harsh punishment. It had no system of prisons; the concept of reforming an offender or locking up dangerous criminals had not developed in this society. State responsibility for order nevertheless was revealed in its stated obligation to offer some payments to the victims of certain crimes. The state also assumed the task of enforcing fair commercial practices and seriously punished those who were convicted of providing poor-quality commodities, be it a house, a boat, or other goods. How widely these provisions were enforced cannot be known, but the claims of the state are revealing.

The Egyptian state developed separately from the states in Mesopotamia. Again, origins are unclear, but small regional kingdoms apparently launched the process, which then led to conquest and the formation of a unified state by around 3100 B.C.E. Two features distinguished the Egyptian state from its Mesopotamian neighbors. First, as we have seen, it experienced greater stability. Egypt's geography—surrounded in part by desert, in part by the Red Sea—gave it much greater protection from invasion than Mesopotamia had. Second, perhaps because of a particular delight in stability, or perhaps because stability made it possible, the authority of the ruler was more heavily emphasized. Here is where cultural and political characteristics reinforced each other, in both civilizations. Gradually, the Egyptian kings, or pharaohs as they came to be called, moved from claiming the support of the gods to claiming that they were among the gods themselves, to be worshiped with elaborate ceremonialism as well as obeyed. Massive monuments conveyed this religious tone while demonstrating the state's capacity to organize the necessary labor. This merger of state and religion is called a theocracy.

Egypt's considerable expanse and the needs for careful administration of the Nile River's irrigation and flooding potentials prompted a considerable bureaucracy. The head of this officialdom was a vizier, who in 1400 B.C.E. was joined by another—one to administer the delta area, one the south. This suggests a growing administrative complexity, and indeed, given the region's prosperity, the Egyptian bureaucracy may have been somewhat larger than its counterpart in Mesopotamia. Villages may have had less independent power, and certainly the organization of labor service loomed large in a society devoted to massive monuments. Officials also collected taxes, acted as judges, administered the treasury (including, sometimes, the temple treasuries), and directed the armies.

Little is known about the states of the Indus River valley, though recent work is filling in some gaps, and scholars are currently debating evidence of considerable decentralization along with signs of some coordinating authority in the well-appointed cities. The early Chinese state is also shrouded in some mystery. It was almost certainly smaller than the governments of North Africa and West Asia, with fewer bureaucrats and less need to emphasize military activities. The most distinctive feature of this state involves the ways in which it was conceived—the political culture it generated, in the notion that the state was the family writ large and that rulers and officials were like parents exercising benevolent and paternalistic control over the people. This quality began to develop during the Shang dynasty, the first historical dynasty (in Northwest China) whose existence has been confirmed, by the 20th-century discovery of their writings on oracle bones. While they, like other ancient people, worshiped animistic natural forces headed by a supreme deity, the Shang-ti, the Shang rulers defined their ancestors as the deities. It was from these ancestors that they sought guidance and blessings, and toward them as well that they displayed a fear of divine punishment. This ancestor worship, probably derived from the earlier tribal or Neolithic agrarian tradition, provided the ruler a strong religious justification; ministers and officials were also clan members and junior followers of this patriarchal lineage headed by the king. The later, imperial-period Chinese concept of rulers and officials as parents of the people derived from this Shang family-state tradition and became a persistent and distinctive feature of Chinese political culture.

Features of the Shang state and society were further developed, revised, and institutionalized by their conqueror, a former vassal, the Zhou family, who came into prominence shortly before 1000 B.C.E. Originating further west in the Wei River valley, the Zhou had the advantage of fertile land and a strong military ability, acquired by constant fighting against their nomadic neighbors. The dynasty proved important to the development of the state in Chinese culture because they introduced a lasting political principle and theory, the Mandate of Heaven. Moreover, they firmly established the concept of family-state, which influenced Chinese civilization for the next millennium and beyond.

The Mandate of Heaven idea was developed by the early Zhou rulers to justify their conquest of the Shang. Though an unusual concept, it illustrates the common tendency to use religious claims to provide legitimacy for early states or ruling groups. Yet both its explicit and implicit meanings profoundly affected Chinese politics and culture. As vassals, the Zhou had owed loyalty to the Shang, so their military triumph had no justification in principle. Yet they needed to appeal to their fellow vassals, and to a lesser degree, to the majority of subjects, to gain acceptance. Thus they began to argue that the final Shang ruler had misgoverned and that, as a result, Heaven, or Tien (a new deity introduced by the Zhou, probably a remote family ancestor), withdrew his mandate of governance. The implications were obvious: Heaven supported the Zhou, but Heaven also insisted on ethical, meritorious behavior on the part of rulers. This idea of explicit responsibility, unusual in the early civilizations, was a vital concomitant to the authoritarian claims of the Chinese state. The combination described Chinese political administration in principle, and often in fact, through many periods of Chinese history. Although Chinese emperors were still hereditary, they were required to govern well to maintain their power; and although not overtly acknowledged, a right of rebellion existed in order to depose oppressive, inept rulers. In these terms, rebellion might be widely accepted as reestablishing legitimate government, with no changes in the basic system involved. Much later, the principle of responsible rule would underlie the development of the Chinese bureaucracy and its training.

Conclusion

Early governments constituted a vital innovation in human history, affecting particularly economic coordination but also the conduct of war. Force and religious beliefs were always combined to make this system work. Despite their recent origins, early states could have important influence on people's lives, especially in their work but to some extent in their family arrangements. At the same time, despite sometimes sweeping claims, they did not provide detailed controls over daily life; the majesty of the state might be feared or respected, but it was also rather remote.

As with culture—indeed, intertwined with beliefs about the gods and about the nature of society—early governments differed significantly from one civilization to the next, setting up important legacies for later world history. The difference between states that claimed divine support and those, such as Egypt, that ultimately claimed the ruler himself was a god is not insignificant. The Egyptian idea may have influenced political traditions of divine kingship later in Africa—though this is not certain—and it was certainly revived, briefly, at a crisis period in the Roman Empire, when arguing that the emperor should himself be worshipped seemed at least worth a try. The dependence of states in the Middle East and North Africa on religious backing contrasted with a looser use of religion in China, where a somewhat different, more secular justification for political power began to emerge. Distinctions of this sort, passed on to later regimes in these same areas, clearly generated different ideas of what the state was. They may have affected the functions actual states sought to carry out. And—though this is hard to test historically—they may even have created different chances for durable political success. Here, as in other aspects of early civilization history, it is worth asking if some traditions were more useful than others.

CHAPTER 4

GENDER STRUCTURES

Introduction through Early Civilizations

Early human history, and particularly the emergence of agriculture and then civilization, fundamentally redefined the meanings of male and female and many of the roles of men and women in human society. Key changes related to the upheavals in population patterns, which increased women's childbearing and child-rearing responsibilities. But gender also related closely to broader formulations of culture, including religion. Developments in these crucial early periods added greatly to the "natural" features of gender, creating the complex relationships between the natural and the humanly constructed that have persisted ever since.

The Paleolithic (Early Stone Age) Period

For most of human history, the only records that remain of gender structures, as with all other aspects of human culture, are physical remnants—bones, stones, marks on the landscape where there were once buildings and fields, pieces of pottery, a few drawings and carvings. Interpreting these to gain insights into early family structures, the roles of men and women, and ideas and practices of sexuality is extremely difficult, for it is often hard to decide what something *is*—a spear point or a scraper, a man's bones or a woman's—and even harder to decide what it might *mean*. Nevertheless, we know that early humans developed gender structures—concepts and practices that differentiated women from men, beyond physical differences—and that later elaborations, in all their variety, grew out of these early forms. These gender structures predated the formation of states and played a major role in organizing human behavior.

Though traditionally, early human cultures are termed "hunting-and-gathering" cultures, recent archaeological research indicates that both historical and contemporary hunter-gatherers actually depend much more on gathered foods than on hunted meat. Thus early human societies might be more accurately termed "gatherer-hunters" or "foragers," a term now favored by scholars. The most important element of early human success was flexibility and adaptability, with gathering and hunting probably varying in their importance from year to year, depending on environmental factors and the decisions of the group. This flexibility may have extended to gender roles, for most prehistorians now question whether men were always the hunters and women the gatherers. Whatever tasks they did, both men and women made tools; the pointed flaked-stone tools that remain from the Paleolithic period were multipurpose and could have been used as peelers, nutcrackers, spear points, plant choppers, and skin scrapers.

The emphasis on the importance of both gathering and hunting has reinvigorated debate about the source of gender hierarchies: If prehistoric women did not have to depend on "man the hunter," how and why did women become subordinate? Answers have ranged widely. Some have focused on physical differences, such as women's reproductive capacities, with pregnancy and lactation regarded as physical burdens that leave women less time for other tasks. Male strength, aggressiveness, and a greater propensity for violence have also been stressed, with warfare viewed as one of the ways in which men claimed a greater share of scarce resources. Sociobiologists have developed a genetic explanation: Because men produce millions of sperm and women relatively few mature eggs, the key to "genetic success" (meaning the transmission of one's genes to the next generation) for men is to impregnate as many women as possible while keeping other men from doing so, whereas for women it is to take great care in bringing up their offspring. Thus it is genes, according to this theory, that explain rape and the seclusion of women and why men skip out on their child-care payments.

All of these answers have been challenged by studies of primates and contemporary foragers and by cross-cultural comparisons, and the weaknesses in all of them have led some scholars to assert that women were not subordinate in the Paleolithic past. In the 19th century the idea developed that the earliest human societies had been matriarchal (female dominated), with female deities and female leaders—an idea still held by a few scholars but largely discredited for lack of evidence. More recently, the idea that foraging societies were egalitarian—with men and women having different tasks but equally valued—has become more popular, based largely on observation of some contemporary foraging societies, such as the !Kung of South Africa or the Mbuti of the Democratic Republic of Congo, or on reports of foragers from the recent past, such as the Innu (Montagnais-Naskapi) of Labrador in Canada. Scholars who accept the idea of an original egalitarianism see the roots of female subordination in something that happened subsequent to tool manufacture and use, that is, in something that happened because of the "agricultural revolution" of the Neolithic period.

Neolithic Period

Because most foraging cultures have some sort of division of labor by sex, and with women primarily responsible for gathering plant products, women were most likely those who first intentionally planted seeds in the ground, rather than simply harvesting wild grains. They then began to select the seeds they planted in order to get more productive crops, and, by observation, learned the optimum times and places for planting. This early crop planting was done by individuals using hoes and digging sticks and is often termed *horticulture*, to distinguish it from the later agriculture using plows. Horticulture can be combined quite easily with gathering and hunting, as plots of land are usually small. Many cultures, including some of those in eastern North America, remained mixed foragers/horticulturists for thousands of years, with base camps they returned to regularly during the growing season. In horticultural societies, women appear to have retained control of the crops they planted, sharing them with group members or giving them as gifts. They had high social status, though rules on what work was male or female were quite strict, and men would be ridiculed for doing women's tasks.

In some areas of the world, beginning with the Middle East, horticulture was successful at producing enough food to allow groups to settle more or less permanently in one area. This food included cereal crops that could be eaten by young children, allowing women to wean their children at a younger age. Earlier weaning meant a woman became fertile more quickly after a birth (nursing tends to suppress ovulation in the mother), so that children were born at more frequent intervals. As we have seen, agricultural villages in the Middle East began to grow quite rapidly.

What can we tell about gender structures in these early Neolithic horticultural societies? As with Paleolithic groups, conclusions are often based on a combination of archaeological finds and comparisons with more modern groups. Most scholars stress diversity over one single pattern. Most horticultural societies adopted living arrangements that were either *matrilocal*, in which husbands left their homes to live with their wives, or *patrilocal*, in which wives left their homes to live with their husbands, but not both. In many cultures, women appear to have been responsible for agricultural work—querns used to mill flour have been found in female graves—whereas men hunted—arrowheads have been found in male graves. It appears that there was little differentiation in status based on sex, as there is not much difference in terms of the quantity or quality of grave goods found with men and women.

Plow agriculture appears to have brought more drastic changes in gender structures than simple crop planting. Here, indeed, is one of the big shifts in gender relations in world history. Beginning around 3000 B.C.E. in the Middle East, cattle began to be used to pull carts and plows; the earliest depictions of this are on Mesopotamian cylinder seals, which also indicate that plowing was a male task. At about the same time, some cultures began to raise cattle for milking and sheep for shearing—rather than both for meat, as had been the earlier practice—thus increasing the amount of what are termed *secondary agricultural products*, such as dairy products and cloth. The spinning and weaving of cloth became a primary female task, though why this should be so is not clear; most explanations note that spinning can be combined with caring for younger children and the overseeing of older children's working, and that the equipment needed was not extensive or expensive and so available to most women. The problem with this is that it does not explain why women did not have access to resources for more expensive tools, nor why they were the ones charged with supervising and training children.

We can never be certain about the reasons for this new gender division of labor, but it happened not only in the Neolithic Near East but also in the vast majority of the world's cultures in which plow agriculture was introduced. In much of sub-Saharan Africa and the Americas, for example, agriculture continued to be carried out largely with a hoe and digging stick, and women continued as the major crop producers. In Asia, plow agriculture and the keeping of domestic animals were and are more common, and women play a much smaller role in farming.

The consequences of plow agriculture and its new gender division of labor are easier to trace than the causes. Plow agriculture significantly increased the food supply but also significantly increased the resources needed to produce that food: Animals had to be fed and cared for, plows made and maintained, storage containers expanded and improved, workers trained and sheltered. For the first time in human culture, material goods—plows, sheep, cattle, sheds, jars—gave one the ability to amass still *more* material goods, and the gap between rich and poor, between plow owner and non–plow owner, began to widen. This social differentiation based on access to animals and agricultural implements came just at the time, as we have seen, that agriculture was becoming a male task, so its impact was different for men and women. With men responsible for the basic agricultural labor, boys were favored over girls for the work they could do for their parents while young and for the support they could provide in parents' old age. Boys became the normal inheritors of family land and of the rights to work communally held land.

Though the effects of plow agriculture on gender structures are relatively easy to document, the reasons behind them are hotly debated. Some analysts put forth a strictly materialist explanation: Female subordination resulted from women's exclusion from the means of production, from their smaller role in the daily production of agricultural goods with the new division of labor. This view has been criticized because it overlooks women's role in the processing of food and clothing, as well as neglecting cultural factors that contributed to the origins of *patriarchy*, the social and political structure in which men, and particularly older men, predominate. Thus other analysts emphasize the association of gender with other cultural dichotomies discussed earlier in this chapter. As agricultural communities changed the landscape through irrigation and building, they increasingly saw themselves as separate from and superior to the natural world and developed a nature/culture dichotomy. Because women were the bearers of children, and because they did not own the irrigated, culturally adapted fields, they were regarded as closer to nature and therefore inferior. As more of women's labor began to take place inside the house or household complex, and as houses were increasingly regarded as owned by an individual or family, women were increasingly associated with the domestic or private realm. Men, whose work was done outside in conjunction with other men, were increasingly associated with the public realm, which increased in complexity and importance as communities grew. Both of these dichotomies—nature/culture, private/public—and their association with women's subordination have been criticized as not applying to all of the world's cultures, but such ideological linkages were important in many areas. A final factor, relating to practical arrangements and cultures alike, involved more frequent childbearing, which, as we have seen, was a key component of agricultural society.

Civilization

Political change, such as the growth of the increasingly hierarchical and bureaucratized cultures of Mesopotamia and Egypt, also brought differing opportunities for men and women. The early river-valley civilizations depended on taxes and tribute as well as slave labor for their support, and so their rulers were very interested in maintaining population levels. As hereditary aristocracies developed, they became concerned with maintaining the distinction between themselves and the majority of the population. These concerns led to attempts to control women's reproduction, through laws governing sexual relations and, more important, through marriage norms and practices that set up a very unequal relationship between spouses. Some historians see the type of marriage established in the river-valley civilizations, in which women were placed under the legal authority of their husbands, as the key reason for the subordination of women, rather than physical differences or the division of labor. Because the vast majority of people married, women increasingly derived what power and authority they held from their husbands rather than from their own abilities, wealth, or status. Women generally married for the first time in their late teens to men who were about ten years older. This age difference added another element of inequality to the marriage, with a woman substituting the authority of one older man—her father—for that of another—her husband.

Marriage in most of the world's cultures, including those of ancient Mesopotamia and Egypt, set up an economic unit in which the properties of the husband and wife were usually combined and regarded as heritable, in other words, as able to be passed down to children or other heirs. It was therefore extremely important to husbands that they be assured that the children their wives bore were theirs. Thus the laws of Mesopotamia mandated that women be virgins on marriage and imposed strict punishment for a married woman's adultery; sexual relations outside marriage on the part of husbands were not considered adultery, a distinction carried on in many later societies. By the third millennium B.C.E., Mesopotamian husbands veiled their wives on marriage; the word for this veiling in ancient Akkadian was the same as the word for shutting a door, for the veil was to protect the wife's honor just as the walls of the house did. Concern with family honor thus became linked to women's sexuality in a way that it was not for men; men's honor revolved around their work activities and, for more prominent families, around their performance of public duties in the expanding government bureaucracies. In actuality, Mesopotamian women may have made some family decisions, but legally they were subject to their husbands; because almost everyone married, widows were the only women who controlled their own property.

Though Egypt was also patriarchal—one writer, around 2000 B.C.E., warned men, "Hold her [the wife] back from mastery"—systematic repression there may have been less severe than in Mesopotamia. Women in Egypt, at least in the upper classes, seem to have been treated with greater respect than their Mesopotamian counterparts. More queens wielded real power, for example. Queen Nefertiti, in the first half of the 14th century B.C.E., was known for her beauty but also for the influence she had over religious reforms in the kingdom. Egyptian religious beliefs were also more egalitarian than those of Mesopotamia. Concern for the afterlife was extremely important in Egypt, and religious beliefs about the afterlife applied equally to women and men; in the Middle Kingdom, for example, both men and women could become stars on the body of the sky goddess Nut, one way in which the afterlife was envisioned. In the absence of sons, daughters were made responsible for carrying on family religious practices,

Representing Men and Women in Egypt. An Egyptian funerary statue of husband and wife from the Old Kingdom, showing both spouses of equal size and suggesting their similar importance. From Gay Robbins, *Women in Ancient Egypt*. Copyright the British Museum, British Museum Press. Reprinted by permission.

honoring both the major gods and goddesses worshiped in their area and the spirits of their ancestors. This may have been true also in China in the early Shang dynasty—before about 1500 B.C.E.—though later, only sons were regarded as capable of honoring the ancestors properly, and not having a son was regarded as a crime against the ancestors.

Religious beliefs and practices were never completely egalitarian, however, and appear to have changed significantly with the development of river-valley civilizations. Based on evidence from contemporary foragers, the earliest human religious beliefs probably involved general forces and spirits linked to the natural world rather than personified gods and goddesses. Some archaeologists see evidence of a more anthropomorphized (human-formed) deity by the later Neolithic period in the Middle East and perhaps elsewhere, a fertility goddess or Great Mother Goddess tied to the fertility of crops and animals. It appears that in the earliest creation stories, this Great Mother Goddess gave birth to the world, in some variations by herself and in some with the help of a male consort, whose origin is not specified. In some creation stories, the Great Mother Goddess *is* the earth. No one knows when these first creation stories began to be told, for they predate writing.

By the time writing and urban civilizations developed in Mesopotamia, the most commonly told creation story was slightly different, emphasizing the role of a male deity over that of a female. The Great Mother Goddess became the substance out of which a male god—his name varied—created the universe, but she was no longer an active force. Cultures often adapt their religious beliefs to fit better with new economic and social realities; the adjusted religious beliefs then give support and sanction to the changed situation. Thus, by 1000 B.C.E., the more advanced of the world's civilizations generally held religious beliefs that mirrored the society around them. The gods were viewed as married and procreating, with a single male god as their leader and half-divinities who often resulted from the sexual exploits of male gods among human women.

The one group in the ancient Middle East whose religious beliefs came to differ significantly from those of their neighbors were the Jews. Their creation story did away with the female deity altogether, with Yahweh, the male creator God, creating the world out of nothing. Yahweh—or in the anglicized variant, Jehovah—is not flanked by a variety of other gods and goddesses but is the only God. Though there are prominent women in early Judaism, women were not allowed to be priestesses; their religious duties and activities revolved around the household rather than the temple. Jews shared with their neighbors the emphasis on procreation and on the authority of the husband and father, codifying these in the laws, moral maxims, and historical accounts that became Hebrew Scripture, a body of works that Christians later termed the Old Testament.

So far we have been talking about men and women as undifferentiated groups in order to emphasize the differences between them created in river-valley civilizations. It is important to emphasize, however, that gender hierarchies intersected with other hierarchies, and that almost all social groups or classes contained both men and women. This means that at least a few women, the daughters, wives, widows, and occasionally daughters-in-law of rulers and other prominent men, sometimes gained great power, either alongside their male family members or when there were no male family members able to govern. Hereditary aristocracies depend on the idea that special powers and rights are handed down from generation to generation; although in most aristocracies men are regarded as having more of these powers and rights by virtue of their gender, women are not completely excluded. Indeed, in ancient Egypt pharaohs, who were considered divine, occasionally married their sisters or other close relatives in order to increase the amount of divinity in the royal household, for all family members contained some of this divinity.

On the other end of status hierarchy, some people in ancient Mesopotamia and Egypt were slaves—owned outright by others—and far more were held to labor service requirements so that their labor, though not their persons, was owned by others (a group sometimes termed *helots*). (See chapter 5.) As we would expect given the division of labor developed with plow agriculture, male slaves and helots performed the majority of tasks associated with crop growing; female slaves ground grain, herded pigs, made pots, pressed oil from seeds. They also produced cloth—often in workshops of several hundred—which was among the trade goods handled by the new merchant class. The division of labor among free peasants and town residents was very similar to that among slaves. Men did most of the agricultural labor and women most of the weaving; the Egyptian Old Kingdom hieroglyphic for weaving is, in fact, a seated woman with a shuttle.

Conclusion

Though, ultimately, we may never know or agree on the source of gender distinctions—biological or psychological differences, the division of labor, the requirements of marriage, the growth of the bureaucratic state, religious ideas—it is clear that some types of gender structures were created in even the earliest human societies. Remnants of our hunter-gatherer past are often used to explain certain sex differences in contemporary culture, such as men's tendency to join with other men in teams and clubs (which ostensibly comes from earlier hunting parties) or women's ability to remember where objects are located (which supposedly comes from the skills needed for gathering roots and nuts). Gender structures that first developed in the Neolithic period are still found in many cultures around the world, with men still responsible for plowing and herding and women for spinning and weaving. Even in the most technologically advanced cultures, sons are still favored over daughters; women's tasks are valued less than men's; and the majority of government officials are male. Thus, though the religious systems—except for Judaism—and the ruling hierarchies and the stone or bronze technology of early human cultures have been gone for millennia in most of the world, certain aspects of their gender structures have endured. Within a common patriarchal framework, however, different societies developed different tones and emphases, as in the distinction between women's informal status in Egypt and that in Mesopotamia.

CHAPTER 5

WORK AND LEISURE IN THE PRECLASSICAL PERIOD

Many major changes occurred in work and leisure during the long early stages of human development, particularly after the advent of agriculture brought about a radical shift in how men and women labored—though information is often scarce. Even after agricultural work patterns were established, the rise of civilizations heightened and complicated the efforts needed to keep new agricultural societies going. For the first time, a small number of members of human societies were able to remain aloof from the daily needs of just getting food. As the Bronze Age opened (around 3500 B.C.E.), people began living in towns, and a select few were able to specialize in nonagricultural professions. This specialization brought about a strict hierarchical ordering of society in which the food-producing masses became subordinated to landlords, military specialists, priests, and merchants. A key role for early states involved organizing labor, often in considerable and surprising detail. Great advances in technology, such as the introduction of the plow, also forced important changes.

This is not to say that hunting and gathering disappeared. To the contrary—the vast majority of the earth's landmass remained in the hands of nonagriculturists during this period, where small bands of people numbering no more than forty to sixty wandered across the countryside, looking for game and plants to eat. It is even possible that the majority of the human population remained in this state in the preclassical period, though more and more people decided to settle down and cultivate fields. Since we have more information about agricultural peoples than about foragers, and because complex labor systems evolved there, we will concentrate on these societies, in particular those that flourished in Egypt and Mesopotamia.

Work in Agricultural Societies. Men in ancient Egypt piling up grain preparatory to thresh-ing. From Charles Francis Nims, *Thebes of the Pharaohs: Pattern for Every City* (London: Elek Books, 1965). Reprinted by permission.

Agriculture was by far the most important work of the bulk of the pop-ulation, even in the societies that relied on cities. Linguistic evidence from Sumeria suggests that the oldest professional names were those of plow-man, miller, and shepherd, terms associated with agriculture and herding. Only later did names such as baker, fuller, brewer, and leather worker evolve.

As we have seen, labor relations between the genders changed with the advent of civilization. As hunters and gatherers, men attended to the hunt while women gathered fruits from plants. It is also likely that women in-vented horticulture and then agriculture. Be that as it may, in most agri-cultural societies men soon took on the major agricultural tasks, preparing fields, sowing, harvesting, and the like. The adoption of an agricultural lifestyle, though it probably improved material life, meant a severe loss of freedom. This was obvious not only for women but also for men, who, once they adopted agriculture, could not roam as they had when they were hunters.

Among agriculturists, women were an integral part of the labor force and, in addition to spinning, watching the animals, child rearing, preparing food, and keeping up the household, had to work in the fields alongside the men during the labor-intensive periods of the year. Thus, for the majority of women—those involved in agriculture—labor demands did not change much. Only in the cities did women's tasks begin to shift substantially. This was especially marked in elite households, where women concentrated on their reproductive functions and were seen more as ornaments than as integral in making a living. At best, they remained resources for forming strategic alliances with other members of elite families. Thus, ironically, as women's labor burdens lifted, their relative status diminished. It is important to remember that the tendency to devalue women's work touched only a small minority of the world's population during this period. Most households were too absorbed in working just to survive to see women's contribution as anything less than essential.

In addition to gender differentiation, greater social divergences made their appearance in this era. Growing specialization among the population led to an increasingly hierarchical society. Those who did not have to labor in the fields felt themselves to be superior to the agriculturists. They constituted a small but significant group, rarely exceeding 5 percent of the population during this period. Those not working in agriculture tended to be more educated and, as writing evolved, more literate, though literacy rates remained extremely low. Even these more urbanized people remained tied in significant ways to the agricultural economy. As one Mesopotamian letter writer suggested, the fields were "the soul of the country."

Merchants, bakers, weavers, and leather workers were obviously directly linked to production from the countryside. Priests were a small but very significant group. Religion evolved in large measure as a way of placating divine beings—rain gods, river gods, mountain gods, and the like—to provide adequate conditions for food production. Many societies in Mesopotamia were highly theocratic, with the priests ruling their people. The first towns in southern Mesopotamia had temples as their centerpiece. In Egypt, the pharaohs were also (at least in theory) gods, thus legitimating their power. Aristocracy and government officials (who were often one and the same) constituted another part of the elites. At first, the aristocracy filled both government and military duties. Their feelings of superiority over the rest of the population came from their leadership role and their ability to protect their settlements from outsiders. As settlements grew, the role of the government increased as well, creating larger differences between the common folk, mostly engaged in agriculture, and elite groups. This can be seen in Egypt, where different social groups were buried in differently sized tombs. Whereas upper officials had elaborate tombs built to assure their afterlife, common workers' graves were little more than holes in the ground.

Specialization took off during the Bronze Age (beginning around 3500 B.C.E. in Mesopotamia). The introduction of this alloy of copper and tin was closely associated with urbanization. The use of bronze rather than stone implements made agriculture, as well as many other activities, much more efficient, creating larger surpluses. This, in turn, facilitated higher population densities. In Mesopotamia, agriculturists continued to live in the towns, farming the plots of land on the outskirts of the settlement. Most people lived in the smaller agricultural villages scattered throughout the countryside, though under the domination of a large town. In Egypt, urbanization was less advanced. There were fewer urban centers, and most people lived in small farming villages.

Technological improvements aided in saving labor for productive tasks, but it is unlikely that common farmers saw their work commitment eased. The introduction of the plow, with which a pair of oxen could do what previously required a dozen people, did not mean that less work had to be done. In the case of Egypt, plowing made the population available for other services, such as the building of more temples and pyramids. It is perhaps no wonder that soon after the introduction of the plow in Egypt, during the Old Kingdom (2778–2300 B.C.E.), many of the greatest pyramids were built.

Life was hard for the vast majority of the population in the river-valley civilizations. In Egypt during the Old Kingdom, a tiny number of landlords controlled vast estates in which the resident peasants were bound to the land. The men were organized into labor gangs of fifty to a hundred. Smaller units of about five men each, perhaps consisting of relatives or neighbors, worked on specific tasks. In the slack season, when the Nile flooded the fields, the peasants were forced to work for the pharaoh in unskilled tasks involved in the construction of the many royal buildings, such as the pyramids, built during this period.

Although most members of river-valley civilizations were agriculturists, a whole variety of labor systems existed. One way to distinguish
among labor systems is to examine the various levels of freedom involved. Slavery existed in all river-valley civilizations, though it was relatively unimportant. There were numerous reasons for this: The river-valley civilizations found it difficult to control war captives, the most common source of slaves in later history. Rulers frowned on the enslavement
of their own people, for it reduced the amount of taxes rulers could
exact, since slaves usually paid nothing directly. Also, slaves did not participate in the state's labor drafts. Selling oneself or a family member
into slavery to pay off debts—the most common means of enslavement—was usually only a temporary measure. Sumerian rulers, for example, issued "Decrees of Fairness" every five to seven years, liberating
any debt slaves as a way to increase the free (and thus taxpaying and
labor service) population. In some civilizations, such as Egypt, enslaving
one's own kind was seen as reprehensible.

Another and far more important category of worker was that of the
semifree laborer. In Shang China, for example, temples and palaces had attached to them a type of permanent worker to whom these institutions
provided all agricultural tools. During the Middle Kingdom period in
Egypt (ca. 2065–1580 B.C.E.), a large part of the population was designated
as *hemwew nisut*, or royal workers. This was an inherited position. Men
worked the fields, and women were assigned to domestic tasks or to spin
and sew in special workshops. They could be moved around at will, though
they were not slaves. In Babylon as well, the government used dependent
persons who were responsible for cultivating state-owned fields, perhaps
one-third of the total cultivated land. So important was their role that their
official name was "bringers of income."

Most important were free laborers, or free *peasants*, though they also
had to work for the state part of the time. This required, or *corvée*, labor
was essential to the maintenance of state in Egypt and Mesopotamia. The
image of thousands of foreign slaves working to build the pyramids, perhaps absorbed from Hollywood films or biblical accounts of the Jewish
exile in Egypt, is simply not accurate for most of this period. While much
unskilled labor was necessary to build these grandiose monuments, a significant amount of work was relatively skilled and could be done only by

properly trained workers, who were usually of higher status than slaves. Rulers valued these skilled and semiskilled workers and provided certain privileges for them, such as (in Egypt) separate workers' housing, substantial food rations, clothes rations, and even a type of oil that probably worked as a kind of suntan lotion. This is not to say that supervisors did not use whips or canes to encourage their workers, but this occurred only for those involved in the most menial of tasks.

Thus, beneath the rulers there were three estates throughout river-valley civilizations: free persons (mostly peasants), dependent workers, and slaves. Since rulers asserted that they (or better said, their office) owned their realm and all the population in it, even the "free" peasants usually owed some type of labor duty in addition to taxes. Furthermore, the state maintained a number of dependent persons who worked on state-owned estates. This category was largest in the Egyptian case (especially during the Middle Kingdom) and smallest in Mesopotamia. We have very little information on China and even less on the Indus Valley civilization.

The status of workers changed over time as well, with a marked tendency toward the loss of freedom, with the notable exception of Egypt. In the case of China, with the accession of the Zhou dynasty from 1100 B.C.E. onward, slave labor became more common; Zhou rulers did not practice massive sacrifices of war captives, as had the Shang. In the case of Mesopotamia, the native inhabitants appear to have lost many of their freedoms as the Babylonian period progressed. This had to do with increasing debt and the salinization of southern Mesopotamia, where hundreds of years of irrigation slowly rendered the formerly fertile fields less capable of sustaining intensive agriculture. When the independent peasants failed to make do, they were forced to sell their lands and thus, almost by definition, lost their civil rights.

Egypt's case is more complex. During the latter portion of the preclassical period, in the New Kingdom (1580–1085 B.C.E.), the use of coerced labor increased dramatically. This tendency toward coerced labor was due to an extraordinary military expansion beyond the Nile valley itself. Though there was a propensity toward expansionism in the Middle Kingdom period, only during the New Kingdom did the pharaohs systematically attempt to conquer much of the Fertile Crescent. Military commanders received slaves as payment, captured from newly conquered territories. In one expedition by Amunhotep II into Asia, the pharaoh claimed to have taken a total of 71,000 slaves from what is now Syria. In contrast, the life of the common peasant in Egypt improved somewhat over the history of this river-valley civilization. Under the New Kingdom, commoners gained more freedom. Each peasant household received a plot of arable land, to be inherited within the family. Apart from paying taxes, the peasants were left much to their own devices.

The loosening of strictures for the Egyptian peasant was undoubtedly related to the influx of foreign slaves. The new slave population during the New Kingdom enabled the greater liberty of the native peasant; slaves picked up the slack left by the free peasantry, since they could be assigned at will, as had been the case with the peasant corvées in earlier dynasties. The result was an early example of a common phenomenon, where the liberty of one segment of the population is dependent on the continuing lack of freedom of another. Indeed, in many economically flourishing agricultural societies, this inequality at work became the norm, as in Greco-Roman civilization or, more recently, the United States South prior to the Civil War.

To summarize, throughout the river-valley civilizations dependent or coerced labor increased. In the case of China and Egypt, slavery of foreigners became more important. In Mesopotamia, foreign slaves had always been prominent because of the region's greater warlike characteristics; in this instance, however, it is possible to note an increase in domestic slavery or dependent labor due to debt, and a concomitant general loss of freedom for the native population. Only the Egyptian peasantry gained greater freedom over time, as foreign war captives took up the labor needs formerly provided by natives. Clearly, civilization went hand in hand with coercive labor practices, and the high levels of civilization—at least most of those aspects we can measure, such as buildings and other monumental architecture—had a substantial human cost.

Leisure Activities

Despite the harshness of life in this period, people also engaged in leisure activities, though they lacked the definition of leisure we maintain in the late 20th century. It is necessary again to differentiate among social groups and the sexes. For example, the elite minority did not have the same bleak and strenuous existence that the common peasantry had. Members of the elites were exempt from much of the common labor and were able to participate in activities not usually open to commoners. As many of the pictures from Mesopotamian and Egyptian sources make clear, activities such as hunting constituted a preserve of elite males. In leisure as in work, gender differentiation was more marked among the elites than among the peasantry, though this varied across civilizations. We know little about elite women's leisure activities during this period, except that they were much more restricted than men's. Only among the Egyptians did both sexes partake of many of the same activities. The beautiful tomb paintings show how men and women dined in the same rooms, served by young girls and entertained by dancers, musicians, and acrobats.

In contrast, among the masses of these agricultural societies, both sexes participated in the same leisure activities, though their roles might be different. The most common activity, and one that continued throughout the existence of agricultural society, was the communal festival. These festivals were generally organized around religious activities. In Mesopotamia, the temples served as social centers, and the festivals in honor of the temple gods constituted a favorite means of relaxation. These religious rituals were usually tied to agrarian rhythms. For example, the festival at the temple of the fertility goddess Baba in Lagash might mark the end of the harvest season. Both sexes participated in these festivals, though women were in charge of food preparation. During these ceremonial occasions, people drank alcoholic beverages and often got rousingly drunk. Beer was the beverage of choice, and getting drunk in the feasts that followed the official ceremonies at the beginning of the festivals was common and expected. Festivals were also times to partake in delicacies that were infrequently available the rest of the year. This was virtually the only time that peasants were able to consume meat; otherwise, meat was too precious even for those owning a few head of sheep or cattle, since livestock represented more a peasant's means of savings than an item of consumption.

Members of the elites also sponsored festivals. Rulers, for example, celebrated their accession to the throne, the commemoration of a battle victory, or the birth of an heir. These types of civic festivals were often closely related to religious ones, since many rulers during this period represented themselves as divine or semidivine. These festivals, with their parades and other activities, showed the power of the lord and represented a confirmation of the legitimacy of the ruler. They also permitted him to show his largesse to the masses, thus tying the common folk to the person of the ruler and thus to the state. This type of festival also legitimated—if only in symbolic terms—the labor requirements the state imposed. These ceremonies were very important to create cohesiveness in the community and confirmed the profoundly hierarchical ordering so characteristic of agricultural societies.

In conclusion, labor systems changed greatly in the preclassical period, probably more rapidly than leisure did, once villages had formed basic festival patterns. As more and more humans switched from hunting and gathering to agriculture, their lives changed significantly. Labor requirements went up considerably, especially for men, who now took charge of much of the agricultural labor. As food surpluses permitted a few members of society to dedicate themselves to nonagricultural activities civilization emerged, and with it a more complex but much more hierarchical society. New technology such as the plow and the use of bronze saved effort in agriculture, but rulers used the labor saved (and often much more) in other activities, such as the construction of monumental buildings and other symbols of autocratic rule. Obligatory labor for the state was the rule in river-valley civilizations. Indeed, in most societies during this period, the position of peasants deteriorated, as they depended more and more on landlords or the state for their living. Egypt was the exception, but even here the increasing use of war captives counterbalanced the larger but still very relative freedom of the native peasantry.

River-valley civilizations established patterns of leisure use characteristic of agricultural societies. Members of the elites had more time and engaged in many leisure activities, such as banquets, hunting, and ritual occasions. Gender distinctions existed most sharply among the elites, in both work and leisure. In turn, among the ordinary folk the most common leisure activity was the communal festival, where whole neighborhoods, villages or towns participated. Many centered on religious activities, timed in accordance with agricultural rhythms, but civic occasions also fostered bonds among neighbors and generally accentuated the great differences between rulers and the ruled.

EPILOGUE

The early civilizations that developed before 1000 B.C.E. have long inspired great awe. Greeks and Romans looked at some of the monuments of Egypt and the Middle East and called them "wonders of the world." Fascination with Egyptian pyramids persists. How could a society with very limited technology amass such majestic structures? What combination of devotion and compulsion would even organize the labor for such efforts? Recent discoveries have extended this sense of wonder to the workings of Harappan civilization along the Indus River. Though now in ruins, the complex walls and urban water systems required a level of engineering genius and massive effort even modern cities might envy.

Other vantage points are also important. Crucial to our understanding of these early civilizations and their legacies is a focus on the precarious control humans had by this point achieved over relevant forces of nature. The long millennia of human evolution had produced a species with unusual brain power and adaptive capacities. Improving tool use allowed the species to expand both numerically and geographically. The development of agriculture offered a substantial population increase, which consumed much of the new bounty, and also new exposures to disease. The margin of subsistence remained limited for most people and, indeed, for whole societies. Increasing control over the environment generated real population growth but also anxieties about sustaining the results. Several societies sought methods of control beyond agriculture itself.

In this context, a number of societies, headed by Mesopotamia, introduced new levels of organization and structure. The creation of formal states and the imposition of systematic inequalities in the labor force and between men and women signaled these changes. Coordination by state officials allowed great improvements in irrigation systems, which, in turn, created larger food supplies. Divisions of labor, though they helped produce greater inequality, allowed the generation of specialists in crafts, politics, and religion. New needs and capacities for organization linked developments in the state and in work; coordinating the regimenting of labor was a vital state function and the basis for state resources. More structured gender rules related to these trends as well.

Yet the new systems were hard to maintain. A limited economy generated few resources to pay state officials. Hence a mixture of compulsion and cultural promotion arose to help cement the whole operation. Because governments had few bureaucrats of their own, they depended heavily on private landlords—members of the aristocracy—to enforce labor rules that would produce enough surplus for state coffers, while usually enriching the landlords as well. Small government military forces, because they had special access to metal shields and weaponry and sometimes also to scarce, expensive animal resources such as horses, helped enforce government edicts and the social order. Religion was used to justify the powers claimed by rulers; disobedience was a crime against the gods. Massive monuments and elaborate ceremonies and costumes celebrated the religious qualities of the state, creating a sense of awe between ruled and rulers. These expressions, which also fed the appetites for luxury of the upper classes, commanded important resources, which tightened the links in the whole system.

Yet the essential features of organized civilization, even if understood in terms of exploiting the advantages of improved agricultural coordination as well as some needs for defense, clearly took on a life of their own. Rulers exhibited a taste for monuments well beyond levels needed to impress the populace. An upper-class sense of the inferiority of ordinary labor was an important cultural by-product but not necessarily an inevitable one. The new imposition of gender inequalities remains perhaps the hardest to explain in terms of organized responses to precarious control over nature. Some division of labor between men and women made economic sense in agricultural societies, as it had in foraging situations. An increased birthrate confirmed the need for women to be able to handle frequent pregnancies and the care of young children (even the many who would die in infancy), and this helped create divisions of responsibility in agricultural households, even as the labor of both sexes remained essential. But the larger assertions of male dominance, particularly in the upper classes, where labor divisions were not as inevitable, suggests a further need for male compensations for their adaptation to agricultural work and, often, to social inferiority. Having women as at least symbolic targets of control may have eased the psychological adjustment to a more organized social pattern.

We cannot know what actual balance prevailed between regimentation and latitude. Early states and labor systems stressed careful organization, and successful public works demonstrate real abilities to coordinate dependent workers. But most people were rural, living in scattered villages; many features of life, including family activities and leisure celebrations, may have had a community emphasis but were quite decentralized, remote from the seats of power. This balance surely helped the systems to function in practice. Even the most cherished gods might be local, the official gods of the state acknowledged but treated as more distant divinities.

One final feature of the early civilizations stands out: The structures each civilization generated helped confirm a sense of separation among peoples in many parts of Asia, Africa, and Europe. The obvious divisions between agricultural civilizations and surrounding hunting-and-gathering or herding groups formed a starting point. It was easy to identify these "others" and label them with contempt. But even other civilized groups, if they were known at all, were regarded as different and inferior—which is one reason that their members, if captured in war, were readily enslaved, just as captured herdspeople or foragers might be. Each civilization was producing its own institutions and, particularly, its own cultural patterns, leading to a sense of identity and distinctiveness. Even though historians in retrospect can see a host of common patterns, the gods of one people were decidedly not those of another—and of course, the other people's gods were impostors, their worshipers to be scorned. The evolution of claims by states enhanced this sense of separation and identity. One god-king could hardly recognize the divinity of a rival. There was no sense of a common humanity.

FOR FURTHER READING

POPULATION/BIOLOGY

G. D. Brown Jr., *Human Evolution* (1995).
B. G. Campbell, *Humankind Emerging* (1992).
J. D. Clark and S. A. Brandt, eds., *From Hunters to Farmers: The Causes and Consequences of Food Production in Africa* (1984).
M. N. Cohen, *Health and the Rise of Civilization* (1991).
Brian Fagan, *The Journey from Eden: The Peopling of Our World* (1990).
———, *People of the Earth: An Introduction to World Prehistory* (1995).
Madhav Gadgil and Ramachandra Guha, *This Fissured Land: An Ecological History of India* (1992).
M. D. Gremek, *Diseases in the Ancient Greek World* (1989).
A. W. Johnson and Timothy Earle, *The Evolution of Human Societies: From Foraging Group to Agrarian State* (1987).
Adam Kuper, *The Chosen Primate: Human Nature and Cultural Diversity* (1994).
Delores R. Piperno and Deborah Pearsall, *The Origins of Agriculture in the Lowland Neotropics* (1998).
Douglas Price and J. A. Brown, eds., *Prehistoric Hunter-Gatherers: The Emergence of Cultural Complexity* (1986).
R. J. Wenke, *Patterns in Prehistory* (1984).

CULTURE

W. T. DeBary Jr. et al., eds., *Sources of Chinese Tradition* (1960).
W. T. DeBary Jr. et al., eds., *Sources of Indian Tradition* (1958).
M. F. A. Montagu, ed., *Culture and the Evolution of Man* (1962).
Denis Sinor, ed., *The Cambridge History of Early Inner Asia* (1990).
Clifton Edwin Van Sickle, ed., *A Political and Cultural History of the Ancient World* (1948).

STATE AND SOCIETY

N. N. Bhattacharya, *Ancient Indian History and Civilization* (1988).
H. Crawford, *Sumer and the Sumerians* (1991).

Cho-yun Hsu and K. M. Linduff, *Western Chou Civilization* (1988).

Allen W. Johnson and Timothy Earle, *The Evolution of Human Societies: From Foraging Group to Agrarian State* (1987).

Jonathan M. Kenoyer, *Shell Working Industries of the Indus Civilization: An Archaeological and Ethnographic Perspective* (1983).

Z. Liu, *Ancient India and Ancient China* (1988).

Michael Loewe and Edward Shaughnessy, eds., *The Cambridge History of Ancient China: From the Origins of Civilization to 221 B.C.* (1999).

David O'Connor and David P. Silverman, eds., *Ancient Egyptian Kingship* (1995).

R. Thapar, *From Lineage to State* (1990).

GENDER

Margaret Ehrenberg, *Women in Prehistory* (1989).

Janet Gero and Margaret Conkey, *Engendering Archaeology: Women and Prehistory* (1991).

Roberta L. Hall et al., *Male-Female Differences: A Bio-Cultural Perspective* (1985).

Gerda Lerner, *The Creation of Patriarchy* (1986).

Barbara Lesko, *Women's Earliest Records from Ancient Egypt and Western Asia* (1987).

Carol Meyers, *Discovering Eve: Ancient Israelite Women in Context* (1988).

Dale Walde and Noreen D. Willows, eds., *The Archaeology of Gender* (1991).

Barbara Watterson, *Women in Ancient Egypt* (1991).

LABOR AND LEISURE

Ann Rosalie David, *The Pyramid Builders of Ancient Egypt: A Modern Investigation of Pharaoh's Workforce* (1996).

Jacques Gernet, *Ancient China from the Beginnings to the Empire* (1968).

Bill Manley, *The Penguin Historical Atlas of Ancient Egypt* (1996).

Isaac Mendelsohn, *Slavery in the Ancient Near East: A Comparative Study of Slavery in Babylonia, Assyria, Syria, and Palestine* (1949).

Gay Robins, *Women in Ancient Egypt* (1993).

Robert J. Wenke, *Patterns in Prehistory: Humankind's First Three Million Years*, 3d ed. (1990).

PART II

The Classical Period, 1000 B.C.E.–450 C.E.

Highlights. After the disruption of several of the river-valley civilizations, another set of civilizations arose that expanded into much larger territories and developed a variety of new devices to integrate these territories. These processes of durable civilization building dominated the classical period, as China, India, and the Mediterranean created cultural, political, and commercial systems of lasting importance. Other societies developed on the borders of these major systems, and several new international linkages arose as well. The classical period drew to a close after about 200 C.E., as the great empires began to falter.

Key Developments. The expansion of major civilizations after about 1000 B.C.E. resulted from several factors. New invaders brought energy and aggression; Indo-European nomads from Central Asia poured into India and, later, southern Europe and the Middle East, combining with local populations. The achievements of the river-valley centers provided experience in setting up bureaucracies and trade routes. The use of iron provided advantages in weapons and agricultural production. Growing populations surged into adjacent regions—for example, the northern Chinese who entered southern, rice-growing areas and the Greek colonists who spread through the Black Sea borders and westward to Italy.

New size meant new demands on coherence. The expanding civilizations formalized cultural systems, creating basic statements of political and social values—such as Confucianism in China—or of religion—as with what became Hinduism in India. Spreading, coherent cultures helped link diverse peoples together, often providing common languages at least for elites, for instance, Mandarin in China. The new civilizations developed greater political capacities, linking diverse regions into solid empires.

China led the parade here, but major empires arose periodically in India and the Mediterranean as well. Finally, commercial links encouraged specialization, as grain-growing areas traded with areas suitable for other crops and products.

The classical civilizations also generated new patterns of social inequality. China ultimately established a bureaucratic class, educated in Confucianism though deriving mainly from a wealthy landlord group. Confucianism urged enlightened treatment of ordinary people, as long as they worked hard and offered respect, but it insisted on orderly hierarchy. India's caste system, developed gradually after the Indo-European invasions, divided people into fairly rigid categories by occupation and birth. Contact among these castes, from Brahmin priests on top to "untouchable" laborers on the bottom, was rigidly controlled by cultural rules. Med-iterranean civilization featured cultivated, landed aristocrats, who dominated most states. On the bottom, slaves, conquered in war, did much production work, along with freer peasants. Classical civilizations assumed the necessity of this kind of inequality, which indeed followed from limited resources and the need for a governing group over more complex societies.

Expansion and integration were gradual during the almost fifteen hundred years of the classical period. Each classical civilization developed distinctive emphases. China moved from the decentralized Zhou dynasty, to more dramatic centralization under a powerful emperor, to the bureaucratic state pioneered by the Han dynasty. Confucianism, developed to combat political fragmentation by urging self-control, mutual respect, and hierarchy, was joined by other belief systems, such as the Taoist religion, and a pragmatic approach to science. Chinese technology advanced rapidly, introducing vital new products such as paper. India emphasized religion and trade, providing the most active international merchants from the Middle East to Southeast Asia. Hinduism arose under the priests and stressed the primacy of otherworldly goals along with duties to one's caste here on earth. Major epics provided unifying stories and values. Another major religion, Buddhism, protested Hindu ritualism and inequality but also highlighted the importance of union with the divine essence and the worthlessness of earthly life. The Mediterranean civilization, arising first under the Greeks, developed a rich artistic and philosophical culture, with strong emphasis on the importance of political life. Greece declined amid

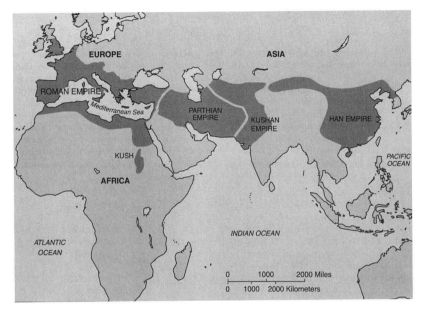

The Major Classical Civilizations, 1st Century C.E. From Peter N. Stearns, *World History in Brief: Major Patterns of Change and Continuity*, 3rd ed. Copyright 1999 by Addison-Wesley Educational Publishers Inc. Reprinted by permission.

internal warfare during the 4th century B.C.E., but a Macedonian royal house spread Greek ideas through much of the Middle East and Egypt. Alexander the Great's conquests set the framework for an active period of Hellenistic culture through the entire region and into western India. Finally, as Hellenistic kingdoms began to decline after about two hundred years, an expanding Roman republic gained primacy in the Mediterranean world. Like Greece, Rome depended primarily on aristocratic rule, though with some voice for ordinary citizens. Unlike Greece, Rome proved adept at creating powerful political structures. The republic turned into a major empire under Augustus Caesar, creating political unity around the Mediterranean for several centuries. During this final Roman period a major new religion, Christianity, developed in the Middle East and spread to a growing portion of the Mediterranean peoples.

During the classical period, agriculture began to arise in additional areas, including Russia, Japan, and northwestern Europe, while agricultural societies also expanded in Africa. This was the beginning point for the great Bantu migration in Africa. (See chapter 2.) In the Americas, early civilization sprang up in additional centers, notably the Andes, while in Central America a complex Mayan civilization arose after the disappearance of the Olmec centers.

Emphasis in the classical period rests on separate civilizations that developed different answers to the issues raised by territorial expansion and growing complexity. China's ultimate stress on a centralized empire and bureaucracy differed from India's emphasis on unifying religious ideas and social systems, with politics a less important ingredient. Resulting differences would have lasting impact, as the values and institutions of the classical period created a basic arsenal for the leading civilization areas. But contacts among the centers took shape as well. Trade routes brought Chinese silk as far west as the Mediterranean. Alexander's conquests created a brief period of mutual imitation between western India and the Mediterranean.

Between 200 and 500 C.E., each of the classical civilizations encountered new problems. Invasions from Central Asia helped topple the Han dynasty, then the Roman Empire, and finally India's last great classical empire, under the Guptas. Epidemic disease wiped out massive segments of the populations of China and the Mediterranean, weakening the economy as well. Growing corruption and political incompetence provided a third stumbling block. Trade and cultural levels fell in several cases. Decline was most severe in the Mediterranean, where political unity was broken from that time onward. Western Europe suffered particularly, while a new Byzantine Empire in the northeastern portion, centered in Constantinople, carried forward Roman institutions, Greek culture, and a Christian church. India suffered political decline, but Hinduism reaffirmed its hold and economic activity remained considerable. China experienced over three centuries of unusual political disunity before reviving classical traditions in the 6th century. Taken together, these developments ended a key period in world history and opened yet another phase.

The rise and fall of the classical civilizations involved new emphases in culture and politics most obviously. It was from these that changes in gender structures and work systems most directly emerged. But culture and politics responded to forces of expansion that themselves emanated in part from new technologies and changing disease and environmental patterns. The decline of the same civilizations, so often debated, owed much to shifts in these patterns as well. The biological and technological underpinnings of the classical period provide the entry into what the period was all about.

II. *Classical: 1000 B.C.E.–450 C.E.*

1000–600	Epic age in India; beginnings of early Hinduism; *Upanishads*
933–722	Kingdom of Israel
933–605	Assyrian Empire
8th–7th centuries	The emergence of Greek city-states; population increased in Greece and Greeks established colonies overseas; Homeric epics, *Iliad* and *Odyssey*; beginnings of Rome
753–509	Roman monarchy
ca. 735–715	Sparta defeated Messenia and enslaved the Messenians
700	Zhou dynasty decline
Late 7th to 6th centuries	Rise of Greek reformers and tyrants: Solon (ca. 630–560), Peisastratus (546–510)
ca. 563–483	Gautama Buddha
551–478	Confucius
509–450	Beginnings of Roman republic; Twelve Tables of Law
500–449	Greek defeat of Persia; spread of Athenian Empire
ca. 500	Lao-tzu and Taoism; editing of the Five Classics
490–479	Persian War
477–431	The golden age of Athens; democracy under Pericles; Phidias, Sophocles, Socrates, etc.
431–404	Peloponnesian War
338	Philip I of Macedon conquers Greece

334–326	Alexander the Great conquers Egypt and the Persian Empire
300–100	Hellenistic period
322–184	Maurya dynasty in India
290–270	Roman domination and control of central and southern Italy
264–146	Rome's Punic Wars
221–202	Ch'in dynasty, Great Wall
202 B.C.E.–220 C.E.	Han dynasty
140–87 B.C.E.	Rule of Wu Ti in China; increased bureaucracy, examinations; spread of Confucianism
133ff.	Decline of the Roman republic
ca. 100	Invention of paper in China.
88	Sulla as consul marches on Rome with six legions; beginning of civil war and power struggle between military commanders
73–71	Slave revolt led by Spartacus almost topples Roman state
47–44	Julius Caesar dictator in Rome
30 B.C.E.–220 C.E.	Kushan rule in India; Hindu beliefs develop
27 B.C.E.	Augustus Caesar and the rise of the Roman Empire
27 B.C.E.–180 C.E.	Pax Romana (the great Roman peace)
20–30 C.E.	Beginnings of Christianity
52 C.E.	Height of gladiatorial games in Rome
ca. 1st century C.E.	Beginning of Bantu migration
180	Decline of Marcus Aurelius in Rome; beginning of the empire's decline
ca. 200	Use of camel for trans-Saharan trade
200ff.	Spread of Indian influence in Southeast Asia
220–589	Nomadic invasions of China; disorder; considerable spread of Buddhism
312	Constantine I tolerant and patronizes Christianity
320–535	Gupta dynasty in India

395   Roman Empire divided into east and west
400   Gladiatorial games outlawed in Roman
       Empire
453   Fall of Rome

CHAPTER 6

POPULATING THE EARTH

Agrarian Civilizations: Diseases, Technology, and Environmental Transformation

Over two millennia, agrarian civilization gradually expanded within and beyond the alluvial valleys. Early in the first millennium B.C.E., however, agrarian civilization became a more dynamic, growing type of human biological and social form that advanced slowly over the world, and in the face of which non-urban-dominated societies, whether foraging or agricultural, shrank back or were overwhelmed. Agrarian civilization became the fourth great population wave. Its demands for food, water, and manufactured goods (tools, housing, clothing) strained environments to their limits and beyond. Some environments demonstrated resistance; others deteriorated beyond nature's capacity to recover, causing populations to decline or relocate. The natural human propensity to population growth was, in civilization, released and structured by two independent developments: One was technological advances, the other diseases.

Technological innovations did not necessarily originate in ancient civilizations. In fact, improvements in strains of crops or animals or the domestication of new ones occurred in diverse geographic settings, the better ones spreading wherever climate and soil permitted. Except for dramatic new crops, most of these developments were small, gradual in effect, and largely elude researchers until their cumulative effect produced changes in settlement patterns or population growth. One of the most important innovations was iron metallurgy. It is not clear where or when iron was first extracted from ores. Rare iron objects are reported as early as 1900 B.C.E., but systematic use of iron and knowledge of its production is usually attributed to the Hittites, an Indo-European people who settled in Anatolia

(Asia Minor) sometime before 1200 B.C.E. Although iron ores were widely available across the world, producing iron implements was a complex process, probably invented not more than two or three times in all history and evidently spread by the migration of expert metallurgists themselves. Nevertheless, by 800 B.C.E. the entire Near East and eastern Mediterranean was in the Iron Age, and by 500 nearly all of Europe; by 800, iron was commonplace in India. Bronze use diminished considerably, but stone implements remained widely employed. Iron implements appeared after the 7th century B.C.E. in Southeast Asia and China.

Iron democratized metallurgy, placing high-quality tools and weapons in the hands of the humble and productive classes. Improved shovels, hoes, axes, and plows facilitated terracing and irrigation works; they speeded up land clearance and timber harvesting and made for faster and agronomically more effective tillage. So iron powerfully increased the productivity of the agricultural labor force and accelerated civilization's growth on rain-watered lands.

Most other nonagricultural innovations involved small mechanical improvements, using human or animal muscle power applied to levers, inclined planes, and pulleys or combinations of these, such as wedges, screws, and wheels of various kinds—treadmills, gear wheels, flywheels. Handyman engineers improved designs over hundreds of years, but without dramatic impact on productive processes. Wind and water power had rich potential but were little used until after 500 C.E. Sailing ships, however, harnessed wind power to transport vast cargoes over long distances, safely, quickly, and with little human effort.

Ships and iron smelting required immense quantities of wood. Mediterranean fleets—the Phoenicians, Greeks, Carthaginians, Romans, Egyptians, and others—each included hundreds of ships containing the timber of thousands of trees, which had to be replaced as they rotted, wore out, or were destroyed by storms or war. Iron furnaces depleted forests so vastly that the furnaces had to be relocated every few years. In medieval Europe, a forge consumed a circle of 4 kilometers' radius in a year, and ancient forges were more wasteful. Wood also fueled pottery making and other manufactures. In villages and cities, acrid smoke rose year-round as fires of wood, crop residues, or dung heated homes, cooked food, or repelled insects. Wherever civilization advanced, forests retreated, as a vanguard of peasants, woodsmen, and metallurgists set to work with fire and iron.

Disease and Civilization

In Afro-Eurasia civilization advanced because diseases, too, cleared the frontiers of primitive peoples, whether hunter-gatherers or Neolithic agriculturalists. To explain how, it is necessary to begin with a few general principles. A disease may be defined as the symptoms or response that a large organism makes to bodily invasion by microparasitic organisms, whether bacteria, viruses, or other tiny life-forms such as amoebas, fungi, or internal worms. All living animals, including humans, have immunological systems that produce antibodies that destroy or neutralize most pathogens. Interaction between humans and the gamut of microparasites is as old as humanity itself. It traces back to the ancient African homeland, where microparasites and humanoids coexisted in a rough equilibrium. Small, isolated hunting-gathering bands gave microparasites little opportunity for multiplying prolifically, while microparasites did their part by keeping human populations in check. When a rare fatal disease invaded a community, it followed one of two possible courses: Either it was completely fatal, in which cases the microparasite itself perished, or, with less virulent forms, some persons died while others survived by developing immunities, which effectively eliminated the disease from the community. On the evolutionary scheme, then, humans and microparasites moved to mutual accommodation; successful pathogens became less deadly to ensure their host's and thus their own survival, while surviving humans passed to succeeding generations at least partial resistance to the most prevalent diseases in their home environment.

This biological equilibrium was disturbed when humans migrated beyond their sub-Saharan homeland. The initial results reduced the impact of disease. Microparasites flourish in warm and humid conditions but multiply and spread with difficulty in the arid, cooler environments into which *homo sapiens sapiens* migrated less than 100,000 years ago. Northern Africa was dry most of the time, although, to be sure, its climate became more humid for several millennia before the rise of civilization. Likewise, the Middle East was dry through the hot summers and cold in winters, when rains fell above the Mesopotamian plain. The rest of northern Eurasia like-wise was considerably healthier than the sub-Saharan homeland. There-fore, when foragers became established in these northern environments, populations increased to new levels, which in part explains the late Pale-olithic population surge and which, after the end of the last Ice Age, pushed some cultures into the agricultural revolution.

Malarias (there are several kinds) and dysenteries evidently increased among Neolithic agricultural societies due to increased population densi-ties and sedentary living, but other diseases failed to become endemic, or constantly present. There are, however, 30 to 50 separate pathogens that humans share with cattle, pigs, dogs, sheep, horses, and domesticated fowl, so regular contact with farm animals certainly became the means by which humans acquired a range of diseases present among societies ever since.

The huge populations of civilization created a new relationship be-tween humans and microbial organisms and a special relationship between disease-bearing and disease-susceptible societies. By the beginning of the first millennium B.C.E., the Nile's population reached at least 4 million, the Indus valley 2 million, and Mesopotamia another 4 million. These num-bers represent an exponential increase in the human species and created fundamentally new environmental and social realities.

The history of disease is largely hidden from historians, inferred mostly from hints instead of overt evidence. It involved a struggle between human immunological systems and an array of bacteria, viruses, and other microscopic organisms, such as worms and amoebas, all invisible until the age of modern science. Ancient peoples little understood diseases, usually attributing them to divine vengeance, unusual weather, or the malevolent magic of evildoers. It is difficult, therefore, for modern historians to know exactly what diseases were at work. This difficulty is compounded by the fact that the first civilized contacts with a pathogen caused horribly spec-tacular symptoms, quite unlike the milder reactions of modern superim-mune humans. Modern peoples are the surviving descendants of countless generations whose at least partial immunities have been passed on to their successors. Because the most deadly strains of microparasites tended to dis-appear by killing their hosts and eliminating themselves, whereas milder forms survived, the effects of killing diseases in civilization have, over the long term, become muted. The story of this changing relationship there-

A General Geography of Disease Environments in Early Civilization

World Areas with sub-zones	Climate	Disease Environment	Major Diseases
Africa	warm, humid year-round	very dense	malaria, smallpox, measles, sleeping sickness, bubonic plague(?)
Mediterranean Europe and North Africa	warm, dry summer; cool, moist winter	moderate	malaria smallpox measles
Nile valley	hot, dry year-round	dense	malaria, smallpox, schistosomiasis, measles
East Asia			
North China	warm, dry summer; cool, moist winter	moderate	malaria, smallpox, measles
South China	warm, moist year-round	dense	malaria, smallpox, schistosomiasis, dengue fever, measles
South Asia			
Indus valley	warm, dry summer; cool, moist winter	moderate	malaria, smallpox, measles
Ganges valley	warm, moist year-round	dense	malaria, smallpox, schistosomiasis, cholera, bubonic plague(?) measles
Northern Europe	cold winters	minimal	smallpox, measles
Australia, Pacific Islands, and Americas	varied climate, temperate to tropical	almost none	"virgin soil"
Arctic	cold	almost none	"virgin soil"

Virgin soil epidemics is a medical term used to describe populations who have contracted one or more diseases for which they have no immunity or previous exposure. Fatalities have been shockingly high. The "virgin soil" reference denotes lack of prior contact with other disease areas.

fore is one of diminishing disease-determined mortality for civilized humankind, worked out differently in specific environmental conditions, largely by biological forces beyond voluntary human effort and quite without people being aware of the processes at work. So what we do know is largely speculative and largely through inferences made from modern medical observations of infectious diseases among animals and among "virgin soil" populations, which epidemiological geography defines as Australia, the Americas, the Pacific Islands, and the remote peoples of Arctic Eurasia. Many of these peoples encountered Afro-Eurasian diseases for the first time after around 1500 C.E., and modern observers commented on their catastrophic impact.

As climates warmed at the end of the Ice Age, and where agriculture created larger sedentary populations after 8000 B.C.E., diseases and human mortality increased. There had been earlier periods of disease increase, after the human migrations out of Africa. Among hunting-gathering bands, however, and even agricultural villages, diseases quickly ran their course. A certain pathogen infected an entire community, killing those with weaker immunological systems while survivors developed immunities that destroyed the pathogen, effectively ending the epidemic. A disease might be reintroduced by outside contacts, by means of strangers or animals. Some diseases conferred lifelong immunities, some immunities of shorter duration, but most could not reinfect a community until immunities diminished sufficiently—usually as older, immune persons died of old age and a new, susceptible generation took their place, a process taking, say, a decade or more.

Urbanization and dense agrarian populations created new disease environments, new conditions for the propagation of pathogenic microorganisms, for whom large concentrations of people made *their* bountiful environment. This is where disease history and civilization history intertwine, both before and during the classical period. Many diseases became endemic, present all the time, and transmitted directly from person to person through bodily contact or breath or by means of contamination of food, water, or garments. Large populations assured a steady supply of susceptible individuals without previously acquired lifelong immunities. These were newcomers: Some were immigrants from distant villages or long-distant frontier areas, more often than not captive slaves; most, however, were young children, newcomers by birth. Many endemic diseases thus came to be identified as "childhood illnesses" but, properly speaking, were the ills of any newly arrived persons. The exact demographic thresholds for most diseases are not known. Epidemiologists do have good information on measles, which appears to require about 500,000 persons to maintain a continuous pool of susceptibles, through which infections pass in successive waves. Over several generations children inherited at least partial immunities to some diseases, which reduced literal dis-ease—that is, symptoms—and reduced mortality. So measles, mumps, chicken pox, and the like eventually became relatively minor childhood episodes for long-civilized generations but remained spectacularly deadly for distant small communities or, as we shall observe below, for civilized peoples coming from different disease environments.

Civilized diseases affected urban centers with greater intensity than they did outlying villages, not only because the former contained far more people but also because ancient cities were filthy. Surrounded by protective walls, cities quickly became tightly crowded. Broad, panoramic vistas with spacious gardens and monumental palaces illustrate many textbooks and entertain tourists, but these were playgrounds for the minority elites; the urban laboring majority dwelt in squalid neighborhoods amid fetid wastes and small, narrow streets. Ancient cities contained many animals. Some pulled carts or hauled pack loads, others awaited slaughter. Resident chickens, goats, and cattle provided whatever fresh dairy products there were, and in Asia and the Mediterranean, pigs were kept in or near households, much as they were in villages. People living immediately outside city walls kept livestock and grew fresh vegetables in soils fertilized by abundant organic wastes of the city. Slaughter wastes, animal and human manures, and household wastewaters accumulated, providing breeding places for flies and mosquitoes, who assisted in dissemination of disease. Water supplies became noxious in arid summers, when rivers and wells became stagnant as their levels dropped. Summers were the dying time for infants. In great epidemics cemeteries became overfull, and harried, often ill survivors dumped bodies in the rivers. Odors of putrefying flesh joined those of manures and offal. All this, of course, created highly unsanitary conditions. Cities stank. Civilization may have been grand and glorious, but it also waded in shit.

These conditions gave ancient cities net demographic deficits, with levels of mortality higher than fertility. To exist at all, cities required a regular supply of in-migrants. These came mostly from surrounding villages and were usually young adults. Some came to a city seeking opportunities as manual laborers or servants in the households of elite families. Many left their villages reluctantly, as surplus children of large families or as exiles from a local feud or their violation of local custom. Some came as conscripted laborers or soldiers; many were slaves captured in raids on distant peoples—pastoralists, hunter-gatherers, or free Neolithic agriculturalists. In a sense, then, urban centers taxed villages twice, once taking agricultural surpluses, again taking young adults in the prime of life to fill the demographic deficits.

Civilized peasantry also migrated to the frontiers, where pastoralists or hunter-gatherers roamed or where simple Neolithic agriculturalists dwelt in independent villages. Sometimes peasants migrated on their own initiative, fleeing oppressive authority or driven by overpopulation and famine to seek new lands. Frequently, civilized peasantry moved into frontier areas in the wake of civilized armies. Armies themselves were dense concentrations who intensified infections; nearly all armies before the age of modern medicine suffered greater fatalities from diseases than from battle wounds. At the same time, the array of diseases civilized armies and peasantry carried with partial immunity became a potent biological weapon that swept the frontiers of simpler peoples—biological weaponry no less potent because no one knew why the primitives withered away so helplessly. Civilized commentators often explained their expansionary victories by their natural superiority or divine favor, but the truth was more elemental: The conquerors simply infected the losers.

So the establishment of endemic diseases set in motion a two-way flow of population that fundamentally altered the structure of the human race. The first was the outward migration of civilized peasantry either in advance or in the wake of military authority, seeking additional land at the frontier and possibly also freedom from the rule of urban elites. This disease-bearing expansion made civilization relentless in its advance across the globe from its several points of origin. The second was the inward population flow, civilized peasants or primitives from distant points driven by personal needs or taken by force to urban centers. This flow guaranteed a pool of susceptibles and demographically perpetuated urban centers. Urban inflow made cities powerful agents of socialization, wherein gathered simple, rustic people often speaking languages different from the urban natives. Civilization was therefore socially stratified and culturally, even genetically, heterogeneous from its very beginning.

This general picture of civilization relentlessly advancing with an epidemiologically armed peasant vanguard suggests a smoother, simpler pattern than actually existed, for three reasons. First, peasantry almost everywhere lived at the edge of survival. Even Neolithic farmers, free of rulers and taxation, endured malnutrition in childhood and the vagaries of crop failure. The hazards were many, the insurance none: bad weather—too dry in growing season, too wet in harvesttime, and in northern climates a late winter, hailstorms, floods—and crops destroyed by insect or fungal infestations or by wild animals. (In Africa and South Asia, elephants occasionally ruined crops or fruiting trees.) In Egypt the phrase "low Nile" signified starving poor who pillaged stores, stole food from pigs, or ate weeds, as well as corpses floating in the river. Illness not only caused death, it impoverished. When most of a village fell ill at planting or harvest, famine would follow surely. Accustomed to such hardship, peasantry were remarkably resilient. A few good years of favorable weather and healthful conditions resulted in rapid recovery of physical strength, increased marriages, healthy babies, and a local population boom. Of course, famine and pestilence eventually returned. Populations therefore oscillated painfully around a rough equilibrium.

Second, each region, each major world center of civilization, had its own distinctive mix of pathogens. When a disease unique to one region was transmitted to another without previous exposures, a vicious epidemic would ensue, lasting for a century or more. The first 4,500 years of civilization (3000 B.C.E.-1500 C.E.) therefore had highly unstable demographic conditions, with long cycles of growth and cycles of catastrophic population collapse, which threw economies into disarray and toppled empires.

Third, the biological responses of the hunting-and-gathering or stateless agricultural regions varied considerably. In warm, humid world areas, where disease environments were particularly rich, as in Southeast Asia and sub-Saharan Africa, native inhabitants enjoyed immunities to their regional pathogenic pool that civilized newcomers from the north did not. In a sense the tables were turned on the more numerous, better-armed civilized peasants and soldiers, the rich microbial environment providing a shield that protected natives from conquest and assimilation. In more healthful climates, tiny populations of hunter-gatherers succumbed utterly to invasion-imported infections. Agricultural peoples living beyond civilization in free villages, however, were more numerous than these pockets of foragers and armed with iron weaponry, so they put up stronger resistance, on occasion even launching military counteroffensives that attest to some level of immunity. Pastoralists were by far the most potent opponents, because their great geographical mobility seems to have imparted some immunity. Agricultural and pastoral tribes who lived near the frontiers of civilization, for instance, Germanic tribes of northern Europe in the centuries 100 B.C.E.–400 C.E. and the Central Asian Turks and Huns, came in contact with their civilized neighbors for trade, occasional treaties, and frequent warfare. From these contacts they acquired technologies, political and religious ideas, and trade goods (which historians are able to discern) and, almost certainly, experience with the diseases of civilization (for which historians have found little recorded information). Their population sizes evidently gave them sufficient reserves to survive epidemic waves, making them powerful threats to the Roman, Gupta, and Han empires in the centuries 200–600 C.E.

Sub-Saharan Africa had an intense microparasitic environment that largely prohibited southward expansion of Mediterranean peoples. Clearings at the edge of forests provided ideal breeding places for insects that transmitted three deadly diseases. Trypanosome is an ancient parasite of wild animals that is transmitted to humans by the tsetse fly, causing sleeping sickness across its domain in West-Central Africa. The mosquito *Anopheles gambiae* proved a most efficient vector for a deadly strain of malaria. Many Africans developed the sickle-cell trait as a genetic defense, which incidentally caused anemia and death in one-fourth of the children who inherited the trait from both parents. The mosquito *Aedes aegypti* spread yellow fever. Areas of Africa also endured guinea-worm infection (dracunculiasis), schistosomiasis, elephantiasis (filariasis), yaws, and leprosy. Hookworm infestations were so intense that West Africans became immune to hookworm anemia.

Year	Asia	Europe	Fomer * Soviet Union	Africa	Americas	Oceania	World
400 B.C.E.	95	19	13	17	8	1	153
0	170	31	12	26	12	1	252
200 C.E.	158	44	13	30	11	1	257
600	134	22	11	24	16	1	208
1000	152	30	13	39	18	1	253
1200	258	49	17	48	26	2	400
1340	238	74	16	80	42	2	453
1400	201	52	13	68	46	2	382
1500	245	67	17	87	57.5	3	476.5
1600	338	89	22	113	13	3	578
1700	433	95	30	107	12	3	680
1750	500	111	35	104	18	3	771
1800	631	146	49	102	24	2	954
1850	790	209	79	102	59	2	1,241
1900	903	295	127	138	165	6	1,634
1950	1,376	393	182	224	332	13	2,530
2000	3,736	511	296	832	830	31	6,236
Annual Growth Rate 0. 1750	0.06	0.07	0.06	0.08	0.02	0.06	0.06
1750 -1950	0.51	0.63	0.82	0.38	1.46	0.74	0.59
1950 - 2000	2.00	0.53	0.97	2.62	1.83	1.74	1.81

* 2000: territories of former USSR

Continental Populations, 400 B.C.E. to 2000 C.E. (data in millions). From J. N. Biraben, "Essai sur l'évolution du nombre des hommes," *Population*, 34 (1979), p. 16. For 1950 and 2000: United Nations, *World Population Prospects: The 1994 Revision* (New York, 1995).

High mortality rates kept population growth in check. The best cultural defense Africans had was isolation, setting small villages widely apart in forest clearings or on the savanna. Besides those of the Niger valley, temporary towns appeared by the first millennium C.E. on the grasslands of the Sudan, Mali, and northern Ghana. Several regions of sub-Saharan Africa participated strongly in international trade and cultural contacts, and the Bantu migrations assured major population movement within the vast subcontinent. But there was no substantial population movement into or out of sub-Saharan Africa during the early civilization or classical periods, and disease patterns provide part of the explanation. And important parts of sub-Saharan Africa had little contact with Eurasian civilizations until after the 15th century C.E.

Quite the opposite, Australia, the Americas, and the Pacific Islands had substantially less disease. They spanned climatic ranges from polar to tropical, but their populations remained the "virgin soil" type, without experience of the Afro-Eurasian microparasitic killers.

This final setting, when combined with agriculture, could lead to surprising rates of growth and density. Much controversy still boils around the aboriginal population of the Americas before the Spanish conquest. In the 1940s, a number of historians, geographers, and demographers at the University of California, Berkeley, estimated on the basis of tribute records that the population of central Mexico (approximately the area of the Aztec Empire) might have reached 25 million inhabitants around 1500 C.E. This finding has remained controversial, for only in the 20th century did the region reach these numbers again. Historians and demographers have argued about the carrying capacity of the land in a preindustrial setting; the kind of ecological decline that took place after Spanish arrival, as a result of cattle and sheep; the use of analogies with other, better-documented regions of population decline (such as the Pacific Islands); and the use of tribute records (after all, only males were listed) for estimating family sizes. Although many historians now believe that the figure of 25 million might be a bit high, most agree that the population decline of the Indians after the European invasion was exceedingly important.

World Civilizations in Environmental and Epidemiological Perspective

Elsewhere, as civilized populations expanded, they fitted themselves into specific ecological niches in a variety of ways and, in the process, occasionally damaged the environment—and themselves. A useful example is Sumeria.

Deforestation of the highlands caused spring floods to become destructive, ruining maturing crops, and the lower Tigris and Euphrates became choked with mud, enlarging saline marshes and creating breeding grounds for malarial mosquitoes. But irrigation, the mainstay of the Mesopotamian economy, also ruined croplands by increasing salinity. Written accounts describe how the land turned white. Barley can tolerate about 1 percent salt level in soil, wheat only half that. Gradually wheat disappeared and barley yields declined, by 1700 B.C.E. falling by 65 percent, according to some studies. Centers of population, wealth, and power shifted northward after 1800 B.C.E.; hence the rise of Babylonia in Central Mesopotamia. Here, too, eventually salination reduced agricultural output and population, between 1300 and 900 B.C.E.

These geographical shifts help shed light on the transformation of Indus valley, or Harappan, civilization. Some 500 years after its peak in 2300 B.C.E., the cities of Mohenjo-Daro and Harappa were deserted. Salination of the soil may have followed the Sumerian pattern. Spring floods became ruinous as deforestation advanced. The Hakra River, which drew the preponderance of the villages and towns, dried up, possibly because an earthquake changed the region's contours. Most of the region's inhabitants continued to occupy thriving villages and towns in the upper Indus tributaries, where Indo-Aryan migrants joined them.

Settlement of the Gangetic plain to the east is usually attributed to Indo-Aryans, initially pastoralists who herded cattle and sheep on the Iranian plain and in lands farther north. After 800 B.C.E. they had settled into the Ganges and Januma valleys, cultivating wheat, barley, millet—staples of the Indus watershed—but now also rice. Also, swampy areas of the mid- and lower Ganges were being cleared, drained, and plowed. The Aryans, who spoke Indo-European languages (Hindi, Bengali), cross-married with indigenous people but retained their culture.

In eastern India, disease was the paramount demographic determinant. The Ganges valley was (and is) warm and humid. As migrants from the west moved into its forests and swamps, they encountered indigenous peoples who had immunities to their native environments. To their encounter Aryans brought military superiority, but Gangetic natives enjoyed the bacteriological advantage. The primitives therefore did not wither away and by all accounts put up fierce resistance. Perhaps because Aryan-Hindu culture was forced to assimilate the forest people, a system of caste developed, socially stratifying Aryan immigrants and indigenes. Over succeeding generations, differences diminished and immunities built up to create the Indian peoples.

As populations grew, trade and manufactures increased and urban centers developed, by the 6th century B.C.E. across the breadth of the Indus and the Ganges river systems. Disease remained a major theme of Indian culture. Temples of worship for a smallpox deity suggest the disease's presence before 1160 B.C.E. Cholera was evidently endemic in the Ganges by the 1st century C.E. Malaria was as intense in the Ganges as in Egypt and Mesopotamia. Yet, at the end of the Mauryan Empire (321–184 B.C.E.), South Asia contained about 50 million people, representing a vast expansion of civilization.

China's demographic expansion is likewise a story of two river systems and two epidemiological regimes. The core civilization, established in the loess uplands of the Yellow River, spread eastward onto the broad North China plain, and by about 400 B.C.E. North China contained some 20 million persons. Expansion southward into the Yangtze watershed proceeded very slowly. By at least the 5th century B.C.E., northern Chinese, "the men of Han" (and mostly men at that), gradually infiltrated southward. Mixing and marrying with indigenous southern Miao, Pai-man, Yao, Chuang, and other ethnic groups, they brought their language and technology while retaining trade linkages to the north. The Han Empire followed after 221 B.C.E.

Extension of the empire encouraged a massive, slow population shift southward. Deforestation of the western Yellow River highlands probably provoked two disastrous changes in the river's course in 3 and 11 C.E.; the resultant floods, famines, and uprisings seem to have driven several million peasants southward. Although under Han authority, southern China remained an economic frontier until at least the 6th century C.E. Even a large population shift confronted a potent epidemiological climate. South China is the land of warm climate, summer monsoon rains, and paddy rice, which meant stagnant waters and abundant diseases. High productivity of wetland rice could sustain large populations, but endemic diseases kept them in check. Waterborne diseases such as malaria and schistosomiasis took a heavy toll, and several kinds of intestinal worms were South China's specialties. Northern Chinese evidently took centuries to acquire the immunities necessary to support large, dense populations, so South China retained large indigenous populations, speaking distinctive tongues and even having different physical appearance.

Mediterranean civilization was mostly healthier than those of India and China. Its warm, dry summers and cool, rainy winters limited growth of pathogens. Apart from the Nile, the rivers were small, usually with steep, short gradients that kept waters fresh and clean. After about 800 B.C.E., urban-centered Phoenicians and Greeks launched settlements westward along the coasts, Phoenicians mostly in North Africa, Greeks mostly in southern Europe. They met little opposition; there is no record of vigorous resistance from indigenous agricultural peoples. Many native peoples, such as the Romans, remained independent but influenced by civilized culture. Population pressure in Greece and Phoenicia is sometimes offered as an explanation for colonization, but growing scarcity of timber and metallic ores was probably also important.

Mountains overlook the entire Mediterranean coast, except for the Libyan plain and Egypt. These mountains supported great forests of oak and pine that were essential to Mediterranean civilization. The Mediterranean lowlands produced grain (wheat, barley, rye), olives, grapes, and other fruit trees, while sheep and cattle grazed in the highlands or on fallow. Most urban centers, particularly smaller ones, provisioned themselves from neighboring villages, but large cities such as Athens, Carthage, and Rome acquired foodstuffs from distant regions by sea. In return they traded wine, oil, and manufactured goods or collected taxes and tribute. The Mediterranean economy, and the Roman Empire that it supported after 30 B.C.E., represented a network of towns and cities near the mouths of small rivers, held together by ships. What the great rivers were to China and India the Mediterranean was to Greece and Rome. Put another way, the Mediterranean system was many small rivers connected by the sea. Two consequences followed from this: First, Mediterranean civilization owed its cohesiveness to seaborne shipping and therefore was uniquely poised for future transoceanic ventures (an issue to be taken up in later chapters); second, the Mediterranean system had an insatiable need for timber, not only for fuel but also to keep a vast and growing fleet afloat.

Throughout most of the thousand years from 800 B.C.E. to almost 200 C.E., Mediterranean civilization grew unchecked by warfare or disease. To be sure there were wars, for such is the way in which empires were built and dynasties changed; but throughout them all, Mediterranean civilization expanded. There were occasional regional or local epidemics and famines, particularly in Egypt. But overall, no massive die-offs gripped the Mediterranean, nor was the region afflicted by large-scale barbarian invasions.

By the death of Octavian Augustus in 14 C.E., the Roman Empire contained about 54 million inhabitants. In that era, the Han Empire enumerated in the world's first genuine census about 60 million, making two empires of roughly comparable magnitudes situated at opposite ends of Eurasia. Guesses for the rest of the world would be about 50 million for South Asia (India, Pakistan, Bangladesh), perhaps another 50 million for Southwest Asia. Even if reduced by half, these estimates obviously show that civilized societies under the protective umbrella of empire attained incredibly large populations by comparison with their progenitors.

As the great centers of civilization grew, they also came closer together. A set of empires and lesser states stretched across Afro-Eurasia, linked by trade in luxury goods along two main routes: overland caravans by means of the Silk Roads on the southern rim of Inner Asia; and a seaborne network through the China Sea and Malay Straits to the Indian Ocean, then by means of the Red Sea or Persian Gulf to the Mediterranean. By the 2nd century C.E., these contacts included sufficient numbers of persons to transmit infectious diseases throughout the entire civilized network. The disease pools of the separate centers of civilization had developed separately; when they flowed together, the results were catastrophic and without precedent. The populations of the Han and Roman empires collapsed. Political and economic disorder followed, resulting in civil war in which armies degenerated to warlordism. As farmers and townspeople fled and rapacious armies marched, diseases spread widely. Violence, famine, and epidemic—the horsemen of the apocalypse—sent populations into downward spirals that continued into the 8th century C.E.

The crisis began with the famous Antonine plague, an epidemic that swept throughout the Mediterranean after 165 C.E., evidently brought by Roman troops returning from Mesopotamia. Killing a quarter to a third of the population over the next fifteen years, this epidemic signals a population encountering a new pathogen. A new epidemic struck in 251–266, and fatalities in the first wave reached 5,000 per day in the city of Rome. These two epidemics may have been the first arrival of smallpox, an ancient disease of India, and possibly also measles.

So began what historians customarily refer to as the crisis of the 3rd century. Symptoms of labor shortages are found in legislation, beginning in the reign of Diocletian (285–305), that required peasants to remain on the land and locked other workers into certain occupations. Historians seeking to explain collapse of the western half of the Roman Empire stress overt events such as military disorder and fiscal problems. Some evoke decline, decay, or loss of vitality. What was lost or declined, however, was life itself; the decay was disease.

China also had its crisis of the 3rd century. Epidemiological evidence is very sketchy. It chief symptoms were increasing violence along the northern frontier, which culminated in a peasant uprising known as the Yellow Turban Rebellion of 184 C.E. The empire slowly disintegrated into rebellions and civil wars, the Han dynasty disappearing by 220 C.E. Political disorder and violence accelerated population migration southward, with millions moving into the Yangtze watershed during the next three centuries.

For the Middle East, India, and Southeast Asia, no imperial administration produced records allowing estimates of population sizes or their declines. Epidemics may have been less lethal in these areas, but economic deterioration and political disorder struck them as well. Smallpox certainly, and measles probably, had been endemic to India for centuries, so there is no reason to suppose these diseases drove down population. The less richly diseased Roman and Han empires at opposite ends of Eurasia suffered the most.

Population decline and new epidemic waves would continue for two more centuries. Meanwhile, hundreds of thousands of primitive agricultural and even pastoral peoples—Germans, Slavs, and Huns from Inner Eurasia—gradually migrated into what had become population low-pressure zones. The mid–5th century found much of classical civilization in midcrisis.

The ancient world ended in a protracted demographic shock, with massive decline and cultural transformation wrought by in-migration of new peoples. Those who experienced the shock could not understand it. Its biological determinants were invisible and, to their sciences, unknowable. They left historians untrained in historical epidemiology no overt clues; much history has groped for an explanation for the end of the ancient world.

A Note on Life Expectancy in Agricultural Civilizations

The concept of life expectancy sometimes defies arithmetical common sense. A life expectancy of 30 years, for example, seems to mean that most people died a few years before or a few years after age 30 but mostly close to that age. Nearly the opposite is true, however. In all societies, ancient to modern, everywhere in the world, the probabilities of dying are greatest at two points in the life cycle, in infancy (defined as the first year of life, before the first birthday) or at old age. Life expectancy therefore is distributed bimodally, with the modes at the extreme ends of the distribution curve— in a sense, almost the reverse of a normal distribution curve. Probability of dying (expressed as qx, age-specific mortality, in a life table) drops sharply after the first few years of childhood, remains low in the years 10 to 30, then rises gradually as age advances.

Life expectancy, therefore, is a complicated mathematical calculation that sums the probabilities of dying at every age, from birth to some age beyond which almost no individuals survive, for example, age 100. The inverse is probability of surviving, expressed as the number of years a person in a given society can be expected to live beyond a specified age. Usually it is given as years anticipated from the moment of birth and denoted by the symbol e/0. But it may also be measured at age 15, which is expressed e/15, or at e/30 or any other age. Because ancient infant mortalities were very high and infant skeletons are difficult for archaeologists to find, ancient life expectancies often are computed for age 15 and older.

A hypothetical example may help. Imagine a population of 100 persons, of whom 50 die before the first year while the remaining 50 survive until age 60. This gives an average of 50 x 0 = 0 plus 50 x 60 = 300, for a total of 300 years lived by 100 persons, or 300/100 = 30 years on the average. Many persons in ancient societies became old. The philosopher and poet Xenophones of Colophon in late-6th-century B.C.E. Greece died at 91. His contemporary, also a poet, Simonides of Ceos, died at 90. The Old Testament says, "The days of our life are threescore and 10." (Psalm 90:10, Revised Standard Version), that is, 70, and goes on to say that a strong person may live to 80. Life expectancies are far longer in modern affluent societies than in ancient ones and vary by region and social class. But high or low, life expectancy everywhere always follows the same probability curve, an excellent example of the biological foundations of history.

CHAPTER 7

CULTURE AND POLITICS IN THE CLASSICAL PERIOD

Civilization patterns were vitally conditioned by environment and disease, but political and cultural initiatives had important impacts of their own. This was true even in the final classical centuries, when disease and invasion claimed the upper hand. The development of the classical civilizations involved major innovations in belief systems and the organization of states—though politics probably changed more, if only because formal states were more recent creations. Each of the classical civilizations built on previous cultures; they used the machinery of government, such as writing systems (Greece, for example, modified the Phoenician alphabet to create a sleeker model), and they used basic ideas already generated, such as the Chinese concept of the state-society relationship as familial. But they also introduced new elements, different from the patterns of river-valley societies. It was no accident that fundamental thinkers in each society— Socrates in Greece, Buddha in India, Confucius in China, all operating in the 5th century B.C.E., at a formative stage—created systematic philosophical or religious approaches that would long continue to influence each civilization and its heirs. Each approach also had political implications, helping to shape and to defend the types of government each society developed.

Political Change: Reinventing the State

Civilizations during the classical period experienced fundamental political change. The relationship between state and society witnessed far more innovation than did basic technologies during the same centuries. The state already existed, of course: Precedents from the river-valley societies provided a basis for further creativity. Classical China inherited political institutions and concepts from the Shang and early Zhou dynasties; Greece benefited from earlier civilizations at Mycenae and Crete and from Egyptian patterns. Nevertheless, change outweighed continuity.

The simplest of historical measurements, the before-and-after test, suggests the extent of change. Governments at the beginning of the classical period were localized and loosely structured, dominated mainly by large landowners or priests. Governments near the period's end were vast empires, with extensive bureaucracies and a range of services. During these centuries of political change, a whole host of developments established issues that would linger in political life to the present day: How much voice should ordinary people have in government? How should bureaucrats be trained and selected? Should governments try to control beliefs, or should they tolerate diversity? With developments of this sort, the basic structure relating state and society was changing, yielding durable new ingredients for the future.

There were several spurs to change. Iron weapons and growing agricultural prosperity gave new powers to political leaders but also new tasks, in supporting wider trade patterns. Larger populations created new needs for state action. Invasions at the end of the river-valley period provided ambitious leaders and conquerors, eager to expand territorially and to strengthen the hold of the state. Not surprisingly, the expansion of government personnel and activities was a crucial ingredient of the integration of the enlarged civilizations of the classical period, helping cause the expansion but also necessitated by it. It was an increase in officialdom that provided the means for wider tax collection—though states also became vulnerable to failures in taxation efforts because of economic decline or loss of bureaucratic control. Another key symptom of the new position of the state was the emergence of explicit ideas about what the state should be and do—the emergence of formal political theory.

The new states maintained functions that had already been developed. Systems of justice actually expanded, with law codes now backed by larger groups of magistrates and by more elaborate theorizing about the goals of the law. Military activities continued, for defense and, recurrently, for expansion. Rulers built great palaces and sponsored other public works, as before. On the whole, however, the use of the state to organize work gangs declined as the state's activities broadened and as various forms of taxation supplemented direct work service. Governments began to take a wider role in certain kinds of economic and cultural activities. Correspondingly, awareness of the state increased, with many people, though particularly at the elite level, becoming more attached to participation in political life.

Redefinition of the functions of the state helped cause innovations in government personnel and frequent debates about what forms of government would work best. Monarchies and assertions of divine support for the ruler continued from the past, but even these systems usually acquired additional justifications, and certainly, a more elaborate bureaucratic base. And government by council, by dictator, or even by a form of democracy developed in certain circumstances as well.

The states of the classical period differed from the modern states. They remained small by modern standards, and they largely avoided certain common modern functions, such as welfare systems and mass education. But these states did produce institutions and ideas that had lasting significance. The idea of jury trial, for example, came initially from the classical Mediterranean, and the notion of merit examinations for selecting bureaucrats from classical China. At the same time, particularly because this was a period of such extensive innovation in the state-society relationship, great variety existed among the major civilizations. Characteristic political styles emerged in China, India, and the Mediterranean that would have enduring impact, but they differed widely from one another. Comparison in this context becomes a vital tool for sorting out the many possible combinations that were explored.

Little information exists about the reactions of ordinary people to the new forms of government. Some must have welcomed less domination over work as well as the new forms of political order. Others, however, may have resented attempts to tamper with traditional culture or to widen the definition of crime. The growing significance of states in the classical civilizations made more people aware of government as a factor in their lives and as an institution whose adequacy might be evaluated. More important governments meant governments that might more readily be seen to fail. Political protest—whether designed to change the state or to put it in new hands—became a periodic feature of social life, at least in China and the Mediterranean. Along with invasions—not a new phenomenon but still important—these protests helped cause recurrent oscillations and, sometimes, major changes in the political process.

Finally, the range of state activities made civilizations depend heavily, though not exclusively, on the quality of leadership provided. Correspondingly, a key symptom and cause of civilization decline late in the classical period involved a growth of political incompetence and a deterioration in the range and quality of government services. Here, too, was an important new ingredient in the larger patterns of world history.

Political changes in China, though gradual and complex, produced the most innovative government of the classical era. Correspondingly, Chinese civilization depended heavily on extensive government action and, usually, considerable political centralization. Government centralization under the emperor was a major achievement, given the vast size of the Chinese Empire during much of the classical period. Though the Chinese imperial state did not spring up overnight, the importance and consistency of its government institutions were unmatched in the other classical civilizations. Hence the durability of basic features of the Chinese state in later periods of history had no counterpart elsewhere. Despite periods of chaos, Chinese leadership always managed to reestablish the state apparatus that had first been invented during the classical centuries.

Several factors helped cause the unusual expansion of the Chinese state. One of these was geography. Early states in Northwest China emphasized military defense to keep out nomadic invaders, but invasions were not so frequent as to unseat systematic political structures, as occurred to an extent in India. Problems of flooding and the need for careful irrigation along the Yellow River also promoted the state, which soon developed other public works, including an elaborate system of canals. And individual leadership played a role, in the form of forceful emperors and the doctrines of the philosopher Confucius, who emphasized the central importance of political order.

Chinese political innovations had several facets. In the first place, China developed an unusually large and explicit bureaucracy—at its height late in the classical period, including about 130,000 people, or .2 percent of the population. This is a modest figure by the standards of a modern state, but it was unprecedented in the classical era. The emergence of a bureaucratic state was also accompanied by growing specialization and by deliberate training. It depended on recruitment according to tests and merit-based recommendations, rather than simply birth or privilege. Finally, the bureaucracy and the emperor himself were imbued with an ethic of responsibility, in which their considerable political power was tempered by a belief that they owed their subjects good service.

The final component in the innovations of the Chinese state involved the growth of its functions. While governments in some river-valley civilizations had wielded great power in certain respects, as in the recruitment of labor service, the range of functions of the Chinese government widened considerably. Maintenance of great public works, administration of justice, and military defense were staples, but the government also branched out into the cultural sphere and into economic interventions. In principle, Chinese political thinking created no clear boundary between state and society. This does not mean that the state intervened in every aspect of private life—it lacked power to do so. But it did mean that there was no particular limit, in principle, to what the state might undertake.

The Chinese state encountered important problems and constraints at many points; its very innovation and ambition virtually assured certain difficulties. Bureaucrats were often opposed by other groups in the imperial court. The government frequently allowed landlords to accumulate important powers, which could antagonize the peasantry. Recurrent social unrest was one result, for the peasants expected the state to assure fair treatment. Given limited resources and technology, actual ability to control localities often fell short of stated goals. Villages and local leaders had considerable power. In more distant provinces—and it could take a full month to communicate between the capital and some outlying regions—the hand of the state might be particularly light.

The development of the Chinese state unfolded in several stages during the classical period. During the long Zhou dynasty, considerable decentralization prevailed, though key military arrangements and doctrines were established. Growing disorder from about 770 B.C.E. onward created increasing demands for more effective political structures, though it was only under the Ch'in dynasty that actual state institutions responded. The feudal system was abolished in favor of regional districts directly responsible to the emperor; hereditary nobles and walled city-states were both brought under central control. It was at this point that government functions began to expand to a wide range of public works, including the Great Wall in the north to protect against nomads—a project that relied on peasant corvée labor. The state also promoted a standardized written language and standardized weights and measures, coinage, and even wagon-axle length (to facilitate road use). It began to conduct a certain amount of trade directly, establishing a precedent for extensive economic functions. Government investments in research promoted practical science, yielding findings about the effects of various medicines and climate patterns. The Ch'in dynasty was followed by the Han, which confirmed the importance of the central administration and its extensive functions but added procedures for training a responsible bureaucracy, relying on Confucian doctrines. The Mandate of Heaven idea was also reintroduced to justify the emperor's rule. Bureaucrats were sent out to all regions to supervise the administration of justice, public works, tax collection, and military recruitment. Regulations and the institution of the censors kept watch over officials to prevent corruption, with various punishments, up to required suicide, for misbehavior. A state school was set up in 124 B.C.E. to train bureaucrats; a hundred years later, this had blossomed into a national university with 3,000 students.

The Indian state did not establish the extensive claims or the continuity of its Chinese counterpart. One of the great Indian empires, the Mauryan (322–184 B.C.E.), did set up roads, hospitals, even rest houses for travelers. The government was also active in promoting religious change, including prevention of the religious sacrifice of animals. On the whole, however, Indian governments emphasized more local systems; the Gupta Empire at the end of the classical period constituted an alliance of regional rulers more than an expanding central state. Indian civilization relied far more on cultural developments and its unusual social structure than on systematic political innovation.

Political systems in Greece and Rome also differed from those in China, but here there was sustained interest in government and experimentation with a variety of structural forms. Monarchy, dictatorship, aristocratic councils, and democratic rule were widely discussed and defined by political theorists and actually implemented at various points during the classical period. This rich array of options, along with Rome's particular emphasis on a rule of law and a strong tendency toward localism, served as the Mediterranean's chief heritage to later political systems. Far less attention was paid to major innovations in government functions or to establishing a far-reaching bureaucracy.

Geography dictated a local focus to politics in classical Greece, with emphasis on cities ruling over surrounding countryside. Relatively few invasions and a favorable population-to-resources ratio, in a mild climate, also reduced the need in Greece for the kind of innovative, centralized, and coercive political structure established in China. Within the *polis*, or city-state, forms of government varied. Initially, tribal systems brought by the invading Indo-Europeans after 1200 B.C.E. encouraged a monarchy supplemented by an aristocratic council. In some cases (as, later, in the Roman republic), a popular assembly of those ordinary people who were regarded as citizens operated as well. Aristocratic councils gained in power, but growing social unrest after the 7th century B.C.E., pitted peasants against landowners, as farmers faced increased crowding and often went deeply into debt. This tension, in turn, brought new tyrants to the fore, holding dictatorial power and bidding for popular support by sponsoring useful public works and some social reforms. Governments increased the building of temples, which provided jobs while also honoring the gods, and they patronized cultural activities such as festivals and dramatic performances. Some governments soon returned to aristocratic rule, but a few, such as Athens, created a direct democracy, with citizens (at least, that minority who could regularly attend) participating in meetings to decide on state policy and selecting leaders by lot. This was not democracy of a modern type, not only because people participated directly, rather than selecting representatives, but also because the vast majority of residents did not count as citizens at all—they were women, foreigners, and slaves. But for those who did have rights, the Athenian democratic concept provided a distinctive answer to the question of how government should be run. Rather than setting up a bureaucracy, people were chosen at random to hold offices, usually for a year. The assumption was that any citizen could do the job, though poor performance might be punished severely by the assembly. Only generals were chosen by talent. The Athenian jury system, the world's first, demonstrated faith that ordinary citizens could judge criminal activity—including crimes against the state. Here, too, the contrast with China's reliance on professional administrators is striking.

After the Greek system deteriorated in the 4th century B.C.E., Hellenistic kingdoms, ruling extensive regions even after Alexander the Great's empire split apart, emphasized greater despotism along lines established previously in Persia. Military officials played vital roles. In the Egyptian kingdom, under the Ptolemy dynasty, a formal bureaucracy developed. The kingdom was divided into administrative units that were directed by officials sent out from the capital. The state ran a number of monopolies, such as salt and mining, like its Chinese counterpart. Exports, currency, and other aspects of economic life were closely regulated. The government claimed ownership of all land, which justified not only taxes but also frequent direction of peasant farmers to plant necessary crops in the interest of preventing famines. Hellenistic governments were culturally tolerant, allowing minorities and city-states great latitude in religion and ceremony. Overall, the Hellenistic period provided an interesting set of precedents, some of which would be resumed later in Middle Eastern history.

In the short run, however, the Hellenistic kingdoms declined, and the next great political impetus in the classical Mediterranean came from Rome. The Roman republic repeated many of the key patterns of the Greek city-states, helping solidify attention to the importance of political forms and the need for widespread interest and participation in the affairs of state. The aristocratic senate was the dominant structure, but ordinary citizens also had their assembly. Again, most people were not citizens, but nevertheless this democratic element was important. Leadership of the republic did not emphasize professionalism. Two consuls were elected by the senate; the fact that they watched over each other—each could veto the other's decision—and also served for short spans (a year) limited their power. As the republic grew, some other administrative posts were established: to conduct censuses and property-tax surveys; to run financial activities; to build public works, including the great port facilities and open markets in and around Rome; and to operate the court system to deal with crimes and civil disputes. Nevertheless, the bureaucracy was not large, because Rome depended heavily on citizen participation. Officials in many posts continued to be selected only for short terms, to prevent abuses of power; and duplicate officials often watched each other closely, as the principles circumscribing the consuls were applied to other bureaucratic sectors.

Rome's commitment to a limited administrative structure, combined with its steady territorial expansion, produced two additional characteristics. First, Romans were usually quite tolerant of other local government systems, as long as these paid financial tribute to Rome and adhered to Rome's military and foreign policy. Only in a few cases, in areas deemed rebellious, did the Romans send in an elaborate bureaucracy of their own. The most notable instance of centralized repression was the destruction of the temple of Jerusalem and then the forced dispersion of the Jews in 70 C.E. Second, military leaders gained increasing power within Rome itself, as well as in the growing empire. Without a large civilian administration, and with growing dependence on territorial expansion, military officials inevitably wielded great authority. In 241 B.C.E., Rome divided conquered territories into provinces, each with a governor who had both civil and military powers; many governors were themselves generals or under generals' control, which enhanced the overall role of the military hierarchy and of key commanders. Julius Caesar was a vivid example of a general who parlayed political control of key provinces and a powerful army into dictatorial rule in Rome itself.

The subsequent establishment of an outright empire inevitably included some expansion of the formal apparatus of government, though Augustus kept many of the old institutions, such as the senate, as window dressing. A group of senators, chosen by lot, served as advisers to the emperor—again, an interesting move that countered any tendency toward professional bureaucratic controls at the top. The emperor appointed provincial governors, but he himself ruled some of the frontier provinces to facilitate military defense. The emperor did now appoint some civil servants, whose loyalty, however, went to him directly, rather than being supplemented by an independent value system, as in Confucian China. Civil administrators helped the government expand the road system, collect taxes, regulate coinage, and monitor the grain supply for the huge city of Rome. The government also sponsored a variety of cultural and religious activities and buildings, while providing popular entertainments and even some free bread for the growing Roman population.

The expansion of state functions was supplemented by growing efforts to promote worship of the emperor, whose statues were displayed prominently throughout the empire. In another move to cement loyalty, selected subjects outside Rome, even outside Italy, were granted Roman citizenship; this helped tie local elites to the imperial structure. The empire did not, however, innovate greatly in the area of government personnel and function. Centralization was modest. Existing states, cities, and urban elites continued to govern in most cases, running their own affairs as long as they paid taxes and accepted the supervision of Roman governors. Even regional kings might continue to rule, as in much of North Africa. Tax collecting, vital for a government that had to sustain a large military establishment, was itself decentralized. Romans paid sales and inheritance taxes, and merchants also paid fees for using the nearby harbor. Provincial tax levels were set by government officials, but these then contracted the levy to tax farmers for actual collection, with the tax farmer who put in the best bid, that is, who promised to highest rate of return, winning the contract. This was convenient for a government without a local bureaucracy, but it resulted in some harsh procedures, because tax farmers could pocket anything extra they managed to collect.

Throughout the classical civilizations, the growth of governments and the development of new political forms created new vulnerabilities. Active states could deteriorate, leaving societies open to more general decline. Changes in political forms—for example, loss of both citizen and aristocratic power in the Roman Empire—could loosen loyalties to the state, reducing support in times of crisis. Worsening leadership and rivalries among powerful ministers in the later Han dynasty reduced the effectiveness of the Chinese state by the 2nd century C.E. Regional bureaucrats became corrupt. Tax collections deteriorated, and with this the quality of public works worsened, contributing in turn to agricultural difficulties and peasant discontent. When new invasions of the Chinese state by a nomadic group, the Huns, were added, as well as the new diseases discussed in the previous chapter, Chinese society experienced significant chaos, which lasted over three centuries. Here, however, the power of the bureaucratic model was such that basic institutions and political ideas were revived in the later 6th century. Invasions and disease also weakened the later Roman Empire: Again, government functions shrank, leading to a more localized, less prosperous economy. In this case however, loyalties to the state also softened in the empire's western portion, and despite vivid recollection of Rome's glory, no real revival of this political model ever occurred. Only in the eastern Mediterranean did a Roman state, headed by an emperor and with a growing bureaucracy, survive the end of the classical period, emerging as the Byzantine Empire during ensuing centuries.

Creating Cultural Coherence

Cultural change in the classical period raises three or four basic questions, including the relationship between culture and the type of government each classical society developed. First, what was the classical culture in each case, and how did it compare with the others? How, also, did it help draw the civilization together, over a wide territory? Second, how did the culture affect other institutions and behaviors? Greek science, for example, emphasized a quest for logical principles in nature. Scientists gathered information, but they were particularly eager to spin rational models. In contrast, Chinese science remained pragmatic, focusing on gaining knowledge that would improve medicine, astrological calculations, or technology. One reason, then, that Chinese production techniques advanced more rapidly than Greek ones involved basic cultural outlooks: Many Greek scientists disdained applications as beneath their high station. Third, how did the newly articulated cultures affect ordinary people, at a time of extensive social inequality? Did they help link ordinary people with elites, or did they separate them further? This is a key question for the social role of classical cultures. Finally, how would the largely separate cultural systems respond to contact? Was openness to outside ideas a quality that emerged in every case?

As intellectual leaders realized the importance of defining clear religious or philosophical ideas, at least to social elites, their focus was on cultural productions within each civilization, not on cultural links among different civilizations. Precisely because cultural integration dominated much of the internal history of the classical civilizations, increased differentiation described the relationships among the major areas during the period. The differences in beliefs between Egypt and Mesopotamia, though real, thus pale in comparison to the contrasts between Confucian China, which was heavily secular, and Buddhist/ Hindu India. The process of firming up a culture as part of regional integration, as well as increasing the elaboration of its expression as wealth increased and the life of imperial courts became more extravagant, created sharper distinctions between civilizations.

Furthermore, relatively little contact occurred among the major civilizations until the final centuries of the classical period. This increased the process of differentiation and also fostered some outlandish legends about other areas. The Greek historian Herodotus, for example, writing in the 6th century B.C.E., was not really aware of China's existence in any coherent way. He did know of India and imagined it a land of fantastic wealth; one of his passages describes the giant ants that dug gold in India's deserts. Legends of this sort might motivate efforts at contact—Alexander the Great's push into India, later on, owed something to the extravagant tales of wealth current in Greece and the Middle East—but they reflected the fact that direct links among civilizations, and therefore real cultural interchange, were extremely rare. In the third century B.C.E., the Chinese geographer Tsou Yen described the world in terms of nine large continents, divided by great oceans; each continent had nine regions, and China was only one of nine on its continent. This view, based on mathematical symmetries rather than any real knowledge, altered earlier Chinese belief, which had emphasized China as the only place in the world, but it neither reflected nor, in fact, encouraged wider contacts.

Civilizations were not entirely self-contained, however. The influence of a culture could spill over into adjacent areas that were not fully brought into the civilization itself; hence, for example, the interaction between Mediterranean cultures and the African kingdoms of Kush and Axum. Though serious contact among major societies was rare, it did occur and brought additional changes in its wake. Hellenism reflected the results of cultural interchange among Greece, Persia, and Egypt, while Alexander's brief penetration of India had striking cultural results. Finally, the dynamism of India's religions created missionary impulses that provided another means of promoting cultural exchange. As Christianity developed in the Middle East, it, too, reached out beyond civilization boundaries. These missionary results were particularly important in the final centuries of the classical era, marking the beginnings of a major transition in world history more generally. Thus the impact of contact, as well as the more pervasive internal integration efforts, set the framework for what was clearly a fundamental period in world cultural history.

Internal Patterns: China and the Mediterranean

As in politics, classical China represents the best example of explicit and successful cultural dissemination within a civilization area, for the imperial government, particularly by the time of the Han dynasty, consciously attempted to create some cultural homogeneity as part of the process of assuring order and stability. The most explicit attempts at cultural integration during the later classical period aimed at the Middle Kingdom, and particularly at aligning some aspects of the cultural framework between north and south. Language was one key project. Populations in the southern region did not speak Chinese. Government-encouraged migrations from the north, as well as education efforts, gradually encouraged spoken, Mandarin Chinese, though the basic linguistic integration took many centuries, stretching beyond the classical period, and even then a number of separate dialects persisted not only in parts of the south and southeast but in sections of the north as well. Standardizing the written language was a related initiative, again directed at unifying the cultural framework, at least for the upper, literate classes. By the 3rd century B.C.E., the Chinese were in a position to produce the first formal dictionary, another key step in linguistic integration, while scholars under the Han dynasty were also encouraged by government patronage to construct a unified history of China and a body of approved, traditional literature. Finally, the government actively promoted the doctrines of Confucius, from the 6th century B.C.E. Confucian emphasis on order, hierarchy, and self-control gave a distinctive flavor to elite cultures throughout China.

China's policy of cultural integration had two limitations, however. First, it paid little direct attention to the lower classes. These people were largely illiterate, which excluded them from the obvious common cultural channels. Confucianism itself insisted on the division between gentry and commoners, who owed each other courtesy but operated on different planes. Lower-class beliefs continued to be permeated by polytheistic religion and associated rituals, such as good-luck emblems over doorways and parades with dragons and other symbols. As long as these beliefs did not interfere with good order—and they were compatible with some gradual, informal acceptance of certain Confucian views—upper-class culture turned a blind eye.

Second, China's frontier regions were not fully brought into the common cultural orbit. Areas to the west, north, and south of the Middle Kingdom experienced far more political instability, rebellion, and invasion than did China proper. The imperial government mainly sought to maintain order and derive tribute; it did not try to acculturate fully, often regarding the frontier peoples as little more than animals. Chinese settlements, however, were planted in certain instances, and criminals might be exiled to the frontiers; schools and other institutions followed this movement. Intellectual communities developed, working in Chinese and with Confucian culture. Chinese example spread agriculture and other technical and economic systems that inevitably affected beliefs and styles. Chinese artistic wares were obviously esteemed by the local upper classes, often found, for example, in tombs. Local leaders might adopt Chinese culture more broadly, using Chinese musical instruments as sources of higher standards of beauty or seeking more formal education as part of building firmer political structures. The result—and echoes of it last to this day in China— was a mixed frontier culture, with both Chinese and local elements. The frontier regions were, finally, a two-way street, particularly in the west, bringing new influences into China as well. The Chinese lute, ultimately the society's most popular instrument, came in from Central Asia, as did new artistic emphases on the human figure. Early Chinese art had rarely depicted people, but western influences changed this, even as China's evocative renderings of these figures maintained a distinctive tone.

The formation of Mediterranean civilization inevitably involved some of the same cultural integration as occurred in classical China. Greek spread widely as the upper-class language of the whole eastern Mediterranean, though there were, unlike China, no particular efforts to cut into the diversity of lower-class languages—with the result of far less overall linguistic cohesion in the region. Latin was widely used later on, and both Greece and Rome sent out settlements to their far-flung empires, which in turn spread common artistic styles and beliefs. Cultural contact in the region was particularly important during the Hellenistic period. Alexander and some of his successors deliberately sought to mix Greek, Persian, and other Middle Eastern traditions in order to provide an eclectic culture that would be more exciting than any one version and also provide the basis for political cohesion. Greek artistic and literary forms, science, and philosophy spread widely in this context. One clear sign of successful mixing is the production of important treatises in Greek from places like Egypt. Hellenism was short-lived, however. Roman cultural efforts were slightly less ambitious, though here, too, the importance of Latin and the spread of citizenship brought intellectuals from the Middle East, North Africa, and Spain to some common education and artistic and philosophical production. Thus some of the leading early Christian writers, such as Augustine, working in Latin with Greco-Roman philosophical concepts, came from North Africa. On the whole, however, Greco-Roman cultural integration was less extensive than that of classical China. There was less emphasis on a common, civilization-wide history (as opposed to separate Greek or Roman myth-histories, which were developed). Despite the importance of Greek and Hellenistic science and philosophy, nothing as sweeping as a devotion to Confucianism developed in the upper classes.

Comparison and Contrast: The Special Dynamism of Religions

Efforts to form some cultural links within each civilization, though varying in intensity, led to important differences in emphasis and identity. India contrasts most vividly with both China and the Mediterranean in its overarching emphasis on religion. The usually peaceful rivalry between Hinduism and Buddhism in India during much of the classical period indicates an interest in otherworldly matters that far exceeded the religious impulses of the other two classical centers. Of course, religion did not describe the whole of Indian culture; there was important secular drama, filled with tales of adventure and happy endings, as well as impressive achievement in science and mathematics. India's main university, Nalanda, emphasized these subjects along with agriculture and medicine. But the religious tone predominated, drawing most artistic production to a depiction of the various deities or toward adornment of the temples.

The differentiation from the Mediterranean is particularly interesting because both regions drew from earlier Indo-European ideas, including religious stories and the panoply of gods and goddesses. Early religion in India after the Indo-European invasion thus included the worship of a war god, Indra, youthful, heroic, ever victorious. Like the Roman Mars or the

Norse Thor, Indra, as conveyed in the Indian epic *Rig Veda*, wields thunderbolts, and he also has the power to release waters. Varuna, a second god, resembled the Mediterranean Jupiter as king of universal order; Agni, god of fire, resembled Vulcan. As in Greece and Rome as well, the Indians of the epic (Vedic) era worshiped other, lesser personified powers of nature, some of them female, such as Ushas, the "rosy-fingered" daughter of the sky, goddess of dawn, described in some of the same terms the Greek Homer used to describe Dawn in his epic *The Odyssey*. Indians and Mediterraneans alike created powerful priests to develop rituals and to intercede with the gods; ceremonies and animal sacrifices were common. They wove stories of the gods into their epic literature, endowing the gods not only with great powers but with human qualities writ large, including quarrels and deceit. These features provided the great epics in both societies with a host of dramatic incidents.

Furthermore, Greek culture directly penetrated into western India in the wake of Alexander the Great's invasions in the 4th century B.C.E. Artistic impact was considerable. Governments in the region issued magnificent coins, with the images of the Greek gods and Hercules along with the local kings. Triumphant columns commemorating the conquests also spread the Greek style. Greek artistic themes, including the heroic representations of the human figure, had powerful influence on Indian art. They were particularly important in defining the artistic representations of the Buddha himself. Previously, Gautama Buddha had been portrayed mainly indirectly, through symbols such as footprints or empty thrones. Now, sculptors began to work more elaborately in stone, with greater attention to the human form. The result was a major change in artistic-religious expression, affecting not only India but also China and other Asian regions where Buddhism later penetrated. A Greco-Indian school of sculpture evolved, particularly in the Gandhara region of the northwest, operating for several centuries and incorporating even Greek-style costumes and hairstyles while representing Indian religious motifs. Here was syncretism—this blending of diverse cultures—with a vengeance. Greek mathematics and scientific concepts also fed ongoing scholarship in India.

But cultural contact was a two-way street. Buddhist monks in the region worked hard and often successfully to convert Greek leaders. The last Hellenistic king in Northwest India was converted to Buddhism directly.

Cross-Cultural Influence in the Classical Period: Greece and India. This statue came from a region, Gandhara, strongly influenced by Hellenism as a result of Alexander the Great's conquests. Artistic ramifications continued into the 2nd century C.E. In this case, Buddha is dressed in a Greek toga, with a Greek hairstyle. Can you think of other examples of using one society's styles to express religious values from another? From *The Cambridge History of India*, vol. 1 (Cambridge: Cambridge University Press, 1971). Reprinted by permission.

A host of Indian monks, along with 500 Greeks, attended the long religious discussion that preceded this king's conversion. Hinduism also won converts, in part because its religion could incorporate additional gods and local cult heroes, thus allowing the introduction of some Greek elements. Explicit conversions were transitory, and no importation of either Hinduism or Buddhism to the Middle East occurred. Contacts with India, however, helped generate a series of more spiritual, fervent religions that nourished the Middle East in the centuries around the birth of Christ—often called mystery religions—reflecting Indian philosophical influences. While most of these religions had a largely lower-class clientele, Indian ideas may have affected the highly intellectual, elite writers in the Stoic school. Thus Seneca, a leading Roman Stoic writer, stated, "God is near you, he is with you, he is within you . . . a holy spirit indwells within us." How much Indian influences mattered in what came to be a dynamic religious environment in the Middle East is impossible to say, but they did encourage new ideas about a spiritual life after death, when souls might live on happily until the full union of souls, and even the concept of divine saviors who might help elevate mortals through their love. The imprint of these ideas cannot be traced as clearly as that of Greek sculpture, but the possibilities of influence are intriguing, both on some philosophical schools in the Roman period and on religion itself. Was this result of cultural contact part of the context in which traditional Jewish religion was modified and the resulting Christian faith more readily received?

The effects of the unusual mutual contact clearly radiated for centuries. Influences extended geographically as well; here was a key source of Chinese importation of a more human-focused art, as Hellenistic and Indian blends reached the western frontier through Central Asia. The contact also pointed up an obvious feature in civilization exchange: Each society recognized strong points in the other as targets of syncretic imitation. Powerful Greek art and stone sculpture made sense in what they could add to Indian representations and available materials. India's religious strength was its cultural signature, and Mediterranean visitors saw this clearly. Neither culture overwhelmed the other, even where imitation went furthest; but a real enrichment, a real process of change and recombination, was undeniable.

Cultural Expansions

Along with the great encounter between Hellenistic and Indian cultures, civilizations developed important cultural outreach beyond their formal borders—a less surprising development, but an important one. Obviously, the wealth and commercial growth of civilizations created both contacts and influence that might persuade others to add new cultural ingredients—just as frontier people did in their interactions with China. Whether a religion or artistic style seemed superior in its own right or whether converts vaguely hoped to associate themselves with a powerful neighbor cannot always be determined; often, surely, both ingredients were involved.

Two cases of civilization's outreach were particularly significant. From the Mauryan dynasty onward, India's commercial ventures and overt missionary activities commingled in Southeast Asia. The emperor Ashoka, after his own conversion to Buddhism, sent many emissaries to Sri Lanka, Burma, and perhaps beyond, beginning the penetration of this great religion in these areas. Expanding trade later encouraged both Buddhism and Hinduism in other areas. A variety of Indian seafarers and merchants settled in the eastern part of the Indian Ocean. At one time, a Hindu kingdom formed in Vietnam, and Sanskrit spread widely in what are now Thailand and Malaysia, providing also a base for the development of regional writing forms. More durable Hindu kingdoms were established on several Indonesian islands, where pockets of the religion survive to this day.

The African kingdoms below Egypt formed a second enclave of cultural penetration, but in this case from the Middle East and North Africa. Again, both trade and missionary outreach were involved. The kingdom of Kush, south of Egypt, continued to flourish in the final centuries B.C.E., even as Egypt itself declined and was then taken over by the Romans. The center of the society moved south, to a new capital city in Meroe. Kush had long nurtured a mixture of independent cultural development and imitation; its writing system and religion were its own, for example, but its monumental art, in temple and palaces, owed much to Egyptian models. From the 4th century B.C.E. onward, the capacity for borrowing was more widely extended. Kush began to trade actively with the Middle East, by means of caravans to ports on the Red Sea and from there both to the Indian Ocean and to the Roman lands. Kushite architecture began to reflect

Middle Eastern influences, while metal pottery picked up some Chinese, Indian, and Greek styles. These motifs were applied to the regional polytheistic religion, as in the figure of the lion god Apedemak.

Meroe began to decline after 200 B.C.E., displaced by a new kingdom, Axum, to the south (the forerunner of present-day Ethiopia). Axum quickly took over the trade with the Middle East. This contact is expressed in the mythical Ethiopian version of the Jewish biblical story of the queen of Sheba, in which the queen's sons, sired by Solomon, became the founders of the royal family of Ethiopia. In fact, Axum began to use Arabic writing and language, while borrowing the Arab polytheistic religion. Some conversions to Judaism also occurred. By 50 C.E., Axum's trade had shifted more strongly to the eastern Mediterranean, where Greek cultural influences were picked up. Greek writing was now widely used. A leading king accepted Christianity as one of the state religions, and a separate Ethiopian strand of Christianity then developed widely. Ironically, this cultural shift, along with an unexplained decline in trade, helped isolate Ethiopia, for its neighbors remained polytheistic or, a bit later, converted to Islam. Ethiopian culture continued its distinctive path, among other things developing a vigorous art around Christian religious themes. The extensions from the Middle East into this corner of Africa were less far-reaching than India's cultural interaction with Southeast Asia, but they showed the power of contact.

As the power of several classical empires began to decline after about 200 C.E., the missionary potential of two key religions expanded. Cultural boundaries became more porous, at least for a time.

The expansion of Buddhism is particularly noteworthy. Buddhism reached different parts of China in different ways. Indian merchants had contacts with southern China through oceanic trade. Other versions of Buddhism spread through Central Asia, while a particular type of Buddhism entered Tibet directly from India, becoming solidly implanted there. The type of Buddhism most popular in China was a modification of the original, called Mahayana, or Greater Vehicle, Buddhism. This strand was less austere than the earlier form and also quite tolerant of other ideas, which could be held along with Buddhism itself as lesser truths. A variety of gods peopled this version, including the deified Buddha himself; and saints (bodhisattvas) existed, holy people who stayed back in the world to guide others to salvation before passing to nirvana themselves. Even with these modifications, which made Buddhism seem more attainable and the goal of nirvana clearer and more reachable, Buddhism was a marked contrast to the beliefs that had predominated in classical China. It spread not only because of active cultural contact but because the political deterioration of China during and after the late Han dynasty weakened the commitment to earlier values, such as Confucianism.

The first transmitters of Buddhism to China may have been merchants, but by the late 2nd century C.E., Buddhist leaders in India and Central Asia were actively sending in missionary groups. By the 4th century, explicit translations of Buddhist texts were underway. Once launched, Buddhism inspired a number of Chinese and Korean students to visit India, the first great student exchange across civilizational lines in world history. Several hundred students were involved between the 3rd and 8th centuries. Many returned to further the work of translation and conversion.

This was the first great religion ever known in China, though Taoism previously had organized some spiritual beliefs. It also constituted the only wholesale cultural borrowing in Chinese history before modern times. The first converts were upper-class Chinese, including patrons in various Chinese governments. Some Chinese combined Buddhism and Confucianism, which demonstrated the eclecticism possible in many Asian cultures. Buddhist monasteries spread widely, often gaining large holdings in land. Gradually, many lower-class Chinese also converted. Buddhism had a massive influence on Chinese art, including music, and Buddhist sculpture virtually commanded the field, in an area not usually of great interest to the Chinese. Initially, Chinese Buddhas were stiff, austere abstractions of the deity, but gradually Chinese commitment to human qualities altered the style toward plumper, more lifelike figures, more aligned with Chinese concepts of human beauty. Buddhist temples spread new architectural forms. In literature, earlier Chinese themes continued, but a vast outpouring of Buddhist work developed as well—later ignored in Chinese intellectual life. Buddhist literature included popular myths and miracle stories but also a variety of appeals for salvation and biographies of holy men.

Not surprisingly, Chinese traditions strongly influenced the ongoing development of Buddhism in East Asia; as is usual in cultural exchange, mutual impacts were vital. The Chinese emphasized careful classifications of different Buddhist sects and various levels of Buddhist truths. Buddhist rituals and magic formulas made sense to many Chinese, for they resembled aspects of Taoism; ceremonies for the dead fit in with traditional ancestor worship. Chinese versions of Buddhist monasticism, including the Ch'an (or in Japanese, Zen) variety, tended to stress constructive work for society, not purely passive contemplation. Buddhist groups served as centers of learning, hospitals, and inns for travelers. Chinese translations altered Buddhism's more tolerant view of women: "Husband supports wife," became "husband controls wife", while "wife comforts husband" became "wife reveres husband." Even the Buddhist emphasis on monastic celibacy was gradually relaxed, given Chinese insistence on the importance of family formation. Finally, Chinese Buddhism developed close ties with the state, sometimes supported by it and often urged to generate political loyalty. These changes, particularly, showed the distance between the Chinese and original Indian versions of the religion.

Nevertheless, despite important syncretism and the changes already introduced in the Mahayana version, Buddhism and Chinese cultural traditions coexisted uneasily. Buddhism downgraded worldly focus, in contrast to Confucian emphasis on the transcendent importance of social obligations and particularly of the state and the family. The power of Buddhist influence on China was a striking testimony to the results new civilization contact might produce during special crises in a society's history. Even as China adapted Buddhism toward greater compatibility, problems remained. The decline of Buddhism in late-classical India removed some of the power from the initial Buddhist impetus in China. Taoism began to change, among other things, seeking to gain greater popular loyalty through a new emphasis on magical healing and other practices. The question of Buddhism's ultimate role in Chinese culture was not fully answered at the end of the classical period or even a few centuries beyond. It would have to be revisited, once Chinese political and cultural traditions were reasserted after the end of political turmoil.

The spread of Buddhism to China (and through it, to Korea and later to Japan) was the great culture contact story of the late classical period. The advance of Christianity from its original center in the eastern Mediterranean raised some similar themes. Here, too, was a religion convinced of its truth (though much less tolerant than Buddhism of other truths) and possessed of a strong missionary impulse that could transcend traditional political and cultural boundaries. As the effectiveness of the Roman Empire declined, many people saw new reasons to turn to a fresh belief system that emphasized otherworldly goals and rewards, at a time when conditions on this earth seemed insecure.

Christianity's principal dissemination, during the late classical centuries, occurred within the Roman Empire, where established merchant routes and even shaky political institutions facilitated the spread of churches. But missionaries fanned out beyond the fluid borders of Mediterranean civilization. The conversion of many Ethiopians is one example of this more extensive influence. Still more missionary activity was directed toward portions of the Middle East beyond Roman borders, and from there to Central Asia. A variety of separate churches formed as Christian efforts merged with local cultures, and as disputes within mainstream Christianity forced dissenters to seek their fortune elsewhere.

The Armenian people, located in Central Asia northeast of Turkey, were the first group to convert to Christianity as a whole country. A missionary won the favor of the Armenian king, Tiridates III, around 300 C.E., and official conversion followed by royal decree. The church soon broke from Greek Christianity over disagreements concerning the nature of Christ. Armenian Christian leaders formed an alphabet, derived mainly from Persian but with Greek influence, in order to transmit religious writings. Religious contact, in other words, led to other cultural developments, though not to a cultural merger across civilizational boundaries.

In the 5th century C.E., Nestorius, the patriarch of Constantinople, developed yet another version of Christ's nature. He argued that it was at once divine and human, which was standard Christian doctrine, but innovated in claiming that only the human portion had been born of Mary; hence, he contended, Mary should not be regarded as the mother of God. His views won a resounding condemnation at a church council in 431. His followers fled to Persia, where their views mingled with local religious beliefs to form what was called Nestorian Christianity. A separate church organization ensued, with active missionary efforts all over Central Asia and into India and China. Nestorian conversions in China were noteworthy until the government cracked down on the religion in the 7th and 8th centuries. A strong Nestorian minority survived in the Islamic Middle East until it was scattered by Mongol invasions in the 13th century. (It reentered China at that point, where it won some renewed tolerance.)

Because the classical period placed such emphasis on the integration of distinct civilizations and cultures, surprising results might accrue when societies came into contact—as in the Indian-Hellenistic interlude. Surprising results also followed the combination of unprecedented commitments to spreading religion and the weakening of the classical civilizations themselves. While missionary activity had been a recurrent part of Indian history during the classical period, it was much newer in China and the Mediterranean, where most cultural efforts had stayed within the civilization itself. Cultural contacts responded to larger shake-ups, and in turn, they created additional disruption and opportunity. These developments, while forming distinctive regional paths as in Armenia, also helped set in motion the larger dynamic of the next, postclassical stage of world history.

Conclusion

The innovations needed to pull larger territories into effective societies underpinned major developments in statecraft and culture alike. Ordinary people in the classical civilizations still might have only irregular contact with government officials, while preserving older beliefs and rituals. But their lives changed with the expansion of government claims and functions and with new patterns of belief among priests and landowners. As culture contacts increased to include the dissemination of dynamic religions such as Buddhism and Christianity, even ordinary people experienced new goals in life, new standards for measuring work or death or family relationships. Developments in work, disease, and gender patterns helped measure the impact of political and cultural change—and also the continued limits to controlling the human condition through formal institutions or organized beliefs.

CHAPTER 8

GENDER STRUCTURES IN CLASSICAL CIVILIZATIONS

The classical period introduced vital new developments in gender relations. Each civilization generated some characteristic family arrangements, including how spouses were selected. More important still was the establishment of clear ideas about gender associated with each of the major cultural systems. Confucianism, Hinduism, and Mediterranean philosophy formulated specific notions about men's and women's qualities and roles. These cultural formulations helped stiffen gender relations, because they could be passed down from generation to generation and become part of basic socialization patterns, creating unexamined perceptions among men and women alike.

The gender structures that developed in the world's classical civilizations built on those created in the earlier river-valley civilizations, rigidifying the existing distinctions between men and women and adding new sources through which these were supported and justified. The growing importance of sons generated a system, particularly in China and the Mediterranean, in which unwanted girl babies might simply be put to death, in a practice called female infanticide. As law codes were expanded, women's legal disabilities grew, and new restrictions were added on women at certain points in their life cycle, such as widowhood. In the epic stories told about the founding of classical civilizations, such as the *Ramayana* in India and the *Aeneid* in Rome, female characters either loyally support the hero or attempt to thwart him on his mission; they do not do great deeds on their own. In the philosophical systems that became the basis for Chinese and Mediterranean civilizations—Confucianism and the Greek philosophy of Plato and Aristotle, respectively— women were regarded as necessary to the natural order of the universe but clearly inferior and in need of male control. Along with these philosophical systems, religious beliefs that regarded women as both inferior and dangerous to men's spiritual well-being grew more widespread during the classical period. Both philosophy and religion developed certain key texts that were memorized, discussed, debated, and elaborated in schools and other types of educational establishments generally open to men only. As the social distinctions between groups within civilizations grew more rigid, high-status men felt it increasingly important to seclude their daughters and wives from other men, and special women's quarters—termed the *gyneceum* in ancient Athens—were built within houses or house compounds.

As they had in river-valley civilizations, women occasionally ruled territories in the classical period; female rulers whose names are known range from Lady Ahpo-Hel of Palenque among the Maya in the Yucatán to Empress Wu in China. Women's rule was often informal—they took over when their sons were young or their husbands were ill—but occasionally they ruled in their own right. Queens and empresses made significant contributions to the development of political structures, intellectual and cultural institutions, and religious systems, but their reigns were usually portrayed later as marked by turmoil and instability, if not worse. A woman who had power over a male ruler, for instance, his wife or concubine, was also generally portrayed in official histories as scheming and evil, with court historians and chroniclers—most of whom were male—developing a stereotype of the weak ruler as one who let himself be advised by women.

Classical civilizations were not monolithic, however, and traditions also developed within them that lessened the distinctions between women and men in ways that were regarded as especially significant. In three of the major religions that developed during this period, Hinduism, Buddhism, and Christianity, women were regarded as capable of obtaining the ultimate spiritual goal—perhaps through a longer and more difficult process than men had to undergo but not cut off from the goal entirely. In all three religions, devotion to gods (Hinduism) or particularly holy figures (Buddhism and Christianity) provided male and female adherents with a feminine ideal and object of devotion. Though in all three religions the most important leaders and thinkers were men,

Ganga and Yamuna with Attendants. A sculpture of the river goddess Ganga (Ganges) from 9th-century India, portraying her as life-giving. Reprinted by permission of the Los Angeles County Museum of Art, the Nasli and Alice Heeramaneck Collection, Museum Associates Purchase.

women were active in winning adherents and in developing their own rituals. These three religions, and also several smaller ones that developed during the classical period, such as Jainism in India, came to offer at least a few women the opportunity to choose a life of religious devotion instead of marriage and motherhood.

Family Structures

Other than individuals who remained unmarried for religious reasons, and—in some cultures—slaves, most people in classical cultures married, and the family group was the central institution. This family group varied in size and composition from culture to culture, and within one culture, according to wealth and social status. In some areas of the world most households were nuclear, made up largely of parents and their children, with perhaps one or two other relatives; in others, an extended family of brothers and their spouses and children lived in a single household or family compound. Wealthier households also contained unrelated servants and slaves and, often, younger relatives whose parents had died or older widows. All these individuals, whether adults or children, blood relatives or unrelated, were generally under the authority of the male head of household, usually the grandfather or oldest married brother in an extended household. Boys as well as girls remained under their father's control until they married, and perhaps beyond if they continued to live in an extended household.

Most classical cultures were patrilocal, with women leaving their own families on marriage and going to live with their husbands, often in a different village. In some cultures, the woman retained strong ties to her birth family and considered herself part of two families, whereas in others these ties were weak, with the woman contacting her birth family only in grave emergencies. In China, for example, a woman was never inscribed on the official family list of her birth family, so that she would never be honored as one of their ancestors by later generations; she was instead inscribed on that of her husband's family once she had had a son. Women who had no sons simply disappeared from family memory. In cultures in which extended families lived together or in close proximity to one another, a woman came under the control of her father- and mother-in-law as well as her husband when she married. Because relationships between mothers and sons were often intense in these cultures that put so much emphasis on male children, a new bride's interaction with her mother-in-law was often very difficult. Spiteful and cruel mothers-in-law became stock figures in the literature and stories of classical cultures—particularly in China and India—reflecting what was often harsh and unkind treatment of young women in real life. (In the Mediterranean and, later, in the rest of Europe, where mothers-in-law usually did not live in the same household with a married couple, this is not a common theme; here, the malicious older woman who causes harm is generally a stepmother.)

Despite conflicts in real life, marriage and motherhood were increasingly idealized during the classical period. Girls were trained from a very young age in the skills and attitudes that would make them good wives and mothers, instructed that their primary purpose in life was to serve their husbands and children. Weddings were central occasions in a family's life, with spouses chosen carefully by parents, other family members, or marriage brokers. Much of a family's resources often went to pay for the ceremony and setting up the new household. Opportunities for divorce varied in the classical world, but in many cultures it was nearly impossible, so the choice of a spouse was undertaken carefully, after much consultation with relatives and often with astrologers or other people who predicted the future. Weddings themselves were held on days determined to be lucky or auspicious, a determination arrived at independently for each couple.

Because most classical cultures were patrilineal, giving birth to sons was central to a continuation of the family line, with women and men offering prayers and sacrifices to accomplish this and marking sons' births with special ceremonies or rituals not performed for the births of daughters. Additional ceremonies were conducted throughout boys' early years to keep them healthy, in an effort to counteract the high rates of child mortality created by diseases. Women also carried out other rituals within the household designed to maintain family harmony, promote the family's well-being, and assure the favor of spirits and deities. Most of the religious systems accepted in classical cultures were highly ritualistic, with the performance of certain rites and ceremonies regarded as more important than holding any specific belief, so that these actions gave meaning to women's lives, making them important in the maintenance of culturally significant values.

The injunction to marry did not simply apply to women, however. Unmarried men in most classical cultures were not regarded as fully adult, and until the advent of Buddhism and Christianity, there were no institutionalized forms of lifelong celibacy for men, though they might spend a period of time as students before they were married or as religious devotees away from their families once they had married and had the necessary sons. Marriage, rather than signifying simply the attaining of a specific age, was the way in which men normally escaped the control of their own fathers. It remained a permanent state for most men; women whose first husband died often lived the rest of their lives as widows—in some classical cultures, they came to have no other option—but men quickly remarried. Having children, particularly sons, was just as important for men as for women, perhaps even more so, and various ways were devised to provide sons for a man whose wife did not have one: taking second or third wives or concubines, legitimizing a son born of a woman who was not a wife or concubine, adopting a nephew or an unrelated boy or young man. A woman whose husband had died before she gave birth to a son might be expected to remarry his brother, so as to produce a son that was legally regarded as the child of her deceased husband. (This practice is called a levirate marriage.)

The kingdoms and empires of the classical world regarded the family as the basis of society—population was generally counted by households, not by individuals, with rights to participate in positions of political and religious leadership determined by membership in certain families or clans. Intellectuals also saw the family as the basis of society in political and social theory, the microcosm of larger society and the place in which cultural values were anchored. In classical China, for example, Confucianism taught that the order and harmony of the universe began with order and harmony in the smallest human unit; if things were disrupted in families, they would necessarily be disrupted in the larger political realms. In Rome as well, military victories and defeats were often attributed not simply to the skill of armies but also to the stability or instability of family life. Classical Athens broke with this to some degree, but here, too, political theorists such as Plato thought that the family and state were intimately related to one another; the perfect state, wrote Plato in *The Republic,* could be achieved only if political leaders were separated from their families at birth, so that they were not tempted to make decisions that would benefit their relatives.

Beyond the Family

Though both women and men derived their identities largely from their families, in both theory and reality, men were also involved in the world beyond the household. The family served as the *basis* for men's place in the world, whereas for women it was the *location* of their place in the world. Though they might learn to read and write, women in classical cultures generally did so within the household, while upper-class men attended schools, academies, and other formal institutions of learning. Women's religious rituals sometimes took them to a neighborhood temple but more often were performed at household altars and shrines. Women's occupations were often those that could be done within the walls of a house, such as spinning and weaving. Increasingly in classical cultures, the only women seen outside the household were those of low status—servants and slaves bringing water from wells or marketing in classical Greece, lower-caste women weaving or making the black eye makeup termed *khol* in India, peasants whose work needs required collaboration between men and women. Thus this spatial separation of men and women was an issue of social as well as gender structures, for the women who were most likely to be found outside the household, in contact with men who were not members of their families, were those of low status.

This link between public appearances and status can be seen most dramatically in the case of women who provided sexual services and entertainment for men, mainly in the cities. Along with women who supported themselves through prostitution, in most classical cultures there were also some who combined sexual services with dancing, singing, and educated conversation, often in government-run brothels. Such women had a very ambiguous position: they were clearly dishonorable, and their children could not be married into good families, but they also might be quite wealthy and highly educated. Even among such women, however, status was determined by level of seclusion; high-status courtesans had their own households or at least remained inside brothels, whereas low-status prostitutes walked the streets.

In many ways, not only prostitutes but all women had an ambiguous relationship to the institutions and structures that were developing in classical cultures, while the male experience was more straightforward. A man in classical Athens or Rome was either a citizen or not and had certain rights and privileges based on his status; a man in classical India belonged to a certain caste and performed the rituals required of that caste; a man in China who took the imperial scholarly examination could obtain a position as a court official or governor. Women in Athens were not citizens, though they could pass this status on to their sons; in India, they married only within the caste of their fathers, but they did not go through a ceremony marking their caste status or need to observe most rituals regarding purity and pollution; in China, they wrote poetry and occasionally histories but could never hold an official position or take the imperial examinations. A woman's position in any of the social groups that were becoming increasingly distinct in the classical period was generally mediated by her relationship to a man and could change on marriage, remarriage, or widowhood. Thus, for her, the rhythm of her personal life cycle—when she married, whether she had children and how many, when her husband died—was generally more important than it was for most men, whose lives were shaped more by large economic patterns or by the political institutions that are generally seen as the central accomplishment of classical cultures. Though individual women often had a great deal of political power, politics was generally conceptualized and to a large degree practiced as a system that regulated relations between men. In all classical civilizations, lower-class women suffered less inequality in relation to men than most of their upper-class sisters. Their work was essential to the family economy, which prevented their being completely subordinated or confined to decorative and marital roles.

Cultural Differences

So far we have been discussing developments in gender structures that were shared by many classical cultures, but these did not work in precisely the same fashion in each civilization. Particular cultures placed different emphases on gender distinctions and supported different kinds of family arrangements, and women had slightly different opportunities to accommodate themselves to patterns of change in each society. Thus comparison must be added to gain an understanding of the overall direction of change.

China

By the period of the Zhou dynasty, certain structures were in place in China that made the life experiences of women and men dramatically different. The aristocracy came to have surnames, which determined the clan to which an upper-class man belonged and to which he owed loyalty and obedience. This loyalty was due not only to living members of his clan but also to his ancestors, for upper-class men were expected to carry out a series of rituals honoring their ancestors throughout their life and to have sons so that these rituals could continue. Honoring the ancestors became an integral part of Confucianism, which also emphasized the balanced but hierarchical relationship between Heaven—the superior, creative element—and Earth—the inferior, receptive one. Proper human relationships, especially family relationships, were those that were modeled on the relationship of Heaven and Earth, hierarchical and orderly. All aspects of family relationships had proper etiquette and rituals attached, which became more elaborate over the centuries and were recorded in books, including the Five Classics that formed the basis of Confucian teachings. Though both women and men were viewed as essential to the cosmic order, women were expected to be subordinate and deferential; these expectations were codified as the "three obediences" to which a woman was subject—to her father as a daughter, to her husband as a wife, and to her son as a widow. The other major philosophical-religious system of classical China, Taoism, promoted stronger notions of male-female complementarity, but even Taoists, as well as later Chinese Buddhists and Christians, grew up in a system that emphasized gender hierarchy.

The most powerful women in classical China were those attached to the imperial household as the emperor's wives and concubines or as the widows of former emperor. The principal wife of an emperor was considered the legal mother of all his children, no matter who their biological mother might be. When an emperor died, this woman became the empress dowager, and she was often the most important woman at court, for she generally chose the spouses for the children of the emperor and often controlled who had regular access to the new emperor. The few women in classical China who became highly learned were generally attached to the imperial household and, despite their own learning, often agreed with Confucian teachings about women's inferiority.

Land in China—the most basic form of wealth—was held largely by aristocratic families, passed jointly from generation to generation by the male members of the lineage. Because daughters left the family on marriage, they had no rights to land, although complicated exceptions were occasionally made for girls who had no brothers, in which they held land in trust for their sons or in which their husbands were adopted into the family. Some peasant families also owned land and, like nobles, passed it down in the patrilineage, although many were completely landless and worked on noble estates. Almost all peasants married, not because of Confucian principles but because marital couples and their children were the basic unit of agricultural production; procreation was an economic necessity, to supply supplementary family labor and replace population lost to disease, and not simply a religious duty.

India

Hinduism and Buddhism were the most important determinants of gender structures in classical India because they shaped all aspects of life, not simply what we might consider the religious realm. Both of these religions came to incorporate many different ideas and traditions, some of which stressed gender hierarchy and some gender complementarity. In Hinduism, higher-caste boys and men went through various ceremonies marking their status and spent a period of time studying sacred texts, while girls and women did not. A girl married very early and then went to live with her husband's family, where she honored his ancestors and performed rituals designed to prolong his life. If such rituals were ineffective, women could expect a long period of dismal widowhood, during which they were considered inauspicious—that is, unlucky—and so not welcome at family festivities or rituals. Though there is some disagreement about this in Hindu sacred texts, most of them teach that a woman can never gain the final state of bliss, known as *moksha*, without having first been reborn a man. Some Buddhist texts also regarded women as not capable of achieving enlightenment unless they first became men, and Buddhism placed all nuns under the control of male monks.

There were also traditions that stressed the power of women. Many of the Hindu deities are goddesses, who range from beneficient life-givers, such as Devi and Ganga, to faithful spouses, such as Parvati and Radha, to fierce destroyers and disease bearers, such as Kali and Durga. Women performed religious rituals either on their own or with their husbands and were active in the *bhakti* movements, popular devotional movements that stressed intense mystical experiences. Hindu stories stressed women's service to men but also gave credit to initiative, cleverness, love, and sensuality—ingredients different from the emphases of Confucian culture in China. For its part, in theory the Buddhist path to enlightenment (nirvana, or *nibbana*) is open to all regardless of sex or caste; one needs simply to shed all earthly desires.

Like Confucianism, Hinduism saw family life and procreation as religious duties; all men and women were expected to marry, and anything that interfered with procreation, including exclusively homosexual attachments, was seen as negative. In Buddhism, the spritually superior life was one that renounced all earthly desires, including sexual ones, and nuns and monks were warned about both homosexual and heterosexual relationships. Buddhism was never completely comfortable with women who gave up family life, however, and the ideal woman in Buddhism—both historically and in sacred texts—was more often than not a married woman with children who supported a community of monks or who assisted men in their spiritual progress, rather than a nun.

Classical Mediterranean Society

In contrast to classical India, gender structures in the Mediterranean, until the advent of Christianity, were shaped more by secular ideas and aims than by religious systems. Ideas about gender originating in classical Athens were sharply hierarchical. Aristotle (384–322 B.C.E.), the most influential philosopher in Western civilization, saw only males as capable of perfection and described women—and all female animals—as "deformed males." Thus the perfect human form was that of the young male and the perfect relationship one between two men. Athens developed an institutionalized system of *pederasty*, in which part of a young upper-class male's training in cultural and political adulthood included an often sexual relationship with an older man. (Formal homosexuality between adults, however, was condemned and open to legal punishment.) In the same way that Confucianism made women's subordination part of the cosmic order, Aristotelian biological and political theory made it part of nature: "The male is by nature fitter for command than the female . . . the inequality is permanent." This inequality was not simply a matter of theory but was also reflected in Athenian life, for citizen women did not participate in education, politics, or civic life and were generally secluded in special parts of the house. Slave women were not secluded; in fact, their work, such as buying and selling goods at the public market or drawing water at neighborhood wells, made the seclusion of citizen women possible. Women from outside Athens were engaged in a number of occupations, the most famous of which was being a *hetaera*, a resident in one of the city-run brothels, in which upper-class men spent considerable time. These aspects of Athenian life—certain types of homosexuality, prostitution, slavery, and the subordination of women—disturbed later scholars of the classical period such as Edith Hamilton and H. D. F. Kitto, who chose to leave them out of their discussions of the glories of Athenian democracy and philosophy.

In contrast to Athens, classical Rome developed a notion of the family that is in many ways close to that of China and India, in that the family, rather than the individual man, was considered the basis of the social order. This family was patriarchal, with fathers, particularly during the republican period, holding strong control over their female and male children and husbands control over their wives. Both men and women married early, at roughly the same age, a marital pattern both supported by and supporting the Roman ideal that husbands and wives should share interests, property, and activities. Spousal loyalty was often used metaphorically to represent political loyalty in a way that would have seemed bizarre to Greek political theorists. During the late republican and imperial period, upper-class men were often absent from their homes on military or government duties in Rome's rapidly expanding territories, which left women more responsible for running estates and managing businesses and property. No Roman woman was named emperor in her own right, but as the wives and mothers of emperors, they frequently influenced imperial politics. Respectable women had more opportunities in public than the Greeks had tolerated, including attending entertainments. Within the family, law gave wives some protection against abuse, modifying the disciplinary inequality of the earlier republic. But women's conditions deteriorated again in the later empire. The classical Mediterranean was home to a wide range of religious beliefs and practices, and in the 1st century C.E. Christianity was added to this mixture. In some of its teachings on gender, Christianity was quite revolutionary. The words and actions of Jesus of Nazareth were very favorable toward women, and a number of women are mentioned as his followers in the books of the New Testament, the key religious text for Christians. Women took an active role in the spread of Christianity, preaching, acting as missionaries, and being martyred alongside men. Early Christians expected Jesus to return to earth again very soon and so taught that one should concentrate on this "second coming." Because of this, marriage and normal family life should be abandoned, and Christians should depend on their new spiritual family of cobelievers—an ideal that led some women and men to reject marriage and live a celibate life, either singly or in communities. This rejection of sexuality also had negative consequences for women, however, because most early church writers—who were male and often termed the *church fathers*—saw women as their primary temptation and developed a strong streak of misogyny. Some of these writers, most prominently Augustine (354–430 C.E.), were dualists who made sharp distinctions between the spiritual and the material, the soul and the body, and identified women with the less valued material aspects of existence. Women were generally forbidden to preach or hold most official positions in the church. Thus, like Hinduism and Buddhism, Christianity offered contradictory and ambiguous messages about proper gender relations and the relative value of the devotion and worship of male and female adherents.

Conclusion

Gender differences had been abundantly clear in river-valley civilizations, but they intensified during the classical period, creating greater gaps between men and women. This change was most evident in the upper classes, though it tended to put pressure on gender patterns in society more generally. Rome during the early empire was a partial exception to this pattern, but in China, India, and Athens, the stipulations and family arrangements accompanying Confucianism, Hinduism, and Greek city-state politics tended to define women's roles and the perceptions of women with growing rigor.

Why did this rigidification occur? To some extent, the creation of more systematic cultural statements, such as Confucianism, almost unwittingly formalized gender ideas, by pulling less systematic inequalities into more elaborate ideological systems and tying gender structures to notions of society and the cosmos. Many historians believe that, on the whole, growing prosperity in agricultural civilizations created the means and facilitated the motivation to treat wives more as ornaments, as a sign of the family's wealth and success, and also to try to isolate and control them more fully, in order to assure male monopoly over their sexual activities and resulting offspring. This explains the particular focus on the upper classes as centers of innovation in gender thinking. Another contributing factor may have been more formal activities of governments, which reduced (though did not eliminate) women's informal power roles in individual families. Certainly, as we have seen, the creation of a more elaborate political sphere spurred men to try to define public life as their own, establishing a new occasion for men and women, the public and the familial, to be separate.

Yet there were tensions about gender within each of the civilizations, and the distinctions among cultures are significant as well. Cultural change, particularly the expansion of Buddhism in Asia and the rise of Christianity in the Middle East and Mediterranean, both strengthened and questioned existing gender structures. This simultaneous challenge and reinforcement would continue in the postclassical period, when contacts between cultures increased.

CHAPTER 9

WORK AND LEISURE IN THE CLASSICAL WORLD

In many important ways, the classical period defined patterns of labor systems and leisure that continued to exist well after the civilizations that spawned them changed or collapsed. Most obviously, the caste system in South Asia emerged during this period, melding religion with an organization of society based in large part on what type of labor each segment performed. Perhaps less dramatic but just as important, the classical civilizations in China and the Mediterranean organized work in structures that would remain characteristic in their successors. In the case of China, free peasants formed the backbone of the labor force, whereas in the Mediterranean world, slavery and other forms of unfree work became important components of labor mix. This chapter examines why these three civilizations created such different forms of labor exploitation.

Leisure activities also became defined in characteristic ways during the classical period. The festivals that emerged during this age, while they often had important antecedents, proved extremely durable. Many holidays became standardized during this age, although many changed in their meaning over time. In contrast to the preclassical period, some festivals lost their religious identities and became secular celebrations. Elsewhere, athletics and spectator sports emerged for the first time as important forms of leisure. Theater developed and became an activity enjoyed by spectators in their spare time. Indeed, while the concept of entertainer had existed previously, there were more of them in this period than ever before.

Comparing the Organization of Work

Before analyzing and comparing different civilizations, it is important to keep in mind certain general characteristics that continued to distinguish labor in the classical world. By this time a majority of people were agriculturists, as agriculture continued to spread and to reproduce the population boom that first occurred in the river-valley civilizations. Nevertheless, most of the earth's territory was still in the hands of hunters and gatherers and, increasingly, herders. In the major civilizations, with the most numerous laborers in the world, peasants formed the most important category. These workers farmed their land (or at least had usage rights over it) but were usually subordinate to a landowning aristocracy. The peasants paid taxes, making it possible for a small group of people at the top not to engage directly in agriculture and to form a ruling group that often evolved into a state. The work of the peasants also enabled the emergence of other groups, such as ritual specialists and priests and, especially marked in this period, merchants who traded in agricultural and manufactured goods. In this sense, peasants were responsible for creating civilization but in most cases were not permitted to participate fully in all its activities.

Chinese Work Patterns

Despite the predominance of agriculture in every civilization, there were important variations among civilizations in how work was organized. In the case of classical China, farmers and farming enjoyed greater standing than in the other civilizations. In the official Chinese social hierarchy, farmers came after the scholar-bureaucrats in prestige. Such was the prestige of farming in classical China that even scholars tried to keep their hand in agriculture, dabbling when they could in plowing or other agrarian activities. After the farmers came artisans and, lastly, merchants, actors, and other presumably disreputable folk. Only booksellers were seen as honorable merchants and were ranked with the scholars. In theory (though rarely in practice), peasants could become government officials; in Han times, discrimination against traders increased, even leading to a prohibition against merchants becoming state officials. Traders were, however, typically much wealthier than the vast majority of peasants, bringing about contradictions between wealth and social prestige. The lack of prestige in commerce did make the wealthy prefer to invest in land rather than trading ventures, leading to increased landlordism.

Plowing and Sowing, from Tomb No. 1 at Jiayuguan, Gansu, 220–316 C.E.

The majority of the population were either peasants who owned their own land or permanent workers who cultivated plots that they did not own but that remained in the same family for many generations. This pattern had emerged in the preclassical period under the Zhou dynasty. The Zhou formed China's feudal period, in which political unity was an ideal rarely, if ever, achieved. Instead, the relatively weak central government and the rival kingdoms gave away land to aristocrats to provide resources for armaments, horses, and other military needs. These aristocrats had to supply loyalty and military services to their benefactors. In return for military protection, peasants paid a certain percentage of their crops to the aristocrats, in what is called a manorial system. The landlords restricted the movement of the rural workers; after all, it was the peasants' work that made the land produce, and peasants' movement elsewhere meant the land, less productive, could yield less to the aristocracy.

The classical period in China was punctuated by a social revolution. In the Ch'in dynasty (221–202 B.C.E.), the emperor decreed the liberty of all manorial peasants, giving them the land they had worked for generations. During the Ch'in period, this decree probably did not mean much less actual work, for it was during this dynasty that the emperor built much of what we know of as the Great Wall. The authoritarian methods to recruit workers brought about widespread discontent and, ironically, led to the Ch'in emperor's overthrow. The abolition of the manorial system was permanent, however, and led to higher population growth, as well as spontaneous migration to the fertile and less densely populated lands in southern China. The consequences of these actions had lasting importance for rural labor patterns. In the first place, instead of millet and wheat, peasants increasingly began to cultivate rice, which grew well in the hot southern climes. In addition, population growth diminished the size of the plots of households, especially in the densely settled eastern portion of the empire. By the time of the Han dynasty (202 B.C.E.–220 C.E.), the standard landholding of one farming family with seven members was considered to be 100 *mu*, or slightly less than 5 acres. The small plot size meant that Chinese peasants had to engage in intensive farming. They had to use deep tilling techniques and irrigation and to invest a much greater amount of labor into their plots, with frequent weeding, fertilizing (this included "night soil," as human excrement was called), careful thinning, and the like. In the south, where winters came late or were mild, cultivators frequently tried to plant and harvest more than one crop annually or to plant a staple crop such as millet in between the mulberry trees.

This intense activity was not enough in years of droughts, overabundant rainfall, or other natural disasters. Peasants needed to generate other income to cover their taxes and pay for other goods that they might want to acquire. The most important subsidiary activity was weaving, done mainly by women, as the ancient Chinese refrain "man as tiller, woman as weaver" suggests. Indeed, the Han considered agriculture and weaving to be complementary, a distinctive trait of Chinese rural life. Even when they were sitting at their doorsteps conversing with their neighbors, women spun fibers or kept busy in other ways. It is possible that weaving brought in almost as much income as farming.

Unlike the preclassical period, when slavery was a relatively important phenomenon, in classical China rural slavery declined markedly, particularly from the Ch'in dynasty onward. One estimate concluded that slaves in Han China constituted less than 1 percent of the total population. Slavery was simply not conducive to intensive agriculture, for only those whose very survival depended on the close care of their crops could be relied on. Landlords could not count on slaves to give the plots the attention they deserved.

Labor in Greece and Rome

Classical China contrasts markedly with Mediterranean civilization, where slavery was much more common. In Mediterranean civilization, slavery was relatively unimportant at the beginning of the classical period under the Greeks but increased as Rome predominated toward the end (until Rome's decline). In addition, other types of dependent laborers remained important throughout the period. Slave populations came mainly from people conquered in the many wars of the classical Mediterranean. A lengthy debate has surrounded the slavery question, especially for ancient Greece. The debate focuses on the number of slaves, on their functions, and above all on the experiences of being a slave. It is clear that slaves composed an important segment of the Greek population, but they were not the majority. In Attica, the peninsula dominated by Athens, for example, slaves constituted less than half of all inhabitants. The vast majority of the population included peasants, craftspeople and casual laborers. Slaves were used as domestic help and also in mining operations—such as the vital Athenian silver mines—where conditions were particularly demanding.

Outright slavery in agriculture was rare. But throughout classical Greece, a whole host of types of dependent rural laborers existed; the most famous were the helots of Sparta, although Sparta probably constituted an extreme. The descendants of peoples living in the Peloponnesian before the Indo-European invasions in the preclassical period, the helots were rural workers who labored to maintain their conquerors, the Spartans. The Spartans were a military aristocracy, the small minority of inhabitants of the region who remained in constant military preparedness, in part to be able to beat back a helot rebellion at any time. The state distributed helots to different Spartans in a serflike arrangement where the helots owed their overlords half of the crops they produced. Similar systems of serflike populations could be found on Crete and in Thessaly and other Greek city-states. More broadly, an arrangement whereby a large proportion of the rural population lived as workers dependent on city residents was typical for Greece generally.

In Roman times, as the republic began to expand militarily, a growing commercialization in farming brought about a more substantial use of slaves in the countryside, for with greater agricultural specialization and the concentration on cash crops on large estates, rural slavery became profitable. The growing of wheat in northern Africa and the cultivation of grapes and olives in coastal Italy and Greece were activities where the use of slaves made economic sense. Even here, slavery began to predominate only after the Second Punic War (200 B.C.E.), when Rome expanded far beyond its previous boundaries. Indeed, before the 3rd century, it is possible that the free Roman peasantry was underemployed and that military service served as a way for the state to extract the surplus from its population while also undergirding Rome's rapid military conquests and territorial expansion. As conquests continued, however, draining the Roman economy of laborers, the rich had to find alternative sources of workers, and they increasingly turned to the supply of slaves available from the conquests of new peoples. The emphasis on commercial agriculture, where intensive care of the crop was not necessary, contrasted clearly with China. In imperial Rome, slaves could easily be used since cultivation of grains (the type of agriculture where most slaves were employed) was an activity where brute strength and not much delicacy was involved.

In both Greek and Roman societies, slavery extended deeply into many occupations, in addition to its growing importance in Roman agriculture. Domestic slaves probably predominated in ancient Athens, and they continued to be important in urban settings in Roman times as well. They included many of the gladiators and chariot racers who competed in the Roman arenas. Slaves were especially important in elite households, fulfilling a host of functions there. Slaves ranged from the messenger boy and the washerwoman to the highly educated Greek tutor who taught the children of aristocrats. Many artisans were also slaves, purchased as children by the master artisan or setting up a shop for the absentee owner, to whom they paid a large percentage of their earnings. Finally, slaves performed particularly brutal labor in the mines, which took a high toll in lost or shortened lives. Slavery was ubiquitous in Mediterranean society, though slaves never reached a majority of the total population of the region.

Attitudes toward manual and especially agricultural labor remained much more negative in the Greco-Roman world than in China. Here was a cultural cause and effect of the role of slavery. Where Chinese bureaucrats dreamed of being able to retire and plow their fields themselves, the Greek and the Roman elites despised working with their hands. This attitude was not fully developed in the early Roman republic, but later, even the Romans adopted the Greek mentality that true citizens existed to think and act in politics, not cultivate the land. Thus the various utopias that Greek thinkers developed included slaves to do the manual work and leave the citizens to do other matters. An added factor was the Greek idea that civilized people lived in an urban setting, where they could participate fully in cultural and political life. Only barbarians and inferiors lived dispersed in the countryside, where high culture rarely penetrated. The ideas of urban areas as centers of civilization and the disdain for manual and agricultural labor were to remain important characteristics of societies in the Mediterranean world.

Domestic slaves in Mediterranean society often had some hope of earning enough money to buy themselves out of slavery. This is not to say that manumission was common (it was virtually nonexistent in the rural setting), but the hope of achieving freedom was an important incentive in keeping labor discipline. The Greek philosopher Aristotle, one of the most prolific political thinkers of the Mediterranean world, asserted that "all [slaves] ought to have a definite end in view; for it is just and beneficial to offer slaves their freedom as a prize, for they are willing to work when a prize is set before them and a limit of time is defined." Slaves became eligible for manumission after they turned thirty years of age.

The variable nature of slavery in the classical world has stimulated the greatest debate. Scholars such as David B. Davis and Orlando Patterson, as well as specific experts on Greco-Roman slavery, such as Moses Finley, have worked on the challenging problem of accurate characterization. Some slaves, particularly in the mines and on the Roman agricultural estates, were treated very harshly, often doomed to short working lives because of foul conditions. Roman agricultural slaves have been compared to later slaves in the Americas, pressed hard for commercial profit as well as deprived of liberty. The only difference involves the lack of clear racial aspects in the Roman case, with slaves derived indiscriminately from Europe, West Asia, and Africa. But urban slavery, in contrast, might be relatively agreeable, particularly when opportunities of manumission beckoned. Work might be lighter than that of free agricultural peasants, which is why some men, and perhaps even more women, deliberately sought slavery as a means of associating themselves with a prosperous household. Here, the difference between urban and rural work, not the slave/free distinction, could prove most important. Generalization, clearly, is not easy, with slavery not seen as being as systematically demeaning as it would later prove in the Americas.

Slavery was not a stable institution, for among the three classical civilizations, the Mediterranean was punctuated by the most lower-class revolts. This included the Third Messenian War in 464 B.C.E., in which the helots revolted against their Spartan overlords and caused the latter to adopt the militaristic society for which they became famous. The Spartan nobility at times engaged in the ritual slaying of the strongest helots to create a sense of terror and prevent them from overpowering the ruling minority. A number of slave revolts also punctuated the Roman Empire, among them the Spartacus revolt that for four years (73–71 B.C.E.) laid waste to the Italian countryside.

Patterns in India

Among all the classical civilizations, India suffered the fewest lower-class revolts, for the caste system created a social stability unmatched even in Confucian China. This system evolved after the Aryan invasions prior to the classical period, in the Vedic and Epic ages, when Indian civilization reconstituted itself on the basis of Hinduism. Indeed, the social system that the castes defined was based largely on job classifications. As Indian civilization slowly reemerged from the devastation of the invaders and people adopted farming more widely, agricultural categories became important. In contrast to China, however, agriculture did not rank high in cultural prestige and was normally reserved for the lower castes. While different castes might practice agriculture in fact, and the importance of food production remained fundamental, there was a cultural distaste for it. A Hindu law code, the Laws of Manu, listed "farming the land" as "for a commoner," specifically criticizing plows for "injuring the earth and the creatures that live in the earth." Classical Indian society esteemed trade and merchant activity to a much greater extent than did either China or the Mediterranean. By the classical period, the following castes had appeared: The Brahmans were the priests, the Kshatriyas the warriors, the Vaisyas farmers and traders, and the Sudras the common laborers. The untouchables, originating in the conquered pre-Aryan population, handled ritually impure tasks such as working with leather or hauling of dead bodies. The ritual impurity of animal products was a relatively late addition, for it is clear that the Aryans had no such taboos in their pastoral society. Needless to say, the latter three castes were by far numerically the most important, with the warrior and Brahman castes forming what might be considered the Indian aristocracy.

To say that these categories were mere job descriptions is grossly to oversimplify the caste system. While the denomination of these castes had some real basis in what type of work Indians did, the castes splintered into hundreds of subcastes, with carefully prescribed roles. Most important, the caste system was based on religious notions that by the classical period manifested themselves through taboos and distinctive ritual actions. Members of different castes and even subcastes were prohibited from intermarriage.

The careful division of Indian society into castes made slaveholding superfluous in classical times. Since all work was caste specific, slaves had little role to play in the Indian economy. Sudras and the untouchables, because they had the dirtiest jobs to perform (both in a ritual as well as a physical sense), took the place of slaves. Even war captives, the most important source of slaves in the Greco-Roman world, usually either were already members of some caste or were placed into a (low) caste position. Tribal peoples, many of whom remained on the Indian subcontinent during this period and who had continual contact with Indian civilization, remained largely outside the caste system. In part because of this, they remained despised by civilized Indians. To become civilized meant for these tribal peoples to integrate themselves into the caste system, a process that occurred as Hindu civilization slowly spread through the subcontinent.

Comparative Issues

The solutions the principal three civilizations came up with to sustain their agricultural societies varied widely. Attitudes toward manual labor diverged considerably as well. In the case of classical China, intensive agriculture brought on by high population densities meant that the independent peasant and the tenant would predominate in the countryside. The exaltation of farming as the most useful lower-class activity meant a categorization of virtually everything else as at best subsidiary or actually pernicious. As a result, the state held commerce, entertainment, and other service activities in low regard. This was not the case in the Greco-Roman world, where agriculture did not carry the same prestige because it became associated with slave labor. This region, where the idea of civilization was associated with urban centers, deprecated the country life. In turn, Indian civilization's answer to justifying the radical inequalities of agricultural societies was embodied in the caste system, where each member had his or her own role to play according to the caste in which he or she was born. The position of the castes, with Brahmans and Kshatriyas at the top, highlighted the fact that religious and military functions received greatest prestige.

Different work systems could have wider implications. Roman slavery, for example, was closely connected to territorial expansion; neither the Indian nor the Chinese work patterns had this link. When Roman expansion ended in the 2nd century C.E. and the supply of slaves dwindled, the whole production system was affected, and more localized, less commercial economic activity was a clear long-term result. Reliance on slaves also helped lessen Greek and Roman interest in technological changes that would improve production. China, with its reliance on intensive labor, was an obvious contrast, with great interest in developments such as water mills and wheelbarrows that would make peasant and artisan labor more productive. Nowhere, to be sure, did technology greatly alleviate manual labor yet, but the difference between East and South Asia and the Mediterranean was marked.

Despite these differences in types of labor and the prestige of manual labor, one must not forget that all three classical civilizations also maintained important similarities. In all cases, the division of labor was based on a deeply hierarchical notion of how society should function. The peasants remained at the bottom (only partially replaced by slaves in the Greco-Roman world) and supported the activities of the other groups in society. While some Mediterranean slaves might achieve freedom, or while some Chinese peasants might rise in status, generally there was little notion of social mobility. With few exceptions, people accepted their station in life and the type of work they did. Another point to keep in mind is that in all civilizations, the vast majority of population, just as in the preclassical period, was involved in agriculture. The Chinese were most realistic in making farming prestigious, though the weak status of merchants was to bring about some problems later on. Quite obviously, during the classical period itself, all three labor systems functioned in providing relatively reliable agricultural surplus for the operations of complex civilizations. Only when new disease levels reduced labor supply, particularly in China and the Mediterranean, did the systems break down.

In contrast to Eurasia, in the Americas civilization was just emerging in the classical period. The civilizations of the Toltecs and the Olmecs in central Mexico, the beginnings of Maya civilization to the south (in an area called Meso-America, comprising Mexico and Central America), and the various Andean civilizations, such as those of the Chavín and Paracas cultures in Peru, began to organize labor and leisure activities in novel forms. As elsewhere, civilization meant greater social divisions, with a tiny elite on the top living off the production of the many peasants. In all cases, the ability to evolve into civilizations rested on the cultivation of maize, which required much intensive care but yielded much in calories. The society that emerged in central Mexico was more hierarchical than those farther south. Sharp differences among slaves, commoners, warriors, and priests were common, with the priests occupying the highest places in society. In the Maya lands, the jungles throughout the region made it possible for peasants to escape, and so Maya civilization appears to have been somewhat less brutal than those farther north. Here, some elaborate irrigation networks meant hard work for the peasants but sufficient surplus to make possible the building of elaborate ceremonial centers and temples.

In the Andes, civilization was predicated on different patterns of work. The genius of Andean civilization was seeing the subtropical mountains not as barriers but as regions that provided the widest possible access to different agricultural goods. This was possible because in the steep mountains the Andean peoples could grow products of different climates over a short space, often within less than a day's walk. Thus villagers could live in the high valleys, at 9,000-foot altitudes, in a moderate climate zone where they could cultivate potatoes. Just a bit lower, farther down the valley, the climate was warm enough for growing maize, whereas on the lowest hillsides, at 4,000 feet, people could grow the coca plant, whose consumption was useful for alertness when doing tiring work. Relatives might live a day's walk up the mountain, on the high treeless *puna* above 11,000 feet, where only llamas and alpacas grazed. For many Andean people, it was possible to maintain self-sufficiency on a household or family level, especially when combined with reciprocal work obligations with relatives and neighbors. Agricultural work, when joined with reciprocal labor, turned into a celebration, with the hosts providing ample food and drink for those who helped them. The need to remain close to the fields meant that few urban centers developed, since productivity was linked to access to a multiplicity of different crops within a short distance. By the end of the classical period, these characteristics were well developed in the Andean region, making possible the production of much surplus and the development of further civilization.

Leisure Patterns

The fact that most human beings in the civilized areas were agriculturists made most popular leisure activities dependent on agrarian rhythms, just as in the preclassical period. The connection of festivals to agrarian cycles also kept leisure closely tied to religion, since two of religion's main functions were to explain how the world worked and to serve as intermediary between the deities in charge of nature and humankind. The end of winter, the sowing season, the harvesting of crops were not only important times in the life of the peasant but were also marked by festivals to celebrate the gods who controlled the earth and the elements.

Religion permeated peasant life in the classical period in ways it does not in our secularized world. Even in the classical period, however, there were some notable variations. Among the major civilizations, India maintained the most religious basis for leisure activities. Hinduism saw not only living according to caste requirements (*dharma*) as a goal in life but also *artha*, the accumulation of material goods, and *kama*, the attainment of sensual pleasure. As a result, we have the literary classic of the *Kama Sutra*, which describes the many ways it is possible to attain *kama*. In other words, sex in its own right was an activity that was religiously endorsed.

The heavy hand of the Chinese state tried to limit festivals. During the Han period, the state made certain festivals official. In an effort to cut down on too much celebrating, however, the state often reduced multiple-day holidays to one day. The specialization and standardization of festivals also impoverished them, for fewer people attended as they became simplified and reduced to one single custom. As the state took a festival over for its own purposes, the celebration lost much of its previous meaning. This occurred especially with the New Year rituals, which, as a cost for becoming part of the official calendar, lost their religious justification of celebrating the triumph of the sun over the forces of darkness.

The Mediterranean world maintained a religious orientation in its festivals, as in the case of classical India. Here, however, certain processes of secularization became evident as well. The Olympics, the gladiatorial contests, and the chariot races for which Greco-Roman civilization is famous originated as religious games. The Olympics became associated with inter-city-state rivalries and often were quite rowdy. The Greeks excluded women from the spectacles, cutting down on their leisure possibilities (in contrast to today, when women constitute the majority of Olympics spectators via television). Generally speaking, however, participation in sports was an important activity among Greek males. Whether this was true leisure is somewhat questionable, since physical preparedness was an important duty of all Greek citizens for military purposes. We know that in the 2nd century C.E. at least 126 Greek cities had gymnasia, where its citizens could practice martial arts such as running and discus and spear throwing. In Athens alone there were nine public gymnasia and many more private ones.

Romans, while exalting sports as well, preferred to be spectators rather than participants. That is not to say that, especially in the republican and early imperial periods, citizens avoided physical exercise. In Greek times, slaves watched while free men performed. By the time Rome had conquered the Mediterranean world, slaves performed and free men watched. Most popular were the chariot races, in which the charioteers were frequently slaves. Unlike in the Greek Olympic Games, men and women sat together in the circus to watch the races, leading some Roman authors to extol the circus as an opportunity to meet members of the opposite sex and have amorous adventures. Successful charioteers, even slaves, were lionized by the public and idolized by male and female spectators alike. Gladiatorial contests, though they grew out of religious games, also became tied to the political ends of the Roman state by the time of Julius Caesar's reign. By the end of the 1st century of the common era, Trajan celebrated his victory over the Dacians with 10,000 combatants at one time.

The increasing extravagance in these games and the mixing of politics with religion also mirrored the increasing pretensions of the emperors in the late Roman period. Later Roman emperors fancied themselves gods and associated festivals with themselves as a way of maintaining political legitimacy. This was quite similar to the Chinese, who also mixed religious with civic festivals. The emergence of Christianity began to curtail this display, once it became the official religion in the Roman Empire with the emperor Constantine (313 C.E.). This curtailment included the gladiatorial games, where some Christians had suffered. In 399 C.E. the emperor closed the gladiator schools, and in the next century the games died out throughout the empire. Chariot races continued, but soon thereafter the barbarian invasions put a stop to all such extravagant spectacles.

Other important leisure activities developed during the classical period as well, many of which persisted for centuries thereafter. Greek drama represents one of the culminating achievements of Mediterranean civilization. Drama was not just for the wealthy but could be enjoyed by slaves and citizens alike. This was mass entertainment in all the senses of the word, in terms of its popularity and through themes such as love, sex, murder, and mayhem, with overwhelmingly secular motifs (though gods often played some roles). Likewise, the classical period saw the development of theater in China, though here popular styles often were adopted by the elites and became formalized. Unlike Greek drama, Chinese drama often had heroic themes that asserted Confucian values and exalted the role of the state. Music also played an important role in China, where it became an integral part of the rituals of the state court. Since music was seen to reflect the cosmic order, what better means to assert the supremacy of the Son of Heaven than music? Whether the state had much success in promulgating its type of music to the masses is not known but doubtful during this period when Confucianism, despite the state's efforts, remained primarily the province of the elites.

EPILOGUE

The classical period lasted for about 1,500 years, which is not necessarily a long time in terms of basic human processes. Predictably, a number of features carried over from the earlier days of the river-valley civilizations and agricultural societies. Most people in the classical civilizations were peasants, working in many of the same ways their river-valley ancestors had done. Many governments continued to use religion to help cement popular loyalties to existing political and social systems. The religions were often new, and the systems extended over wider geographical areas, but key functions persisted. Societies remained patriarchal; key changes occurred, but in the main they merely deepened inequalities between men and women that had been created with the advent of agriculture. Fundamental biological characteristics that had been established with agriculture continued as well: There was no brand-new population regime. Further growth of cities and wider commercial contacts created new problems of contagious disease, which underlay some of the great crises of the classical period, but through most of the period, key societies expanded population size on the basis of increasing food production through opening additional land to agriculture. Disease conditions varied; crucial new elements, created by growing contact, entered the classical scene in the final centuries.

New features of the classical period did not, then, affect all aspects of people's lives. Several forces in the period were particularly striking in promoting change. The adoption of iron tools and weapons was crucial throughout much of Afro-Eurasia, in creating new possibilities for military force and for agricultural productivity. Here was one of the principal bases of the classical period in the first place, distinguishing it from what had come before. Technological changes during the period itself were more minor, and they affected Asia more than the Mediterranean and Africa.

The rise of stronger states, covering larger territories, was a vital component of the classical period. While its role in work systems did not expand (except, to an extent, in China), the greater power of government contributed to gender relations, reducing the informal power of women and highlighting the special public functions of upper-class men, and may have affected leisure as well.

Cultural change was even more significant as a force in daily life, for the new religious and philosophical formulations spread over wide areas as part of the drive to create new links among disparate peoples in the expanded classical civilizations. Belief systems reflected growing differences among major civilizations in the attitudes toward work. Cultural change directly caused shifts in gender relations, greatly contributing to more rigid inequalities. Belief systems also helped enforce labor systems, particularly with India's caste apparatus; this was one reason that state-run labor operations declined. Culture counted more than state power in defining work systems (except in some of the cases of slavery).

Changes in politics and culture associated with the rise of the great classical civilizations might seem to overshadow the rhythms of population growth and disease. Indeed, connections are not always clear. But civilization expansion depended on basic iron technologies, expanding food production possibilities. Different disease patterns helped shape the character of the civilizations themselves. China's two disease pools, between north and south, complicated the integration of this expanding civilization, which may explain the emphasis on deliberately generating strong political and cultural systems, compared to the more disease-free Mediterranean. Biology, in other words, made Chinese integration more difficult, requiring more explicit political efforts. The rise of new religions such as Hinduism, Buddhism, and, later, Christianity mirrored new needs to come to terms with growing problems of disease and death, first in India, then more generally. A search for religious solace increased, compared to the earlier civilization period. Expanding civilization contacts—the fruit of improved political and commercial organization—changed the disease pool, and epidemic crises then showed that proud states and cultures had not gained dominance over the biological environment. Overintensive agriculture, resulting in deteriorating soil conditions in parts of the Middle East and North Africa, added to the pressures on population, at least in the Mediterranean world.

Before the final crises, the classical period saw the civilization form at a high point. Expansion brought new peoples and areas into the major civilizations. Equally important, the major civilizations themselves improved their self-definition, generating clear statements of basic cultural values and political institutions. Even systems of patriarchy and work patterns reflected the distinctive orientation of each civilization. Correspondingly, it was in the classical period that several civilizations, particularly India and China but also the Middle East to a degree, developed structures and expressions that would prove amazingly durable, lasting well beyond the classical period itself. Hinduism, Confucianism, and the Chinese state institutions would change in response to new forces, but they would preserve a recognizable core into the late 20th century. The emergence of well-articulated, separate civilizations makes comparison a prime analytical tool for assessing people's lives in the classical period, to see how different governments, cultures, and gender systems operated in juxtaposition with one another.

Yet a tension existed, even in the classical period, between distinct civilizations and more unifying factors. The major civilizations experienced some similar trends. Their particular gender systems differed, for example, but the gap between men and women increased in virtually every case. This means that some underlying forces were at work. Everywhere, the task of producing cultures and states that would help pull together larger territories generated common results, despite major differences in specifics. Everywhere, philosophers and religious leaders produced justifications for inequalities in society and at work—even though the Greek philosophical argument for slavery differed from the Hindu support for caste, and both, in turn, from the Confucian sense of hierarchy.

Important contacts supplemented common processes. Indian culture affected the Mediterranean and, later, China on the strength of contacts. Trade and migration facilitated the spread of disease, one of the deadly unifiers of humankind across civilization boundaries. Also important was the capacity of the major civilizations to spread aspects of their operations to still wider areas—including additional parts of Africa, Southeast Asia, and Korea.

One of the principal legacies of the classical period, then, was the tension between well-defined civilizations, often proud of their self-proclaimed superiority over other peoples, and the capacity for increasing contact. As the classical heritage lived on in major civilizations, so did the need to deal with new forms of cultural exchange and the crosscutting forces of disease or migration. Work systems for ordinary people depended on distinctive cultural and political structures, but they also responded to exchanges of techniques and ideas. Gender was slightly less responsive to exchange, for men's and women's roles were often held as basic to the beliefs and power relations of particular civilizations, but it, too, would be affected. As the classical civilizations declined, opportunities to test identities against new kinds of contacts would increase.

FOR FURTHER READING

POPULATION/BIOLOGY

Jared Diamond, *Guns, Germs and Steel: The Fate of Human Societies* (1997).
J. Donald Hughes, *Ecology in Ancient Civilizations* (1975).
Massimo Livi-Bacci, *A Concise History of World Population* (1992).
John R. McNeill, *The Mountains of the Mediterranean World: An Environmental History* (1992).
William H. McNeill, *Plagues and Peoples* (1977).
William H. McNeill and Ruth S. Adams, eds., *Human Migration: Patterns and Policies* (1978).
Stephen Plogar, ed., *Population, Ecology and Social Evolution* (1975).
Clive Ponting, *A Green History of the World: The Environment and the Collapse of Great Civilizations* (1991).
I. G. Simmons, *Changing the Face of the Earth: Culture, Environment, History* (1989).

CULTURE

Jerry H. Bentley, *Old World Encounters: Cross-Cultural Contacts and Exchanges in Pre-Modern Times* (1993).
Martin Bernals, *Black Athena: The Afroasiatic Roots of Classical Civilization* (1987).
R. A. Markus, *Christianity in the Roman World* (1974).
N. Ross Reat, *Buddhism: A History* (1994).
Benjamin I. Schwartz, *The World of Thought in Ancient China* (1985).
Jean W. Sedlar, *India and the Greek World: A Study in the Transmission of Culture* (1980).

STATE AND SOCIETY

Hans Bielenstein, *The Bureaucracy of Han Times* (1980).
Arthur Cotterell, ed., *The Penguin Encyclopedia of Classical Civilizations* (1993).
Peter Green, *Alexander to Actium: The Historical Evolution of the Hellenistic Age* (1990).
Andrew Lintutt, *Imperium Romanum: Politics and Administration* (1993).

M. Ostwald, *From Popular Sovereignty to the Sovereignty of Law* (1986).

Paul S. Ropped, *Heritage of China: Contemporary Perspectives on Chinese Civilization* (1990).

H. Scharff, *The State in Indian Tradition* (1988).

Vincent A. Smith, *The Early History of India from 600 B.C. to the Muhammadan Conquest* (1925).

GENDER

Peter Brown, *The Body and Society: Men, Women and Sexual Renunciation in Early Christianity* (1988).

José Ignacio Cobezón, ed., *Buddhism, Sexuality and Gender* (1992).

David M. Halperin, John J. Winkler, and Froma I. Zeitlin, eds., *Before Sexuality: The Construction of Erotic Experience in the Ancient Greek World* (1990).

Stephanie Jamison, *Sacrificed Wife/Sacrificer's Wife: Women, Ritual and Hospitality in Ancient India* (1996).

Mary Jo Maynes et al., eds., *Gender, Kinship, Power: A Comparative and Interdisciplinary History* (1996).

Pauline Schmitt Pantel, ed., *A History of Women in the West: From Ancient Goddesses to Christian Saints* (1992).

Beryl Rawson, ed., *Marriage, Divorce and Children in Ancient Rome* (1991).

Robert H. van Gulik, *Sexual Life in Ancient China* (1961).

LABOR AND LEISURE

Derk Bodde, *Festivals in Classical China: New Year and Other Annual Observances during the Han Dynasty 206 B.C.–A.D. 220* (1975).

T'sung-tsu Ch'u, *Han Social Structure*, ed. Jack L. Dull (1972).

M. I. Finley, *The World of Odysseus* (1954).

Allen Guttmann, *Sports Spectators* (1986).

Cho-yun Hsu, *Han Agriculture: The Formation of Early Chinese Agrarian Economy (206 B.C.–A.D. 220)*, ed. Jack L. Dull (1980).

G. E. M. de Ste. Croix, *The Class Struggle in the Ancient Greek World from the Archaic Age to the Arab Conquests* (1981).

Thomas Widemann, *Greek and Roman Slavery* (1981).

Ellen Meiksins Wood, *Peasant-Citizen and Slave: The Foundations of Athenian Democracy* (1988).

PART III

The Postclassical Period, 450–1450 C.E.

Highlights. The dominant themes of this new period of world history, different from those of the classical centuries, emphasize changes in migration patterns, culture, and trade. Technology shifts that supported trade and agriculture and the geographical extension of political capacities in state building form secondary themes.

The period was launched by the devastating epidemics that had helped bring down the classical empires and that now led to new migration patterns in the Middle East, China, and Europe. In culture, the spread of world religions emphasizing otherworldly goals across previous civilization boundaries was the key development. The new Islamic religion was the most important single system at this point; along with the rise of the Arab peoples in politics and world trade, Islam propelled a new Middle Eastern civilization to dominance in international power. Contacts among major societies in Asia, Africa, and Europe created a new international network that spurred the exchange of goods, ideas, and techniques. Finally, civilization as a form spread to additional geographical areas, and the number of distinct civilizations increased. These developments—the rise of Islam, the spread of world religions, the new world network, and the spread of civilization—did not create a homogeneous framework. Specific civilizations responded to the themes distinctively. But a common set of issues did exist.

Key Developments. Islam arose on the Arabian Peninsula around 600 C.E., under the influence of the prophet Muhammad. Muhammad, claiming inspiration from Allah, the one true God, wrote his revelations in the Qur'an, the holy book of the new religion. He used Jewish and Christian beliefs but added to them a stronger emphasis on acceptance of Allah and a set of rules for religious and personal behavior that, if followed, would

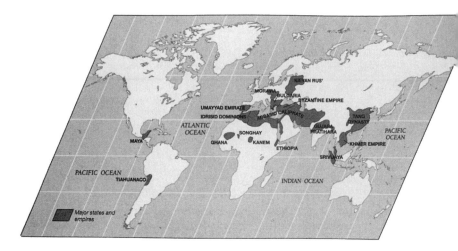

The Postclassical World Takes Shape, ca. 900 C.E. From Peter N. Stearns, Michael Adas, and Stuart B. Schwartz, *World Civilizations: The Global Experience*, 2nd ed. Copyright 1996 by HarperCollins College Publishers. Reprinted by permission of Addison-Wesley Educational Publishers Inc.

assure people of what should be their chief goal, salvation in heaven. Converted Arabs began a pattern of conquest that would take them through the Middle East and North Africa and into Spain, Central Asia, and India. Many other peoples in these areas began to convert to Islam, while expanding trade and missionary activity also brought the religion to sub-Saharan Africa and Southeast Asia. In their new home territories, the Arabs established a loose empire under a Muslim ruler called a caliph, who in principle directed religious and political affairs simultaneously. Arab achievements included active trade through the Indian Ocean down Africa's coast and also eastward to the Pacific, in the Mediterranean, and across the Sahara desert to the rising kingdoms of West Africa. The Arabs also embraced a vibrant artistic, literary, and scientific culture.

The rapid spread of Islam was only part of the dissemination of major world religions—religions capable of leapfrogging across other political and cultural boundaries. Even earlier, as we have seen, Buddhism had fanned out from India (where, ironically, it became a minor force as Hinduism rallied) to Sri Lanka and many parts of Southeast Asia, and also to China and on to Korea and Japan. Christianity, advancing rapidly during the later Roman Empire and spilling into other parts of the Middle East and Northeast Africa, now began to convert virtually the whole of Europe. Catholic Christianity, with an institutional church headed by the pope in Rome, commanded missionary efforts in western and Central Europe, while Orthodox disciples, backed by the Byzantine Empire in Constantinople, gained greater adherence in eastern Europe, including Russia. The two branches split formally in the 11th century. Overall, the spread of world religions reflected the need for otherworldly rewards amid the chaos caused by rising death rates and the decline of the classical empires. Literally millions of people converted to new faiths, abandoning or modifying older polytheistic beliefs and secular commitments. A new world religious map was forged as a result, and many of its contours have changed little since the postclassical age.

Islam and other missionary religions played a major role in creating new, more intense international contacts. Trade in a variety of luxury products—silk, but also spices and porcelain—intensified among the most advanced urban centers in China, India, the Middle East, and the Byzantine Empire. Europe and Africa connected to these trade routes. Upper-class Europeans by the 12th century became attached to imported products such as sugar. In eastern Europe, trade routes reached from Scandinavia through western Russia to the Byzantine Empire, where exchanges with Arabs occurred. Africans offered gold, slaves, and other items for trade with the Middle East. Somewhat separately, an East Asia network arose involving annual trade between China and Japan. Contacts of this sort facilitated diffusion of ideas and techniques. Arabs adopted the Indian numbering system, and Europeans then copied the Arabs. The compass traveled from China to the Middle East and thence to Europe; paper, previously invented in China, followed the same course.

The expansion of civilization resulted in part from assimilation of prior achievements in classical centers on the part of neighboring or invading peoples. In Central America, Mayans and then other peoples, including the Aztecs, built on technologies and artistic styles of the earlier Olmec society, spreading larger empires in the region. African civilizations expanded to the south of the Sahara; the massive migration of Bantu peoples from West-Central Africa continued, bringing agriculture to much of the south and east, where several major states arose. The greatest kingdoms, such as Ghana and Mali, were in West Africa. The Byzantine Empire, solidifying major features of the previous Roman Empire but blocked from expansion in the Mediterranean by Arab success, targeted Christian missionary activities and trade to the west and north, facilitating the development of Slavic societies. Several societies, including Russia, deliberately imitated the more advanced centers. Russia copied religion, a modified alphabet, art, and some political ideas from Byzantium. Japan launched massive imitation of China, importing the alphabet, artistic styles, Buddhism and elements of Confucianism, technology, and key social ideas. Japan retained its own flavor, failing in efforts to copy China's centralized government, but the advantages of using established examples were obvious. African kingdoms imported Islam to further learning and political bureaucracies, as well as religion per se, even as most ordinary Africans retained adherence to polytheism.

Of the major centers, only the Americas remained isolated from the world network and resultant imitations. In consequence, they could not import technologies such as iron and the wheel; they had no contact with any world religion; and they operated in a separate disease pool in "virgin soil" conditions, failing to develop immunities to diseases common in Afro-Eurasia. American civilizations were advanced in many ways, both in Central America and in the other center in the Andes, ultimately dominated by the extensive Inca Empire; but they were different and proved vulnerable as a result when contacts were forced on them after 1492.

Even within the world network, each civilization reacted differently to world religions, contact, and civilization expansion. China retained the clearest hold on past traditions. It did import Buddhism but ultimately imposed limits against it, lest Buddhist otherworldliness distract from the political and social goals of the empire and Confucianism. The two main dynasties of postclassical China, the T'ang and the Song, sought to manage changes within an adaptable but traditional framework. India retained Hinduism and the caste system but experienced the growth of a Muslim minority and regional kingdoms set up by invading Muslim rulers. African civilization resembled western Europe in being loosely organized and divided politically, depending on contacts with the Arab world and benefiting from growing merchant activity. But Africa was comfortable with its Islamic contacts and also had abundant goods for trade. Europe, a Christian society resentful of Islam and suffering also from a poor international trading position because of a lack of export goods such as gold, began to adopt a more aggressive stance, seeking to exploit new trade routes that might address key problems. Different civilizations also exhibited different patterns in population and agriculture. China, Europe, Africa, and Central America became the settings for substantial (though diverse) shifts in agricultural production. Differential impacts of migration and disease helped explain the economic patterns of large societies. Civilizations, in sum, remained varied, even as a new world history framework took hold.

The dominant themes of the postclassical period begin to change in the 13th century. Arab civilization remained strong, but trade activities declined somewhat, and the central government of the caliphate began to collapse. At the same time, an important nomadic group in Central Asia, the Mongols, successfully invaded China. They also conquered Russia; pressed into the Middle East, where they unseated the caliphate; and threatened Southeast Asia and Central Europe as well. Under the Mongols between the late 12th and the late 13th century, a series of interlocking empires stretching from Russia to China facilitated international contacts. A number of Europeans visited China, whence they brought back technical knowledge, including printing and explosive powder; soon, improvements in the printing press and the invention of guns to project explosives gave European society new strengths. It was in the Mongol period also that an epidemic of bubonic plague spread from China through the Middle East and Europe, causing massive death and illustrating the power of international contacts on the biological level. Mongol political power began to decline in the 14th century and was followed by a brief period of Chinese trading expeditions, but these ended, by a policy decision, in the 1430s. The world network remained vital, but its leadership was again open for newcomers. Finally, in the 15th century, Russia began to expel Mongol rule, while the Byzantine Empire finally disappeared in the face of attacks from a new Turkish-led Ottoman Empire. The world cast of characters was changing substantially, while new technologies, including navigational devices, improved ships, and guns, began to determine a new international framework.

TIMELINE

III. Postclassical: 450–1450 C.E.

476–800	Germanic tribes invade western Europe; struggle for order and stability
500s	Hun invasions in South Asia; beginning of the Rajput (princedoms) period
500–800	"Dark Ages" missionary work in northern Europe
500–1350	Height of manorialism in western Europe
527–565	Emperor Justinian in the Byzantine Empire
570–632	The life span of Muhammad and his establishment of Islam as a religion and political community
581–618	Sui dynasty in China
7th century	End of Olmec culture; rise of Mayans in Central America
610–753	Spread of Islam across Arabia, southern Europe, North Africa, and India
618–907	T'ang dynasty in China
632–738	Islamic expansion beyond Arabia
650–1700	Extensive use of military slaves in Middle Eastern states (Abbasid, Mamluk, and Ottoman empires)
661–750	Umayyad caliphate
700ff.	Spread of Hinduism in southern India
711	Islamic invasion of Spain
712	Arab raids in Southeast Asia
732	Franks defeat Muslims in France
750–1258	Abbasid caliphate

800–814	Charlemagne's empire
800–1300	Height of manorialism in Japan
813–833	Islamic capital transferred to Baghdad
855	According to legend, Rurik king of Kievan Russia
900	Movement north by Mayans, intermingling with Toltecs
906ff.	Decline of the caliphate, growing Turkish influence
10th to 13th centuries	Kingdom of Ghana
960–1127	Northern Song dynasty in China
962	Germanic kings revive "Roman" empire
980–1015	Conversion of Vladimir I of Russia to Christianity
1000–1200s	New levels of manufacturing in Song China
1018ff.	Beginning of Christian reconquest of Spain
1054	Great Schism, the split between western Christian church and Byzantine Orthodox church
1066	Norman conquest of England; strong feudal monarchy
1073–1085	Reform papacy of Gregory VII
1096ff.	Crusades
1100ff.	Rise of Incas
1127–1279	Southern Song dynasty in China; rise of commerce and great commercial cities
1192ff.	Muslim invasions in India, leading to Delhi sultanate
1194ff.	French Gothic cathedrals
1200ff.	Rise of the Sufi movement
1200ff.	Mayan decline
1200–1274	Thomas Aquinas and flowering of scholasticism
1203–1204	Capture of Constantinople by Fourth Crusade

1206	Temujin named Genghis Khan of Mongols; Mongol invasions of China
1236	Capture of Russia by Mongols (Tatars)
1253	Formation of Thai state (Siam)
1264–1368	Yuan dynasty (Mongols) in China
1268	Mongol conquest of Baghdad and end of the Abbasid caliphate
1275–1292	Marco Polo to China
1279	Toppling of Song dynasty by Kublai Khan and Mongols
1281	Failure of second Mongol invasion of Japan; "divine wind" typhoon
13th to 14th centuries	Kingdom of Mali
1300ff.	Italian Renaissance
1300–1400	Black plague infects significant populations in China, western Europe, Middle East
1336–1573	Return of Japan to feudalism
1338ff.	Decline of Delhi sultanate
1338–1453	Hundred Years' War
1350ff.	Formation of Aztec Empire
1368	Mongols driven from China by Ming dynasty
1368–1644	Ming dynasty; peak of emperor's power
14th and 15th centuries	Height of the Swahili (East African) city-states
1400	Height of Incan Empire
1405–1433	Ming maritime expeditions to Southeast Asia, Indian Ocean, Arabia, and the east coast of Africa

CHAPTER 10

POPULATING THE EARTH, 500–1500 C.E.

Introduction

At the levels of high politics and culture, as well as at the biological foundations, the 5th and 6th centuries saw the end of classical civilization. Convergence of Afro-Eurasian disease pools and massive population declines provoked economic and political disorder, which in turn contributed to further decline, a cycle that created a population trough lasting roughly six centuries, from about 180 to 750 C.E. Population collapse led to large-scale migrations, mostly of peoples who formerly dwelt on the periphery of civilization. Over the next few centuries civilization, as a form of human organization, became vastly larger and geographically redistributed by, first, the rise of Islam in the 7th and 8th centuries and, second and third, the massive expansion and relocation of the Chinese and European economies and populations from around 650 to 1330. These expansions were abruptly interrupted by the Black Death, a second massive epidemic wave that probably began in East Asia in the mid-1330s (possibly earlier) and spread across Eurasia, reducing populations by a third or more. Plague remained endemic for centuries afterward, but its virulence slowly diminished. Population growth and economic development resumed by at least 1450, if not earlier. These changes resulted in new cultural syntheses and political systems, fundamentally different from their ancient predecessors.

Most important, by the later part of the postclassical period, China and western Europe became two dynamic economic and social systems at opposite ends of the Old World, whose interaction in the developing world network—by overland routes such as the Silk Roads or by seaborne connections by way of the Indian Ocean—affected most of Eurasia. These contacts, facilitated by the expansion of Islamic merchant activity, promoted biological homogenization across Eurasia and Africa, that is, the diffusion of plants, animals, diseases, and peoples. Beginning in the 15th century, biological homogenization grew into a global phenomenon as these two systems initiated oceanic voyages that put them in contact with the wider world. Europe, not China, led the way across the oceans, for reasons that lay partly in their agrarian and demographic transformation, though ultimately, European cultural and political impulses were the direct causes of the more aggressive expansionism.

Disease and Migration: A New Framework

The processes affecting population in the postclassical period began with in-migration of peoples who had dwelt beyond the limits of civilized empires. Europe west and south of the Rhine-Danube frontier offered fertile plains, broad valleys, and a mild climate, as well as a network of roads, harbors, and towns that could sustain large populations. Central and eastern Europe had become overcrowded, even at lower population densities, given the region's poorer soil, harsher climate, primitive agricultural technology and chaotic tribal violence. Since the 1st century B.C.E., small numbers of Germanic peoples had infiltrated the northwestern provinces of the Roman Empire, often with imperial consent, where they served as soldiers or settled down as farmers. By the 3rd century C.E., disease and disorder created a demographic low-pressure zone in western Europe, with low population levels that tempted invasion. Meanwhile, warfare among rival tribes was intensified by the violent westward advance of Inner Asian Huns. Orderly immigration gave way to invasion when several hundred thousand Goths crossed into the empire. They came less as rapacious invaders than as desperate refugees. To Gallo-Roman and Italian observers, the invaders seemed like great hordes. They must have been startling on the move together: carts, herds, warriors; old men, women, and children. Estimates suggest modest numbers, possibly 200,000 Ostrogoths, 100,000 Burgundians, and the Vandals who crossed Gibraltar into North Africa numbering not more than 80,000. Successive tribal waves crested in the 400s, bringing violence that was destructive of life, trade, and urban centers.

Crisis continued as the Justinian plague (so called after the Byzantine emperor, 527–565) struck Constantinople in 542 and was followed by at least fifteen succeeding outbreaks, the last ending in 750. Plague did not reappear until the mid–14th century, well known to us today as the Black Death. Diagnosis of the Justinian epidemic as bubonic plague is based on a detailed description left by the Byzantine historian Procopius. Other diseases passed through the Mediterranean in these two centuries, but plague was the conspicuous killer. It probably originated in the great African lakes district, south of what is today Ethiopia, appearing first in Pelusium, an Egyptian seaport. From there it spread to Alexandria, Palestine, and Syria and to urban centers and large river-valley populations all around the Mediterranean. Death tolls are uncertain; in Constantinople, one-half to one-third died in the first wave of 542–544.

The plague bacillus *Yersinia pestis* penetrated the body by way of mucous membranes of the mouth or lungs or through tiny wounds in the skin. The bubonic form resulted usually from an infected flea, whose bite inoculated the bacilli. Dead tissue formed large, black, gangrenous spots on the skin. After a few days, a large, hard swelling appeared in the lymphatic glands of the groin, neck, or armpit—the bubo. After eight or ten days the victim either began to recover or died. In some cases a pulmonary abscess developed, and the coughing victim's breath transmitted bacilli to others, creating the pneumonic infectious variant that spread quickly and was 100 percent fatal, death occurring within two or three days.

Fleas are specialists, each type adapted to a specific animal species. Unfortunately, the rat flea that carries plague, *Xenophylla cheopsis*, can also live on humans. For a long time it was thought that black rats carrying fleas were the necessary means for plague's dissemination. But *Pulex irritans*, a flea of humans, can also transmit plague. Moreover, the rat flea also infests several other rodents, among them brown rats, which, being shy of humans, prefer sewers or open fields; large marmots known as *tarabagons*, which are found in Central Asia near Lake Baikal; prairie dogs of North America; Middle Eastern gerbils (*jirds*); and rats around the African lakes. In rodent warrens burrowed underground, fleas and plague bacilli find their refuge, where they remain to this day. The bacilli are also fatal to rodents, so the disease spreads haphazardly as rodents enter abandoned warrens where fleas lie waiting. In the postclassical plagues, when infected flea-bearing rodents fanned out and took up residence in buildings and ships, human centers of infection sometimes developed, and massive epidemics frequently followed.

The plague of 542–750 had enduring consequences for civilization. First, Europe north of the Mediterranean was spared the plague, and possibly the severest effects of the earlier smallpox and measles epidemics, being cooler, thinly populated, and without cities. Its population therefore grew, albeit unsteadily due to Germanic migrations and political disorder, while Mediterranean cities and their nearby districts were ravaged. Germanic populations increased and changed the linguistic and ethnic composition of Britain and northwestern Europe, as did Slavic colonization of the Balkan Peninsula in the 5th through 8th centuries. Vigorous population growth in Scandinavian coastlands propelled Viking raids in the 9th and 10th centuries and establishment of colonies in Iceland (875–900) and even Greenland (985–986). Second, shaken by demographic and revenue losses, the Byzantine and Sassanian empires put up feeble resistance to Islamic expansion out of Arabia after 643. Not that Arabs were immune; plague struck an Arabic army in Syria in 638–639 and spread through Mesopotamia, killing soldiers and native inhabitants. In the Umayyad caliphate (661–749), plague reappeared in Syria and Iraq, as well as Egypt and North Africa. Population shifts alone do not explain the Arabic-Islamic transformation of the entire Middle East and North Africa.

Disease and disorder contributed to further population decline and migration in China also. At the beginning of the 3rd century, the Han dynasty had disappeared, and waves of barbarians settled in the north, which the fragmented states of the former empire reluctantly accepted. By the 4th century, a blending of nomadic and Chinese culture made the frontier invisible. In 310–312, a great epidemic is reported to have killed 98 percent of the population in Shensi Province. In the year 322, 20 to 30 percent succumbed across wide areas. A Chinese medical text possibly dating to the 4th century describes boils and pustules that could have been smallpox. A more certain work dates an epidemic of "barbarian boils" (*luchuang*) to the year 495, during a war in the north. Note that this means the barbarians, too, had acquired smallpox, and that some Inner Asian folk were becoming hardened to the diseases of civilization. By the 11th century, Chinese pediatricians wrote about smallpox casually.

Just when bubonic plague arrived in China historians disagree. Venturesome scholars assert it arrived in China possibly as early as 610. In 642, a document described plague as common on the Kwangtung coast (South China) but rare in the interior, which is a pattern identical to the Mediterranean. Plague broke out again in the coastal provinces in 762, killing about half the inhabitants of Shantung Province. A last wave in 806 killed nearly half of Chekaing's people.

Patterns of migration were very distinctive in China. In the Mediterranean, much urban population fled to the countryside, but not far. For one thing, there was nowhere to go southward; beyond the coastal fringe, Africa offered sparse mountain refuge and, beyond that, only desert. The Middle East was already densely settled. If the Mediterranean experienced any large-scale migration northward, historians have not discovered it. Many survivors of pestilence probably chose to remain because they inherited lands and other possessions from their deceased countrymen. The immigration of Germans, Slavs, and Arabs numbered at most several hundred thousand each, the Vikings far fewer. By contrast, Chinese people moved far and often, sometimes following earlier migration paths. Millions moved southward into the Yangtze watershed during the troubled 3rd through 6th centuries. Most were peasants moving to new rural areas, but some fled cities seeking rural refuge. Many migrants moved in waves, one group moving a short distance, say, 50 to 100 miles, pushing out others, who moved a similar distance. Not all went southward; many moved within North China, and some went farther north. Overall, however, these troubled centuries resulted in a generalized shift of population southward to an area that was an underdeveloped frontier.

Beyond China, relatively little is known of the great epidemic waves. Situated at opposite ends of Eurasia, the British and Japanese islands offer examples of the impact of diseases on isolated populations in nearly "virgin soil" conditions. Detached from the mainland and without regular trade contacts, epidemics struck so infrequently that immunities became established quite late, and at great human cost. Populations therefore remained low. Neither supported 1 million persons before the common era. Estimates are possible only for the English portion of the British Isles, the first giving 1.1 million in 1086. Japan reached 1.5 million perhaps about 400 C.E., maybe 4 or 5 million by 600 C.E., then fluctuated radically until the disease regime stabilized at the end of the 14th century.

For Japan, frequent contacts with the mainland are signaled by the arrival in the islands of Buddhism from Korea, and by an epidemic in 552. A missionary band in 585 brought an epidemic of skin sores and fevers—smallpox, probably. The great epidemic of 735–737 is the first well-reported smallpox outbreak in the islands. A massive killer in 994–995 wiped out half the population, according to one account. In all, 8th-century Japan had 34 epidemics; the 9th, 35; the 10th, 26; and the 11th, 24. These were primarily smallpox, mumps, measles, influenza, and dysentery. They coincided with the introduction of Chinese institutions and arts as Japanese courts sent ambassadors and traders to China and Korea. Eventually, the Japanese became hardened to mainland diseases, and populations rose steeply by the 13th century.

The British Isles suffered similarly: infrequent epidemics with massive die-offs that kept population low through radical oscillations. Between 546 and 1087 C.E., 49 separate epidemics are recorded, whose diminishing severity suggests gradual acquisition of immunities. In England, population barely passed 1 million in 1086 but by 1346 had more than tripled, to 3.7 million. At farthest Europe, Iceland experienced virgin soil epidemics worst of all.

Populations Diverge: Growth versus Stagnation, 700–1330

After the end of the worst plague period, Europe and East Asia began a long cycle of growth that eventually accelerated to the modern population explosion. Growth of such magnitude was not universal. The ancient homelands of civilization in Mesopotamia and Egypt, or more broadly, the Middle East and North Africa, stagnated and even declined.

The Nile valley had reached its demographic limit even before the Christian era. At about 5 million, the population was at a maximum not surpassed until the 19th century. Farther west, the rest of North Africa fluctuated between 4 and 5.5 million in all. The Roman era saw a shift from pastoralism to agriculture and terraced cultivation extending into the hills. The epidemics and violence that swept the Mediterranean after around 180

C.E. reduced lowland populations sharply. Abandoned fields and terraces silted river deltas, and malaria became so rampant that agricultural peoples retreated to the mountains. After the Arab conquests, population and cultivation returned to the lowlands; marshlands were properly channeled, and with new crops such as sugarcane, rice, and citrus fruits, populations grew and trade and urban centers recovered.

The Middle East, including the Mediterranean coast, Syria, Persia, and Arabia, experienced modest population growth in the 8th and 9th centuries. Before and after the Arab conquest, the agricultural environs of Baghdad produced bumper crops by means of a network of four major canals connecting the Tigris and Euphrates. At this time Mesopotamia supported about 1.5 million persons. Partly because of the city area's rich agriculture, the Abbasid dynasty made Baghdad its capital in 750. As the Arabic ruling elite consolidated political authority, the bureaucracies of taxation, administration, and military affairs grew and contributed to expansion of old urban centers and growth of new ones around military sites. Urban populations also grew as Eurasian trade revived after restoration of the Chinese Empire in 589 and as the rise of a commercial and landed aristocracy stimulated artisanal (craft) production. By the 11th century, however, the upper Mesopotamian lands became salted and sterile, as Sumeria had three millennia earlier. Oppressive state taxation to finance wars and elaborate construction of fortified cities, mosques, and palaces caused peasants to flee their villages or resort to banditry. Yet the opulence and advanced learning of Islamic high culture continued even as the economic and demographic basis eroded. Finally, even illusory high culture collapsed in the Mongol invasions of the mid–13th century, which, in 1258, destroyed Baghdad and reputedly 800,000 inhabitants of the region. This heartland of Arabic Islam never fully recovered from the crisis.

India is the great population unknown. Historians have guessed population sizes on the basis of literary references to cities and the geographical extent of the Gupta Empire (320–500 C.E.), but even the empire's boundaries were uncertain and changing. Standard histories describe the late classical period as India's golden age of peace and prosperity. But some scholars suggest a decline of trade and urban life that coincided with expansion of villages and agriculture throughout the Ganges basin and southeastern Coromandel lowlands. Recent archaeological studies suggest small populations, particularly before the 10th century. India's dense disease environment and persistence of huge forested tracts suggest populations were not large. High estimates put population for the entire subcontinent at about 50 million in the 1st century C.E., rising to 100 million by around 1000, with low estimates at half these numbers.

There is no direct evidence of plague or other major epidemics. Smallpox and measles had been endemic to India for centuries, so there is no reason to suppose they drove down population. A brief incursion of Huns around 460 was confined to the northwest. Between 400 and 1000 there were at least four famines in northern India, one in 941 associated with cannibalism. Political instability after the Gupta dynasty's end, famines, and maybe occasional pestilence probably prevented growth from 400 to 1000. After 1000, population grew in cycles of disaster and recovery. The four-month rainy season was the key to India's fertility, and failed monsoon rains meant disaster. Although besieged by disease, India's scourge was drought and famine.

To conclude, in the 3rd through 8th centuries the great epidemic waves, political and economic collapse, civil wars, and barbarian invasions reduced populations of the classical empires by half or more. Population low-pressure zones magnetically pulled hundreds of thousands of primitive agricultural and even pastoral Germans, Slavs, and Huns from Inner Eurasia; likewise, Arabic peoples, who were already largely urbanized and disease-hardened through long contacts with the Persian, Egyptian, Greco-Roman, and Indian civilizations that surrounded them. The Arabs created and sustained a chain of ideologically compatible states across North Africa and the Middle East that ensured intensive contacts between East and West, guaranteeing thereby that Eurasian civilization would not again shrink into separate disease pools.

By roughly the 10th century—earlier in China, later in Britain and Japan—ethnically reconstituted civilized populations became hardened to a larger, more homogenized disease pool, which at its eastern and western extremities now included most of the more deadly pathogenic microorganisms (but not all—nature still had a few more tricks up its sleeve). From this point onward, the biological foundations of history shifted and settled into a new form, in a sense creating the demographic foundations of the modern world.

Postclassical Economic and Demographic Revolutions in Africa, Europe, and China, 650–1300

Three remarkable technological and demographic breakthroughs occurred in the postclassical period. Those in western Europe and China are well known to historians; another in sub-Saharan Africa has been revealed mainly by new archaeological research. Broad areas in these parts of Africa, particularly the eastern Great Lakes region, saw substantial advances of agriculture and population, probably led by iron production and implements. Archaeologists label the period the "Later Iron Age" and associate it with formation of large towns such as Mapungubwe, Ntusi, stone cities of the East African coast, and the great cemetery of Sanga in today's Republic of Congo. After 500 C.E., a new type of heavy iron hoe opened up new lands in the Zambezi River valley that previously had been too densely sodded for cultivation. Cattle herding increased as forests were reduced. In southern Africa, large-scale territorial polities developed. Populations increased sharply in regions that today include central Zambia, western Uganda, and southwestern Tanzania. Foraging peoples were displaced or reduced to clients of powerful agricultural and cattle-herding communities, spread by the migrating Bantu peoples. Industries produced new, high-quality tools and household objects. A web of long-distance trading networks spread across all South and Southeast Africa by the 14th century.

The new European economy developed largely in the absence of governmental authority. The Roman Empire never was restored. New political systems rose on the foundations of the new economy after it had been mostly constructed. In China, by contrast, the economic revolution developed mostly within the empire, reconstructed after 589 as, successively, the Sui, T'ang, and Song dynasties. Imperial bureaucracy promoted economic development by disseminating information, by constructing transportation systems, by taxation and finance, all of which accelerated and shaped economic and demographic growth. These two contrasting patterns of development eventually made all the difference in world history.

The European revolution was achieved chiefly by cultivating more land: opening a frontier on the Northwest European plain, made accessible by development of a new tool, the heavy wheeled plow, and clearing away dense virgin forests with the old standbys, ax and fire. Populations grew considerably. Some new crops and techniques developed in southern Europe, but their potential was not realized until centuries later. The Chinese agricultural revolution involved two massive improvements: opening up new lands on its southern frontier and developing a new, complex set of improvements in agricultural techniques and crops. These demanded a vastly greater labor force and stimulated a great increase in population. Both revolutions resulted in a shift in the focus of their respective civilization's center of gravity—Europe to the north and west, China to the south.

Before the 11th century, in a sense there was no European civilization. The Roman Empire had been a Mediterranean system, as much African and Asian as European. Rome's authority only lightly affected the northwest, even after centuries of nominal rule. This remained frontier country, far and remote from the Mediterranean center, covered mostly by dense, virgin forest, and sparsely populated by small agricultural settlements in forest clearings or on pockets of thinner upland soils tillable with scratch plows. Roman agricultural technology was of ancient Near Eastern origin, its principal implement the simple scratch plow (the *ararum*), suited to the light soils and arid climate and producing meager yields. By contrast, the Northwest European plain was a broad expanse of rich clay and loam soils, with a cool climate, abundant rainfall, and long, damp springtimes ideal for the growing of grain, forage crops, and livestock. It includes what today is the northern half of France, northwestern Germany, the Low Countries and extends to southern England, Denmark, and southernmost Sweden.

The heavy wheeled plow made this fertile frontier accessible to cultivation. Probably invented in Central Europe, it began to affect the Northwest European plain in the 6th and 7th centuries. Designs varied; its essentials were a moldboard that cut under the sod, rolling it completely over as the plow advanced. Requiring considerable power and a rigid frame to keep the moldboard in place, it was set on wheels and pulled by six to eight oxen—an expensive apparatus by the standards of the age. Communities therefore had to be large to afford them, and typically they were only a few plows and teams per village. Deeply burying the sod left bare soil ready for planting after a single pass over the land, thereby eliminating cross-plowing and reducing labor needs. Fields became long and narrow—long to reduce turning around the slow, cumbersome plow and team, narrow so that soil became mounded at the field's center, which drained off excess water into dead furrows between the narrow strips. To restore the soil's fertility and to provide time for a field to be plowed for autumn planting, it would be left fallow from midsummer's harvest to the autumn of the following year. During this time, livestock grazed first on the stubble and, after winter, on new growth of naturally occurring grass and weeds. Peasants then manured, plowed, and planted the field. In some fertile regions, a three-field cycle permitted springtime planting of peas, beans, or a new crop, oats. These spread out the year's labor and widened the range of crops, reducing risk of crop failure. Where oats were grown, horses attained some importance, and the era saw development of horseshoes, horse collars, and other improvements in harnessing. Although certainly faster than oxen, horses were generally too expensive for farming, so the former predominated until the 18th century. Horses did quicken overland transportation and remained important in warfare.

The system expanded slowly at first. Violence among rival Germanic kingdoms and clans, then Magyar and Viking raids, inhibited its potential until the 10th or 11th centuries. Clearing away the vast forests in the early centuries was an extremely slow process, but the forests themselves were a great resource for timber and fuel. By the 11th century the agrarian foundations were in place; manufacturing and trade increased, and urban centers developed.

In Mediterranean Europe, where cropland had receded during the centuries of epidemics and violence, it expanded again as population recovered. By the 11th century, new crops and techniques became apparent, many arriving by way of contacts with Islamic North Africa and Iberia. These techniques included construction of a web of irrigation canals, of which the Po River valley in northern Italy was a prominent example. For example, Milan built two great irrigation systems in 1177 and 1229, the Naviglio Grande and the Muzza. Others were constructed in Tuscany, Provence, and Roussillon at the foot of the Pyrenees. Canals not only irrigated the countryside in great herringbone networks, they also brought water to cities on the plain.

New crops brought from India and Southeast Asia by way of Islamic trade routes included rice, cotton, and sugarcane, which were successfully introduced in Italy, Sicily, southernmost Spain, and the Mediterranean islands—sugar especially in Crete and Cyprus, rice especially in the lower

Arno and Po valleys by the 15th century. Sorghum came from sub-Saharan Africa in the 9th century, and mulberries and silkworms from China beginning in the late 10th century to such places as Brescia, Italy, where the new agricultural industry spread slowly in the hills immediately above the Mediterranean coast. Durum wheat arrived from North Africa, the vital ingredient for pasta. New fruits and vegetables included asparagus, eggplant, artichokes, apricots, cantaloupes, and citrus fruits. An important addition was *luzerne*, or alfalfa, originally from Persia or Iran, whose cultivation spread slowly in the 1200s and 1300s in northern Italy and Provence. Centuries later, *luzerne* would have tremendous impact on northwestern agriculture, and cotton and sugar would define Europe's place in the Atlantic economy. The 11th through 15th centuries gave European agronomists and investors time to learn about these crops.

Growth in Europe therefore followed two different patterns: in the south, recovery of an older agrarian and urban system, with innovations; and in the north, establishment of an entirely new system. Population grew everywhere but more dramatically in the north. Trade increased not only in regional products but also between northwestern Europe and the Mediterranean. The north offered woolens, forest products, hides, and iron; the south offered wine, sugar, and luxury goods by way of eastern trade connections, for example, silks, spices, porcelains. Wind and water mills spread widely, especially important in grinding grain, timbering, mining, and textile manufactures. They remained Europe's premier mechanical energy source until well into the Industrial Revolution.

A network of small but numerous urban centers emerged in the north. The shift in population densities and trade from the 11th to 15th centuries may be estimated by the location and size of the major European cities. In the 11th century, most of them bordered the Mediterranean—the largest, at 450,000 persons each, were the capital of the Byzantine Empire, Constantinople, and of the Umayyad caliphate, Cordoba. By the 15th century, Muslim and Byzantine control of the Mediterranean had largely ended; Constantinople and Cordoba proportionately shrank. Meanwhile, northern cities grew, with Paris reaching 275,000; Bruges, 125,000; and Ghent, 70,000. Other cities rose to become major Mediterranean forces: in Italy, Milan at 125,000, Venice at 110,000, Genoa at 100,000; in Spain, Seville at 70,000 and Grenada at 100,000.

Meanwhile, Chinese agriculture was transformed in the 8th to 12th centuries by innovations that fit the southern climate and soils. The heart of the revolution was wet rice cultivation. Traditionally, rice had been grown widely across Asia by "dry" cultivation, that is, sowing seeds in plowed or hoed fields watered by rainfall only, the same as wheat or oats in Western agriculture. Growth was slow and yields were low but acceptable where land was abundant and labor scarce. South China offered a warm, semitropical environment with a long growing season (year-round in the far south), and abundant monsoon rains. The labor demands for rice cultivation were extensive, the techniques complicated, the yields enormous. Wet rice cultivation had developed at several places in southeastern Asia in preceding centuries, but only on a limited scale. It involved planting in fields that were made flat and bunded, or dammed up at their perimeters, then flooded and plowed to create a bed of mud into which presprouted seedlings were transplanted in tiny bunches by hand. Diffusion of these techniques, and innovations in them, became, in effect, the Chinese agricultural revolution.

An important set of innovations involved soil preparation. The moldboard plow appeared in dry cultivation in northern China about the mid–3rd century C.E. In soft, wet fields it required little power, for a single ox or water buffalo or even 4 to 5 men could pull it. To enrich soil, peasants applied manure—urban and rural, human and animal—mixed with crop residues, river mud, and, where available, lime. Transplanting seedlings sprouted in specially prepared, highly fertile seedbeds saved seed, guaranteed uniform placement and growth rates of plants, facilitated weeding, and assured that plants would attain maturity simultaneously in a plot. Thorough weeding increased yields considerably and was achieved by draining fields when rice was about half grown, followed by careful weeding between rows and along field edges.

Selective breeding and introduction of new strains resulted in different varieties of rice. By the Song era, virtually all the older varieties used in the mid–T'ang dynasty had been replaced. The new strains included some of the genetics of *champa* rice, a fast-growing, drought-resistant variety introduced from central Vietnam and widely adapted in the 11th century. Besides varied adaptability to different soils and moisture conditions, strains matured at different rates. Harvesting thus was spread out over the months. Different maturation times also ensured against dry spells. If one variety or field failed, another might succeed. On lands that could not be irrigated, traditional dry rice or the new *champa* could be used. Wheat appeared also as a dry-field crop by the end of the 10th century. In the far south, the year-round growing season allowed double and even triple cropping, with faster ripening strains and transplanted seedlings. In dry fields, too, wheat, rice, and beans alternated in rotations. These innovations greatly increased yields and, thereby, population densities.

Lands were also opened up along the coasts as marshes and river deltas were drained, leveled, and brought into cultivation. Into suitable hillsides rice terraces were cut and dammed. For these, water-control systems were essential, to carry away unwanted water and to bring water when and where needed.

Hydrological technologies were obviously crucial. The techniques were complex, but basically they involved building dams to raise water levels above stream beds in order to divert water into irrigation canals that made incredible webs across the terrain; these were opened and closed by sluice gates, some big, some small, or by just a clod of earth. Areas with streams and steep gradients had an advantage in using gravity to move water. Mountain terraces allowed rainwater to be trapped in terraced and bunded fields, then trickled down or released. Flatlands presented a problem, as did dry times, when water had to be raised by pumps. The simplest such pump was a bucket on a pole, known as a well-sweep. Others, such as the *noria*, were great waterwheels with paddles or bamboo pots that raised water the height of the wheel, then dumped it from above. The simple treadle pallet pump was a small, portable device that raised water as it was pedaled like a bicycle. Wind power was not developed in China until after this economic revolution, around the 16th century.

Handicraft manufacturing and industries increased. Rising textile manufactures extended cultivation of hemp and cotton. Mulberries and silkworms became a distinctive feature of Chinese peasant communities. The trees were grown beside houses, along roads, beside ditches, in gardens, almost anywhere, and they grew quickly, as trees go. Silk thread and cloth were produced by peasants in their idle hours, by women, or, especially, by old or young or disabled persons. In short, their production fit into agricultural space and into work routines conveniently. Tea bushes and lacquer-producing trees spread in several regions. China led the world in iron production, particularly cast iron; in 1078 the Song Empire produced some 114,000 metric tons, as against 68,000 tons in industrial England in 1788. Chinese porcelain manufactures became world renowned in these centuries; kilns and workshops multiplied in many areas, with the best pieces produced near capital cities. These traded widely across Asia by land and sea.

China's economic revolution had a final component that was largely missing in Europe: improvements in transportation and communications, mostly by governmental direction. The T'ang and Song governments maintained and improved roads and bridges. Between major cities, roads were paved or surfaced with stone and brick. Water transportation became the bloodstream of China's economy. The immense network of navigable waterways of the Yangtze and its tributaries was extended to North China by canals. In the Sui era (589–617), navigable routes of canals and canalized rivers connected the Yellow and Wei Rivers and connected the lower Yangtze to Hangchow. In 608 the first truly big Chinese canal reached to Loyang and Peking (Beijing). It was over 40 meters wide, with an imperial road running parallel. On its banks at strategic points were enormous granaries, the biggest able to store 33 million bushels of grain. By the Song era, the network was more than 50,000 kilometers long and floated a virtual town of boats and people at some points.

From the 11th century onward, Chinese seafaring activities expanded. The coastal seas became a highway for heavy junks (ships) sailing north and south on seasonally altering monsoon winds. The Song era began China's golden age of cartography and geographic knowledge, which culminated in the great maritime expeditions of 1404–1433.

These ships and barges, inland and seagoing, accelerated the circulation of staple and luxury goods. A growing urban bourgeoisie in China demanded porcelains and fabrics but also foreign imports of incense, ivory, coral, ebony, sandalwood, and rhinoceros horns. Chinese silk and porcelain exports reached startling heights. Copper coins of the Song spread through every Asian state and across Inner Asia. The imperial administration maintained an elaborate monetary system that circulated an immense volume—even paper money by the 11th century, along with certificates of deposit and promissory notes.

The economic and demographic revolution spawned an urban revolution. Cities throughout eastern China outgrew their walls. The capital city of the southern Song era, during Mongol control of the north, was Hangchow, which reached a million persons and more by 1275—the world's largest city, which no European city would equal until the 19th century. The Yangtze basin became the most urbanized, but North Chinese cities grew too. Overall, about 10 percent of the Chinese population dwelt in cities, but with a total population of over 100 million persons, it was the most urbanized society in the world.

Hence the Chinese economy became the world's most commercialized in both rural and urban sectors. Its high-output agricultural production and high-density population grew to levels that only continued success of all parts of the interdependent system could sustain.

Black Death: A Question of Impact

The several centuries of astonishing economic and demographic growth at opposite ends of Eurasia ended in the pandemic outbreak of bubonic plague, known to Western history as the Black Death. Somehow plague had become established in the grasslands of Inner Asia, probably endemic in Yunnan Province since the early T'ang period. Overland caravan traffic reached a peak under the Mongol empires of the 13th century. Thousands of persons in commercial caravans or in supply and military forces traveled the vast distances. In the mid–13th century, Mongol troops and supply traffic somehow carried flea-infested rats from Yunnan to Central China, thence across Central Asia. Plague struck the travelers first, then swept through the swollen Chinese and European populations, with devastating effect. The exact dates of plague's arrival in China are uncertain; population decline and fleeing refugees derived at least in part from the Mongol invasion of North China. To the west, plague's arrival in Crimea is dated to 1346, with the first wave of deaths across Europe dating 1346–1350. (Middle Eastern parts were hit at about the same time.) It remained endemic for the next three centuries across most of Eurasia, with some outbreaks in India and the Middle East continuing into the 20th century. Repeated outbreaks of plague joined the familiar list of other diseases to drive populations erratically downward, reaching bottom at about the mid–15th century. China's population fell by half between 1200 and 1393, Mediterranean Europe by a similar proportion.

Historians of the Western world are impressed by the Black Death and its economic and psychological consequences, and indeed, these were many and far-reaching. But in broad global and temporal perspective the Black Death seems smaller, particularly compared with the disease impacts at the end of the classical period and the massive die-off of Native Americans after 1492. (See below, chapter 14.) It interrupted Chinese and European growth for a century and a half, a far shorter span than the earlier wave of epidemics and violence, from 180 to 750. Civilization was not drastically reoriented or restructured. By 1500 much of Eurasia had recovered, and the Atlantic regions were already sending expeditions into the seas and nearby islands in search of profit and colonial opportunities. By this point, new interventions would also affect economic and population patterns in Africa.

Conclusion

Populations were very different by around 1450 from what they had been at about 500. First, they had increased enormously, recovering from the bottom of a demographic trough (ca. 500–750) to attain new heights. The peak was attained in the 14th century; it plunged for a century or so in the Black Death, then returned to nearly its former peak by 1450. A century later, by 1550, populations surpassed former sizes.

The geographical range of civilization vastly extended. South China and northern Europe were fully integrated into the system of Afro-Eurasian civilizations. Peoples formerly not part of civilization—Germans, South Chinese peoples, Arabic peoples—were now assimilated. Inner Asia developed quite differently. Here, pastoral empires proved ephemeral, the vast expanses of Inner Asia evidently too loosely organized to sustain enduring states at this point. Finally, plants, animals, diseases, weeds, and peoples had circulated with new intensity. Most of these contacts were anonymous, but there were surely many thousands of them. Bubonic plague's diffusion, to some historians, stands as a symptom of this greater interaction; but if the Justinian plague had, in fact, reached across Asia from China, the Black Death inaugurated nothing. It simply reflected continued interdependency, not a major innovation in population biology. The diffusion of South Asian crops—sugar, cotton, *luzerne*, assorted fruits and vegetables—and the appearance of Mediterranean traders in East Asia are also indicative of greater exchanges. Sugar, cotton, and *luzerne* were highly significant for global interaction that would span the world's oceans over the next few centuries.

CHAPTER 11

CULTURE AND POLITICS IN THE
POSTCLASSICAL PERIOD

The postclassical period was not, on the whole, a period of major political change, except in the sense that formal states spread to new areas such as northwestern Europe, Russia, and additional parts of Africa and Southeast Asia. The capacity to form large empires—a recurrent characteristic of the classical period—largely declined, though China retained its strong state tradition; Islam developed some political unity around much of the Mediterranean; and important empires arose in the Americas. Loose political organization, however, symptomatic of state development in new regions but also the decline of political focus in places like India, was more characteristic.

Cultural innovation, however, was a pervasive development, thanks to the active spread of new or newly vigorous religions and the widespread process of active imitation of other societies, in which cultural components took a key role. When Japan looked to China or Russia to Byzantium, the copying of basic cultural apparatuses, including writing, artistic styles, and religious and philosophical concepts, formed the most essential contact, along with trade relations. None of the imitative areas took over the core culture entirely—Russia, for example, preserved a distinctive musical tradition and simply lacked the resources to copy Byzantine architecture in full. But along with religious conversions, the spur to change was obvious.

It is not easy to relate the huge changes in disease and migration patterns, as well as the spread of new agricultural methods, to the shifts in politics and culture. More productive agriculture helped support new political developments, refining the Chinese imperial system, for example, and promoting the strengthening of governments in Europe and Africa. Migrations and religious contacts interacted: Some peoples converted to new religions as part of the process that would draw them to civilization centers, while religions, in turn, may have helped connect migrants to established populations. Major epidemics also encouraged efforts to seek spiritual solace. But cultural changes also had independent impact, among other things creating important new divisions among the peoples of Afro-Eurasia, even as economic contacts increased.

Culture: Religion, Division, and Global Interaction

The Process of Culture Contact

The new cultural horizons that helped define the postclassical period were symbolized and furthered by the rise of world travelers. Muslim venturers journeyed through North Africa and the Middle East, also visiting Persia, India, islands in the Indian Ocean, China, Europe, and sub-Saharan Africa—the most famous traveler, Ibn Battuta, covered as much as 73,000 miles. During the Mongol interlude, Europeans visited China, Southeast Asia, Central Asia, and India. Travelers' accounts spread knowledge—and myths—about different cultures.

Contacts changed thinking, just as the massive religious conversions did. Europeans converting to Christianity gradually moved away from the partial tolerance of homosexuality that had characterized the classical Mediterranean, coming to view heterosexual activity as alone normal. Muslims generated important new ideas about the state. Muhammad urged obedience to government no matter what its form, for religious goals should be primary; but he also suggested that good government would protect and further the faith, which could lead to political unrest when rulers seemed to be ignoring religious norms. All three world religions—Islam, Christianity, and Buddhism—challenged traditional ideas of social inequality. They accepted inequality on this earth, though sometimes urging charity, but they also argued that everyone had a soul or shared in the divine essence, which could complicate older views of systems such as slavery. The same ambivalence—accepting inequality but arguing for equal souls—applied to gender relations. In another sphere: Europeans, learning a better numbering system from the Arabs, were thereby aided in developing an improved quantitative sense by the 12th century, which would spill over into science and religion alike. Cultural change was ubiquitous, its impact widespread.

Change varied with area. China had already imported Buddhism, which many Chinese in various social groups found attractive as political stability suffered after the fall of the Han dynasty. But a new, strong dynasty, the T'ang, increasingly regulated Buddhist activities from the 7th century onward, seeking to make sure that Buddhist monks would support the state. Later this dynasty turned against Buddhism more systematically, closing most monasteries and seizing lands, forcing as many as 250,000 monks and nuns back into secular life. During most of the postclassical period, China focused on teaching Confucian culture to the bureaucracy, spreading the system's hold in southern China, while beginning to preach basic Confucian values to ordinary people as well. A fairly traditional elite culture was here used to cement regional and social loyalties.

China's cultural mix was not fully exportable. Japan, however, imitating China actively and sending students to the mainland to learn Chinese and Korean ways, copied not only the alphabet but artistic and literary styles as well. Buddhism had a major impact in Japan, and Confucian ideas spread to a degree as well. Older values, such as the Shinto religion, persisted alongside the new elements, while ideals of feudal loyalty and honor gained primacy over Chinese political imports. Confucian social ideas, such as the downgrading of merchants and women, had an impact but were not taken to the full Chinese extreme. And the sheer openness to imitation differentiated Japan from China. Nevertheless, a powerful overlap emerged, and Japan also learned from China that there was not much gain in attempting to contact other parts of the world.

Areas open to Islam experienced far more cultural change than China did. Indeed, Islam's appeal to ordinary people—through the prospect of charity in this life, heaven in the next—clearly helped the religion link disparate groups and regions. Initially, to be sure, Arab Muslims were content to leave local beliefs unchanged, as long as religious minorities paid extra taxes. But the sheer success of Islam and the desire to gain both religious and practical benefits by converting to Arab or, at least, Muslim culture had powerful effects. Some regional religions, such as Zoroastrianism in Persia, virtually disappeared through the process of conversion. Islam itself developed new missionary impulses. A more mystical version, the Sufi movement, arose in several parts of the Middle East by 1000 C.E., stressing the holy power of local, religious leaders, whose visions and ecstatic dances could excite mass fervor. Sufi visionaries helped draw many ordinary people to the religion and also spurred missionary activity in Central and Southeast Asia. Even India was affected, as Sufi missionaries utilized Hindu stories and religious sites to help their appeal. An important Muslim minority resulted, while within Hinduism a syncretic movement arose, the *bhatki* cult, that accepted monotheism and spiritual equality—which helped limit Islam's appeal to lower-caste Indians. But most Hindus resisted, and Muslim invaders' scorn for Hindu values tended to reaffirm traditional commitments; an example is the Turkish writer who talked of "the innate perversity of the Hindu nature. . . . [Hindus] believe that there is no country but theirs . . . no religion like theirs. They are haughty, foolishly vain, self-conceited, and stolid." The sensuality of Hindu art also differentiated the two religious groups, causing another set of mutual suspicions.

Islam and the Arab language spread down the coast of East Africa. Arab traders intermarried with the African elite, and a mixed language, Swahili, became a common currency along the coast. But the lower classes were less involved in this process, and key Arab ideas, for example, about the isolation of women, were not widely adopted. Correspondingly, Arab travelers to sub-Saharan Africa like Ibn Battuta, while praising strong rulers and Islamic devotion, criticized the public freedoms for women. Cultural alteration and contact remained diverse—change was widespread, but regional variants continued to predominate as people struggled to combine older identities and familiar ways with attractive new ideas.

Cultural patterns in western Europe involved another set of distinctive directions, though the two basic processes of conversion to a world religion and assimilating new contacts operated here as well. Ardent missionary efforts spread Christianity steadily to the north, to Germany, the British Isles, and ultimately Scandinavia. As always, there were important compromises with older beliefs, as syncretism inevitably accompanied major new cultural forces. The popularity of worshiping individual saints preserved remnants of polytheism, even though the old gods were attacked. Holy days were set up to coincide with well-established rituals. Christmas was thus located in December, to pick up the popularity of celebrating the winter solstice, while the idea of Christ as Prince of Light linked to older

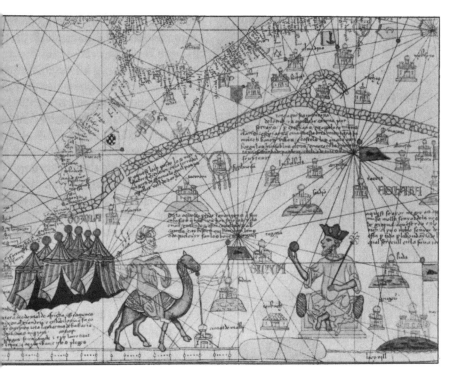

Africans and Islam. This map by a Jewish mapmaker in Spain in 1375, Abraham Cresques, shows the emperor of Mali (in sub-Saharan Africa) holding a golden scepter in his hand. The emperor, Mansa Musa, made a famous pilgrimage to Mecca in 1324, complete with massive resources in gold. His trip caused a sensation in Egypt and led to the impact of mosques and other Arab-style buildings back in Mali. Mansa Musa was the great patron of learning at the crossroads city of Timbuktu, long one of the major Muslim centers. Reprinted by permission of The British Library.

concerns about reviving the sun at this season. Yet the new religion dominated art and literature. Intellectuals struggled to accommodate classical and Arab science with religion, usually careful to insist on the primacy of faith and of otherworldly goals. The monastic movement combined ardent Christianity with other important values, such as hard, regular work—the source, some have argued, of an unusual Western belief in the relationship between diligence and goodness. Religious leaders also insisted on punctuality for prayers, which ultimately supported the development of more precise timepieces. By the 13th century, one monastery was able to set alarms for sleepers—and by this point, Europe had a clear world lead in time-keeping and the importance of time, even as it remained technologically backward in other respects. Again, cultural change could have sweeping consequences, with unexpected results over the long term.

Cultural Rivalries and New Rigidities

Cultural change in the period had one other outcome: the formation of mutual hostilities. China, as we have seen, tended to draw away from external influences after the experience of Buddhism. Invasion by the hated Mongols confirmed the focus on the superiority of regional values.

A fiercer cultural rivalry developed between Islam and European Christianity. Many Muslims looked down on Europe as backward and crude. Europeans, for their part, developed an admiration/hate relationship as they traded more actively with the Muslim world and, in the Crusades to reconquer the Holy Land after 1091, gained other contacts as well. On the one hand, Muslims had scientific and philosophical knowledge and artistic styles that gained wide respect. Copying Arab science (itself partly derived from Greek and Hellenistic sources) spurred Western rational philosophy and even helped set in motion a small current of empirical scientific research. Christian knights who resided in the Middle East in the Crusades period learned of more sophisticated products and manners. As one observer put it, "Even Muslim observers admitted as much: Everyone who is a fresh immigrant from the Frankish lands is ruder in character than those who have become acclimatized and have held long association with the Muslims." Here was an important source of new themes in Western cultural life. But very little flowed in the other direction. Few Muslims thought they had much to learn from Europe, though there was individual recognition of the fighting prowess of some of the knights. Europeans in general continued to be regarded as gross, smelly, and backward, and Muslim tolerance of local Christian minorities deteriorated during the final postclassical centuries as a result of the process of beating back crusader attacks.

For their part, Christian hostility to Islam itself remained fierce. When Christian forces began to reconquer Spain, from the 10th century onward, they pressed Muslims hard to reconvert. Missionaries wooed upper-class Muslims with philosophical arguments while trying to force the lower classes into compliance (though many slaves freely converted as a means of gaining freedom). In 1492, the Spanish Christian rulers finally expelled all Muslims (and Jews) completely if they would not convert.

Mutual hostilities help explain why the pace of cultural imitation did not increase at the end of the postclassical period, despite important new contacts. Thus the Mongol conquests facilitated travel and technological exchange, but outright cultural impact was slight. Mongol rulers themselves sought advice from Muslims, Buddhists, and Christians, along with Confucians; they liked diversity. But established cultural areas did not venture much new learning, for foreign styles and beliefs now seemed too strange. Flexibility was, if anything, declining. No students flocked from one region to the next as they had when the world religions first spread. Europe's Catholic leaders saw the Mongol Empire as a chance to send missionaries to China, and some intrepid souls gave this a try, claiming to have baptized a large number of Chinese. But there were no durable gains, and when the Mongols were expelled, the Catholic presence vanished without a trace. Tolerance in the Middle East declined as well. Under Sufi influence, Islam became more narrowly religious, attacking science and philosophy. Turkish immigrants to the Middle East, previously converted, also emphasized a less tolerant version of Islam than that of the Arab traditions. In Europe, concurrently, Christian leaders began to attack remnants of pagan beliefs, trying to insist on stricter Catholicism. A revived interest in Latin classics and artistic styles, associated with the early Renaissance, points up an additional theme for this period but also promoted a sense of Western cultural distinctiveness and superiority. Even Japan reduced its admiration for China, convinced that Mongol control of China but failure to invade the Japanese islands demonstrated Japan's superiority and ability to stand alone.

Only a few pockets of flexible contact remained, such as India. In general, prior cultural developments had created sharper boundaries. Imitators, having gained by their imports, stopped wanting to imitate. On the international level, cultural change slowed for a while. In individual regions where significant alterations were taking place, as in western Europe and, soon, Japan, outside influence and impact were both limited. In most areas, assimilation of the huge shifts that had already occurred predominated, as a key cultural period in world history drew to a close.

New Forms of State Building

Political Diversities

The dominant themes of the postclassical period raised several general political issues. In states operating within the previous classical centers, a key issue involved rebuilding or consolidating after the decline of the great empires. In areas around this region that were actively copying cultural and political forms, the leading question was how much advanced state structure could be imported; and here the answer was usually qualified, for efforts to create large bureaucracies or empires foundered in places such as western Europe and Japan for lack of resources and experience. Quite generally in Afro-Eurasia, governments had to respond to the growing importance of major religions and religious institutions. The rise of trade provided new resources for states—a crucial development in West Africa, for example—but also raised questions about the relationship between governments and merchants. Different situations and traditions prompted varied responses to these issues. Political diversity across the postclassical world increased as a result, where organized states prevailed at all. At the same time, there were relatively few major innovations in governments' functions in this period, except in state support for religious rules.

The strongest states, not surprisingly, developed on the basis of prior achievements in the classical period. The Byzantine emperors, ruling in the northeastern Mediterranean, preserved a number of Roman practices along with Orthodox Christianity. They claimed religious authority and exercised considerable control over the church. A large bureaucracy involved extensive specialization (in foreign affairs, treasury, justice, and the military) and explicit training. Government regulation of the economy was extensive, and the system was highly centralized. Surrounded by enemies, particularly the forces of Islam, Byzantine rulers devoted great attention to military organization and recruitment and to diplomacy.

Particularly under the T'ang dynasty, China revived and consolidated its earlier political forms. The restoration of centralized imperial administration occurred in the 6th century and immediately involved major new public works, such as a great canal linking North and South China. Improved methods of military recruitment and taxation followed from government reforms of landholding patterns by the T'ang emperors and their predecessors, creating a larger free peasantry for several centuries. The T'ang created a council of chief ministers of the specialized departments, improving coordination, while employing "remonstrators" to criticize imperial behavior—a creative implementation of Confucian beliefs in responsible elites. The T'ang also expanded the examination system for bureaucrats, emphasizing Confucian classics, current affairs, and poetic composition, and allowing a limited recruitment of talented people from the lower classes. The government retained firm control over merchant activities, even as trade and urban classes expanded rapidly, and also regulated cultural affairs, ultimately turning against Buddhism while promoting Confucianism and monitoring the Taoist religion and its priests. The government role in economic change and in the transportation infrastructure contributed greatly to China's population surge and urban growth, discussed in chapter 10.

The most important new political center of the postclassical period was Islam, where the Muslim caliphate carved out a new unity between the Middle East and North Africa while institutionalizing some of the political implications of the religion itself. In principle, the Islamic state was intended to protect and enforce Islam on the whole community (while tolerating religious minorities), implementing divine laws as interpreted by Islamic scholars, the *ulema*. The chief ruler, or caliph, held to be the successor to the prophet Muhammad, administered the huge territory carved out by Arab conquests, at one point extending into Spain in the west, Persia in the east. The same expansion, of course, brought new political demands and experiences. Arab rule depended heavily on careful military organization, with garrisons stretched through the caliphate. Contact with Persia brought growing adoption of elaborate ceremonies and court rituals to enhance the prestige of the caliphs. At the same time, like Persians and Romans before them, the Arabs allowed substantial local self-rule; a large central bureaucracy on the Chinese model, with representatives in every area, did not develop. Specialization of functions did increase, but except for the religious expectations (often disappointed by caliphs whose interests were frequently mainly secular), there was no elaborate expansion of the role of government in society at large. While the government organized some public welfare, for example, Islamic emphasis on charity left most of this activity in private hands. Several caliphs supported education and scholarship, but the extensive expansion of Islamic education depended more on religious than government auspices, with Quranic schools developing around individual mosques.

The Expansion of Societies with States

For the long run, the spread of often rather loosely run states to new areas constituted the most important political development in the postclassical period. In Europe and Japan, a system called feudalism developed to provide some political coherence, after attempts to create a more conventional empire failed. In Africa, large regional kingdoms in which rulers often claimed to be gods depended in fact on careful negotiation with local elites; several kings also utilized a bureaucracy trained in Arabic and the Islamic religion to supplement their administrative efforts.

After the collapse of the western Roman Empire in 476 C.E., various Germanic tribal leaders tried but failed to re-create the Roman model. Several Germanic kingdoms were established, two of whose leaders employed the title of Roman emperor; the most notable attempt at empire occurred under Charlemagne, around 800, but ended in division into smaller units. Internal weakness, including the lack of an educated elite, and outside invasions inhibited political stability. In this situation, local military leaders began to form personal bonds in the interests of mutual defense. Lords would grant lands and protection to lesser warriors, or vassals, who would pledge military support in return; all parties could afford the horses and armor necessary for battle in this period. This network of mutuality and loyalty was feudalism, and it permitted the construction of regional groupings that gradually reduced endemic warfare and raiding. Kings in places such as France operated as large feudal lords, seeking to use ties with vassals to enforce larger loyalties, even though they did not monopolize military force. Gradually this system permitted the formation of larger kingdoms; by 1100, kings of France and England ruled loosely over a substantial number of regional vassals, who in turn (as lords) commanded the service of lesser vassals. Alongside these feudal monarchies, the Catholic Church developed its own bureaucracy in the interest of regulating local church activities and collecting funds for support.

The net result of these various patterns was the emergence of more complex political units, which were, however, constrained by a number of factors. In principle and often in fact, kings were limited in the religious area by the powers of the church. Feudalism provided opportunities for political expansion, but it inhibited the growth of large central states; among other things, lords were supposed to ask vassals for advice before undertaking major initiatives. European kings did develop the beginnings of their own bureaucracy in the final centuries of the postclassical period, with some limited specialization of functions (finance, justice, military). But vassals often forced kings to create new institutions—called parliaments—to represent them and other powerful interests. Parliaments focused on their claim to approve any new taxes as a means of restraining arbitrary behavior by kings. With many different government units crisscrossing western Europe, feudalism also provided a strong military orientation to the emerging states, with frequent wars and enduring rivalries.

A similar system developed in Japan, after an initial effort to import a centralized, Chinese-type model, complete with Confucian bureaucracy, failed in the 8th century. Powerful landed aristocrats successfully opposed a strong government. Emperors were retained for religious functions, but regional warfare revived among powerful noble families. Here, too, the central government lost its control over military force. Local chieftains set up a network of feudal loyalties instead, granting warriors, the samurai (meaning, "those who serve"), land in return for military service. Larger networks of loyalty could create a limited central state, called a shogunate, as in the period 1185–1335; the Kamakura Shogunate reduced internal warfare and created a small central bureaucracy, though a looser feudal system returned after its decline. Japanese feudalism differed from its European counterpart in a greater stress on personal loyalty—lords and vassals were regarded as fathers and sons—and far less emphasis on contractual obligations of the sort that could lead to parliamentary institutions. In principle, vassals' devotion to lords should include even suicide when a lord was killed in battle. This intense system provided its own building blocks for solid organizations in later Japanese history, with strong emphasis on authority and group cohesion.

As trade and cultural activity intensified in sub-Saharan Africa, several political patterns developed in addition to the strong monarchy already established in Ethiopia, which was based on patterns inherited from Kush and Axum. Commercial city-states organized on the Indian Ocean coast, mixing Arab traders and African elites in merchant-led administrations. Important parts of West Africa, such as the Ibo territory in present-day Nigeria, with flourishing agriculture, elaborate artistic forms, and a substantial population, did not develop formal states—thereby providing some of the most interesting cases of ongoing stateless societies, with smaller communities and kin groups organizing informal decision making.

In much of West Africa, however, beginning with Ghana, large regional kingdoms developed from the late classical period onward, profiting from active trade routes with North Africa across the Sahara. Like many monarchies, the systems seem to have evolved from village headmen directing extended family communities, claiming religious as well as political powers, though also employing a council of the leaders of prominent families. African kings used elaborate ceremonies, sometimes speaking only through interpreters, who repeated the king's words in a loud voice. Religious status might involve claims that the kings required no food. At the same time, the Sudanic kings employed educated Muslims as bureaucrats, who brought literacy and administrative experience to the governments. As usual, governments developed some specialization among record-keeping, financial, and military functions. By the time of the great empire of Mali (1210–1400 C.E.), most kings were themselves Muslims, sometimes undertaking the pilgrimage to Mecca; but in a political mix similar to cultural syncretism, they combined their sincere devotion with continued claims to divine kingship.

While the leading African states were larger than government units in western Europe and Japan, they did not have extensive functions. Warfare commanded the greatest attention, along with careful levies on merchants. The system worked well, however, and persisted into the 19th century—indeed Africa, along with China, displayed the greatest amount of political continuity from the postclassical period until modern times. In the period itself, the formation of African states, like the emergence of states in Japan,

northern Europe, and Russia, demonstrated the growth of political opportunities and needs in an ever-widening range of agricultural societies, enhanced by contacts with the more experienced administrations of China,
Islam, and the Byzantine Empire.

Conclusion

Not surprisingly, developments in culture and in politics meshed in crucial
respects during the postclassical period. The growth of world religions
helped limit state activities in many areas. While religious training provided sources of bureaucrats in states as diverse as the Sudanic kingdoms
and the Mongol empires, religious interests on the whole distracted from
intense political concerns. Otherworldly goals might seem more important
than the details of state consolidation. Religious beliefs and institutions
often played a greater role in holding a society together (if loosely) than
governments did. Thus shared Christianity and some common trade provided a rough unity to western Europe despite widespread political divisions, frequent war, and relatively weak governments. As the caliphate declined in the Middle East, the same was true for the heartland of Islam.
Correspondingly, the impact of new beliefs on aspects of daily life, such as
work and gender relations, was usually greater in this period than the interventions of government. Here, however, other factors, such as growing
trade and the biological results of international contact, played a role as
well in causing modifications in the basic patterns of life.

CHAPTER 12

GENDER STRUCTURES IN THE POSTCLASSICAL PERIOD

The gender structures that developed, rigidified, and expanded in the classical period were both strengthened and challenged during the postclassical period. Increasing contact between civilizations often introduced new notions about the proper relations between men and women. This led in some cases to radical changes, such as the adoption of Muslim norms across a broad geographic area. In other cases it led to a strengthening of older ideas, such as the sharpening of Confucian doctrines about female subordination during the Song dynasty, a response to the challenge of more egalitarian Buddhist ideas.

In many parts of the world, such as Europe, Japan, Central America, the Andean region, and West Africa, large, loosely centralized states were established that were ruled by hereditary monarchies. In these states, individual women often gained great power, either ruling in their own name as queens or empresses or, more commonly, ruling in fact during the minority of a son or when a husband was incapacitated. Ideas about how the right to rule should be handed down varied considerably throughout the world, and in a few places, such as the Andean region under the Inca, women inherited their right to rule independent of the male ruler. In some areas, such as many parts of Europe, daughters could inherit territories if there were no sons, and in others, such as parts of Africa, combinations of brothers and sisters ruled jointly. Among the elites, then, a woman's class and family standing could to some degree outweigh the restrictions created by gender.

In general, however, the creation of states out of earlier, less formal structures of government heightened gender distinctions, rather than lessening them. Rulers generally relied on an educated elite of bureacrats and government officials to run their larger territories, and such individuals were almost always men, trained in schools or special training programs that were closed to women, such as the universities of Paris and Timbuktu. Rulers also relied on large armies to conquer new territories and prevent rebellions in areas already conquered, another avenue of influence that was closed—with very few exceptions—to women. To cement alliances with these new territories, conquerors often took women as wives for themselves or for their officials, generally choosing women from the most prominent families as a symbol of the extent of their conquest. Thus women were forced to travel hundreds of miles from their homes in order to join the household of a ruler or official for whom they might be one wife or concubine among many. Polygyny was often a mark of the increasing social stratification in larger states, for the number of wives and concubines a man could support was a mark of rank and wealth.

The growth of states meant increased demands for tribute and taxes, which were generally levied on the basic household unit of a marital couple and their children. (Despite polygyny among certain elites, most men married only one spouse at a time.) In most of the world during this period, taxes and tribute were paid not in currency but in the labor or products of both women and men. Sometimes tribute demands also shaped the gender division of labor; when certain items such as cloth or rice were favored as tributary goods, all family members might work to produce them, thus breaking down older patterns.

In some parts of the world, people themselves were part of the tribute, and existing systems of slavery often expanded. In some areas, such as Russia, the majority of slaves were men, used for heavy agricultural labor and estate management, whereas in others, such as Italian and Islamic cities, the majority were women, purchased to do household tasks. Many of these women also had sexual relations with their male owners, though cultures varied widely in how the children who resulted from such unions were regarded. Because in many of the world's cultures most people owed labor or goods as part of their taxes to higher authorities, the line between being slave and being free was not sharp, and people crossed it in both directions; stories about slaves who became the favorites of rulers—for men, through their intelligence, and for women, through their beauty—and thus gained power for themselves and their children became a standard part of the historical tradition.

Although queens and a few slave women gained a public role in some circumstances by their links to ruling dynasties, for many other women, this was a period of withdrawal. In China, Japan, and much of the Islamic world, women were physically secluded, with special parts of houses constructed for them—termed *harim* (which means "forbidden area") or *zenana*—and their contacts with the outside world were sharply limited. If they left their houses, they were to be secluded behind the curtains of a chair or behind a veil. Seclusion and veiling constituted a mark of class status as well as of religious or cultural norms and appear to have begun among the upper classes, although the practices gradually were adopted even by quite poor families whenever possible. Seclusion was generally accompanied by a young age of marriage for women—and sometimes for men—with the woman traveling from her birth household to her husband's upon marriage. Seclusion created special women's spaces where men were only rarely present, giving some women power within the *harim*, or women's quarters.

In Europe, the Americas, Southeast Asia, and parts of Africa, most women were generally not secluded, a fact that male travelers from areas of the world in which women *were* secluded found surprising. In Europe and parts of the Americas, some women did live in all-female communities cut off from the world, but these were religious institutions rather than households, and the women dedicated themselves to the service of specific deities, often symbolically marrying that deity to indicate their special status. Marriage to a deity also provided women in other parts of the world, such as India, with an acceptable alternative to human marriage, and through this or through mystical visions or other types of spiritual experiences, women occasionally gained power not open to them in the secular world. To a large degree, however, the major world religions that won increasing numbers of adherents during this period offered men more opportunities than women, and women often developed their own less formal religious practices, such as special rituals for childbirth and healing or the worship of female saints, which the official churches frowned on but did not prohibit.

Islam

The impact of Islam on gender structures is hotly debated, in large part because that impact has become so pronounced with the rise of Islamic fundamentalism or revival in many parts of the world in the last several decades of the 20th century. Some historians point to the fact that the Qur'an, the most authoritative religious text for Muslims, holds men and women to be fully equal in God's eyes—both genders capable of going to heaven and participating in religious pilgrimage—and argue that restrictions on women under Islam came either from pre-Muslim Arabian practices or from practices already going on in areas that the Muslims conquered. They thus see such matters as the veiling of women as not essential to Islam. More scholars note that the Qur'an does make clear distinctions between men and women in social practices, however—it allows men to have up to four wives and to divorce their wives quite easily, while setting a daughter's share of inheritance as half that of a son's—and that the body of religious law that grew up in the first several centuries of Islam's development gave religious sanction to practices such as seclusion and veiling, for which the references in the Qur'an are ambiguous.

There is no dispute that women played a major role in the early development of Islam. Muhammad's first wife, Khadija, was a merchant and his first convert; he took no other wives until after her death. His youngest wife, Aisha, and daughter Fatimah were important transmitters of Muslim traditions and were clearly not secluded, though it is the statement in the Qur'an ordering seclusion for the Prophet's wives (possibly for their safety, given their prominence) that was later used to justify requiring seclusion for all women. Aisha even led troops into battle from the back of her camel, and early Muslim women prayed and attended religious ceremonies in public.

As Islam expanded, it took over territories where women were already secluded, and the ruling caliphs began to favor this first for their own households and then as an official policy for all women. Seclusion became part of official Muslim law—the *shari'a*—which is regarded as having divine authority, with marriage viewed there as a reciprocal relationship in which the husband provides support in exchange for the wife's obedience. In contrast to Muhammad's first wife, respectable women did not pursue a trade outside the household, though they did invest in real estate—acting through male agents—because Islam protected the rights of women to hold property independently. The seclusion of women was possible in large part because of the expansion of slavery, for slave women—who came from outside Islam and were unveiled—could carry out many of the basic tasks, such as shopping or getting water. Slave women also served as concubines—the Qur'anic limitation of four wives at any one time did not apply to concubines—and their children were regarded as fully legitimate and free. Seclusion of women gradually spread from the cities to the countryside, although it was rarely as pronounced there, both because rural women's labor outside the house was necessary and because most men a woman encountered in a small village were probably her relatives anyway.

The Qur'an recommends marriage for everyone, and women generally married at quite a young age; men often married later, when they had established themselves. This age differential, combined with polygyny, meant that young men, especially those who had left their native villages for the greater opportunities in the cities, frequently had difficulty finding wives; they often formed armed youth gangs and, particularly in the 10th and 11th centuries, terrorized urban residents and attacked the daughters and wives of well-to-do families. The Islamic marital pattern may have contributed to Islam's toleration of homosexual relations between men; though officially forbidden by Muslim law, they were not punished with any great severity, and in the period of the Abbasid caliphate (750–1258), homoerotic literature praising beautiful young men became a popular genre among some urban circles. (We know very little about homosexual relations between women in the Muslim world.) Heterosexual relations outside marriage and concubinage, especially adultery with a married woman, were punished much more seriously.

Because Islam regarded sexuality within marriage or other approved relationships as a positive good, contraception was acceptable and, judging by discussions in medical and legal texts, a fairly common practice; in contrast to Christianity, sexual relations in Islam did not have to be justified by reproduction, though having children, and particularly having sons, was seen as essential to life. A woman often had very close relationships with her sons that continued throughout her life; in some areas, a man acquired a new name once his first son was born, signifying his increased stature.

The Spread of Islam

Though the stereotype of the spread of Islam is one of military conquest, intermarriage played an important role in the growth of the religion. Arab traders often married local women to gain access to economic and political power through kin connections, and then these women served as brokers between two cultures, one imported Islamic and one indigenous. In Asia and Africa, Islamic law and practices mixed with existing traditions, creating a wide diversity in marital practices, religious rituals, and norms of behavior for men and women.

In India, Islamic ideas mixed with those of a reinvigorated Hinduism to encourage increasing restrictions on women. Both religions favored the veiling and seclusion of women—termed *purdah*—although the strictness and exact rules of these practices varied according to social status and location. The spread of Islam encouraged the practices and also a greater division between men's and women's work roles, not only in the Muslim minority but among some Hindus as well. Hindu families often attempted to marry their daughters off at a very young age— by the year 1000, the recommended age was between eight and ten— which increased the likelihood that they would experience a long period of widowhood. Restrictions on widows begun in the classical era grew harsher, and gradually, the practice of *sati*, a widow's self-immolation on her husband's funeral pyre, became a praiseworthy alternative to the dismal life of a widow. The origins of sati—the word means "good wife"— are uncertain and hotly debated, but by the 11th century it was a fairly common practice among upper-caste families, and mounds of stone honoring the women who had provided spiritual benefits for their families in this way came to dot the landscape. Though Muslim rulers opposed sati, they did little to limit it in practice, and not until the 19th century did reformers begin a concerted effort to end it.

In contrast to India, gender structures in Southeast Asia during this period appear to have been much more egalitarian; some historians even view the hundreds of cultures of Southeast Asia as the most advantageous for women in all of the premodern world. Judging both by internal sources and the reports of outsiders, women in Southeast Asia engaged in trade and agriculture, owned and inherited property, acted as negotiators in political

Women in Africa. A bronze statue of a queen or queen mother from medieval Benin in western Africa, one of many portrayals of female rulers in the postclassical world. From Heinrich Lott, *Die Frau im Alten Afrika* (Munich, 1978). Reprinted by permission.

disputes, and played important parts in religious rituals. Though traditions that stressed female subservience were introduced into some parts of Southeast Asia—into Vietnam from China and into Malaysia and Indonesia from India and Islam—local traditions that allowed women a greater role were never completely subsumed.

It is difficult to make any generalizations that apply to all of the vast number of cultures in Africa during this period, but many of them were matrilineal and had systems of marriage that involved a bride-price rather than a dowry. Thus girls were seen as a source of wealth rather than a drain on their families, for the cattle or land their husbands offered in order to marry them would allow their own brothers to marry. Most cultures in Africa accepted polygyny, with families living in house compounds in which each wife had her own house, cattle, fields, and property. The division of labor varied widely, but in most areas women were responsible for growing and processing roots and tubers, which were often the staple crop; even in the larger towns that grew up in East and West Africa in the 12th century, women still tended crops in the gardens surrounding the towns. Because they often owned property and goods independently, women also worked as traders in market towns and sometimes over wider geographic areas.

African kingdoms often had complex systems of rulership, in which women held power directly in an office known as "Mother of the King" (who may or may not have been the actual mother of the king) or as a joint or coruler, with particular duties. Both men and women acted as leaders and priests in indigenous religions, which generally honored male and female gods and spirits through complex rituals designed to assure the health and prosperity of the community. Christianity in Ethiopia and Islam in North and West Africa excluded women from positions of religious leadership, and women may have been slower than men in accepting both of these religions. Arab travelers noted that even Muslim Africans usually ignored veiling and concealing dress. Cultural blending had varied results on gender where Islam was involved.

Europe

In the centuries after the collapse of the Roman Empire in western Europe, people often conceptualized their society as divided into three groups—

those who fight, those who pray, and those who work. Though women did not regularly fight, in most parts of Europe they could inherit feudal estates and take oaths of vassalage and were expected to defend their estates if attacked. In the early Middle Ages (ca. 500–1000), when feudal monarchy was very limited, the wives of rulers were often in charge of the finances of the kingdom in the same way that women were often in charge of the finances of households, as there was no separation between the king's private household affairs and those of the kingdom. As monarchies became more complex in the later Middle Ages, the role of the queen became more ceremonial, though individual queens might still hold a great deal of power.

In contrast to most other parts of the world, upper-class men in Europe were officially monogamous—Christianity espoused monogamy and increasingly even criticized institutionalized concubinage. This did not mean, of course, that there was no sexual double standard or that rulers did not have mistresses, but it did draw a line between legitimate and illegitimate children and make the lines of succession clearer. European territories began to favor *primogeniture*—the automatic handing down of a territory to the eldest son, regardless of competence—and slowly this trickled down to families of lesser social standing, although it was not adopted in all of Europe. Where it was, however, it placed all daughters and younger sons at a disadvantage, for they received a much smaller share of the family holdings, whether these holdings were vast estates or a one-room house.

The segment of society devoted to prayer included both men and women. During the early Middle Ages, Christianity spread slowly throughout Europe, with churches, convents, and monasteries gradually dotting the landscape. Convents offered women physical protection from the violence and instability that often plagued medieval society and also the opportunity for leadership, as the head of a convent was an abbess, usually chosen by the convent residents themselves. A career in the church offered even more opportunities for a man, as positions of leadership such as bishop meant that one was also in charge of a large territory and, as such, could gain both wealth and power. The Christian church came to hold about one-tenth of the land in Europe, and so its officials—all of them male except for abbesses, who generally held fairly small territories—rivaled secular rulers in their prestige and authority. In Western Christianity, clergy were increasingly expected to be celibate—not married—and their holdings could not be passed down to a son as secular holdings could, because priests' children were not regarded as legitimate. In Eastern Christianity, priests were allowed to be married, although nuns, monks, and bishops were not. In both areas, Christianity grew steadily more hostile to homosexuality throughout the period, often identifying it with Islam or with heretical beliefs; secular laws against homosexual activity prescribed increasingly savage penalties, and officials sometimes saw the clergy as particularly prone to the "vice of sodomy."

Christianity was not simply an institution of clergy in Europe but was also the belief system of the vast majority of the population by the 12th century. In the same way that Islam was often shaped by existing cultural patterns, Christianity was as well, so that the worship of various nature deities or holy places was transformed into the veneration of saints, who, along with Jesus' mother, Mary, became important figures of devotion. Most people learned about such holy figures and other elements of Christianity orally or through visual depictions in the churches and cathedrals around them, with female figures playing a more important role in popular understandings of Christianity than in the learned theology taught in the all-male universities.

Individuals who worked far outnumbered those who fought or prayed in European society, which in the early Middle Ages meant primarily working on the land. Christianity discouraged slavery in Europe, and gradually, most slaves became serfs—personally free, though owing labor services that tied them to a piece of land—although this changeover took several hundred years and was never complete; when cities began to grow in the 12th century, young women were often brought in as household slaves from areas outside of Western Christianity. (Like Islam, Christianity preferred slaves who were not believers.) Most parts of Europe depended on grain-based agriculture, with a gender division of labor typical of that in grain-growing societies: Men were responsible for clearing new land, plowing, and the care of large animals; women were responsible for the care of small animals, spinning, and food preparation.

Although we often think of feudal Europe as a time of aristocratic domination, in fact villages in many parts of Europe were quite autonomous, with their own courts and decision-making bodies. In these institutions, only male heads of households could play a decision-making role, although women were generally free to bring a case to court or make a complaint. In contrast to Africa, married women's property was considered part of their husband's holdings, so that in practice only unmarried women or widows actually showed up in court. This group might be a fairly large share of the female population, however, for in contrast to many other parts of the world, women married at an advanced age in parts of Europe—as late as 22 or 23—and a significant share of the population appears not to have married at all. Being a widow did not bring severe restrictions and, in fact, could bring opportunities for independent action unavailable to married women.

Toward the end of the Middle Ages, the European economy grew increasingly specialized by region, with vast grain-growing areas in the east supplying growing cities in Italy and the Low Countries with basic foodstuffs, and with the production of such items as wine and silk developing in certain areas. The merchants who handled this international trade, and who became fabulously wealthy through it, were almost all male, although women occasionally invested in their ventures or sold the products of international trade, such as pepper and oranges, at local markets. Women were often employed in the production of items for trade—whether slaves or serfs in Russia growing grain, girls in Italy unwinding silk cocoons, or village women in Denmark drying fish. In some of these areas they, with the boys and men who worked alongside them, were paid wages for their work; the earliest wage rates extant in Europe, from the 14th and 15th centuries, set women's wages at half to two-thirds those of men.

East Asia

In the T'ang and Song dynasties, the rulers of China put great emphasis on social and political order, viewing order within families as the basis of stability in the state. In a few instances this worked to women's advantage. The only woman to hold the title as well as the office of emperor in China's long history, Empress Wu (ruled 690–705), used Confucian ideas of loyalty owed to one's mother and Buddhist ideas of the godlike ruler—along with her administrative and political skills—to build up her power and stabilize her reign.

The emphasis on authority within the family was detrimental to most women, however, as it was accompanied, particularly in the Neo-Confucian movement of the Song period, with an increased emphasis on male superiority and on the disruptive power of sexuality. Sexual attraction was regarded as so strong that individuals alone could not control it; walls, laws, and strong social sanctions were needed to keep men and women apart. Women of the middle and upper classes were increasingly secluded in many parts of China, and even peasant houses were walled; boys and girls were cheap to hire as servants for tasks that needed to be done outside the walls. Widows from the upper classes were forbidden to remarry, and those from lower classes could receive government rewards if they did not.

Female seclusion was also accomplished through foot binding, a practice that began in the Song period among elite women and gradually was adopted by the vast majority of the female population in central and northern China. Foot binding began when a girl was about six; the toes of her foot were bent under the ball and wrapped tightly with long bandages so that their growth was stunted. Gradually her foot assumed a pointed shape that erotic literature described as a lotus blossom, and the intense pain of the earliest years lessened somewhat, though the bandages were required for the rest of her life to maintain the foot in its small size. Foot binding did not totally immobilize women, for peasant women worked in the fields and in cloth production with bound feet, but it prevented them from traveling great distances. Bound feet became a requirement for marriage, so that mothers bound the feet of their daughters in the hopes that they might make a better match; they continued to do so until the 20th century, even when the practice was officially forbidden.

Foot binding was not accepted by other East Asian societies, such as Korea and Vietnam, though they did adopt Confucian notions from China that restricted women's capacities to perform ceremonies of ancestor worship and inherit family land. Women's rights to land also decreased in Japan, but this was largely the result of the growing importance of the military under the shogunate, as land was increasingly given only to those who fought.

In the earlier part of the postclassical period, Japan stood in sharp contrast to China as a society in which women played a significant public role. The Japanese emperors trace their family ancestry to a female deity, the sun goddess Amaterasu, and half of the rulers of Japan during the period 592–770 were empresses who ruled in their own right, not simply as regents. Women were religious leaders in traditional Japanese religion (which later came to be called *Shinto*), though this also included negative ideas about women as a source of pollution through menstruation and childbirth. In the Heian period (9th–12th centuries), while Japanese men were imitating Chinese classics, women such as Murasaki Shikibu and Sei Shonagon were creating the masterpieces of Japanese literature; in no other of the world's cultures did a work by a woman reach the stature of *The Tale of Genji*, Murasaki Shikibu's main work. Daughters were more valuable than sons among upper-class families because of complex patterns of marital politics, and husbands often went to live with their wives upon marriage, instead of the more common virilocal (male-centered) pattern. Both matrilineal and patrilineal family ties were viewed as important. Many of the ideas about sexuality found in other of the world's postclassical cultures were simply absent from Japan: Virginity in brides was not discussed, nor was homosexuality stigmatized, and marriage was not regulated by either church or state.

By the 13th century, the military was becoming increasingly important, and Confucian ideals of discipline and self-control were expected of the *samurai*, the warrior class. Like the wives of nobles in Europe, samurai wives managed the estates of their husbands when they were away and were expected to defend them if necessary; long, curved spears were viewed as the best weapons for women, and suicide was the ultimate honorable choice if surrender was imminent. Less-exalted women worked in all aspects of agricultural production and in certain areas became famous as divers for seaweed and other ocean products, living in matrilocal communities that continue to today. (Similar communities of women divers have existed for centuries on Cheju Island in Korea.)

The Americas

Although there were groups with settled agriculture and fairly dense populations in many parts of the Americas during the postclassical period, most of these did not have a writing system, and so it is difficult to gain a clear idea of their gender structures. For example, we know groups in the

Americas developed hybrids of corn and other crops, but we do not know whether this was men's or women's work. Much of what we know comes from a slightly later period, after contact with Europeans, and this contact may very well have altered earlier structures. The American civilizations about which we know the most, such as the Aztecs and the Incas, were also undergoing great changes in their gender structures in the centuries immediately preceding the European explorations, because of changes in their political and economic systems. Thus the gender structures described by the earliest European colonizers and missionaries may actually have been quite new, rather than representing "traditional" values or patterns of behavior.

This is clearly the case in Mexico. The Maya, who developed a complex civilization in the Yucatán during the 3rd to the 9th century, traced the ancestry of rulers through both the male and the female line. As in many African societies, women were prominent as the wives and mothers of rulers but also occasionally as rulers and priests in their own right; they were buried with a large number of grave goods, and their names, such as that of Lady Ahpa-Hel of Palenque, were sometimes recorded. Judging by artistic evidence, women planted root crops and engaged in weaving and food preparation while men cleared land.

The Aztecs, who took over central Mexico in the 14th century, appear also to have been relatively egalitarian originally, but this changed with greater emphasis on military conquest as the Aztec Empire expanded. Political power was increasingly concentrated in a ruling class of priests and warriors, all male, with upper-class women's role defined largely in terms of their reproductive capacity. Women who died in childbirth were to be honored like warriors, but while they were alive, they were to stay inside, weave, and bear children, although their seclusion was never as complete as that of upper-class women in the Islamic world. Upper-class boys and girls both had the opportunity for formal schooling; for boys this stressed military and governmental skills, and for girls, weaving. Aztec leaders frequently married the daughters of rulers in the tribes they had conquered, using marital politics as a means of cementing political alliances and conquests in the same way that European nobles did. For commoners, the most significant effect of Aztec conquest was an increase in tribute demands, with women paying their share of the tribute in cloth and prepared food such as dried fish or tamales, while men paid theirs in corn. (Tamales were, in fact, seen as ritual equivalents of the human sacrifices that the Aztec rulers also demanded; the pot in which they were steamed was seen as a symbolic womb, and they were generally eaten only on special occasions.) Both women and men sold themselves or were sold into slavery, and women slaves, generally those taken from conquered groups, were used as prostitutes in state-run brothels for soldiers.

In the Andean region, pictorial evidence from Mochica and other cultures of the first millennium C.E. shows women preparing food, weaving, bearing, nursing, and carrying children, while men are shown in battle and carrying out government activities. Both sexes are shown as religious leaders, though only men appear in certain rituals. Before the Inca conquest of the 15th century, people lived in autonomous kin communities, with lines of descent reckoned through both sexes; girls inherited access to resources such as land, water, and herds through their mothers, boys through their fathers. Religious beliefs reinforced this reciprocity with male sky deities and female earth deities, all with their own festivals and religious hierarchies. Women were seen as especially linked to earth deities, such as the Mother of Corn, which is why they put seeds in the ground while men dug holes with digging sticks.

Inca conquest did not dramatically upset these communities initially, but gradually, the Inca emphasis on combat gave men added prestige and offered them opportunities in the Inca army and bureaucracy that were not open to women. Both to symbolize and to reinforce their conquest, the Inca took women from conquered tribes, sometimes making them the wives of important Inca nobles, as the Aztecs did, but sometimes also marrying them to the Sun, who was the most important god for the Inca. These women married to the Sun were termed *acclas*, and they lived in special houses where their virginity was guarded, emerging to participate in rituals symbolizing the conquest of other Andean peoples by the people of the Sun, the Inca. The Inca also worshiped the Moon in a religious hierarchy headed by the queen (the *coya*), who was usually a relative as well as the wife of the chief Inca, but there was no group of young men corresponding to the *acclas*, and the *coya* and other noblewomen never received young men as rewards of conquest in the way that the chief Inca and other men received young women. One month of the year was especially dedicated to ceremonies honoring the Moon, but during the other eleven the Sun and the male priests and officials who directed his worship were paramount. Because both the Aztecs and the Incas needed soldiers for their conquests, great emphasis was placed on reproduction, with adults in essence required to marry and with strict laws against abortion, homosexuality, and adultery; how much these were actually enforced is difficult to say, however.

Conclusion

The postclassical period framed a number of specific developments in gender relations, for the most part leading to greater segregation and, often, measurably harsher treatment of women. Most societies witnessed increased inequality and new practices that stressed women's dependence on men. Prior traditions and their spread to new areas, as well as the rise of states that restricted women's informal power, were involved in these trends.

This pattern occurred despite the spread of religions which urged that women had spiritual qualities along with men, and in some cases it may have arisen in reaction against these cultural forces. No huge changes occurred, globally, to unseat dominant patterns of patriarchy. But there was great variety from one society to the next, while certain of the new contacts among societies (notably, the spread of Islam and the Chinese influence on Japan) were powerful enough to alter gender assumptions, usually, again, toward greater inequality.

CHAPTER 13

LABOR SYSTEMS AND LEISURE IN THE POSTCLASSICAL PERIOD

Few large-scale changes in work patterns occurred in the postclassical world. The main story is one of continuity from the classical period. Slavery continued to play a large role in parts of the Mediterranean, with some modifications. While large-scale agricultural slavery diminished from Roman levels, in the new Islamic world domestic slavery persisted, with the addition of a largely new category, military slavery. The poverty of western Europe largely eliminated slavery there, which was replaced by the institution of serfdom. Chinese and Indian civilizations maintained patterns set in the classical period, with intensive agriculture and the caste system, respectively, characterizing each civilization's labor system; though we have seen that labor-intensive agriculture accelerated in China. In the new American civilization centers, work patterns in most cases did not change substantially; rather, the new Amerindian civilizations built and systematized labor systems elaborated in earlier periods.

The breakup of the Mediterranean world into three separate civilizations—western Europe, eastern Europe, and the Middle East—brought about a diversity even greater than in the classical period, with marked differences among the civilizations that rose from the ashes of the Roman Empire. Certain common characteristics, such as a tendency toward manorial relations, emerged before the first millennium c.e. In the case of the Byzantine Empire, slavery and commercial agriculture persisted initially as hallmarks of the labor system. The restriction of the empire to the eastern portion of the Mediterranean, however, and the inclusion of Anatolia (present-day Turkey), with its large independent peasantry, into the core of the empire propelled a greater proportion of peasants into the mix than had been present in classical times. Slavery persisted in the coastal areas and islands of the Aegean Sea and in the olive- and wine-growing regions, as well as in urban centers and the mines. As elsewhere, slavery continued only in areas that were prosperous, for slaves cost considerable amounts of money; owners could justify the purchase of slaves only in areas where it was possible to make profits through commercially grown crops or where members of the elites kept large households to maintain their prestige. Here the continuities from the classical period, at least initially, were most obvious, as they were in the Byzantine forms of government and culture.

Slaves, Soldiers, and Peasants in Islamic Civilization

Islamic civilization was a close second in preserving classical Mediterranean patterns, and this showed in its mix of labor forms, with a large segment of the working population toiling as slaves. Along with continuities from the classical period, however, Islamic law and Arab custom modified work patterns significantly, adding new elements to the mix. Islam improved the position of the Arab slave by changing him or her from mere chattel to a human being with a set religious and social status in Muslim society. Under Islamic law slavery was permitted, but only nonbelievers could be enslaved; yet while Muslims were not to be enslaved, slaves who converted to Islam or those Muslims who were born to slavery were not automatically set free. Muslims were not permitted to sell themselves into slavery, nor to sell their children. Finally, under Islam, agricultural slaves, who usually lived under the worst conditions, were much rarer than in classical times. True, the imported African slaves in the salt mines of the Sahara desert rarely survived five years, and the Zanj slaves who drained the salt marshes of Basra in southern Iraq lived in horrendous conditions. Slaves were most common in Islamic society, however, in the domestic, commercial, and military spheres, where a close proximity to their masters and daily personal interactions made life somewhat more bearable. Thus the lot of slaves improved under Islam, compared to Roman times.

Though slaves converted to Islam were not automatically freed, high rates of manumission made it impossible for the slave population to reproduce itself. This was a logical development, given the incentives that Islam provided for manumitting of slaves—manumission was considered a good deed for a Muslim—and the close relations between masters and slaves that naturally occurred in intimate setting of the household. Moreover, unlike among Jews or Christians, sex between masters and slave women was permitted, and many masters freed the children born of their union. This meant that to keep numbers up, the slave population increasingly had to be purchased from elsewhere. Two groups in particular were common as slaves in Middle Eastern society, both from the fringe areas of the Islamic world: Slavs and sub-Saharan Africans. In addition, Turkish and Caucasian slaves existed in significant numbers in certain regions.

A novel development in Islamic society late in the postclassical period was the extensive use of military slaves. This system, initiated with Turkish slave-soldiers in the early 8th century, reached its full flowering in the declining years of the Abbasid dynasty, from 950 onward. In the fiercely competitive world of Islamic politics, where assassinations and coups were frequent occurrences, controlling a group of loyal military specialists was an extremely valuable asset for any ruler. During this period, nomadic elites and slave-soldiers formed alliances to dominate the regional kingdoms that asserted themselves throughout the area. In the eastern part of the Middle East, Turkish boys purchased at a tender age and trained in martial skills and Islamic doctrine constituted the bulk of elite military specialists. Some slave-soldiers even were permitted to remain Christian in the Turkish kingdoms. In Egypt, the Mamluks (originally meaning "white," from their Slavic origins, but later referring simply to the military slave caste) ruled the country for two and a half centuries before their conquest by the Ottomans in the early 16th century.

Feudalism and Manorialism in Circum-Mediterranean Civilizations and Japan

Feudalism and serfdom emerged early in the postclassical period in the western part of the Roman Empire; serfdom, indeed, began before the Roman Empire fell. Barbarian invasions beginning in the 3rd century meant a rapid decline in state control and public order. As the Germanic tribes continued to pour across the border, government control virtually broke down. In this chaos, free peasants felt obligated to find a defender and often exchanged servile status for military protection from strongmen who had the resources to hire armed retainers and create private armies. In many cases, these were the men who had obtained the *latifundia*, or landed estates, from the Roman government. The peasants who exchanged their labor for defense—serfs—clustered around the manors in which their lords lived and were obligated to provide labor for cultivating their lords' land, the surplus of their own production, or both. Virtually all other sources of income vanished in what for western Europe are known as the Dark Ages, since trade and manufacturing drastically declined. In contrast to the Middle East, where, under Islamic rule, urban centers grew and prospered, cities declined in population and became small fortified settlements that often did not survive barbarian attacks.

Even as the cities shrank, agriculture in the northern reaches of western Europe increased in production with the advent of the moldboard plow. Probably adopted from Slavic peoples to the east, this plow made its appearance in the 6th century and was commonly in use by the 9th century. The moldboard plow not only transformed northern European agriculture and population levels, it also brought about social reorganization, since it required the use of eight oxen, an expensive proposition for peasants of the medieval northern Europe. Peasants had to share their resources in ways not necessary in the south, where the lighter scratch plow needed only one animal to drag it. The exploitation of the land in the north reflected this new social organization, as the peasants combined their fields into large, open swaths and farmed separate strips within the large communal fields. Communal labor became more important, and peasant councils on the manors provided for a limited amount of self-government.

The 12th century saw the culmination of western European civilization in its medieval form, as improved agriculture brought about rising population levels and increasing trade. Trade, in turn, stimulated the growth of cities and fairs. Merchants established guilds, organizations that represented the interests of traders and fought for rights and privileges for commerce. Great feudal lords saw the development of urban economies as a good thing, for in this way they did not have to depend exclusively on the resources of their vassals for income. As a result, many lords provided the merchants with certain privileges and exemptions from duties. Included was the right of a serf to become a free man or woman after remaining in towns for a year and a day. Feudal lords also permitted some of the younger sons of peasants to leave for the city, as manors became overpopulated. Thus rural-to-urban migration emerged, along with a slight but significant growth in an urban labor force that relied largely on wage labor, rather than on manorial obligations. In terms of work patterns, the most distinctive result emerged in urban manufacturing. Here, craft guilds regulated conditions of training (apprenticeships) with rules that assured proper skill levels and the quality of goods produced; artisan masters were prevented from accumulating undue wealth, for the guild ethic was hostile to untrammeled competition or inequality. Guilds also opposed rapid changes in techniques, preferring stability. Even as these distinctive urban work systems developed, it must be kept in mind that the overwhelming majority of workers in late medieval western Europe still lived in the countryside.

The prosperity of the High Middle Ages broke down in the 14th century. However transitory, the results of the Black Death, reducing population between 25 percent and 33 percent in western Europe, created havoc on the regional economy. Initially, the labor shortage brought about higher wages, but in response, some states began to set maximum-wage laws. Manorial lords attempted to maintain customary manorial obligations, while peasants agitated to have them commuted to cash payments in a rising wage economy. In the context of recurring epidemics, the peasantry began to revolt, bringing about large-scale rural uprisings against manorial obligations. The Peasants' Revolt of 1381 in England, the chronic rural disturbances in France called the Jacquerie, and the Ciompi insurrections in 14th-century Florence are examples of these violent conflicts. The aristocracy brutally suppressed these revolts with their far superior weaponry, but it is clear from the disturbances that peasant life had taken a turn for the worse in the late postclassical period.

The decline in serfdom was permanent, however. The scarcity of labor in the aftermath of the bubonic plague (the disease returned various times in subsequent centuries but killed off many fewer people) made it difficult for the aristocracy to retain the manorial system. The insistence on custom often favored the peasants, as in the 12th and 13th centuries, when they insisted on commuting their obligations into money payment, based on customary prices for goods and services. Moreover, peasants had other opportunities, such as moving to the cities and escaping the grasp of manorial lords completely. The lords of the manor could do little about the increasing autonomy of the cities. The new national monarchies that arose during the later postclassical period usually favored the urban merchants in disputes with the landed elites, for the merchants served as a counterbalance to the power of the mighty aristocracy, as well as an increasingly important source of taxes and loans.

In the postclassical period, serfdom and feudalism also developed in areas far from European civilization, for instance, in Japan. The organization of labor there was different from that in the wheat-growing Mediterranean region, for Japanese villages relied on irrigated rice cultivation. Not only did rice support a denser population than existed in regions that relied on wheat, but in Japan, the communal practices needed for effective irrigation and the sharing of water resources fostered a much greater sense of cohesion and community than in Europe or the Middle East. Although the Japanese initially tried to imitate the Chinese system of centralized government (which would not have permitted feudalism or serfdom to emerge), a series of weak emperors allowed a full-blown manorial system to evolve, with the peasants enserfed by the local samurai.

The State and Labor in Prosperous China

The spread of civilization to Japan had been occasioned by the brilliance of the T'ang dynasty in China (618–907), from which the Japanese borrowed many concepts. Unlike many other agricultural societies, China did not fall into a manorial system. During the early T'ang dynasty, the government imposed a system in which peasants were given equal allotments in fields, an organization that the imperial bureaucracy enforced through the registering every three years of all households throughout the realm. The T'ang dynasty thus continued the Han dynasty's control over the countryside, reinforcing an independent peasantry as the ideal for a prosperous country. Only as the T'ang dynasty declined did manorial systems begin to crop up. With the advent of the Song dynasty (960–1279), however, the state again redistributed the manorial holdings to the peasants, who once again became independent smallholders.

Chinese patterns in the countryside were also different in part because the T'ang and Song dynasties experienced considerable technological improvement and enhanced economic dynamism over earlier periods in Chinese history. Indeed, the postclassical period was one of the high points of Chinese civilization. Though the Islamic Middle East rivaled China in its commerce (and indeed, during the Song period, Muslim traders dominated commerce in coastal China), the reliance on slaves and on manorial relations in much of the Middle East meant that landlords had few incentives to improve agricultural machinery. The Middle Eastern solution to increase productivity was to add more low-paid workers rather than to make work more efficient. In China, however, terracing and the draining of marshes added significant new land, while the development of rice seeds that ripened earlier and were drought resistant increased yields in the 11th century by permitting up to three crops a year on certain plots. As the Chinese state spread southward, the emphasis on rice cultivation, the most productive Old World crop, furthered prosperity. New farming implements designed for rice cultivation, including the wheelbarrow, as well as the use of night soil (human feces) from the cities as fertilizer, composting, and other practices made Chinese agriculture even more productive. The highly labor-intensive agricultural system already in place in Han times reached its climax during the postclassical period. Most important, during the T'ang and Song periods, peasants increasingly specialized in the crops that would grow best in their region, rather than producing everything they needed for a year's consumption. For example, the hilly regions of South China generated different varieties of tea, which the peasants sold in return for rice. Specialization thus brought about greater trade, for peasants had to acquire elsewhere the foodstuffs they did not grow themselves. Trade increased also because of the state's construction of the sophisticated system of canals that tied together the great Chinese river systems in the most densely populated portions of the country.

In agricultural civilizations, trade was the most important stimulus for the growth of cities. Only trade could generate sufficient surplus to create complex urban societies that did not rely solely on goods produced in the areas surrounding the cities. A distant second in promoting the growth of cities was the presence of strong government, for effective rulers could concentrate in urban settlements the wealth they siphoned off from the countryside in the form of taxes. Western Europe in the late postclassical centuries experienced city growth through the quickening of commerce, as the Islamic Middle East had done earlier on an even larger scale, but China during the Song dynasty, because of the combination of vibrant trade and a strong government, created an urban culture previously unseen in world history. This was especially the case in the coastal cities, where maritime trade also expanded rapidly. The settlement of Arab traders along the coast, in combination with Chinese technological advancements in oceangoing vessels, created dynamic commercial centers and ports. While foreigners played a substantial merchant role, given the cultural disdain for trade, in the interior the Chinese themselves acted as merchants, some becoming very wealthy. Even many bureaucrats in the Song period became involved in trade, but since officials were still not permitted to engage in merchant activities, they put relatives or even servants in nominal charge of their enterprises.

By the Song period, considerable manufacturing took place as well in the urban centers. While most private workshops were small, employing no more than a few individuals, state-run enterprises could be relatively large. In Kaifeng, the capital of the northern Song, the government employed more than 2,000 workers on 400 weaving machines to make high-quality textiles for the imperial court. The state established shipyards where up to 3,000 ships could be built. In what is now Kiangsi Province, the Song government employed more than 100,000 miners to extract copper from its mines. Arsenals scattered throughout China occupied almost 10,000 workers to produce materials used by soldiers, such as saddles and stoves as well as weapons of all kinds.

The state dominated virtually all manufacturing. This meant that, in contrast to medieval western Europe, guilds did not form, because the state did not permit them. The state conscripted artisans into its labor force, harshly punishing those who tried to escape their duties or did not perform as expected. Manufacturing in China was probably the most advanced in the world at the time, but it rested on a strong state and the oppression of the artisan class. As a result, when the T'ang and Song dynasties fell in political power, the urban economy declined. The effort to organize large masses of workers, successful at the time, did not leave an enduring heritage. Chinese urban manufacturing would revive later, but on somewhat different bases.

The Development of Complex Labor Systems
in the Americas

As in China and the Middle East, the postclassical period was one of great flowering of complex societies in the Americas. Some of the most elaborate and, certainly, the most extensive civilizations developed in Meso-America (central Mexico south to the Panamanian isthmus) and in the Andean region. Labor systems in the civilized portions of the Americas evolved over hundreds and often thousands of years, prior to the European invasions of the 16th century. (See chapter 7.) Work patterns in civilized America revolved around two plants: maize (corn) and the potato. The former, a Meso-American specialty, spread to the Andes as well. Corn is an astonishing plant, one that can produce many more calories than Old World plants in a relatively short growing season and with relatively little work. A family of three in Meso-America could produce twice as much as they needed to live on in 120 days of work, something not equaled even in the intensive agricultural rice system of China. Potatoes also were important, for these Andean plants produced far more calories even on marginal lands than an equivalent field of wheat, the staple crop of the Mediterranean world. Reliance on these highly nutritious foods made possible very high population densities in central Mexico and the development of civilization in regions, such as jungles and high mountain ranges, that were not conducive to the production of large surpluses in Eurasia. By themselves, the American crops should have reduced the onerousness of rural work.

In this context, several features of the labor systems of high civilization in both Meso-America and the Andes differentiated work in the Americas from labor in all the other civilizations during the postclassical period. Most notable was the blend of sophisticated methods of agriculture with relatively unsophisticated technology. Metallurgy existed in the Americas but was used only for making ornaments. The indigenous peoples had no plow and did not use wheels, other than for children's toys. Furthermore the Amerindian civilizations used little animal power for their agricultural tasks. Only the Andean peoples had the llama, a camel-like mammal of the high mountains, which they used to carry loads of no more than 100 pounds' weight. The American societies had no chickens, donkeys, or cattle, as in Eurasia or Africa; instead, they had dogs, turkeys, and guinea pigs.

Instead of a plow they used digging sticks. Even so, they created complex cultures and an agricultural surplus that brought about—at least in central Mexico—high population growth. Some scholars have estimated that the area of central Mexico, which the Aztecs dominated, had a higher population density than even China at the same time. Indeed, it is likely that the population of central Mexico (the region surrounding Mexico City) regained the number of people it contained at the end of the postclassical period only in the 20th century.

Corvée labor was essential to the building of civilization in the Americas. In this sense, labor systems in the Americas resembled those of river-valley civilizations rather than contemporary societies in Afro-Eurasia. Only China still relied heavily on corvée labor in the postclassical period, though not to the same extent as the American civilizations. Merchants played an important role in Maya and Aztec societies in Meso-America, whereas in the Andes there were virtually no merchants and few markets in Inca territory. Andean civilization emphasized as an ideal self-sufficiency in virtually all foodstuffs on the household level. Since Inca territory was located in the tropical and subtropical mountains, it was possible for the inhabitants to cultivate most plants of all different ecological levels within short distances from one another on the steep slopes. By the 15th century, both Inca and Aztec societies had developed bondsmen who were attached to the aristocracy and served them exclusively, often in skilled tasks. In neither case could these people be bought and sold as slaves, living otherwise ordinary lives with their families. This was a relatively late development, however, one that was truncated with the Spanish conquest.

The Maya had the most egalitarian labor system of the American civilizations. The topography of the Maya area and the lower density of population than in central Mexico made it possible for the commoners to insist on more egalitarian treatment. If the Maya peasants did not like their conditions, they could simply disappear into the jungle to form a new community. Thus, Maya leaders had to be cautious in their treatment of commoners. It is possible that the decline of Maya civilization in the lowland jungles of Central America between 750 and 900 C.E., and the transfer of civilization to the north in the Yucatán Peninsula, was related to a refusal of the peasants to accede to the demands of their nobility.

Work in the Americas. Andean men and women engaged in joint labor sowing seed, from a book by Guaman Poma, an author of Andean origin, published in 1613. Reprinted by permission of Siglo Veintiuno Editores, Mexico City, Mexico.

Not all American civilizations relied exclusively on labor exactions. By the late 15th century, in the regions under Aztec control, the conquered peoples paid a larger amount of their surplus to their overlords in tribute than through corvée labor. Through tribute in foodstuffs, for example, the Aztecs were able to sustain the large population of their capital, Tenochtitlán, as harvests from the hinterlands surrounding the lake in which the city was located became insufficient. Among the Aztecs, a new category of tribute, that of sacrificial victim for the increasingly bloodthirsty gods, became increasingly important. While this in some cases led to the murder of thousands of men (and some women and children), this made little difference in the labor pool, due to the very high population density of the region.

The Incas, while not fixated on the blood of freshly killed sacrificial victims, were also authoritarian. They expanded the long-standing custom of Andean ethnic groups to send out agricultural colonies to different parts of the region, often located many days' or even weeks' distance away. Many large Andean ethnic groups did this to take advantage of the different ecological niches in the mountains and valleys, but the Incas refined this technique for their own advantage. They sent members of some of the most warlike groups in the empire to frontier regions to defend their empire from incursions by hunting-and-gathering peoples. Resettled peasants also were obliged to produce corn and potatoes for the Inca state, to be redistributed to granaries throughout the empire. These were relatively new developments in the late 15th century. According to Garcilaso de la Vega, the son of a Spaniard and an Inca princess, when the Inca armies conquered a region, they divided the land up into three parts: one for the Inca state, one for the Sun cult, and one for the community. The subjects were then obliged to work on Inca and the Sun's land, called the *mita,* as their contribution to the Inca state. While somewhat idealized, this account shows the overwhelming importance of labor in tribute assessment. The local headmen also received the peasants' surplus through labor exactions—used for cultivating their own fields—rather than through taxes in goods. This system kept the peasant communities essentially intact.

Many scholars in the 19th and early 20th centuries believed that the Incas had created a perfect state in which benevolent administrators took care of the grateful population. A French Socialist, Louis Baudin, asserted that the Incas had created the first perfect communist state. Later research has shown that this was not the case. For one, the Incas transferred populations by force from one region to another. The Incas also had subservient populations, at times similar to slaves, called *yanacona,* who were forced to work at the tasks their masters decided. In some cases, these *yanacona* were highly skilled laborers, such as silversmiths, but in many instances they constituted the agricultural workers who cultivated the aristocracy's fields. In any case, workers did not just labor according to their needs, but had to provide for their overlords. Inca society was very hierarchical and in no way a workers' paradise.

Leisure Patterns

During the postclassical period, there were few innovations in leisure activities. This is not surprising, given the strong patterns set during the classical period and the persistence of agricultural civilization. Indeed, in some places the sophistication of leisure activities decreased somewhat, as was the case in western Europe. Public professional entertainment diminished in the circum-Mediterranean civilizations. The emphasis on sensual restraint in both Christianity and Islam and the prohibition of the consumption of alcoholic beverages in the latter initially stifled some leisure activities. This did not necessarily imply major change, for as we have seen, most festivities were closely tied to religious holidays.

In the case of the Middle East, music and poetry flourished in ways they had not before. Perhaps the most characteristic element of postclassical leisure activities in Europe and Asia was the wandering minstrel or the small professional theater group. Known as *Minnesänger* in medieval Germany and troubadours in France and England, Middle Eastern, Indian, and Chinese societies all had similar men and women who traveled through the countryside, performing at markets and fairs and, if they were fortunate, at the local aristocrat's household. Since literacy remained a rare phenomenon in the postclassical period, these singers and actors played an important role in disseminating news, gossip, humorous stories, and the great myths of each civilization. In western Europe the *Song of Roland, El Cid,* and *Tristan and Isolde* provided stories of adventures or unrequited love that fired the imagination and livened up an ordinary peasant's life. In the Middle East, the great story cycle of the *Thousand and One Nights* was recounted everywhere, from villages to the marketplaces of the great city. In India, actors performed portions of the great religious plays of the *Bhagavad Gita* and other Hindu sources.

With the continued development of urban centers, especially in the Middle East and China, new, more individual forms of entertainment took hold among the elites. Writing and listening to poetry, often in highly complex forms, became popular. Although some of these poems were for popular consumption, the creation of often abstract and metaphorical styles meant that, as never before, these types of entertainment were to be the province of the highly educated elites. In the Aztec world, poetry often reflecting deeply pessimistic themes, such as death, also became popular among the elites.

In China, the addition of Buddhism to the major religions in the T'ang dynasty enriched the festivals celebrated, especially with the establishment of the All Soul's Festival, where the Chinese traditional veneration of their ancestors blended well with the Buddhist honoring of the dead. The emphasis on state-directed festivals in China continued from Han times and gave the Chinese festival season a more secular cast than in other civilizations. These celebrations must have been impressive, on one occasion leading to the parading of 200,000 guards and soldiers. Since at least classical times, these festivals were designed to create a higher loyalty to the reigning Chinese dynasty and to display vividly the power and legitimacy of the government.

Community festivals remained the most important forms of leisure during the postclassical period, however, and they enlivened many special days during various parts of the year. Closely tied to religious holidays, which were, in turn, frequently associated with important points in the agricultural cycle, these festivals demonstrate the overwhelming importance of peasant life and civilization's dependence on agriculture. The whole community would turn out for these festivals, which offered social companionship and fostered the cohesion of the village. In Eurasia, the spread of world religions also meant a mingling of new religious dates with older festivals, as occurred in western Europe with the blending of the winter solstice celebration and Christmas. This holiday entailed communal feasts and gift giving, involving much of the village population.

Reliance on community festivals marked the Americas as well. State labor exactions were joined with community festivals to make work more palatable. In the Andes, the whole community turned out to work the fields of the Inca. After the day's work, the headmen gave a feast for the village, providing music and dancing and thus turning this obligation into a festive occasion. Also in the Andes, many of the festivals entailed ritual drunkenness. Peasants drank large quantities of *chicha*, corn beer made by fermenting corn with human saliva, for these feasts. Andean peoples perceived drunkenness as a kind of sacred state that freed the mind to act and say things in different ways and helped cement social relations within the community. On other days, people did not imbibe many alcoholic beverages, though the highly nutritious *chicha* was a staple of the daily Andean diet. For their part, the Aztecs severely limited alcoholic beverages, making them available only to old men and women. High officials could be punished by death if found intoxicated in public. The Aztec prohibition of alcohol was similar to Islamic custom, save for the exception for the elderly.

The Americas exhibited other distinctive patterns in leisure forms. Throughout Meso-America, the indigenous peoples played a ball game in which noble players (commoners were not permitted to play) attempted to hit a rubber ball through a stone ring mounted on the side of the ball court. Players wore pads on much of their body, to avoid scraping their skin and to hit the ball correctly, for the hands could not touch it in play. In few games did players score, and indeed, if someone got the ball through the ring, then all the audience's jewelry and other valuables were forfeit to the winning player. When this occurred, the stands often emptied in a mad rush to avoid paying the reward. The common folk in Meso-America played a kind of dice, on which they gambled, at times excessively.

The persistence of basic leisure patterns was the dominant theme of the postclassical period, as even religious occasions were blended with older feasts and dances. Repetition and community solidarity were key leisure goals. With the decline of Greco-Roman civilization large sporting events faded, as no new civilization built the kinds of stadiums characteristic of the classical Mediterranean. Sports activities, however, as well as drama, continued in the postclassical world in a more modest form. European artisans and peasants played rough ball games (the precursors of football), often as part of festival competitions. Urban and aristocratic society even supported professional entertainers, though mostly among the transient groups, who gained little prestige. Rural leisure, in contrast, continued to generate local entertainment, often crude but deeply popular.

EPILOGUE

The postclassical period is one of the most significant and interesting periods in world history. Four developments had lasting influence. First, the spread of world religions and the creation of a new religious map set a cultural framework that still affects the operations of most societies today. Second, the creation of new links among societies—the world network—also created a durable framework. Even though international contacts operate differently today, they build on the exchanges, including the appetite for products, ideas, and technologies from other areas, that were set up by the year 1000. Third, the redefinition of key civilization areas—the separation between the Middle East/North Africa and southern Europe, for example—and the spread of civilization as a form of human organization—in Africa and in northern Europe, for example—again had long-lasting consequences.

Finally, we have also seen that the postclassical era harbored massive population movements and agricultural shifts. Spurred initially by the devastating plagues that helped set migration in motion, biological change was also promoted by new technologies, such as the moldboard plow in China and Europe, and by massive exchanges of crops in Afro-Eurasia. Areas particularly marked by disease, migration and new food production changed more rapidly than apparently more demographically stable areas, such as India.

Yet, for all these important developments, certain patterns of daily life retained remarkable consistency. This was not, for instance, a decisive era in the history of gender. Important shifts did occur, often making women's lives more difficult, as with Chinese foot binding. The spread of world religions had some impact, as Buddhism and Christianity provided new opportunities for religious vocations for women, apart from marriage. But there were few fundamental redefinitions.

Changes in work were more significant, amid great regional diversity. The development of more intensive agriculture in Central America and Africa, the rise of new agricultural techniques and guild manufacturing in Europe, and, above all, the new labor-intensive farming pattern in China deeply altered the lives of those involved. Even so, with the partial exception of China, there was no revolution in work regime. Continuities from the past, including peasant traditions and, in some places, slavery, remained strong. Leisure, furthermore, retained familiar contours, altered mainly by new religious additions to the calendar and rituals of certain festivals.

Several factors explain why patterns of life for ordinary people retained much of the shape already established in agricultural societies. Many of the key framework shifts in the period did not yet have decisive impact on the structures of daily life. Contacts among civilizations in the world network did not usually affect ordinary people too deeply, except through the spread of new crops; contacts would have more, sweeping effects when the network intensified, but this occurred after the postclassical period had ended. Most trade, for example, involved luxury crops that did not reach ordinary people or even affect their systems of work. Technology contacts were limited except for the new plows, though by the end of the period, Europe's borrowing of Chinese explosive powder began to alter the nature of war in ways that affected basic social structure and experience. The spread of the world religions counted for more, as hundreds of thousands of people changed their beliefs to embrace Buddhism, Islam, or Christianity. But for many, new beliefs were blended with old, so that ideas about work or gender or leisure were not completely transformed. Often religions had more impact in these areas later, when there was further assimilation of the new ideas. It takes time to alter basic human structures, and the forces set in motion in this period sometimes had more impact subsequently.

Furthermore, the absence of huge, systematic changes in politics and technology limited the forces impinging on ordinary people. Neither work nor gender was deeply affected by new methods of production, except in particular regions.

Yet the spread of agriculture (as in western Europe and Africa) and the immigration of people into agricultural areas (as with previously nomadic Arabs and Turks in the Middle East) did mean the exposure of hundreds of thousands of people to work and gender standards with which they had previously been unfamiliar. Turks adopting Middle Eastern ideas about women or Scandinavians setting down to agriculture were experiencing massive change. Their work and gender demands were not revolutionary in world history overall—the changes, again, were incremental—but they were new to the people involved, as agricultural systems became more widespread than even before. Here was one of the era's major legacies to ordinary life.

Finally, the development of new civilization areas created or highlighted considerable diversities, which usually overrode any overarching patterns of change in the structures of ordinary life. Many of the changes that did occur, in the treatment of women, for example, have to be discussed in the context of a particular society—such as the Middle East or China—rather than across the board. To be sure, Islamic influence on sub-Saharan Africa and India or Chinese influence on Japan spread certain developments to larger regions. But we have seen that even Muslim Africans (except in North Africa) did not closely imitate Middle Eastern patterns for women (demonstrated, for instance, in their general neglect of veiling). Japan was affected by China's patriarchal system such that the status of women deteriorated, but it did not adopt foot binding. Even areas of especially dramatic change stood out for regional particularisms. China's move to more intensive agriculture differed greatly from Europe's agricultural expansion, with different implications as well for later world history. Despite some shared contacts, including foods and diseases, opportunities for regional diversity remained striking.

FOR FURTHER READING

POPULATION/BIOLOGY

Robert Gottfried, *The Black Death* (1983).
Kenneth Kiple, ed., *The Cambridge World History of Human Disease* (1993).
I. G. Simmons, *Changing the Face of the Earth: Culture, Environment, History* (1989).
E. A. Wrigley, *Population and History* (1974).

CULTURE

Ignacio Bernard, *Mexico before Cortez: Art, History, and Legend* (1975).
J. H. Billington, *The Icon and the Axe: An Interpretive History of Russian Culture* (1966).
G. S. P. Freeman-Grenville, *Historical Atlas of the Middle East* (1993).
Seyyed H. Nasr, *Science and Civilization in Islam* (1968).
J. R. Strayer, *Western Europe in the Middle Ages* (1982).

STATE AND SOCIETY

Nazih N. Ayubi, *Over-stating the Arab State: Politics and Society in the Middle East* (1995).
Brian Bauer, *The Development of the Inca State* (1992).
Peter K. Bol, *"This Culture of Ours": Intellectual Transitions in T'ang and Sung China* (1992).
Inga Clendinnen, *Aztecs: An Interpretation* (1991).
Graham Connah, *African Civilizations: Precolonial Cities and States in Tropical Africa: An Archaeological Perspective* (1987).
Philip Curtin et al., *African History: From Earliest Times to Independence*, 2d ed. (1996).
Basil Davidson, *West Africa before the Colonial Era: A History to 1850* (1998).
Charles Diehl, *Byzantium: Greatness and Decline*, trans. Naomi Walford (1991).
Ross Hassig, *Aztec Warfare: Imperial Expansion and Political Control* (1988).
Judith Herrins, *The Formation of Christendom* (1987).
Peter Jackson, *The Delhi Sultanate: Political and Military History* (1999).

Ira Lapidus, *A History of Islamic Societies* (1988).

James T. Liu, *China Turning Inward: Intellectual-Political Changes in the Early Twelfth Century* (1988).

Tamara Sonn, *Between Qur'an and Crown: The Challenge of Political Legitimacy in the Arab World* (1990).

GENDER

Leila Ahmed, *Women and Gender in Islam: Historical Roots of a Modern Debate* (1992).

André Burguière et al., eds., *A History of the Family*, vol. 1: *Distant Worlds, Ancient Worlds* (1996).

Joan Cadden, *Meanings of Sex Difference in the Middle Ages: Medicine, Science and Culture* (1993).

Patricia Buckley Ebrey, *The Inner Quarters: Marriage and the Lives of Chinese Women in the Sung Period* (1993).

N. A. Falk and Rita M. Gross, *Unspoken Worlds: Women's Religious Lives in Non-Western Cultures* (1980).

David F. Greenberg, *The Construction of Homosexuality* (1988).

Clare Lees, ed., *Medieval Masculinities: Regarding Men in the Middle Ages* (1994).

Eve Levin, *Sex and Society in the World of the Orthodox Slavs, 900–1700* (1989).

Irene Silverblatt, *Moon, Sun and Witches: Gender Ideologies and Class in Inca and Colonial Peru* (1987).

LABOR AND LEISURE

Peter Duus, *Feudalism in Japan* (1969).

Murray Gordon, *Slavery in the Arab World* (1987).

Robert S. Hoyt, *Europe in the Middle Ages* (1965).

Friedrich Katz, *The Ancient American Civilizations* (1972).

Bernard Lewis, *Race and Slavery in the Middle East: An Historical Inquiry* (1990).

Laurence J. C. Ma, *Commercial and Urban Development in Sung China (960–1279)* (1971).

Daniel Pipes, *Slave Soldiers and Islam: The Genesis of a Military System* (1981).

Linda Schele and David Freidel, *A Forest of Kings: The Untold Story of the Ancient Maya* (1990).

PART IV

Early Modern World History, 1450–1750

Highlights. World history after 1450 was gradually reshaped by new power alignments among major civilizations, most notably the rise of the West but also the emergence of land-based empires in Asia and eastern Europe. A new kind of world economy developed, supported by new military and shipping technology, while the inclusion of the Americas affected virtually all major societies. Disease patterns changed decisively, while population growth in Europe and parts of Asia surged beyond any previous precedent. The period 1450–1750 is called "early modern" to note the formation of many durable developments, such as a literally global economy, but also some important differences from a more fully "modern" world.

Key Developments. The framework of world history during the three centuries after 1450 was dominated by several interrelated changes. Slowly but steadily, western Europe rose to a top power position in military and economic terms. Initially, its strength internationally concentrated on naval power, where new sailing ships, navigational devices, and ships' cannons allowed it to dominate sea routes and conquer many islands and ports. New trade and transportation technology intensified international contacts, creating a fuller world economy, where position in trade powerfully shaped internal economic systems, labor patterns, even politics. Regions pressed to trade raw materials, for example, operated at a disadvantage, importing more complex and expensive goods—such as guns—made in the West in exchange for cheaper items, such as sugar, that now had to be produced in growing quantities. Trade was controlled by Western countries, limiting local capital and merchant activity. Governments were kept weak to facilitate economic exploitation. Forced labor, either slavery or harsh serfdom, predominated, to assure low-cost output. As part of the Western-dominated, intensified world economy, the Americas and, by the 18th century, Pacific Oceania were brought into world contacts for the first time, while trade in West Africa was reoriented to the Atlantic with the rise of a massive export of slaves. The results transformed American history, while bringing new crops and other products to Afro-Eurasia. Areas that had previously developed in isolation were subjected to European colonial rule, bringing new cultural forms; then largely dependent, raw-materials-producing economy; and devastating population loss due to previously unknown contagious diseases. Spain and Portugal set up vast empires in South America and the Caribbean, followed by other colonial expansions in North America. Massive movements of people brought Europeans as well as African slaves to the Americas, Europeans to Australia and parts of Africa, and, later, Asians to several areas.

These key developments were shaped by technology. Guns and sails helped spur Europe's advance from the 15th century onward, as Europeans capitalized on techniques imported from Asia to solve long-standing trade inferiorities. After this initial spurt, technological change was more gradual.

Throughout the early modern centuries, technology was complemented by changes in economic and political organization. New trading companies applied capitalist investment and profit seeking on an unprecedented scale. Fed by new revenues, European governments became better organized by the 17th century, expanding bureaucracies and functions alike. By the 18th century a few other regions, such as Russia, sought to copy some of the West European political changes.

Western Europe pioneered in most of the key technological and organizational developments of the modern era. But important regional initiatives marked the first centuries of this era. Huge new land empires developed in Asia and eastern Europe—Russia, the Ottoman Empire in the Middle East, the Muslim Mughal Empire imposed over the Hindu majority in India, and a revived Chinese Empire. Japan developed a more efficient shogunate, eliminating internal warfare and establishing Confucianism and a Confucian bureaucracy as key cultural and political components.

Powerful empires in Asia, as well as strong governments in Japan and many African kingdoms, showed tendencies to react against the trends of

Western intrusion and world economic interaction. Several Asian societies adopted new policies of isolation that actually reduced their commercial and cultural contact with the rest of the world. Others, such as the new Ottoman Empire in the Middle East, attempted to avoid new levels of contact, with considerable initial success. European military technology did not allow penetration of well-organized land masses, which was why Chinese, Japanese, and Ottoman policies were successful through the early modern centuries. Even these societies (particularly China), however, were affected by the new agricultural exchanges with the Americas, an important complication to an already complex picture.

India and sub-Saharan Africa proved to be intermediate cases. India under the new Mughal Empire experienced significant changes apart from world trends. But the Mughal Empire began to weaken in the late 17th century, allowing increased penetration by Western commercial companies. In the 18th century, British forces gained increasing ascendancy, and they introduced new controls over Indian manufacturing and agriculture that brought growing dependency in the world economy.

Sub-Saharan Africa was pulled into the new world economy from the outset, particularly through the slave trade. This huge change had population as well as economic impact in West and Southwest Africa, and it involved immense human suffering. But African governments remained strong, regulating most of the trade though not deriving the principal profits. The cultural impact of European activities was also modest. Here was an important case of substantial continuity along with obvious innovation.

Latin America and a few island areas, such as parts of Indonesia, became parts of an unprecedented overseas colonial outreach, guided by Spain, Portugal, Holland, England, and France. Loose administrations kept political control in these areas, and in the Americas, significant migration from Europe in addition to the importation of African slaves altered the population structures. From the Americas came new products, with impact on many other regions of the world.

World economy, rise of the West, and the impact of exchanges with the Americas all define the early modern period. But increasing diversities and interruptions of contact define it as well, which means that different traditions and political-technological circumstances produced diverse reactions to new global forces.

TIMELINE

IV. Early Modern: 1450–1750

1450	Northern Renaissance in Europe
1453	Constantinople falls; end of the Byzantine Empire; rise of Ottoman Empire
1462	Much of Russia freed by Ivan III (Ivan the Great) from Tatars
1464–1591	Kingdom of Songhai in Africa
1479	Formation of single Spanish monarchy
1480	Expulsion of Tatars from Russia
1493	Beginnings of Spanish government in the Americas (second voyage of Christopher Columbus)
1498	Vasco da Gama (Portugal) to India
16th century	Portugal acquires trading rights and some trading stations in Siam, Burma, Indonesia; Spanish, Portuguese, and Dutch ports on West African coast
1500–1519	Spanish conquest of West Indies, including Puerto Rico, Cuba
1501	Introduction of African slaves in Latin America
1517	Martin Luther's 95 Theses; beginning of Protestant Reformation
1519–1521	Ferdinand Magellan's expedition around the world
1520–1566	Süleyman the Magnificent
1520–1580	Height of *encomienda* system in Spanish America

1526–1761 (officially 1857)	Mughal Empire in India
1527–1542	Viceroyalties established for Central and South America
1531	Francisco Pizarro's conquest of Inca Empire
1533–1584	Ivan the Terrible, first to be called czar; boyar power reduced
1542	Portuguese traders to Japan
1549	First Portuguese government in Brazil
1550–1649	Religious wars in France, Germany, Britain
1557	Macao taken by Portugal
1562	Beginning of British slave trade in Africa
1569	Catholic Inquisition set up for Spanish America; limitation of intellectual freedom
1574–1800	*Mita* forced mine-labor system in Andean Spanish America
1577–1598	Hideyoshi general in Japan; more centralized government and new isolation policy
1588	Defeat of Spanish Armada by English
1591	Fall of Songhai Empire
17th century	British and French forts on east coast of India; scientific revolution in Europe
1600s	Rise of serfdom in eastern Europe; beginnings of rapid population growth, especially parts of Asia
1600–1750	Proto-industrialization in western Europe
1600–1800	Height of African slave trade
1600–1868	Tokugawa Shogunate
1608	First trade concessions from regional princes in India granted to England
1613–1917	Romanov dynasty in Russia
1641	Capture by Dutch of major spice trade center in Indonesia; beginning of control of island of Java
1643–1715	Louis XIV in France; absolute monarchy
1644–1912	Qing dynasty
1652	Dutch colony on Cape of Good Hope

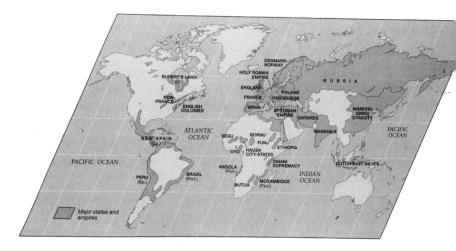

The Early Modern World, 1450–1750: The Rise of Overseas and Landed Empires. From Peter N. Stearns, Michael Adas, and Stuart B. Schwartz, *World Civilizations: The Global Experience*, 2nd ed. Copyright 1996 by HarperCollins College Publishers. Reprinted by permission of Addison-Wesley Educational Publishers Inc.

1670–1740s	Height of sugar plantation system and slavery in northeastern Brazil
1688–1690	Glorious Revolution in Britain; parliamentary regime; some religious toleration; political writing of John Locke
1689–1725	Peter the Great
18th century	Mughal decline; rise of Sikh state (1708ff.) and states of southern India; Enlightenment in Europe
1700–1800	Sugar plantation system and African slavery expand in the Caribbean
1717ff.	Spanish colonial control increased in Latin America; the "Bourbon Reforms"
1727	Chinese-Russian frontier treaty

CHAPTER 14

POPULATION OF THE EARTH

Growth, Decimation, and Relocation

Introduction

The years 1450–1750 bracket two earth-transforming demographic and biological phenomena. They were interrelated and mutually reinforcing.

The first was a substantial increase in Eurasian populations, the first phase of the modern population explosion. Globally, considerable regional variation prevailed, some areas growing rapidly, others not. Growth was particularly great, though uneven, from around 1475 to 1620; it then slowed until the early 18th century.

The second phenomenon was geographic expansion across the world's oceans, bridged in the 15th and 16th centuries by European maritime technology, which resulted in world-straddling migrations of African and European peoples (roughly in that chronological order), whose arrival decimated the indigenous peoples of the Americas, Australia, and Oceania but then repopulated these areas.

As a result of Eurasian population growth, through most of the era many rural areas became more densely inhabited, while urban centers grew. Civilizations pressed into their frontiers. Chinese populations expanded not only southward, but also westward into Inner Asia and northward beyond the Hwang-he basin. European populations also expanded overland, moving eastward, led by Russian populations migrating across North Asia. In Eurasia this process was as ancient as civilization itself, not at all unique. Now, however, Atlantic and Mediterranean Europeans brought epidemiologically armed Old World agrarian civilization across the world's oceans, creating exchanges on an unprecedented scale between entire continents—full of people, plants, animals, diseases, insects, and other biota. The arrival of this biological package caused populations previously isolated from Africa and Eurasia—that is, the remaining virgin soil regions—to collapse, with die-offs reaching 90 percent over a century or so after first contact. This was not an unprecedented phenomenon in human history; earlier civilization expansions—for example, in the Mediterranean during the classical period—had reduced local populations through contacts with new diseases. Never before, however, had decimation occurred on such a large scale, and with such sweeping consequences in world history.

What is known about these population trends comes from political and religious institutions that assembled information on the people under their authority. Limited at first, population data improve over the centuries. Historians distinguish between a prestatistical and a statistical era, roughly before and after 1800. Church and state officials in Europe and imperial authorities in China compiled data for the earlier centuries, China even before 1450. Most of the world came much later into the statistical spotlight. For the centuries before 1800 we know much less about the populations of the Middle East, South and Southeast Asia, and less still about the Americas, Africa, Australia, and Oceania. Where data are scarce, scholarly controversies have raged freely, particularly over pre-Columbian American populations and African populations during the Atlantic slave trade. Nevertheless, the broad outlines of global population trends can be traced, and for some parts of the world, the specific demographic and economic forces can be described.

The Atlantic Crossings: Frontiers by Sea

The period's first major population change resulted from seemingly limited new commercial goals that translated into massive new fields for diseases. Population growth (and particularly European growth during the postclassical period) provided the push for overseas expansion, but at first indirectly. In the first three centuries of the early modern period, masses of European farmers did not clamber aboard ships to the American frontier. Rather, the initial ventures emanated out of urban centers, where affluent investors recruited small numbers of sailors, military adventurers, and navigators, sending them out into the world to gain riches—for the investors, who mostly stayed safely at home. Initially, then, the objectives were trade in Oriental luxuries, the quest for gold, and the establishment of sugar plantations.

Ocean-worthy ships and knowledge of the Atlantic sailing conditions were prerequisites. Since the 11th century, urban centers in the European river valleys opening onto the Atlantic Ocean, and North and Baltic Seas had sent out ships for fishing, seal and whale hunting, coastal transportation, and seaborne trade between the Mediterranean and Atlantic. By the 14th century, improvements in the design of ships and sails and accumulated knowledge put the nearby West African coast within reach of regular voyages.

Spanish and Portuguese investors began their first overseas imperial venture in what historians refer to as the Mediterranean Atlantic, the expanse of ocean connecting the Iberian Peninsula and the Azores, Madeira, Canary, and Cape Verde island groups. While trading for gold with West Africans, they discovered the Canary and Madeira island groups could produce sugarcane, having the requisite hot, wet climate and abundant wood fuel. A group of people known as the Guanche were the only occupants, found only in the Canary Islands. A Stone Age agricultural people isolated for thousands of years, they numbered about 100,000 around 1415, when they became the victims of Spanish and Portuguese slave raiders. The Guanche became the first people to be driven to extinction by European imperialism. Arduous slave labor on sugar plantations and warfare took a heavy toll, but above all the Guanche died from what epidemiologists term *virgin soil epidemics*—exposure to diseases for which there was no built-up resistance. Millions of the peoples of the Americas, Australia, Oceania, and sub-Arctic Asia would later fall in the same fashion. As the Guanche perished, African slaves took their place. Small numbers of African slaves had been part of the Mediterranean labor force since the early Roman Empire, but now their numbers increased. In the last decades of the 15th century, about 1,300 African slaves per year found their way to Europe, mostly to Portugal and Spain, and about 500 per year to the Atlantic islands.

The Mediterranean Atlantic became Europe's launching point to the rest of the world. With Vasco da Gama's voyage farther south, around

Africa's Cape of Good Hope and across the Indian Ocean in 1498, Portuguese mariners established a sea route to India and East Asia. Spanish, Dutch, and later French and English merchants and mariners followed. These seagoing connections intensified biological and demographic interaction among Europeans and Asians of all kinds.

The Columbian Exchange and the Plantation Complex

Christopher Columbus, too, left from the Canary Islands. His second voyage to Hispaniola in 1493 included 17 ships, some 1,500 men, numerous livestock, plants (particularly sugarcane roots), seeds, tools, and unintended parasites (which included diseases), rats, mice, and weeds. His voyage began, in effect, a biological invasion, a replacement of indigenous American species with Eurasian and African types—plants, animals, diseases, and, of course, people.

Nobody knows exactly how many Native Americans there were in the 1490s (see chapter 6), but what happened to them is certain. About 90 percent of them died in the 1st century and a half of their contact with Europeans and Africans. Estimates for central Mexico suggested 17 million people in 1532, scarcely over 1 million in 1608. Isolated from the Afro-Eurasian interactive biological mass since before the Neolithic age, they had constituted the world's greatest virgin soil population, numbering between 70 and 100 million, greater than all Europe and roughly equivalent to South Asia or China.

They were preeminently agricultural. Maize was the main crop, the most productive of the world's grains. It had been in cultivation for thousands of years, and Americans had adapted it to a variety of growing conditions across most of the hemisphere. Combined with beans, chili peppers, squash, pumpkins, and lesser crops such as potatoes and manioc, Native American agriculture produced vast surpluses and supported elaborate political systems in Mexico and Peru. The eastern forestlands of the Mississippi basin and the North American coast supported large agricultural and horticultural societies. In the semi-arid grasslands north and south of the tropical belt, limited agriculture and foraging sustained fewer numbers. Only the cold-weather timber and subpolar lands of the far north and south were exclusively hunting-gathering zones.

Populations of the Americas were different from Afro-Eurasians in two important respects. First, they had not contracted the crowd diseases of Afro-Eurasian civilizations, which they had left behind ten thousand or more years earlier, when their Paleolithic ancestors crossed the germ-free Arctic regions of Northeast Asia and North America. Second, they had not acquired diseases from animals, as had Afro-Eurasian farmers. Their domesticated animals were llamas, alpacas, guinea pigs, dogs, and turkeys, and little else. Among the few diseases were yaws, possibly syphilis (epidemiological experts disagree on this one), and tuberculosis. But smallpox, malaria, yellow fever, schistosomiasis, influenzas, and the array of childhood diseases—chicken pox, measles, mumps, whooping cough—were wholly absent, and they turned out to be the big killers.

"The Columbian exchange" is a concept historians use to explain what happened when the expanding frontier of Western civilization reached out into the Atlantic to the Americas. The American side of the Columbian exchange refers to the entire package of plants, animals, diseases, insects, pests, weeds, and, of course, people that invaded the New World. Together they utterly transformed not only the society and population but the entire ecosystem of the New World.

From Columbus's second voyage in 1493, Native Americans perished massively. The first epidemic of influenza in Hispaniola in 1493 killed many thousands, brought, evidently, in a small herd of swine from the Canary Islands. The Spanish men aboard these vessels were not humanitarians. They had come to the Americas to enrich themselves and win the esteem of the investors and the clerical and secular authorities back in Europe. Impatient for profit, especially to acquire gold, they enslaved, murdered, raped, and plundered the Native American population with astonishing brutality—astonishing not only to us but also to contemporaries. They were unusually brutal men, in a brutal age. Native Americans soon became scarce, and war bands went out to other islands and the coastal mainland to find replacements. They spread death wherever they went, and by 1600, scarcely an American Indian survived.

Smallpox did not arrive until 1518. Most Europeans who made the ocean crossing came from coastal towns and caught smallpox while still children. As adults they were immune; those few individuals aboard ship who might have carried smallpox usually died or passed through the contagious state of the disease before arriving in the New World. There are several hundred strains of smallpox; immunity to one usually gave immunity to the others. In the early 16th century, *Variola major* appeared, a particularly deadly strain with mortality at 30 per 1,000 cases, as compared with the more benign *Variola minor*, whose death toll was about 15 per 1,000. Spanish and Portuguese usually got the latter while children, but *Variola major* found ready victims in West Africans, most of whom were from small rural communities with little smallpox of any kind. A group of African slaves working in placer mines in Hispaniola in 1518 are believed to have been the first to bring smallpox to the New World, and the deadlier strain at that.

When Hernán Cortés set out for Mexico City in 1519, he had among his troops some Africans with contagious cases of smallpox. The Spanish troops, immune since childhood, experienced nothing, but the Aztec and other Indians of Mexico died out horribly. Other epidemics followed, some smallpox, some other diseases. Infection ravaged northward, and also southward to the Inca capital at Cuzco by 1524. While the main attack of Spanish and diseases came in Central America, it is important to understand that points of contact, and thereby contagion, occurred all along the Atlantic coast, from far north in Newfoundland to the far south in Brazil. In 1501 a Portuguese vessel took some slaves from Newfoundland. Meanwhile, fishermen and fur traders established contacts with Native Americans all along the northern coasts. Far to the south, Portuguese ships en route to the Indian Ocean swung wide into the Atlantic to ride prevailing winds around the Horn of Africa. They stopped to take on provisions and to trade for aromatic woods with coastal Americans. Some Portuguese realized the possibility of sugar growing there, and by 1550, whole plantations were in operation. They took local natives captive and, as captives died of disease and overwork, ranged wider along the coast and interior for replacements. At these points and between, all along the coast, contagious diseases came ashore, while from the Caribbean and Mexican centers of infection they moved along the interior north and south.

Besides diseases, violence and slavery killed many. Probably, venereal infections spread among indigenous women by European invaders reduced their fertility. Cultural despair, a loss of the will to live, led to suicides, infanticide, and women deliberately refusing to conceive and rear children in a world that had become horrible. In central Mexico, environmental deterioration due to overgrazing by cattle and sheep made population recovery to former levels impossible.

The consequence was an utter collapse of the Native American population. Indian populations dropped steadily for a century and a half of contact. In coastal lowland regions they died out utterly. In the highlands of Mexico and Peru, cooler altitudes reduced the germ count and kept enough people for population growth to resume. Thus these regions continued to retain a core of indigenous people and at least some modicum of indigenous culture—including language. The overall result, however, was an immense demographic void, a demographic vacuum. European populations did not pour into this vacuum immediately, however; instead mostly Africans did, and the concept of "the plantation complex" explains why.

The plantation complex had its origins in the slave-labor sugar plantations of the medieval Mediterranean, which, as we have seen, relocated to the Atlantic islands in the mid–15th century. The complex became established in northeastern Brazil between 1500 and 1550, then spread northward to the eastern Caribbean in the 17th century, where British, Dutch, and French investors established sugar operations. Sugar production was intended for export to Europe and hence stayed close to coastal areas for seagoing transportation. The essentials of the plantation system were production of a high-profit cash crop in one part of the world, with investment capital coming from European urban investors, that was destined for transportation and consumption in Europe mostly, although eventually also in European overseas colonies. The system developed first in sugar production but spread to other crops eventually—in North America, tobacco, rice, and cotton; elsewhere in the world, coffee, tea, cocoa, and rubber.

Africans came to supply the labor for plantations. European indentured servants were tried for a while, and Native Americans enslaved or used as forced labor on agricultural estates (*encomienda*) also were tried, but both groups suffered high fatalities in the tropical climates of the Americas amid the new population mixing. Between 1550 and 1750, several million Africans made the Atlantic crossing, going to mostly Brazil and the sugar islands. Many Africans also found their way into mining operations: silver in Peru, gold in Brazil. In Brazil, about as many Africans worked in gold mines as worked on sugar plantations.

The African slave trade also transformed the tropical Americas by introducing African diseases. These included yellow fever and *falciparum malaria* (a severe form of the disease), which were by far the deadliest. The tropical Americas went through an amazing epidemiological transition. Pre-Columbian, they were the world's healthiest and most populated tropical region. But European and African diseases made them one of the world's least healthy regions, while ironically, their productive capacity in sugar and bullion made them the most desired. Africans, however, chiefly inhabited the region. The mosquito *Aedes aegypt* infects humans with yellow fever by its bite. If infected in childhood, the victim shows minor symptoms and almost always recovers and enjoys lifelong immunity. For adults, however, over, say, age 20, yellow fever causes serious illness and high rates of fatality. Africans usually acquired yellow fever and immunity as children in Africa, but Europeans arriving from Europe, not born in the tropics, died at alarming rates. *Falciparum malaria* was more complicated. The great variety in the species of plasmodia made each region, each locality, unique and immunity was localized to one's home. Further, only repeated inoculations could keep local immunity strong. So, when Africans moved from one part of Africa to another, or when they moved across the Atlantic, they entered zones for which they had no immunity. As a general rule of human or animal biology, travel over long distances results in relocation in a new epidemiological zone, where some kind of viral or bacteriological parasite lies in wait. Historians call this the relocation cost, and military medical personnel have combated it since the development of modern medical technology in the latter half of the 19th century.

The establishment of these diseases and the labor conditions of plantation slavery created peculiar demographic conditions in the Americas. First, Native Americans were massively swept away from the tropical regions. Second, Europeans could scarcely survive. In 1600, the Spanish Caribbean held only 75,000 to 80,000 persons. (Before 1492 it had at least 6 million native inhabitants!) Of these, only one in ten was

Spanish; the rest were African or of mixed African, American, and European parentage, a *mestizo* population created by the union of Iberian men and African or Indian women. Mostly adult males migrated to the colonies in the first two centuries, 1500–1700, with few women and therefore few children. Given the high mortality, only a constant inflow of new Europeans could sustain enough population for masters, military, and administrators. Africans fared only a little better. While most were immune to yellow fever, falciparum malaria did afflict them severely, as did smallpox. The oppressive working conditions, arduous labor in intense heat, and malnutrition (since slaves were poorly fed), caused African mortality to be extremely high as well. Only regular new supplies of slaves from Africa kept populations at adequate levels. Some African women, perhaps one in four, did find their way to the colonies, but malnutrition and diseases, particularly diseases of the reproductive organs, resulted in extremely low birthrates. Infants were often underweight at birth and underfed and ill in infancy, and they suffered extremely high mortality rates. Nevertheless, gradually, a population that was largely racially mixed, African, European, and some Native American, did become acclimated to the horrendous conditions.

The demographic effects of these conditions are curious. As we have noted, most of the migrants to the New World in the years 1492–1820 were Africans, in all about 10 million, as compared with about 2 million Europeans. Most African slaves, about 95 percent of them, went to the Caribbean and South America; only about 5 percent went to North America. In the cooler climates of North America and temperate South America, European populations tended to cluster. There they settled, that is, created genuine settlements or colonies of Europe. Africans were far fewer in North America, but they survived at higher rates. Women, few in number at first, were healthier and tended to conceive and give birth to healthier babies, who were born in roughly equal sex ratios—about one male for each female. After a few generations, and as the trans-Atlantic slave trade ended in the early 1800s, the sex ratios became normal for adults too, about equal, and natural population growth got underway. Consequently, although North America received only about one-twentieth of all slave imports, it began the 20th century with about three-tenths of all African Americans in the New World.

Other Population Retreats

The dramatic effect of European and African diseases in the Americas formed the most important demographic result of the Columbian exchange in the short term, but it was not the only one. Sub-Saharan Africa experienced a confusing interplay between factors promoting and factors deterring population growth, with the result being an apparent stability even as populations in Europe and Asia increased.

European traders brought a number of American plants to Africa, where they were quickly adopted. African populations had been capable of significant growth previously, but with some limits because of pressures on available crops and animals, including frequent lack of protein. Now, peanuts, sweet potatoes, and corn, all high-yielding plants, were introduced, quickly outstripping indigenous crops and stimulating population growth. All this added to the growth trends that African agricultural improvements had set in motion since the 11th century.

But the massive slave trade drained population in two ways. First, from the 16th through the 18th century, millions of people were directly removed from the West African population. Second, a disproportionate number of these people were young, of childbearing age, and their loss further restricted African population potential. (Polygyny increased in response to the disproportionate loss of males, but it had limited effects on population.) The loss of life went beyond the export of people, for almost as many died on the way to the slave ships as were sent off. One estimate says that of 100 seized in their homeland, only 57 reached a slave ship at the coast. Warfare involving slave catching, overland transportation of slaves, and coastal trading increased disease—particularly mortality from malaria and from newly imported strains of smallpox. The exact effects are unknown, but smallpox certainly ruined the San people, or bushmen, of South Africa. The normal hardships of drought and famine also restricted population growth and compelled the poor to sell their children and even themselves into slavery. The net effect for sub-Saharan Africa was a decline in population, which did not return to its level of 1600 until the 19th century—a remarkable similarity to the Americas. In essence, much of the population expansion possible because of new foods was forcibly reexported to the Americas, which is why there was no growth overall. And here there was no significant immigration. Europeans were quite susceptible to tropical illnesses such as malaria and yellow fever. (White sailors on slaving vessels sometimes died at a rate of 50 to 70 percent.) The result, until new medicines were introduced in the later 19th century, was very limited European penetration of Africa.

European contact with Australia and Pacific Oceania was more straightforward, in the American mode—but later. Europeans touched in Pacific areas occasionally in the 16th and 17th centuries. Their visits were infrequent, however, and they often had been so long at sea that active diseases such as smallpox and influenza had run their course (or killed prior to arrival). But the populations of the Pacific Islands and Australia were virgin soil in terms of diseases that could be brought in from Europe and Asia, and the disaster began to occur as European commercial voyages, explorations, and even settlement began in the late 18th century. Here, furthermore, Europeans were often quite aware of their disease potential and deliberately spread contagion-bearing products, such as blankets, to local inhabitants as a means of clearing them from the land. Key diseases included smallpox and influenza again but also tuberculosis and venereal infections. The result was tragically familiar. Observers had, by the late 18th century, developed statistical reasoning and reported accurately. Some examples among many include the following: The population of the Hawaiian archipelago in 1778, when Captain James Cook arrived, is estimated at 242,000 to 800,000 persons; a hundred years later, only 48,000 remained, and many were of only partly Hawaiian parentage. When measles came to the Fiji islands in 1875, brought by the king of Fiji and his son, who had been visiting Sydney, Australia, the single epidemic killed 40,000 of a total population that numbered 150,000. In southeastern Australia, about 95 percent of the aboriginal population died off in just over sixty years; in New Zealand, the native Maori population dropped by 75 percent within a century.

As in the Americas, the result was both need and opportunity for immigration, though the process occurred later, mainly after 1800. Europeans began to pour into Australia and New Zealand and some Pacific Islands. But in crucial cases, large numbers of Asians were also exported, often as indentured labor during the 19th century. Chinese, Japanese, and Filipinos

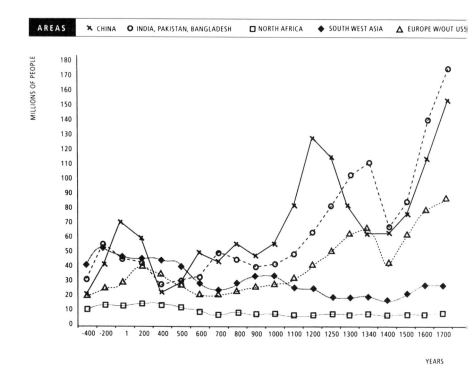

| AREAS | ✕ CHINA | ○ INDIA, PAKISTAN, BANGLADESH | □ NORTH AFRICA | ◆ SOUTH WEST ASIA | △ EUROPE W/OUT USS |

Regional Population Levels over Time, 400 B.C.E.–1700 C.E.

were brought in to work the growing sugar and pineapple fields of Hawaii, for example.

Both in the Americas and in the Pacific regions, the massive importation of new peoples from the various parts of the Old World ultimately stemmed population loss and reversed the flow—though, given the magnitude of the mortality rates among local peoples, this did not occur overnight. Three factors were at work. In the first place, local peoples who did survive the disease onslaught often developed and passed along new levels of resistance that gradually curbed the impact of epidemics. This effect was limited; in many areas, disease and poor treatment continued to impose unusually high death rates on pure-bred American Indians and Hawaiians, for example. In the second place, many immigrants intermarried with locals, producing a mixed population—called *mestizos* in Latin America—that had much higher disease resistance. In the Americas, not only Europeans but also Africans interbred with native Indians. In Hawaii, native Hawaiians mixed with the imported Asian groups. Many of the mixed populations developed unusually high birthrates, quickly outstripping natives and pure-bred Europeans alike. In the third place, some of the immigrant groups themselves developed high birthrates, taking advantage of abundant resources and the need for family labor. Europeans in British North America for example, during the 17th and 18th centuries, had far larger families than their counterparts back home. The French in Quebec present an even more dramatic story: Fewer than 5,000 French Canadian families were formed before 1700. (Other immigrants died or went home before marrying.) To provide labor, French Canadians began marrying early and, when a spouse died, remarrying commonly; they also cut the intervals between births (25 months, compared to 29 months in France). The result was an average of 6.3 children per couple and a doubling of the population in less than thirty years; by 1750, French Canadians numbered 50,000.

Developments of this sort returned the Americas to overall population expansion by the 18th century, though the relative gap with Eurasia remained strong. By this point also, however, additional results of the Columbian exchange were generating a dramatic population explosion in key parts of Eurasia itself.

Population Revolutions

The Columbian exchange was not a one-way street. It brought new diseases, animals, and people to the Americas, to the great disadvantage of existing groups. But it also brought American products to Afro-Eurasia, and here the new types of food were far and away the most important. From this exchange, in turn, combined with other factors, massive population increases emerged.

Beyond the population upheavals of the Americas and the distinctive patterns that now emerged in Africa, global populations expanded slowly in the 16th and 17th centuries. Both Europe and East Asia saw new growth, but limited by high mortality rates and frequent epidemics. Yet the new foods of American origin were gradually establishing themselves, and along with improvements in regional agricultural practices, this would lead to startling breakthroughs by the 18th century. By this point, the unprecedented march of modern world populations had begun.

Impacts on China

China was a vital population center. Strong population advances, based in agricultural changes had occurred in the postclassical period, leading to the new migrations southward. Then new epidemics intervened, at times reducing population levels. A population of 100 to 120 million in the early 13th century had plummeted to 70 million a century later, possibly as a result of the great epidemics of the period. Up to 150 million again by 1600, it had fallen to 83 million in 1651. Then it rose again to 150 million in 1700, maybe 275 million in 1779, and an astounding 330 million by 1800. These figures are estimates, of course, and may exaggerate change. Nevertheless, the instability is obvious.

Population gains frequently led to inadequate food supplies, including outright famines, and deteriorating nutrition also opened the gate to more disease. New contacts with European traders in the 16th century brought problems in addition to the already common bouts with malaria, smallpox, and the like, as well as frequent rural deaths and debilitating illnesses from parasitic diseases because of unhygienic conditions. From European contacts came syphilis, some new childhood killers such as scarlet fever, and, later, cholera. None of this had the disastrous effects of the Columbian exchange in the Americas, for China was already part of the basic Afro-Eurasian disease pool, but massive die-offs could temporarily result. The 16th century had many epidemics. In 1586–1589 and again in 1639–1644, China suffered its two worst epidemics in recorded history, but their medical causes are unknown. Death rates reached 20 to 40 percent across wide areas of eastern China. Overall mortality rates commonly limited the effects of a high birthrate, for China, like most of Asia, emphasized early and nearly universal marriage, with greater fertility than prevailed in western Europe. But there were some restraints in this aspect too, as scholars are discovering. Many couples married young but did not cohabit for several years, and birthrates after age 30 were lower than in Europe—both patterns highlighting deliberate sexual restraint.

But in the 16th and 17th centuries China experienced a major expansion trend and then a new collapse. Rapid growth up to the early 17th century is explained by restoration of unity and peace in the Ming era. As plague and violence receded, populations simply recovered to their pre-Mongol, preplague levels. No special agricultural improvements were added to those of the pre-Mongol era, but existing techniques were more widely extended. Total areas in crops increased substantially, by about one-third from 1400 to 1600, while population doubled. Much cultivated land bore two or three crops annually. Although highly productive American crops made their appearance—maize, peanuts, sweet potatoes—they had little influence until the beginning of the 18th century.

Population growth created a growing demand for textiles, too; more people needed more clothing. Textile fibers were nonfood agricultural products: cotton, silk (from silkworms fed on mulberry leaves), and wool. Peasants everywhere had customarily produced their own clothing, tools, and household utensils. From the 16th century onward, however, rural industries developed in which peasants, or at least rural residents, produced textiles and other manufactured goods for payment at piecework rates or for sale in distant markets.

The collapse of the early 17th century nearly equaled that of the plague; maybe a third or more of the population was lost. Historians offer two possible explanations that involve comparisons with Europe, which experienced a population crisis of lesser proportions at the same time. One explanation stresses climate change. The early 17th century became significantly colder, reaching its lowest temperatures in 1654. The grasslands and livestock in Mongolia to the northwest and Manchuria to the north were reduced, and both Mongols and Manchus placed new pressures on China's defenses. Within China itself, crops were scaled back and migrations and peasant rebellions increased, and these doubtless contributed to diffusion of epidemics. The Ming dynasty succumbed, falling definitively in 1644. Political disintegration worsened the situation until the Manchus consolidated their control in the 1680s as the Qing dynasty.

The pattern of fluctuation shifted dramatically in the 18th century. China's population stood at 102 million in 1686; a hundred years later it had tripled, to an unprecedented 313 million. What had happened? With birthrates already high, the key change must have involved a reduction in death rates, and this, in turn, involved a shift in food supplies. Here scholars debate the relative role of two changes. First, changing regional harvest and planting patterns and rising investments in the land increased crop yields per acre, particularly in the rice-growing regions. At the same time, second, the accumulating impact of the adoption of American crops contributed powerfully. China gained knowledge of these crops—sweet and white potatoes and corn—during the 16th century through trade with the Philippines, where Spanish colonial administrators had introduced them to bolster the local food supply. The crops were easy to grow, in China as elsewhere, and exceptionally rich in caloric value. They may have improved food sources, particularly for poor peasants in less fertile and mountainous regions. With better food, children survived in greater numbers, adding to the population directly and also to the number of potential parents later on.

Agricultural changes may have been bolstered by climate shifts (a warming trend, which improved crop output), and overall population health by the growing use of inoculations against smallpox (using human rather than cowpox, but effective nevertheless). Other contributions to population growth may have resulted from modest improvements in urban hygiene or in herbal drugs, such as quinine to combat malaria. Governments and charitable organizations improved medical care for the urban poor, while a growing practice of burying dead bodies reduced contagion in the cities. But the improved food supply headed the list in reducing the impact of disease on Chinese population levels and in ushering in a prolonged period of massive growth. In turn, the bulk of the Asian population gain in the early modern centuries concentrated in China, as the giant country made the first breakthrough to a new demographic structure.

The result was not pure gain. Many people lived in dire poverty. Begging increased. The work and investment needed simply to sustain growing numbers may have retarded Chinese economic flexibility in other respects. Certainly, China's historic lead in technological change evaporated, possibly because with so much cheap labor the motivation declined.

Impacts on Europe

The full results of the Columbian exchange on western Europe were oddly delayed, though when they arrived, in combination with other factors, they generated an unusually rapid population surge. Given Europe's world position at the time, this surge had obvious international implications, as surplus Europeans began to spill over into other areas, particularly temperate zones where local populations were sparse or declining.

Europe had expanded its areas of cultivation in the postclassical period, as well as developing some new agricultural equipment and foods. This had produced solid population growth until the Black Death of the 14th century. By the 16th century, though recurrent plagues continued, significant growth resumed (probably about 5 percent during the century as a whole). But this was followed by greater stability around 1650. Here was an important contrast with China: The European family system was in full sway by this point, and it was designed to limit population pressure on the land by a combination of relatively late marriage ages (late 20s for most peasant spouses) and a high percentage of people who never married at all. Furthermore, Europeans long resisted introduction of most American foods—they were more conservative in this regard than the Native Americans, who began to incorporate Eurasian food products quite rapidly. European suspicion of the new foods was based in part on the fact that they were not mentioned in the Bible. Beliefs that foods such as the potato carried disease spread widely.

Yet there was change, and it set the stage for more dramatic developments later on. Europe's population grew slowly but steadily. Between 1475 and 1620, the overall gain was 50 percent. Urban populations also increased considerably, stimulated by the expansion of European seaborne commerce with Africa and South and East Asia and by colonial ventures in the tropical Americas. Mediterranean Europe had been the important urban and commercial region, but in the 16th and 17th centuries, northwestern Atlantic towns and cities grew more rapidly and became Europe's dominant area. The Netherlands became the most urbanized country in Europe: In the early 16th century, about one-fifth of its population resided in towns larger than 10,000 persons, and by 1620 that number had grown to more than half—a first in human history. London at the beginning of the 16th century contained 50,000 persons; this number rose to 200,000 around 1600 and to 400,000 by 1650. In the early 18th century, London contained 10 percent of the British population. Paris, at 200,000 persons in 1350, climbed to 400,000 by 1550 and 500,000 by 1700.

Growth of both urban and rural populations increased the demand for agricultural and manufactured products. Agricultural prices increased five times between 1475 and 1620—real increases, not inflation. These pressures launched western Europe's modern agricultural revolution, a slow process that reached maturation only in the mid–19th century. It built on the foundations of earlier agricultural developments, and its objective was to increase output. Landlords and agricultural entrepreneurs sought greater profit; peasants sought subsistence or additional income to pay their taxes and buy necessities. Historians sometimes credit aristocrats with innovating because, being literate, this class left account books and writings about agriculture. But the essential innovations came from peasant gardens, where they had been practiced for centuries.

The modern agricultural revolution involved applying techniques used and crops grown in peasant gardens or small plots—turnips, *luzerne*, and clovers. These had been grown without fallowing every growing season, spring to winter, as food for barnyard animals—rabbits, the family cow, a fattening pig. When transferred to the large fields, these crops increased output tremendously. The innovations occurred at many sites in the 16th century, for example, in northern Italy and in Provence in southeastern France. Continuous cropping had long existed in market gardens near cities; abundant supplies of city manure, animal and human, and high prices for fresh produce provided the means and incentives, respectively. In the Netherlands and southern England, urban pressures advanced agriculture widely, and the techniques came to be known as "Dutch farming."

Bringing clovers, *luzerne* (alfalfa is an American equivalent), and turnips—fodder crops, livestock food—into the fallow land, which had been part of the crop rotation cycle in the large grainfields, was the heart of the agricultural revolution. Pasture lands planted to grasses and clovers also entered into the rotation cycles. These techniques increased output in several ways. First, more livestock could be fed. They, in turn, produced more meat, milk, cheese, wool, hides, and harness power. Some wealthy landowners improved stock breeding to make healthier and more productive animals. Second, the increased livestock produced more manure, which increased soil fertility for all crops, especially grain. Third, legumes fixed nitrogen in the soil, an essential plant food that boosted grain production. Eliminating fallow meant, in effect, increasing land in production, meaning not only more production but more labor needed in agriculture.

Besides increasing yields per existing units of land, another important technique for increasing output was to increase areas in cultivation. Europe still contained broad expanses of land not yet "improved," that is, land not yet cleared of forest, brush, or rocks or marshy areas, inland and coastal not yet drained and diked. Enclosures were a way to bring wastelands in villages into production as pasture or plow land, by legally redefining their ownership and fencing or otherwise "enclosing" them. In England in the 16th century, strong demand for wool led about one-eighth of English land to be enclosed. The result was more pasture and more land in cultivation. Extension of cultivation went on continuously from the 16th to the mid–19th century, with the better lands added to production in the earlier centuries.

These improvements required more, not less, labor in agriculture, so agricultural populations continued to increase. More land was in cultivation, and higher production of grain, fodder, and animals required more workers. Agricultural, or at least rural, people also found livelihood from development of rural industry, or proto-industrialization. Villages near major towns, especially seaports or navigable river valleys, became producers of textiles, ironware, and pottery. In central Germany and in Normandy in France, linen manufacturers developed, as both rural and factory industry. Woolens became important in many areas—the Netherlands, eastern Spain, and much of England and France. With its excellent supplies of iron ore and coal—the latter increasingly the preferred fuel for smelting after 1709—England became a major producer of small iron products such as nails and hand tools, many of them manufactured in backyard village workshops.

Another important support for growing rural populations was the high-yielding food crops from the Americas, particularly maize and potatoes. Their use spread gradually because it took peasants a long time to learn how to grow them, and Native Americans did not come along to show them how. By contrast, European crops and animals in the Americas caught on quickly, because thousands of Europeans came with them and not only showed but forced Native Americans to raise them. But gradually, potatoes first, corn later became known in Europe, and by the mid–17th century, these crops were growing in many places.

Despite these new resources, by the 1630s populations had reached the limits of growth in many regional economies. The "little ice age" may have been a factor in halting growth, but even before it, wages had decreased. Urban vagrancy and roads filled with beggars characterized the end of the 16th and beginning of the 17th century.

Population growth slowed to a standstill, and in several ways. Historians of the 1950s to 1970s developed a new field of research known as historical demography. Using mostly church or parish records of baptisms, burials, and marriages, they discovered remarkable things about the lives of the lower classes—peasants and urban workers—who constituted the vast majority, and therefore the groups who determined population growth trends. The most is known about crisis mortality. Epidemics and famines swept through villages at intervals of three to seven years, raising death rates to crisis levels. Populations would recover for a few years; then another die-off would occur. Apparent population stability therefore was actually cruel oscillation; death rates averaged thirty to thirty-five per thousand but would rise to 50 or 70 or higher in a crisis, then fall to the 20s for a few years. As disease spread around the world in the 16th and 17th centuries, there were many mortality crises.

Furthermore, the European marriage system tightened to limit birthrates. Historical demographers have discovered what they first called the "European marriage pattern," with its two characteristics: relatively late marriage for women—above age 25 usually—and a high proportion of women (and men) who never married—about one-fourth. It was these features that restricted birthrates, since birth control was virtually unknown, and illegitimacy was rare. The age and frequency of marriage fluctuated with economic conditions. In the 16th century, marriage was nearly universal, and the age of marriage had fallen to the low 20s, which increased birthrates. With the onset of hard times in the 17th century, celibacy and the age of marriage rose, and birthrates declined. Another important set of controls included infanticide and abortion, which have been largely hidden from European public knowledge but which researchers have come to appreciate were widespread methods of limiting the number of children lower-class families produced.

Then, in the late 17th century, what had been evolution followed by stabilization changed to population revolution. Increasing contacts with the Americas brought more sophisticated knowledge of the advantages of the new foods, particularly the potato. Originally a cool-weather mountain crop in the Americas, potatoes did well in the Pyrenees, Alps, and Scottish highlands. They also grew well in the long, damp springtime of the Northwest European plain. Whatever hesitancy peasants may have felt about eating potatoes quickly passed when famine threatened; after all, people who in famines desperately consumed grass, weeds, the bark of trees, and even each other hardly would have hesitated to eat a potato. By the later 18th and the 19th century, American foods had become the principal foodstuffs of many rural folk. Various agricultural publicists promoted adoption of these foods, and peasants found that potatoes could allow subsistence on smaller plots of land. (Fried potatoes began to be sold on the streets of Paris in the 1680s—the original French fries.) Governments, eager to promote population growth as a source of military and economic strength, also backed the potato.

Along with new foods, some landowners began to introduce other innovations. As in China, the nutritional base for a population revolution combined regional changes with the use of American foods. Dutch and English farmers drained more swamps and so increased cultivable land. Agricultural reformers further promoted the use of nitrogen-fixing crops, such as the turnip. Improvements in available tools, such as growing use of the scythe instead of the sickle for harvesting, and better methods of stock growing also spread. All this took shape from the late 17th century onward, building on the earlier agricultural changes. At the same time, rates of epidemic disease declined, in part because of more effective government controls over the passage of people and animals along traditional plague routes from the Middle East. As in China, however, it was the change in foods that really counted.

These developments provided the framework for an unprecedented surge. In virtually every area of Europe, the population increased by 50 to 100 percent in the 18th century, with the greatest growth coming after 1750.

The Hapsburg Empire grew from 20 million to 27 million people; Spain rose from 5 to 10 million; and Prussia rose from 3 to 6 million. France increased from 20 to 29 million and Britain from 9 to 16 million. Growth would continue throughout the 19th century. In Europe as a whole, population rose from 188 million in 1800 to 401 million in 1900. This was an upheaval of truly impressive proportions. Its significance may be measured by comparing the rate of expansion with the 3 percent increase in Europe's population during the entire century between 1650 and 1750. Clearly, a demographic revolution was taking shape around 1750, comparable in scope to what was happening in China though a bit later.

The population explosion resulted from a break in the traditional, if approximate, balance between births and deaths in European society. In England between 1700 and 1750, approximately 32.8 people were born annually for every 1,000 inhabitants, and 31.5 people died. Similarly, in Lombardy in the late 18th century, 39 people were born and 37 people died for every 1,000 inhabitants. Clearly, a major alteration had to occur in either the birth or the mortality rate before the expansion of population could begin. In fact, both rates changed: Families began to have more children, and a lower percentage of the population died each year. Lower infant death rates meant more people living to produce children of their own, though falling adult death rates also increased the number of older Europeans. Much is still unknown about the precise developments in population rates in the 18th and 19th centuries, but certain general features seem clear. During the period 1750–1800, for example, the population of England grew at a rate of over 1 percent a year. Approximately 80 percent of this growth can be accounted for by a decline in mortality; by 1800, only 27.1 per 1,000 people died per year. But there was also a startling rise in the number of children born annually.

While historians continue to debate the precise balance of causes involved in these dramatic changes, basic outlines are clear: Better food and a reduction in the epidemic disease cycle allowed more children to live to adulthood, which increased the population directly and also provided more parents for the next generation—a double impact. Rapidly increasing populations provided a new labor force for manufacturing. In the 18th century, this mainly involved hundreds of thousands of people, mostly rural, producing thread, cloth, and other products for market sale (and

usually supplementing this labor with a bit of agriculture). This manufacturing expansion helped sustain the growing population (though sometimes amid miserably low wages), but it could also encourage a higher
birthrate. Some people, able to earn money by their late teens, began to engage in sex earlier; the rate of illegitimate births went up. Others realized
that having an extra child or two might help the family economy by providing additional worker-assistants. And of course, new foods improved
nutrition and, with this, sexual vitality. It was no accident that the age of
puberty began to decline in 18th-century Europe, from previous levels of
16 to 18 years of age. While death-rate decline was the most important
source of Europe's population explosion, various changes on the birthrate
side, though quite short-lived, pushed the population up as well.

Conclusion

The centuries since 1500 had brought massive change. Diseases had decimated key populations. This, in addition to population growth elsewhere,
brought new, transoceanic opportunities for voluntary or forced migration, spreading the numbers of Europeans and Africans located outside
their continents of origin. A wider array of foods as well as better agricultural procedures fueled rapid population growth in a number of selected
areas.

Yet the early modern era, before 1750 or so, did not produce a general-
ized or global rise in population. Three of the six habitable continents, the
Americas and sub-Saharan Africa, experienced population declines, due
largely to the transfer of Africans, Europeans, and their diseases. The mixing of their major diseases also restrained populations in Europe and Asia.
The decline of plague, combined with economic development, increased
Eurasian populations at regionally uneven rates, and the early diffusion of
American high-yielding crops began to provide new foods. Yet China and
western Europe reached a ceiling on growth, imposed in part by climatic
cooling in the later 17th century.

Finally, the uneven picture of world demography showed in other
parts of the world. On the populations of South and Southeast Asia
much less is known, but these show considerable differences from Europe or China. In these southern climates, the cooling trend of the

mid–17th century reduced precipitation, thereby increasing periods of drought, which for wet-rice agriculture were disastrous. Trade statistics show unmistakable declines. In India, the record of famines is so distressing that no worsening in the 17th century seems possible: In the 16th century, droughts caused at least 13 famines, and in the 1560s and 1570s, famine was almost continuous. Plague swept through central and north India in 1595–1598. Malaria and smallpox were ever present, and the Ganges valley harbored cholera. India experienced at least 11 famines in the 17th century. In 1769–1770, a famine in Bengal killed one-third of the population, and the jungles reconquered croplands. Nevertheless, the period 1450–1750 saw large-scale extension of agriculture on the subcontinent, for example, in East Bengal, where Muslim aristocrats with land grants led peasants to cut and burn the jungles to create new rice lands. Trade connections opened by Portuguese, Dutch, English, and French shipping stimulated production of cotton textiles, an Indian specialty until the late 18th century. Despite the frightful record of famines and epidemics, agriculture and manufactures supported population growth. At the beginning of the 16th century for South Asia—India, Pakistan, Bangladesh—a high population estimate would be 100 million persons, rising to 175 million by 1700.

Southeast Asia was a different case. It numbered perhaps 23 million persons in 1600 and only about 33 million in 1800. The region contained vast tracts of forest and lowlands susceptible to cultivation but not yet settled. There were large trading cities and pockets of intensive wet-rice agriculture with correspondingly large populations. The remarkably slow rate of population growth compared with India, China, or Europe was due less to high mortality than to low fertility; women seem to have deliberately restricted their number of infants by aborting third and subsequent children. Another factor may have been endemic warfare between rival states or clans. Battle deaths were few, but enslavement and fleeing kept families small and mobile. European rule and Christianization in the 17th and 18th centuries may have reduced violence and released cultural restraints on fertility. Diseases did take their toll. Malaria existed but was not much feared. Smallpox was the dreaded disease, and possibly, new virulent strains came with European traders; syphilis certainly did. There is no mention of plague or cholera in Southeast Asian history at this time.

Japan's population followed a different rhythm but nonetheless grew considerably. Around 1488, it stood at about 8 million; it rose to at least 13 million, maybe more, by 1600, then leaped to 25 million. Population doubled in the 17th century, unaffected by a cooling trend or warfare. Greater isolation protected Japan from some of the global disease spread, particularly from cholera and tuberculosis. A census taken in 1721 shows that population peaked at about 30 or 31 million; it then did not grow again until after 1860. Japan's population history therefore contradicts both Europe's and China's, showing rapid growth in the 17th century while they stagnated or declined, then stagnation while they grew incredibly in the 18th and 19th centuries. Japanese urbanization in the early modern period increased remarkably: Edo in the mid–18th century had 1 million persons; Kyoto, 500,000; Osaka, 350,000. The period of population stagnation was maintained by great instability, frequent famines, and epidemics. High levels of infanticide and abortion kept fertility limited as well.

Only in the 18th century did a more clearly global trend begin to emerge. The Americas and then Africa began to emerge from their population declines, aided in the Americas by immigration and the development of mixed populations. China and Europe moved into their periods of unprecedented increase. Patterns remained uneven, in part because of the previous differentiations, but global expansion emerged as the dominant theme. The spread of disease still served as an important control, but its incidence declined by the 18th century, partly because more regular international contacts helped build up resistance levels worldwide. For better or worse, the human species was beginning to forge a new relationship with nature.

CHAPTER 15

CULTURE AND POLITICS IN THE EARLY MODERN CENTURIES

Key changes in political institutions altered the relationship between states and ordinary people at several points during the early modern period, adding to the forces of change within major civilizations and in the world at large. The development of new state-society relations was a consistent theme in world history during this period. Cultural change was crucial as well, but it operated selectively at first, intensifying clearly, and with greater international scope, during the 18th century.

Political Change: The Expanding State

The early modern period opened with a flurry of political developments: a relatively new dynasty consolidating in China and major new empires covering much of the Middle East and the Balkans (the Ottomans) and, soon, India (the Mughals). Japan's period of innovation began in the late 16th century, with a new central administration that modified the effects of feudalism. Russia's rulers, now called czars or caesars, launched a policy of expansion and limited state growth even earlier. Of the major civilizations, Africa long displayed the greatest political continuity, with its ongoing pattern of regional kingdoms. Elsewhere, political change was the rule.

Ultimately, it was western Europe that generated the most important pattern of political innovation. Beginning in the 17th century, feudalism declined and the powers of central governments increased. States took on new functions and strove for more coherent organization. Functional expansion and rationalization were the order of the day.

The power and example of the new European nation-state put pressure on several other societies in the world. European colonies in the Americas did not possess strong states, despite claims of power; it would not be until the 20th century, for example, that governments in North America rivaled their European counterparts in range of functions. In Asia, problems with administering large territories that surfaced in the 17th to 18th centuries provided new opportunities for European interference. Russia was the first large outside society to imitate western Europe explicitly, around 1700.

Changes in the West European State

Feudalism declined as the basic framework for political administration in western Europe by the 17th century. Monarchs learned new ways to claim power, beyond the loyalty of their vassals. They used classical language from the Roman Empire, revived by the Renaissance. They talked of a "divine right" of kings to rule. The Protestant Reformation, in weakening the Catholic Church, reduced religious controls on the state; in some Protestant areas, particularly where Lutheranism predominated, the state ran the new church. Wealth from world trade enriched state treasuries, allowing new activities. Growing use of cannons and gunpowder reduced the power of feudal armies, while a rising middle class provided potential bureaucrats loyal to the state, not to the aristocratic class. Strong remnants of feudalism persisted, but the state took on new dimensions.

Some of the results are familiar from the more efficient governments that had long existed in societies such as China. State bureaucracies expanded, and administrators became more specialized in areas such as finance, justice, war. The central government began to install regular representatives in outlying areas to represent its interests. Functions expanded to include growing attention to cultural matters (royal governments, such as the 17th-century French monarchy, often patronized the arts); to economic administration, as governments more consciously regulated tariff policy and even tried to set conditions for production; and to welfare, as policies—often fairly harsh—toward the poor developed. The clearest example of expanding government and bureaucracy occurred in France's absolute monarchy, which took shape in the 17th century; King Louis XIV, in particular, claimed broad powers, though he devoted his greatest energies to war making. But the example was followed in many other states, including rising areas of eastern Europe such as Prussia and in the west, in the 18th century, Spain and Portugal as well. The Prussian monarchy in the 18th century, for example, began to sponsor new agricultural methods and foods such as the potato in order to improve the state's financial base and to increase the population—a clear sign of government's new claims and capacities in the economic sphere.

Two features of the transformation of the Western state were particularly distinctive. First, many expanding monarchies began to link themselves to the idea of a nation—that is, to a geographical unit that defined itself in terms of a common language, culture, and historical experience. This definition may have been somewhat artificial—common cultures in fact had to be created—but the result could be powerful nevertheless. Louis XIV used government resources to help purify the French language. Boundaries between nations, as between France and Spain, became more meaningful. At a time when most Asian and East European empires embraced many races and cultures, the European state pattern was unusual.

Key European governments also began to think in terms of rationalization—that is, in terms of orderly procedures deliberately calculated to improve effectiveness. Armies provided a key example. European armies took on uniforms for the first time in the early modern period. They were organized into defined units, such as regiments, with a clear hierarchy of officers in command. Provisioning services were organized so that armies could be supplied without raiding the area in which they were operating. Army hospitals and even military pension schemes capped this reorganization of military life. Punishment was another area open to innovation: With greater resources and a desire to reduce crime, many European governments began to establish prisons for criminals (though older punishments, such as torture and frequent death penalties, persisted). In a related development, particularly by the 18th century, some governments began to set up rudimentary formal police forces.

The impact of a new kind of European state should not be exaggerated before the end of the 18th century. Most people still encountered governments only sporadically, in their capacities as tax collectors and military recruiters. Furthermore, two important countries held back from the expansion of monarchy that was occurring in France and parts of East-Central Europe. Britain and Holland participated in rationalization to a degree—one of the first prisons was established in Amsterdam. But their governments remained smaller than usual. Here, the greatest innovation involved political structure, not function. A major civil war occurred in England during the 17th century; several issues were involved, including religion, but a key dispute involved the relationship between king and parliament. In a settlement in 1688, the British monarchy accepted a more powerful parliament, with greater powers to initiate laws and check executive action; a number of individual rights, including limited religious freedom, complemented this structural change. Here and in Holland, the idea of a constitutional, parliamentary monarchy was being created, along with more sweeping new political ideas that talked about popular sovereignty and inalienable individual rights. These ideas were carried over into the American Revolution during the 1770s, resulting in a new state without a monarch at all but with clearly divided branches and firm protections for the rights of male citizens.

Political Change outside the West

The development of the modern state in western Europe had little general impact until the 18th and 19th centuries. European colonies did not reproduce the kinds of government being established in Europe itself. Spanish and Portuguese administrators in Latin America set up impressive offices in a few urban centers. Spain governed two huge provinces, called viceroyalties, from capitals in Mexico and Peru and later added centers in Colombia and Argentina. The systems were centralized in principle, but actually, except for military programs to keep order, government powers were quite limited. Church missions, Indian villages, and, above all, the landed estates of the new elite did most of the work of defining labor regulations and settling disputes. English colonies in North America were slightly different, featuring elected assemblies that gave local leaders greater political experience. But their reach was limited as well, as the territory of what became the United States remained rather loosely governed. Even in the 19th century, American governments would remain fairly small.

New Asian empires introduced important political systems. In the Middle East, the Ottoman Empire emphasized strong military organization, forcibly recruiting loyal soldiers, called Janissaries, from conquered territories such as the Balkans. Considerable effort went into organizing provisions for the massive capital city, Constantinople (Istanbul in Turkish). Except for taxes and military recruitment, most provinces were loosely administered, with considerable tolerance for local diversity. Though the sultan, as leader of the state, claimed absolute power, top bureaucrats gained great authority, often amassing considerable private fortunes. Provincial rulers increasingly escaped tight central control. The government did generate a centralized legal code in the 17th century and used the army effectively to keep order. But there were no major innovations in political form or function.

The same pattern basically held true in the Mughal Empire in India, formed after successful Muslim invasions around 1500. Again, large armies and efficient tax collection proved essential to administration, though the new rulers carefully recruited bureaucrats from various religious groups and set up a network of provincial governors. Ambitious efforts to regulate some Hindu customs—such as sati, the practice of suicide by widows—and to create a common language for the empire largely failed.

Both the Ottoman and Mughal empires began to deteriorate by the later 17th century. Ottoman rulers could no longer expand their conquests, which reduced the capacity to reward loyal government officials. Corruption among provincial administrators increased. The Mughal regime became less tolerant of the Hindu majority, provoking increasing resistance, and also attempted an overambitious expansion into southern India, which overtaxed government resources. Increasing European interference developed in India, and the British East India Company (a private operation, though with a British government charter) effectively took over much of the subcontinent during the 18th century. No major new political system resulted, however, as the East India Company relied on local political leaders and devoted most of its efforts to winning profits from its new domain.

China was another empire that encountered new administrative difficulties by the 18th century. The Ming (1368–1644) and then Qing (1644–1912) dynasties had provided effective rule on established Confucian, bureaucratic principles. The government easily limited contacts with European merchants and missionaries. Central schools for training bureaucrats expanded, and regulations governed relations with outlying villages and provinces in increasing detail. But imperial control faltered by the later 18th century. Bureaucrats became more self-seeking, while collection of tax revenues deteriorated amid growing population pressure and social unrest. A chief minister of the last effective emperor, Qianlong, tried for corruption in 1796, had amassed a fortune worth the modern equivalent of over a billion dollars. China was becoming another empire whose size surpassed its capacity for sustainable administration, despite an unprecedented tradition of political success.

Two societies outside western Europe did introduce significant political change in the 17th and 18th centuries. Japan banned most contact with the West and other parts of the outside world around 1600. The Tokugawa family sponsored a process of political centralization; Tokugawa shoguns maintained feudalism but limited internal warfare and created a separate government bureaucracy, while also promoting Confucian education. Administrative efficiency improved, though there were cycles of political weakness, difficulties in tax collection, and social unrest.

In Russia, czars sponsored a steady process of territorial expansion from about 1450 onward. Administration depended on close ties with the aristocracy, who served the state in return for growing control over landed estates and serf labor. Under Peter the Great (reigned 1689–1725), the government copied some Western measures—the first case of importing new principles of the modern Western state. Bureaucratic training improved, while a new council supervised the bureaucracy as a whole; the hierarchy of army officers also was regularized. The government sponsored expansion of armaments productions and the metallurgical industry. But little new contact between state and people developed, as the czars were content to tighten the system of serfdom, leaving most actual governance to the landlord class.

Culture Change: Regional Diversity and Compelling Contacts

In contrast to the previous, postclassical period, cultural issues did not shape the world framework during the early modern centuries. As in politics key changes occurred, but within individual societies, not through wider contact. As in politics also, the most important shifts involved western Europe (and European colonies in North America by the 17th century). The Protestant Reformation split the unity of Christianity. Protestants also pushed new ideas, for example, about the importance of family life, that helped transform popular culture. The scientific revolution of the 17th century was more significant still. New discoveries about gravity, planetary motion, and the circulation of the blood helped propel science to the dominant position in intellectual life, surpassing religion at this level. Beliefs in an orderly nature and in progress of knowledge had wide-ranging implications: They encouraged education, as philosophers argued that children were not defined by original sin but could be shaped through learning. In the 18th century Enlightenment, leading intellectuals argued that political and social life should be rationally planned and studied, as with physical nature. Traditional ideas about religion and about the importance of the aristocracy were attacked; new notions of democracy, even socialism and feminism, surfaced.

The changes in European culture were remarkable not only for the new directions they suggested but for their relationship to popular beliefs. European elites developed new disdain for ordinary people in certain respects, particularly in the area of popular leisure. And by no means were all cultural trends homogeneous. But many ordinary people picked up a host of novel ideas, particularly by the 18th century. Beliefs in magic declined (though only after a period of heightened fear and persecution of witches). Efforts to replace magic with more rationally organized arrangements show up in the rise of lost-and-found offices for misplaced property, which gradually did away with appeals to traditional experts, called cunning men, who sought items with magical sticks. Ideas about family changed, with growing belief in the importance of love as a basis for marriage. In 1500, if a European woman had told her parents that she could not love the man they had arranged for her to marry, she would normally have been ignored; by 1750, even courts of law might support a daughter in her pleas for love, undoing parental arrangements. Even children began to be redefined: Seen as toy- or animal-like before, at least until they were capable of work, they began to be idealized as innocent, educable creatures by the 18th century. At all levels, from science and religion to popular views of the social environment, European culture was shifting rapidly during the early modern centuries. The rapid spread of literacy, prompted by the advent of the printing press in the 15th century and also Protestant interest in reading the Bible, served as one basis for various new trends.

Japan was another center of rapid cultural change, featuring the advance of Confucianism and related education. Secular values gained ground. By the 18th century, Japan had the world's highest rate of literacy outside the West and North America.

Western contact brought huge cultural shifts to Latin America. As Spanish and Portuguese rule spread after 1500, missionaries and government officials alike worked to eliminate the high culture of the American Indian civilizations, for example, destroying most works of Mayan writing; the Spanish bishop of Yucatán so feared traditional religion that he burned all the ancient books around 1540. Missions taught Catholicism and European languages, while a new, European-born elite created cathedrals and government buildings in the reigning Western styles. Among Indians and *mestizos*—the mixed-blood population that soon became a majority— Christianity spread rapidly, though it was usually combined with older beliefs and rituals in the familiar syncretic pattern. Magical healing and Christian prayer mixed, and traditional religious offerings were brought to Christian altars. In Mexico, Christian crosses were covered by Indian religious cloth, the *huipil,* which allowed Mayans to worship both the Christian God and the older gods in the same ceremony—a compromise the priests found it politic to ignore. Massive cultural and artistic change occurred, but the hold of older styles and beliefs persisted, gradually creating a new culture, neither Western nor Indian. The practices of imported African slaves added another important ingredient to the mix in many areas.

In Africa and Asia, Christian and other Western beliefs had far less impact in the early modern centuries. A few Africans in port cities converted, but most retained older, polytheistic beliefs or adhered to Islam. The most massive popular conversions, at the end of the 18th century, were to Islam. In Asia, Christianity gained ground in the Philippines, much as in Latin America, as the Spanish authorities pressed for conversions. Even here, family habits such as communal bathing and ancestor worship persisted despite Christian condemnation. In West Asia, the Ottoman Empire ignored both Christianity and Western science, even preventing the establishment of printing presses lest traditional sources of cultural authority be undermined. Islam itself spread to part of the population of the Balkans, now under Ottoman control, but otherwise, basic styles and belief patterns continued without major change in this vital region. Japan initially showed some interest in Christianity, but at the end of the 16th century the new government, fearful of outside interference, persecuted the Christians; by 1616, the policy of virtually complete isolation was in effect. China, eager to gain bits of scientific and technical knowledge (including contact with superior Western clocks), allowed entry to a handful of Catholic missionaries. But the missionaries mainly adopted Chinese ways, and their contacts were limited; Chinese culture experienced no fundamental change. Missionaries in India had greater success, winning tens of thousands of adherents among the lower castes on the southwestern coast. But this stiffened resistance among Hindu priests, who shunned contact. In the 1600s a Jesuit missionary, Robert De Nobili, sought to win high-caste favor by learning Sanskrit and dressing and eating like the Brahmin priests. But he failed to win Hindu converts, and other Europeans denounced his abandonment of European values.

Overall, outside the Americas, most people reacted to growing European power by tightening their commitment to existing religions and regional cultures. Europeans themselves varied in their interest in proselytizing; Protestants, for example, did not yet display the missionary zeal of Catholics, and the new scientific culture spreading in the West had yet to find its international prophets.

The 18th century formed a transition period, as Western influences became more ubiquitous. China, to be sure, cracked down harder on the missionaries. The Ottomans, however, began to send ambassadors to Europe, who brought back styles and information. A new sultan's palace imitated the new residence and gardens of the French king. Western physicians and printing presses were haltingly imported, though a Muslim press was tightly restricted, printing only 27 books between 1727 and 1784. Japan, still isolated, began to allow translations of European scientific and medical works (though still forbidding religious materials). The biggest change—a genuine, if limited, cultural Westernization—occurred in Russia, from Peter the Great onward. Long interested in Western artistic styles, rulers now imported scientific, mathematical, and technical training, as well as clothing styles and art forms, including the ballet. The goals were to create more efficient bureaucrats, to demonstrate czarist power, and to avoid embarrassment in Western eyes. Ordinary people were not affected, as it was the landlord class that took on foreign ways and consequently seemed even more remote. Nor was the Orthodox religion unseated. Nevertheless, elite culture did change as noblemen increasingly lived as Westerners, often spending long periods visiting the West. By the early 19th century, Russian poets and composers began contributing to European Romantic culture. Russian leaders were now debating how Western to become, with some intellectuals urging radical, Western-style reforms, and others arguing that imitation had gone too far, that Russian values were superior.

Conclusion

Both political and cultural trends were uneven during the early modern period. Political change showed greater coherence, in the widespread development of stronger states and empires. A key cause involved new armaments: Many states, headed by the European colonizers, rode on the backs of cannons, at least in part. The empires of the period—both European overseas creations and the landed empires of Asia—are known as gunpowder empires. But not all regions were involved in new state building. And the durability of government forms was highly variable. The early decline of effectiveness of the Ottoman and particularly the Mughal Empire contrasted with longer-lasting European colonial states (which survived into the 20th century) and the new Russian Empire (which almost reached the 21st).

The early modern centuries saw massive cultural change but in specific cases, not across the board. European culture changed greatly; so, under the missionary spur, did the culture of Latin America. Japan developed important new emphases. But many other regions sought to confirm existing belief systems and even to use isolation as a means of defense. There simply were no global trends, even though the potential for international interaction increased. Indeed, it became clear that protecting distinctive cultural traditions might be a result of interaction.

CHAPTER 16

GENDER STRUCTURES, 1450–1750

Gender structures in the early modern centuries were powerfully shaped by new international population movements and commercial contacts. The contact between cultures in the postclassical period that had worked to change gender structures had often been carried out through the transmission of ideas and construction of institutions by individuals or small groups of people; the spread of Neo-Confucianism and Islam are both examples of this. Beginning in the late 15th century, international contacts often involved the movement of large numbers of people over vast distances, such as Europeans traveling to the Americas, and later to Asia and Australia, to conquer and settle, or Africans being taken as slaves to the Americas or to parts of Africa far from their homelands. In all of these movements, the gender balance between men and women was never equal, so that traditional patterns of marriage and family life were disrupted and new patterns formed.

In many areas, these new patterns involved marriage or sexual relations between individuals from widely different cultures and often with different skin tones and facial features; such skin tones were increasingly defined as "race," a category that came to be regarded as inherited through the blood, so that the children of parents from different cultures were regarded as "mixed-blood," or *mestizo*. Particularly in areas where there was substantial immigration of persons from different continents—such as Europeans and Africans in Central and South America or Europeans and Asians in southern Africa—elaborate racial hierarchies developed, which state and church authorities tried to codify and rigidify. Attempts at maintaining racial hierarchies, whether through laws or less formal means, always involved regulating sexual behavior, for the "racial mixing" regarded as worrisome was not that which occurred on a day-to-day basis in households or on plantations but that which resulted in children. "Race" is a category that can be maintained only through preventing or regulating certain types of sexual relationships, which, until the 20th century, meant attempting to prohibit all relationships between women of a higher status and men of a lower and defining the unions between men of a higher status and women of a lower, or between men and women of the lowest status, as less than true marriage, so that their children were not fully legitimate. (This also applied to class hierarchies in societies such as China, where there were not clear racial hierarchies; class boundaries were maintained by strict prohibition of any union between a higher-class woman and lower-class man and by the definition of most relationships between a higher-class man and lower-class woman as concubinage or prostitution.)

Despite attempts to keep the "races" apart, however, the fact that the vast majority of merchants, conquerors, slaves, and settlers who traveled great distances were men made this impossible, and in many parts of the world a *mestizo* culture emerged in which not only blood but religions, family patterns, cultural traditions, and languages blended. Women acted as intermediaries between local and foreign cultures, sometimes gaining great advantages for themselves and their children through their contact with dominant foreigners, though also sometimes suffering greatly as their contact with foreigners began when they were sold or given as gifts by their families or taken forcibly.

The migration of large numbers of men also had an influence on gender structures in the areas they left. Two-thirds of the slaves carried across the Atlantic from Africa were male, with female slaves more likely to become part of the trans-Saharan trade or to stay in West Africa. This reinforced polygyny in Africa, because slave women could join households as secondary wives, thus increasing the wealth and power of their owner-husbands through their work and children. (They were often favored as wives over free women as they were far from their birth families, who could not interfere in a husband's decisions.) In parts of Europe, male migration also led to a sexual imbalance among certain social groups. Because Christianity and Judaism did not allow polygyny, solutions in Europe were more difficult than in Africa; some women entered convents; some paid higher and higher dowries to attract husbands; and some simply remained unmarried, becoming an intellectual and economic problem in a culture that regarded marriage as the proper path for all women.

The goods that were carried in international trading networks also shaped gender structures. Consumer goods such as sugar and coffee required vast amounts of heavy labor, leading to the development of plantation economies in tropical areas, with largely male slave workforces. These slaves wore clothing made from cloth that was often produced in European households, where traditional gender divisions of labor were broken down because of the demands of the international marketplace, so that men, women, and children all spun and wove. The new consumer goods—foodstuffs, clothing, household furnishings—were purchased by middle- and upper-class Europeans and their descendents in North America and Australia, with women's role in such households gradually becoming more oriented toward consumption than toward production. Class status was signified by the amount and quality of goods in one's home, all of which required purchase, cleaning, care, and upkeep, which became the work—though unpaid—of the women of a household, aided perhaps by a servant or two.

Greater contact among cultures, along with other developments in this era, also changed the ways in which people thought about gender, particularly for those who thought of themselves as at the top of racial hierarchies, such as the Japanese or people of European background. Concern with the sources of differences between the races was accompanied by concerns about why and how the sexes were different, and new ideas emerged that grounded female inferiority not in a divine plan or the order of the universe but in the female body, in the same way that the "inferiority" of certain races came to be regarded as grounded in their bodies. Groups regarded as inferior, as well as religious or political opponents, were frequently charged with sexual practices regarded as deviant, and gender and sexuality pervaded the language and pictorial representations of conquest, colonialism, and conflict. For example, the pope, the leader of Catholicism, was described and shown as the "whore of Babylon" by his religious opponents, while America was depicted as a naked woman in a feather headdress or described as a virgin land waiting to be penetrated.

Both gender and race intersected with other hierarchies in many cultures, such as that of age. In some societies, including many in North

America and Asia, age brought an improvement in status for individuals of both sexes; among the Iroquois in eastern North America, for example, older women chose tribal leaders and older men acted as advisers. In other areas, such as in many parts of Africa, older women in particular were regarded with ambivalence, sometimes able to participate in men's rituals, forbidden to younger women, but also feared as having special connections to the spirit world as shamans or witches. In Europe during the 16th and 17th centuries, older women, particularly those who were widowed or single, came to be regarded with great suspicion; this combined with religious ideas and social pressures to cause an upsurge in witchcraft accusations, with perhaps 100,000 people, most of them women, executed for witchcraft.

Accusations of witchcraft were only one way in which cultures responded to perceptions of disorder and instability, but they point out that these responses were rarely gender neutral. The dramatic changes occurring in these centuries—the discovery of unknown continents, drastic population decline and then expansion, conquest, the shattering of religious institutions, revolutions and civil wars—led many cultures to feel as if their worlds were being turned upside down and that all traditions and hierarchies were threatened. Thus the hierarchy that was closest to home—that, indeed, was *in* the home—needed strengthening and enforcement at all costs, and so, many areas tightened restrictions on women. Neo-Confucianism spread to Korea and Japan, which joined China in limiting women's mobility and right to property. In Europe and China, learned men—and a few women—engaged in a vigorous debate about the intellectual and moral capabilities of woman, generally agreeing that she was deficient in reason but possibly proficient in morality. As the Ottoman Turks expanded their empire, they extended Islamic practices, and women in urban areas were increasingly veiled and secluded; this also occurred in the Mughal Empire of India and in parts of Africa, with the spread of Muslim orthodoxy to those areas.

On the whole, women's opportunities lessened in many societies during the early modern centuries, though this varied by geographic area. Gender structures changed the most during this period in western Europe, the Americas, and Africa, while in eastern Europe and Asia, continuity outweighed change for most people.

Opportunities and Restrictions in Western Europe

European history during the early modern period is often portrayed as a series of intellectual movements—the Renaissance, the Reformation, the scientific revolution, the Enlightenment—set against a background of political and economic changes—the rise of the nation-state and the expansion of capitalism. Though none of these developments was explicitly about gender, all of them shaped ideas about women and men and spawned institutions and opportunities as results of these ideas. Conversely, all of these developments—what is usually described as the "growth of modernity"—were influenced by previously existing gender structures, and all of them created greater tension between gender hierarchies and gender egalitarianism.

During the mid–15th century, the development and mass use of the printing press with movable metal type assisted an expansion of literacy in Europe, which was furthered by economic changes, in which literacy became an essential requirement in certain occupations, and by the Protestant Reformation, which encouraged Bible reading among some groups. Formal schooling opportunities for boys increased steadily in urban areas, though those for girls lagged far behind. Reading and writing were taught separately, with girls who were taught to read often not taught to write, because they attended school for a shorter time than their brothers and because writing was seen as dangerous for a woman, who might then express her own thoughts rather than simply reading those of others. Institutions of higher education, whether universities or the new humanist academies that were established as a result of the Renaissance, were for male students only, with the few women who received an advanced education doing so at home with private tutors; the talents most highly praised in men, such as ability in public speaking or writing, were suspect in women, for as one educated man commented, "An eloquent woman is never chaste."

Religious institutions also shaped gender structures, both in Europe and in the European colonies. During the 16th century, about half of Europe broke with the Roman Catholic Church, and separate Protestant churches were established in many countries and territories. Though they differed somewhat as to doctrine, all of the Protestant churches rejected the notion that clergy should be celibate and saw no value in the monastic life;

thus monasteries and convents were closed, and priests who staffed parish churches generally married and had children. Unlike Catholicism or Buddhism, there was no special religious vocation open to women in Protestantism, who were told to express their devotion domestically, through marriage and motherhood. Women were to be men's "helpmeets," though spouses were also urged to be "companions." Family life was proclaimed as the ideal for all men and women, an ideal that fit well with the standard living arrangement of largely nuclear households, which already predominated in those parts of Europe that became Protestant. Some scholars, most prominently the French historian Philippe Ariès, have noted that this emphasis on family life included new ideas about childhood. Ariès stresses that educational reformers and middle-class parents came to regard childhood as a separate stage in life, rather than viewing children as miniature adults, and they advocated treating children more kindly. Other historians have debated this view, noting that there is evidence for kindness to children and concern for their well-being in many cultures long before the early modern period, and that the cruelest treatment of children actually came after this "discovery of childhood," when children were sent to work in factories, mines, and sweatshops. There was, however, a new emphasis on the importance of motherhood by the 18th century, which added to the familial culture surrounding many women.

The nuclear family was reinforced as a unit not only through thousands of sermons and published moral guides and stories—increasingly written by Catholics as well as Protestants—but also through laws that prohibited married women from owning their own property or carrying out economic transactions without their husband's permission, or that allowed parents to disinherit their children if they married without their permission. (Married women were granted property rights again only in the mid–19th century in most of Europe.) The Protestant championing of marriage did not lessen the average age at marriage, which remained high, but it did lead to a suspicion of unmarried men as well as unmarried women. In Catholic Europe, priests, monks, and nuns remained unmarried, though nuns were increasingly ordered to be more firmly cloistered, that is, shut behind their convent walls. The exciting new roles of defender of Catholicism within Europe and missionary to lands outside Europe were to be for men only.

In the centuries after the Reformation, governments in both Protestant and Catholic Europe became increasingly concerned with regulating the sexual and moral life of their subjects. Public brothels, which had been a common part of European city life in the Middle Ages, were often closed or prostitutes required to wear clothing that clearly distinguished them from respectable women. Sexual behavior that disrupted marriage patterns and family life, such as adultery and premarital intercourse, was prosecuted more stringently, particularly if this behavior resulted in a pregnancy. Unmarried women in France, England, and Scotland were ordered to report if they became pregnant and could be charged with infanticide if they had not made a report and the child subsequently died, even if the death was from natural causes. Harsh laws were passed against homosexuality—usually termed sodomy or buggery—prescribing death by burning, although they were enforced erratically and did not prevent the development of urban social networks of male homosexuals in many of the larger cities of western Europe, such as Venice, Florence, Paris, Amsterdam, and London.

The emphasis on discipline and morality in post-Reformation states has been linked by the German sociologist Max Weber to economic changes, for Weber saw discipline (what he termed "the Protestant ethic") as essential to the new economic forms that developed in Europe at about the same time. Most scholars no longer view religious change as the cause of capitalism, but they do point out the ways in which economic structures and religious aims reinforced one another. In western European cities, for example, craft guilds that arose to organize and control production followed the male life cycle—apprenticeship, journeymanship, guild mastership—and generally excluded women from full membership. Women worked in guild shops, but on an informal basis, as "helpmeets." By the 17th century, journeymen resented even this informal participation and increasingly asserted that the most honorable workplace was one in which only men worked. Women's place, argued the journeymen in agreement with Reformation pastors, was the domestic realm. These sentiments were reinforced by women's actual legal and economic disadvantages, for women inherited less than men and could not control their property independently if they were married. Not surprisingly, most of those who were active in international and regional commercial ventures were men, although women did invest in joint-stock companies and import-export firms.

Colonialism, Castas, and the Catholic Church in Latin America

Changes in the gender structures of Europe during the early modern centuries came largely from developments within Europe itself, whereas those in Latin America came from the impact of European colonialism. During the initial period of Spanish and Portuguese conquest, existing patterns of marriage and family life, as well as everything else, were completely disrupted. American Indian women, including those who were already married, were captured, sold, and given as gifts, often to men who had wives in Europe. Some women developed close relationships with European men; others killed themselves and their children to prevent capture; still others led and participated in rebellions against European powers. The Spanish Crown initially hoped to keep native and European populations apart, using native leaders, *caciques*, as mediators between them; but the shortage of Spanish women, as well as other factors, made this impossible, and in the early decades after conquest, there was a great deal of intermarriage. This lessened somewhat in the middle decades of the 16th century, when racial origins became a consideration in inheritance, the ability to attend school, and entrance into a convent or the priesthood. Sexual relations between European men and native or *mestizo* women continued, but these were more likely to be concubinage or prostitution. One's legal status and social rank came to be based on a complex system of socioracial categories, termed *castas*, that was in theory based on place of birth, assumed race, and status of one's mother but was very difficult to enforce. In practice, except for individuals who had clear connections to Spain or who lived in isolated native villages, one's *casta* was to a large extent determined by how one looked, with lighter-skinned *mestizos* accorded a higher rank than darker, even if they were siblings. *Mestizo* men who wished to become priests or attend a university could sometimes even buy a license making them "white," though no one officially admitted that this clearly demonstrated how meaningless racial categories were.

This concern about *casta*, color, and bloodlines, combined with families' desires to hold onto property and privileges, created a pattern of intermarriage within the extended family among the elite. The Catholic Church prohibited close intermarriage, so distant cousins were the favored spouses, with older women in the family often in charge of keeping track of who could marry whom. These interconnected family networks were important means of gaining and holding economic and political power and also linked families to the church, with male members of powerful families holding important church positions and female members entering the most exclusive convents.

Among those of lower *castas*, who held little or no property and lived largely by their labor, marriage was not a major family matter and, indeed, might even be prohibited. This was particularly the case in those colonies, most prominently Brazil, that saw a massive influx of slaves from Africa. Although the Portuguese Crown remained generally tolerant of European-indigenous marriage, it disapproved of all marriages with Africans, and marriages between slaves were allowed only with the owner's permission. Most slaves in Brazil continued to be imported from Africa, and even in the 19th century men vastly outnumbered women, thus preventing the development of a family pattern centered on marriage.

The Frontier and the Family in North America

The gender structures that developed in North America were quite different from those in Latin America because of initial differences in the European arrivals' cultural heritage, religion, and levels of intermarriage with the indigenous population, as well as later differences in speed of economic development. While in most parts of Latin America a *mestizo* population developed quite quickly, in North America the density of the indigenous population was lower, and there were more women among the early groups of French and English colonists than among the Spanish and Portuguese. Thus there was much less intermarriage between indigenous and European people in North America, and their gender structures remained quite separate.

It is difficult to make any generalizations that apply to all Native American groups. Some tribes, such as the Hopi and Zuni of southwestern

North America or the Algonquian of the Middle Atlantic region, appear to have been matrilocal and perhaps matrilineal, with women and men both owning property and carrying out equally valued religious ceremonies. In other tribes, the most important rituals and positions of leadership were limited to men, though women might help choose these leaders or have a particular sphere of influence, such as choosing marital partners. In many tribes there was a strict gender division of labor in theory, with men responsible for hunting and women for horticulture, gathering shellfish, and preparing food, although this division was often less strict in practice. Many groups stressed the complementarity of the sexes in both economic life and cosmology; just as Mother Earth and Father Sky were dependent on each other, so were women and men, and very few individuals remarried unmarried. Along with this, however, many groups also had a few individuals termed *two-spirit people*, men-women or women-men (later anthropologists often termed such individuals *berdaches*), who wore the clothes and carried out the tasks of the other sex. In some groups, this was a lifelong status, perhaps the result of a family's need for children of both sexes; in some it was a temporary one, with specific ceremonial or religious duties. "Family" was often defined by spiritual linkages along with those of blood, and the connections with an extended family or clan were extremely important to most individuals.

The earliest contacts between Native Americans and Europeans were primarily for trade, but missionaries soon accompanied the traders, bringing with them an ideal of family life that stressed husbandly authority and wifely obedience. Converts were thus caught between two value systems, one of which valued hierarchy and the other consensus; among many groups, women were less likely to convert than men and maintained their cultural traditions. As European immigration brought increasing numbers of settlers, warfare between whites and Native Americans increased, which tended to emphasize men's importance among both groups.

European women were in short supply in the colonies until about 1750, but this meant that those in the colonies married younger than their counterparts in Europe and that almost all of them married. White families tended to be larger than those in Europe, as children were needed for labor. As it did in South America, the slave trade brought in about twice as many men from Africa as it did women, but laws against miscegenation prevented marriage between blacks and whites, and in the mid–17th century, laws were passed in the colonies that made all children of slave women slaves, no matter what their father's race or condition. Marriage between slaves was dependent on the will of the owner, with spouses and parents never certain that they would not be separated from each other or their children.

Though Europeans brought with them strong notions about hierarchy within the household, the fact that their North American colonies were initially thinly settled frontiers meant that family patterns and gender roles differed from those of the more thickly populated Europe. Married women were legally subject and subordinate to their husbands, and children to their parents, but the family was both more and less important as a unit. Because other institutions such as churches, schools, and governing agencies were nonexistent, distant, or weak, the family was the site of much religious training, education, and social control. Laws and sermons created an ideal for men of responsible patriarchy, of governing their household as a "little commonwealth," as their European counterparts did. In contrast, disgruntled individuals, particularly males, could leave their families and find employment and perhaps land elsewhere, an alternative ideal that developed in songs and literature of the lone frontiersman and, later, the cowboy unencumbered by family obligations. These two ideals of male conduct would continue to conflict in white North American culture long after the frontier period was over, with women viewed as either dependent or deserted. The realities of colonial and frontier life, however, often opened opportunities for women—even for those who were dependent or deserted—who worked alongside husbands and fathers or independently in fields, shops, or taverns and traveled across the country in the westward expansion.

Slavery, Polygyny, and Generational Conflict in Africa

Until the 19th century, western Africa participated in the world economy most prominently as a supplier of people, and the trans-Atlantic and trans-Saharan slave trade reinforced already evident tendencies in gender structures. As they had been before the development of the trans-Atlantic trade, most slaves in western Africa were women taken into households as domestic servants, secondary wives, or concubines; these women came most often from the non-Islamic stateless people to the south but occasionally from as far away as eastern Europe or the Black Sea region, brought in by European traders. Women as well as men in western Africa owned and traded slaves, for owning slaves could free a woman from her normal domestic or agricultural tasks and give her time to trade. These women traders sometimes later became the trading partners or wives of European traders, translating and providing commercial opportunities for their partners/husbands.

Because the population density in western Africa was low, there was competition for labor rather than land, with the usual solution—polygyny—augmented by slavery. Wealthier men acquired both wives (and their children) and slaves (and their children), with perhaps two-thirds of rural wives living in polygynous marriages. The production of children was central to a household's survival, so that fertility was a constant concern in religious and magical rituals and barrenness or impotence ascribed, as it was in Europe, to witchcraft. Men usually had to pay a bride-price to acquire a wife, and this, combined with concerns about fertility, meant that men married very late and women very early. The bride-price also set up a generational conflict between men, as households had to decide whether family resources would best be spent acquiring a first wife for a son or another wife for the father. Some analysts have seen this generational conflict as the source for the intense initiation rituals that young men often had to undergo; only those who had gone through such rituals would be allowed to join the ranks of fully adult married men. Initiation rituals were also required to join the secret societies that were an important part of many African religions. These societies were usually limited to initiated men, although there were also a few for initiated women. Women's religious authority came more often from their powers as shamans, spirit mediums, or diviners, however, through which they acted as intermediaries between the living and the dead.

This pattern of polygyny and generational conflict was also found in many groups in eastern and southern Africa, made perhaps even more intense by the lack of large-scale slavery until the 18th century. The way in which one became a powerful and wealthy "Big Man" was by acquiring many wives and children and, in some parts of eastern Africa, also by acquiring many cattle. Cattle, which were owned exclusively by men, were both economically and culturally important, and women's status in cattle-owning societies was lower than in societies of eastern Africa that did not own cattle. The conflict between older and younger men in cattle-owning societies was extremely intense; younger men in some groups lived in military outposts and did not marry but developed a warrior culture that prized physical bravery and daring, somewhat similar to that in ancient Sparta.

Continuity despite Change in Eastern Europe and Asia

The vast migrations of peoples that so altered the gender structures of Europe, the Americas, and Africa did not affect most of Asia or eastern Europe, except in a few specific areas. In eastern Europe and the huge territories of Russia, marriage remained a family decision and was very early—at age 12 to 13 for girls, 16 to 18 for boys—with the couple living with the parents of one spouse, usually of the husband. In terms of the economy, eastern Europe and Russia remained primarily agricultural, with most people dependent peasants on large estates; gender divisions of labor continued, with women usually in charge of animals and garden crops and men mostly plowing and harvesting.

One place that did see significant migration was the Spanish and Dutch areas of Southeast Asia (primarily the Philippines and Indonesia), where the policies of the Spanish Crown and the Dutch East India Company encouraged the development of a *mestizo* culture similar to that of South America, especially in the cities of Manila and Batavia. In these two cities, indigenous women often married Europeans, converted to Christianity, and developed their own culture that blended styles of dress, foods, and patterns of behavior; their children were considered fully legitimate, with their daughters forming the next generation of marital partners for European traders.

In China, Japan, and India, the European population was generally limited to a few male traders and missionaries who rarely developed permanent relations with indigenous women. Here gender structures continued to be shaped primarily by internal forces, and continuity with earlier patterns outweighed change. In China, for example, though at first the

Qing (Manchu) emperors tried to abolish foot binding (and prohibited Qing women from adopting the custom), they gave this up and largely left Chinese family life and traditions in tact. The intense emphasis on filial piety and the procreation of sons that we discussed in chapter 12 continued; even the eunuchs who served in royal and noble households often married and adopted sons, and consensual male homosexuality was prohibited for the first time in 1740, largely because it was seen as an unfilial avoidance of procreative sex. Among certain urban groups the growing commercialization of the economy made wealth a more important determinant of family status, with the result that dowries often rose to exorbitant levels; the wife's dowry might be one source of the money needed to buy concubines, generally the daughters of poorer families sold by their parents. Although wealthy and powerful Chinese men usually did not have as many women as their counterparts in Africa, officials, merchants, landlords, and scholars continued to be expected to have at least one concubine along with their wife as a mark of status. What change there was generally came from Neo-Confucian ideas that subordinated women: In 1646, stricter proof requirements were introduced for rape charges, allowing a charge of rape only if the woman had been seriously injured or killed in her struggles. Widows who refused to remarry or even committed suicide were praised in stories and sayings, and their families were able to display banners or inscriptions honoring their virtue.

The acceptance of Neo-Confucian ideas and the development of a warrior culture during the Tokugawa period (1603–1867) in Japan similarly emphasized gender hierarchy, along with other forms of social hierarchy. Upper-class women could not inherit property easily and were often used as hostages at court to assure their husband's loyalty to the Tokugawa government. A woman could be readily divorced—though she could not divorce her husband—and was often regarded as a "trial wife" until the birth of her first son. In contrast to the ideal of companionate marriage developing in Europe, husbands and wives in Japan were urged to have a quite formal relationship. Men's needs for emotional intimacy were to be met by male and female entertainers and prostitutes, the males often associated with Kabuki theater—a stylized form of drama in which all parts were played by males after 1629—and the females with the geisha tradition, a distinctive group whose services to male clients blended conversation, entertainment, hospitality, and—sometimes—sexuality. Women's needs for emotional intimacy were to be met by their children, with even conversation among women outside the household a cause for criticism.

Conclusion

Most of the developments in the early modern era led to greater disparities between male and female experience in many of the world's cultures and a reinforcement of gender hierarchies. Changes in trade and production placed greater premium on men's work, with women's labor increasingly defined as not real work but "helping," "housework," or "caring." Increasing contacts between cultures led to sharper restrictions on women, with arguments about women's inferiority and efforts to assure their domesticity helping to provide identity in an uncertain environment. But several factors also worked against these trends: Women who served as intermediaries between races could gain a special role; those in thinly settled frontier areas had opportunities unavailable in the more tightly regulated older cultures; those in areas in which business and social life was organized through families—which included most of the world in the early modern era—often retained some power over economic and political developments. Forces that both reinforced and challenged existing gender hierarchies in the early modern period would become even greater in the modern era, as political, economic, and intellectual revolutions would call all hierarchies and structures, not simply those of gender, into question.

CHAPTER 17

LABOR AND LEISURE IN THE EARLY MODERN PERIOD

The years from 1450 to 1750 were a period of rapid and fundamental change in labor patterns throughout the world. For the first time in world history, labor patterns shifted substantially in one civilization as a result of pressures from another. A new pattern in world history had emerged, linking the economies of different civilizations together, which, in turn, affected labor systems as well. The surge of western Europe onto the world stage was crucial. As western Europe became the most powerful civilization in economic and military terms (just as Islamic and Chinese civilizations had been in the postclassical period), it brought into its orbit a number of other civilizations. This was the case with the Americas, which western European powers outright conquered, but also with Africa and parts of eastern Europe, which became suppliers of raw materials and, in the African case, human labor for the West. In addition, western Europe's transformation into a military and trade leader caused profound changes in labor conditions within its own boundaries.

Although several key civilizations, such as China and the Islamic Middle East, experienced relatively little change, another overarching theme is that throughout most of the world, labor conditions worsened. In the first part of this period, landlords in eastern Europe forced peasants into serfdom. With the extension of western European power into the Americas, planters and mine owners began to rely heavily on coercive labor systems to produce raw materials in the new colonies. Africa was sucked into this system as a supplier of slaves for the plantations in the Caribbean and other regions of North and South America.

Slow Change in China and the Middle East

After 1400, few innovations either in agricultural technology or in labor systems emerged in China. This does not mean that during the Ming (1368–1644) and the early Qing (1644–1912) dynasties nothing changed. The integration of the Americas affected the agricultural economy of East Asia as well, with the 16th-century introduction of New World crops such as potatoes and corn. Corn was especially important, since it could be grown on marginal land and thus contributed to an increase in human population in China. Despite some changes, such as the new crops, that made it possible to double agricultural production over the early modern period, the foundation for Chinese agriculture remained set in the time-honored method of applying ever more human labor onto the fields. In addition, the expansion in population in China during this period, as detailed in chapter 14, meant that one of the prime fertilizers, night soil, played an increasing role in agriculture. After the 14th century, agricultural implements did not change, and bureaucrats, always eager to improve yields, looked toward the classic agricultural treatises to improve production. This worked sometimes, but other times the blind acceptance of ancient writers' claims of fantastic yields and the unsuitability of certain methods to the many different conditions in China made it difficult to improve production significantly. The dependence of bureaucrats in Ming China on ancient texts, with little original thinking or innovation, shows clearly why, despite considerable prosperity and population pressure, labor systems of Chinese civilization did not change much.

One possible incentive for change came in the first three decades of the 15th century, when the Ming emperors sent vast trading expeditions to the Indonesian archipelago, India, and the East African coast. This had the potential to transform at least the Chinese coastal cities as manufacturers and entrepôts of trade on a worldwide scale. The experiment in privileging trade (and merchants) was cut short, however, when the Chinese state realized that it would be difficult to keep control over the greatly expanded merchant activity. The traditional suspicion of merchants (who, since classical times, were seen as taking resources away from agriculture) reasserted itself, and in 1433 the government ended the state-sponsored expeditions, indeed, prohibiting anything but minor trade with China's neighbors.

In the Middle East, labor systems also did not change substantially, though Islamic culture was by no means averse to trade. Slavery and other types of coerced work continued to be an important component of Middle Eastern labor systems. Military slavery, the *devsirme* system, where the Ottoman Turks recruited young Christian boys from the Balkans to become members of the Janissaries, continued and in fact reached its apogee during the early modern period. But the composition of the slave force in the Middle East, now dominated politically by the Ottomans, changed: As Russia expanded southward into the prime slave-recruiting area of the Caucasus, the number of Slavic slaves diminished, and the African component increased as Islamic civilization expanded into the African continent. Also, larger numbers of women composed the slave caravans sent from sub-Saharan Africa to the Middle East, to provide a sufficient supply of servant women and nubile girls for the harems of wealthy individuals.

An Emerging World System

The major story of the early modern period, outside the admittedly important exceptions of China and the Middle East, was one of substantial change. As western Europe began to dominate militarily and economically, it brought into its economic sphere civilizations that it conquered outright as well as ones that remained politically independent. The Americas, Australia, and South Asia fall into the first category, whereas most of Africa remained free of direct European rule until the very end of the modern period, while nevertheless experiencing the tremendous impact of the European demand for slaves. As a result of emerging western European dominance, many parts of the world were incorporated into an economic system with western Europe at the center. This new world system brought about substantial changes in labor patterns even in regions where political control remained in the hands of non-Westerners.

Indeed, some scholars, headed by the leading world-economy theorist, sociologist Immanuel Wallerstein, have offered a generalization about the labor systems in the early modern era, arguing that they were absolutely determined by world economic position. Thus western Europe, dominant in the new international trading patterns, needed to shift to wage labor to recruit a flexible labor force that could, however, be dismissed in bad times.

Egyptian Mamluk of the 15th Century. These military slaves often were well treated, dressed in luxurious clothes, and sometimes became rulers themselves. Reprinted by permission of The British Library (ADD.18866 F113).

Societies in the dependent economies, producing cheap foods and raw materials for world trade, needed coercive labor to cut costs. This explanation has merit, but it has also been debated. Was slavery in the Americas really cost cutting, except in the special sense of responding to labor shortages that resulted from the ravages of disease? What about tight serfdom in Russia, which arose before Russia was heavily involved in world trade at all? Was there really as clear a pattern as the world economy schema would imply?

Labor systems changed especially in the Americas, as a direct consequence of the conquest of the region's major civilizations by Iberian invaders. Even where indigenous groups had not developed full civilizations and maintained a combination of hunting and agriculture, as in much of North America and many regions of South America (such as Brazil), the introduction of Europeans altered work patterns substantially. In addition to gold and silver (which only the lucky few found), the major prize of the conquest of the Americas was the vast labor reserves that the Indian population represented and the lands they occupied. Depending on the region, Indians were put to work in state-run work gangs, hunted in the jungles to be sold as slaves, or attracted to European agricultural estates and mines to work for pay. Where they could not be used, they were often expelled from the land. The conquest of the Americas implied a worsening of conditions for the indigenous peoples and an increase in the amount of labor they performed.

As the Spanish made contact with the natives in the Americas in 1492, they first saw them as people who could be coerced to do the Europeans' bidding at will. Christopher Columbus, in one of his letters, wrote that the Indians "would make good and industrious servants." The Spanish Crown preferred to avoid outright enslavement of the native populations. After a long debate with the most learned men of the realm, the Spanish Crown acknowledged by the 1540s that the Indians had souls and should not be enslaved unless they were cannibals. Afterward, the Crown permitted the use of the Indians' labor but not their enslavement. At first, the conquistadors gave out whole Indian villages in *encomienda*, which meant that the grantee could use the labor of the Indians as well as require goods as tribute. But the Crown did not want a new feudal class to emerge in the Americas, built on the manorial obligations of the Indians. Instead, it took over labor recruitment itself, having royal officials distribute a certain percentage of Indians to the Spanish colonists. Indians also paid tribute to the royal coffers, not to the conquistadors. As the indigenous population declined because of diseases—the massive population loss in the Columbian exchange—this system faltered. Spanish landowners began to attract Indians to their estates, sometimes giving them goods up front that they had to work off or sometimes simply offering them refuge from paying tribute.

In the extremely rich silver mines in the Andean highlands of present-day Bolivia, the high density of the peasant population from the former Inca Empire made possible another arrangement. In return for a 20 percent tax on silver production, the colonial state, beginning in the 1570s, required one-seventh of the Indian population in a vast area around the mines to work in the silver mines at Potosí. This system was called the *mita*. The state reorganized Andean communities, forcing people to amalgamate in villages, where Spanish authorities could more easily control the labor draft and the payment of tribute. As a result of this system, Indians were forced to work in dangerous conditions for 12 hours daily, without enough money to pay for food and lodging. Their families came along to help out and earn extra money, and the Indian workers on their days off often had to return to the mines to earn enough to survive. Many Indians died or never returned to their home communities. The *mita* system continued until the wars for independence in the early 19th century destroyed colonial institutions in Spanish America.

Decline of the indigenous population, especially in the tropical islands of the Caribbean and the coastal areas of South America, created a severe labor shortage in the Americas. The situation was exacerbated when Europeans found that certain crops, such as sugarcane, grew well in these areas and that there was a large market for these products. A ready source presented itself in Africa, where Portugal and other European countries had established trading posts and initial slave-buying operations in harbors along the coast. Soon African leaders, enticed by European guns, cloth, and rum, raided into the interior of the continent to gather slaves for sale in the coastal ports, mainly along the Atlantic. Slavery had existed in sub-Saharan Africa before the 1600s, but only after European demand increased did it begin to distort the African economy in distinctive ways. Some African states became more militaristic as they increased raids on enemy territories to gather slaves. Within certain African regions, especially in West Africa, people who fell into debt were enslaved and sold off to the Europeans in port. Thus western Europe's increasingly insatiable demand for sweets and American silver substantially launched the slave trade, and that led to the rapid expansion of the plantation complex. (See chapter 14.)

Dreadful conditions greeted the slaves even before they were put to work on the plantations in the Americas. For the period 1600–1800, possibly as many as 10 million Africans were forced to make the long voyage across the Atlantic, never to see their homes again. Of this number, the vast majority ended up in the Caribbean and along the northeastern coast of Brazil. The "Middle Passage" was horrific: people (mainly men, but including a minority of women) were crammed into slave ships, shackled to the beams, with virtually no room to move. Slavers packed in as many people as possible in order to achieve maximum profit. It is not surprising that the monthlong voyage, with poor food and lamentable hygienic conditions, meant the death of a substantial number of the human cargo. Death rates of 20 percent were expected, and if dysentery or another disease swept the ship, most slaves (and many crew members) might die before they reached port.

Once the slaves reached the other side (if they were so fortunate), they could look forward to a lifetime of servitude. Slavery was harsh everywhere, and while some slaves were better off than others, there was less variation than there had been in the classical world. Workers on the coastal plantations, hacking sugarcane in the tropical sun, and those in 18th-century Brazil, standing in cold mountain streams all day, panning gold nuggets out of the water, were the worst off. Many died, literally worked to death. Slaves who served as servants in urban houses were better fed and lived longer. One way of measuring relative conditions is to look at how long slaves survived. Boom economies led to greater exploitation, for it was easier to buy a new slave than to treat him well. In prosperous regions, such as the 17th-century Caribbean, slaves had to be imported continuously, for the population had fewer births than deaths. In some key cases the lack of purchase opportunities led to somewhat better treatment, as in the tidewater plantations of Maryland and Virginia in the 19th century, where working conditions were less harsh and slave populations reproduced themselves.

It is difficult to exaggerate the importance of the slave trade in the coastal regions of Africa, but in terms of labor conditions it is not the only story, especially when one looks farther in the interior and in regions remote from the principal slave ports. In eastern Africa, for example, while some slave raiding took place (though mainly to supply the Middle East and North Africa), a flourishing trade network in luxury goods such as ivory, betel nuts, and textiles existed, sustained by Arab traders. Most people in the interior remained peasants, whose life expectancy may even have increased with the introduction of new food crops from the Americas, such as potatoes, sweet potatoes, and corn. Indeed, during this period Bantu-speaking peoples were responsible for the continued expansion of agriculture farther into the southern part of Africa, at the expense of hunters and gatherers and herders.

Labor conditions deteriorated elsewhere, for example, in eastern Europe. Two different trends were responsible for this "second serfdom," which was more demanding than West European manorialism had been in the postclassical period. In Poland in the 17th century, increasing exports of wheat and other foodstuffs to the West gave greater power to landlords at the expense of peasants. As peasants fell into debt, they were forced to work on the large export estates not as free laborers but as members of households bound to the land. This process also occurred in Russia, but for slightly different reasons. As the Principality of Muscovy shook off the last remnants of the Golden Horde Mongols (called Tatars) in the 15th century, the Muscovite rulers relied heavily on the aristocracy, called *boyars*, for military assistance. In return, Moscow supported the aristocracy's bid to enserf the peasants in order to provide sufficient funds for these military enterprises. Newly conquered lands provided new people to work the estates, and war captives also supplemented the labor force. As the system evolved, the Muscovite princes (called czars beginning with Ivan the Terrible in the 16th century) prevented political decentralization, as had happened in feudal western Europe, by forcing the leading boyars to live in Moscow and join the imperial bureaucracy. Only on the eastern and southern margins of the emerging Russian Empire was it possible to maintain a relatively free existence, as did warlike Cossacks, who also defended the frontiers against invaders when they themselves were not harassing travelers and peasants farther inland. Elsewhere, expanding serfdom involved large amounts of work service for the landlords, who increasingly gained extensive disciplinary powers to enforce their demands. Serfs modified exactions by working slowly and by maintaining large numbers of traditional festivals, but they lost considerable control over work itself. Serfdom was officially abolished in the Russian Empire in 1861, but labor relations remained relatively coercive throughout eastern Europe into the 20th century. East European serfdom was an unusual case of a harsh labor system imposed by landlords over their own people.

The General State of Labor in the Early Modern Era

The new world system that emerged with western Europe at the apex forced changes in labor systems even in regions outside European control. The worsening of labor conditions in many places had to do with the economic reorganization of the world into those who produced primary (or raw) materials and those who manufactured goods. This was especially the case in newly conquered regions, such as the colonies in the Americas. The 18th century was the high point of African slavery, when thousands upon thousands of human beings were taken from their homes and forced to work as chattel for planters in the Americas or as slaves in the Middle East. Even parts of eastern Europe were feeling the negative effects of Western commercial influence, with the strengthening of serfdom.

In civilizations such as China and the Islamic regions of the Middle East, where western Europe had little impact in the early modern period, labor conditions did not change substantially. This was also the case in India, though penetration by Western powers (initially Portugal, then France and Britain) began to change labor conditions there after 1750. Thus, the early modern period presents a picture of great change in many regions, with some substantial islands of calm in the strongest civilizations outside the West such as the Middle East, China, and India that until this point had dominated world history.

Leisure Activities

It is difficult to generalize about leisure patterns in the early modern period. In certain ways little changed, since agriculture and its rhythms continued to determine types of leisure. The basic set of religions, which to a large extent flavored the ways in which people celebrated, did not vary much in this period in Africa and Eurasia. Worsening labor conditions, which often implied working more hours, restricted leisure activities to some certain extent. This was not always the case, however. At times, celebrations and leisure activities intensified in a period when working was more difficult, because leisure activities such as dancing and drinking became important means of releasing oneself from the daily tribulations of living. In the case of African slaves in Brazil, for example, the plantation slaves' celebrations were intense affairs, with African drums and dancing until exhaustion.

The region where leisure activities changed the most in this period was doubtless that of the Americas. The introduction of millions of slaves from the African continent meant an integration of African culture into the patterns of everyday life, including leisure. In both North and South America, African slaves contributed much to changes in leisure patterns far beyond their own circle. This is evident in particular in musical forms and in dance. New dances emerged, such as *candomble* in Brazil, which became an amalgam of dance and a self-defense system. Since slaves were not permitted to possess or use weapons, they developed this dance from African forms to protect themselves without weapons. Even European colonists accepted fragments of African rhythms into their music and dances (especially where the African influence was greatest, such as Brazil and the Caribbean).

Likewise, the European influence was felt throughout the region, even in some of the most isolated regions of the continent. Where the Indians accepted Christianity, the feast calendar changed substantially. South of the equator, the festivals associated with the agricultural cycle lost their original meanings, since Easter (the celebration of the resurrection of Christ), for example, long associated with the fertility rites of springtime Europe, there fell in autumn. The festival in the Southern Hemisphere took on a more religious cast and emphasized more the suffering and death of Christ, without the heavy emphasis on rebirth that characterized the Northern Hemisphere. Christmas took the place of the time of fertility and rebirth, the colonists and the Indians worshiping Christ as a child, with many of the implications that were implicit in the Easter celebrations in the Northern Hemisphere. The summer solstice in Europe, which fell close to Saint John's Day, was instead the winter solstice in South America, where people lit fires and drank long into the night on the night of Saint John, to frighten away the forces of darkness.

Since the Spanish and Portuguese missionaries could not minister to all the Indians directly, and Indian conversions remained partial especially in rural areas, the Christian celebrations kept much of their non-Christian content. Indeed, periodic inquiries by Spanish priests into the habits of the Indians invariably uncovered a non-Christian foundation that colonial officials found impossible to erase. Thus, many of the dates for celebrations changed somewhat for the indigenous population, but the meanings behind the celebrations remained steeped in the textures of everyday life that had existed before the conquest.

Important leisure changes also occurred in western Europe, associated with cultural shifts and with new work patterns—though there was no revolutionary upheaval as yet. The rise of Protestantism undermined Catholic festivals in many parts of Europe and cut into traditional leisure (just as it cut into previous gender patterns). Many Protestants criticized popular pasttimes such as gambling and dancing. Even Catholic authorities sought to discipline popular leisure, to remove pagan remnants that had long been tolerated. Finally, some European governments tried to regulate games, such as primitive forms of football, that caused too many deaths.

None of this reduced traditional leisure too seriously, except for brief periods such as the years of Puritan rule in mid-17th-century England. More important was a growing distaste by elite Europeans for the doings of the masses. Not just religion but an increasing refinement of manners that had started in the Renaissance caused the drinking and brawling associated with traditional festivals to be scorned. Aristocratic groups developed new audiences for musical and dramatic performances, in palaces or other exclusive sites. The old custom of landlords joining in with their peasants in periodic celebrations, which could allow the peasants to let off steam, began to decline. Increased interest in more regular work habits as part of Europe's growing economy pushed in the same direction. There was no new leisure regime yet, though a few innovations occurred that created new spectator opportunities—such as the first European circuses. But there were signs that some of the purposes of traditional leisure were eroding, or at least encountering new obstacles. Here, as with work in the world economy, were trends that would accelerate after 1750.

EPILOGUE

Beneath the surface of world history—the rise of certain societies and the doldrums of others—basic economic and population forces reshaped the contours of daily life from 1450 through 1750. Growing commercial activity encouraged or required more production for the market, in manufacturing, agriculture, and mining. Almost every major society was drawn in, though at different times and on different terms. Exchange of foods and new agricultural methods promoted a steady increase in world population, even in societies otherwise fairly isolated. This, along with disease-induced population disasters in key regions, promoted new, transoceanic patterns of migration, some voluntary, some forced through slavery or indenture.

Commercialization and population growth worsened the quality of life for many people during much of the early modern period. We have seen that many of the new economic systems shunted women to the side, leaving the newer forms of work increasingly in male hands. Population growth meant new family responsibilities, for example, and these fell disproportionately on women's shoulders. Key cultural changes in both western Europe and East Asia restricted women as well. The rise of science and Neo-Confucianism downgraded women's capacities. Work conditions tightened, most notably in expanded slavery and in serfdom. The early modern centuries saw the birth of new ideas of progress, with doctrines of the scientific revolution and the European Enlightenment. But whatever the new hopes, progress was far from reality for many people, in many basic aspects of their lives.

Patterns of change challenged many traditional identities, especially those rooted in local communities. Market economies required more interaction with strangers and with impersonal economic forces. Migration and colonial domination brought new contacts. Many societies fought to

Slave Labor in the Americas. Slaves seeking gold or diamonds in the streams of Minas Gerais, Brazil, faced arduous conditions. They had to bend over in cold mountain streams from dawn to dusk, to filter gems or precious metals from the sand. From Robert Edgar Conrad, *Children of God's Fire* (New York, 1983). Reprinted by permission of the author.

retain older identities, struggling, for example, to limit trade and missionary intrusions during much of the period.

Diversity in the world's societies continued, along with change. Some new diversity was caused by change, as in the new gap between western Europe and an economically weaker Latin America. Distinctiveness also resulted from different traditions. The greater isolation of China and Japan was novel, but it reflected older ideas about superiority and (particularly in the Chinese case) a cultural disdain for merchant activities. The lack of interest in western science in the Ottoman Empire followed in part from older Islamic scorn for western Europe. One result of diversity was the absence of any clear global cultural patterns. Important changes in belief systems occurred within individual societies, but there were few crosscutting currents. Their early modern period saw widespread interest in strengthening the state, whether through the land-based empires of Asia or the newly efficient states of western Europe and Russia. Separate states helped maintain regional identities. Even basic population patterns moved in different ways, thanks to the impacts of disease, slave trade, and new foods. The early modern period, in sum, unleashed a host of new forces, but they pulled in various directions depending on regional circumstances.

FOR FURTHER READING

POPULATION/BIOLOGY

Mauro Ambrosoli, *The Wild and the Sown: Botany and Agriculture in Western Europe, 1350–1850* (1997).

Noble David Cook, *Born to Die: Disease and New World Conquest, 1492–1650* (1998).

————, *Demographic Collapse: Indian Peru* (1981).

William Cronon, *Changes in the Land: Indians, Colonists and the Ecology of New England* (1983).

Alfred Crosby, *The Columbian Exchange: Biological and Cultural Consequences of 1492* (1972).

William M. Denevan, ed., *The Native Population of the Americas in 1492*, 2d ed. (1992).

Ping-ti Ho, *Studies on the Population of China, 1368–1900* (1959).

Ann Janetta, *Epidemics and Mortality in Early Modern Japan* (1987).

Kenneth Kiple, ed., *The African Exchange: Toward a Biological History of Black People* (1987).

Joseph Miller, *Way of Death: Merchant Capitalism and the Angolan Slave Trade, 1730–1830* (1988).

J. C. Riley, *The Eighteenth-Century Campaign to Avoid Disease* (1987).

David Stannard, *Before the Horror: The Population of Hawai'i on the Eve of Western Contact* (1990).

CULTURE

Michael Adas, *Machines as the Measure of Man: Science, Technology, and Ideologies of Western Domination* (1989).

Evgenii Anisimov, *The Reforms of Peter the Great: Progress through Coercion in Russia*, trans. John Alexander (1993).

Peter Burke, *Popular Culture in Early Modern Europe* (1978).

Gerard Chaliand, *The Penguin Atlas of Diasporas* (1995).

K. N. Chaudhuri, *Asia before Europe: Economy and Civilization of the Indian Ocean from the Rise of Islam to 1750* (1990).

Richard Maxwell Eaton, *The Rise of Islam and the Bengal Frontier, 1204–1760* (1993).

Carlos Fuentes, *The Buried Mirror: Reflections on Spain and the New World* (1992).

Graham W. Irwin, ed., *Africans Abroad: A Documentary History of the Black Diaspora in Asia, Latin America, and the Caribbean during the Age of Slavery* (1977).

James Kritzeck, ed., *Islam in Africa* (1969).

Francis Robinson, ed., *The Cambridge Illustrated History of the Islamic World* (1996).

Howard Morley Sachar, *The Course of Modern Jewish History* (1990).

J. Spence, *The Memory Palace of Matteo Ricci* (1984).

Sheldon Watt, *A Social History of Western Europe, 1450–1720* (1984).

STATE AND SOCIETY

Philip Curtin et al., *African History: From Earliest Times to Independence*, 2d ed. (1995).

Peter Duus, *Feudalism in Japan*, 3d ed. (1993).

John F. Richards, *The Mughal Empire* (1993).

Charles Tilly, *Big Structures, Large Processes, Huge Comparisons* (1985).

———, ed., *The Formation of National States in Western Europe* (1975).

James D. Tracy, ed., *The Political Economy of Merchant Empires: State Power and World Trade, 1350–1750* (1991).

A. D. Twitchett and Frederick Mole, eds., *The Cambridge History of China: The Ming Dynasty* (1998).

GENDER

Joel F. Harrington, *Reordering Marriage and Society in Reformation Germany* (1995).

Asunción Lavrin, ed., *Sexuality and Marriage in Colonial Latin America* (1989).

Mary Beth Norton, *Founding Mothers and Fathers: Gendered Power and the Forming of American Society* (1996).

Claire Robertson and Martin A. Klein, *Women and Slavery in Africa* (1983).

Susan Schroeder, Stephanie Wood, and Robert Haskett, eds., *Indian Women of Early Mexico* (1997).

Richard Trexler, *Sex and Conquest: Gendered Violence, Political Order, and the European Conquest of the Americas* (1995).

Rubie S. Watson and Patricia Buckley Ebrey, *Marriage and Inequality in Chinese Society* (1991).

Merry E. Wiesner, *Women and Gender in Early Modern Europe* (1993).

LABOR AND LEISURE

Peter Bakewell, *Miners of the Red Mountain: Indian Labor in Potosí, 1545–1650* (1984).

François Chevalier, *Land and Society in Colonial Mexico: The Great Hacienda* (1963).

Murray Gordon, *Slavery in the Arab World* (1989).

Arcadius Kahan, *The Plow, the Hammer, and the Knout: An Economic History of Eighteenth Century Russia* (1985).

Peter Kolchin, *Unfree Labor: American Slavery and Russian Serfdom* (1987).

Hugh Thomas, *The Slave Trade: The Story of the Atlantic Slave Trade, 1440–1870* (1997).

Immanuel Wallerstein, *The Modern World System* (1980).

PART V

The Long 19th Century, 1750–1914

Highlights. This relatively short world history period combined trends from the previous, early modern period, such as the intensification of the world economy, with decisive new factors. Heading the list of innovations was the Industrial Revolution in western Europe and the United States, which produced a dramatic new society and economy and greatly extended the power of the West in the wider world.

Key Developments. The Industrial Revolution created factories as the key production units, organizing labor on an unprecedented scale. Governments expanded still further, taking on tasks such as mass education.

After the Industrial Revolution took hold, furthermore, Europe was able to put pressure on all parts of the world, no matter what their proud traditions. Increasing ineffectiveness in several empires compounded this development. European imperialism triumphed in many areas, backed by new weapons and transportation systems. India, in fact, fell to British control even before industrialization, as a once-vigorous Mughal Empire became intolerant and provoked new Hindu resistance while its political dynamism declined. By the 19th century, all parts of the world had to consider whether and how they might imitate European industrial power and government forms. A few centers reacted relatively quickly. Most parts of North America, headed by the new United States, applied key Western political ideas and cultural forms, adding new components of their own, and also began to industrialize rapidly. Russia, which had launched a pattern of selective imitation of the West early in the 18th century, extended this into the first phase of industrialization by the 1890s. Japan was another quick study, replacing its feudal regime in 1868 and moving toward rapid economic change. Much of the rest of the world hesitated or found itself powerless to shift gears so quickly. Latin America won political independence but encountered growing Western economic penetration. China and the Ottoman Empire suffered growing Western intervention, as reform efforts proved inadequate. Africa, which had maintained political independence, had to adapt to the end of the slave trade. After 1860, European countries took political control of the African subcontinent and introduced new forms of economic domination.

Patterns in the long 19th century were complicated in several ways, beneath the surface of mounting industrialization and Western imperialism. Western examples were themselves complex. In addition to the Industrial Revolution, western Europe and the United States (as well as Latin America) experienced a surge of political revolution from 1770 to 1848. Political revolutions highlighted new principles of individual liberty; wider political participation, sometimes including democracy; and the importance of parliamentary, constitutional regimes. They also inspired new movements of nationalism. These ideas could be exported, and in some cases they were used in opposition to developments such as imperialism. In the West, new ideas combined with economic change to alter relationships between men and women. The same combination led to a new movement to limit birthrates. The international implications of some of these developments would be more significant in the 20th century than in the 19th, but some initial responses emerged.

Finally, of course, different parts of the world encountered the dominant forces of this period in different ways. Some places became colonies, while others remained at least technically independent. Some, like Japan, moved quickly to major reforms; others hesitated. Prior traditions and different contemporary circumstances produced new diversities around the world, even as the capacity for international contact steadily increased.

Forces of change embroiled Europe itself in new tensions by 1900. Imperialism increased national rivalries within Europe. Industrialization led to more massive armaments, such as repeating rifles, machine guns, and new battleships, and government military purchases proved increasingly important to industrial prosperity. Alliance systems in Europe created hostile camps, with Germany at the center of one group and France, Russia, and Britain linked in another. The framework produced the first great modern war, and with it, a set of new international developments.

The long 19th century ended with World War I, as European countries engaged in massive internal warfare while other parts of the world began, gradually, to seize greater initiatives. The results would eventually set a new stage for contemporary world history.

V. The Long 19th Century, 1750–1914

1750	Industrial Revolution begins in western Europe with mining, textiles
1764ff.	British control of Bengal
1770	Invention of steam engine by James Watt
1774	White Lotus Society risings in China
1775–1783	American Revolution
1780s–1790s	First writings by modern feminists—Mary Wollstonecraft and others
1787ff.	Sierra Leone founded as British colony for freed slaves
1789–1799	French Revolution
1790s–1840s	Beginnings of demographic transition in western Europe, United States; gradually falling birthrates
1794	Haitian uprising against France, led by Toussaint L'Ouverture; independence and end of slavery there
1807–1834	Trans-Atlantic slave trade abolished
1808	Formation of governing junta in Venezuela
1810	Independent government in Argentina; leadership of Mexican revolt by Miguel Hidalgo y Castilla
1811ff.	Reforms in Egypt by Mehemet Ali
1812	Failure of Napoleonic invasion of Russia
1814	Acquisition by British of Dutch South Africa
1815	Congress of Vienna
1820s	United States begins to industrialize with textile manufacturing

1820–1829	Greek war for independence
1823	Independence of United Provinces of Central America
1827–1829ff.	Reorganization of British rule in India; development of civil service, new legal codes
1830sff.	Rise of liberalism, nationalism
1830, 1848	Revolutions in several European countries
1830	Takeover of Algeria begun by France
1830ff.	Formation of firmer Bantu governments in southern Africa
1834	Abolition of slavery in South Africa
1839–1842	Opium Wars in China
1844–1846	Mexican-American War; occupation of Mexico by United States; upper California, New Mexico acquired by United States
1848	Writings of Karl Marx
1850sff.	Development of railroad in India
1852–1853	British war with Burma; growing influence gained by Britain
1853	Perry expedition to Japan
1854ff.	Expansion of French from Senegal
1854–1856	Crimean War
1856	Gain of virtual independence by Romania
1857–1859	Second Opium War
1858	Professional baseball begins
1858ff.	Takeover of Indochina begun by France
1859	Charles Darwin, *Origin of Species*
1859–1870	Italian unification
1860s	Soccer evolves into sport in England; Japan begins to industrialize
1860s–1870s	Reforms in Russia by Alexander II in judiciary, local governments
1860	German trade station set up in Cameroons
1861	Beginning of British expansion in Nigeria; Russian emancipation of the serfs
1861–1865	U.S. Civil War

1864–1871	German unification
1867	Discovery of South African diamonds; increase in importation of Indian laborers
1868–1912	Meiji period in Japan
1869	Completion of the Suez Canal
1875ff.	Explosion of European imperialism in Africa
1876	Promulgation of Ottoman constitution, guaranteeing individual freedoms, setting up parliament
1876–1911	Porfirio Díaz president in Mexico
1877–1878	Russo-Turkish War; independence gained by new Balkan nations
1878ff.	Expansion of British, French interior expeditions in West Africa
1879–1907	European alliance system
1880s	Russia begins to industrialize
1880sff.	Growing commercialization of Latin American economy
1885	Formation of Indian National Congress
1885–1886	British takeover of much of Burma
1886	Discovery of South African gold and development of railway; steel industry begun in India
1888	Slavery abolished in Brazil
1894–1895	Sino-Japanese War
1896ff.	Rise of Young Turk movement
1896–1899	Revolt against Spain in the Philippines
1898	Formation of Marxist Social Democratic Party in Russia; Spanish-American War; acquisition of Puerto Rico by United States; protectorate over Cuba
1899–1901	Boxer Rebellion in China
1899–1902	Boer War
1914	World War I

CHAPTER 18

POPULATING THE EARTH

Explosion, Migration, and New Controls

The period 1750–1914 witnessed a nearly vertical rise in population, encompassing most areas of the world, though to different degrees. Asian populations almost doubled. European populations nearly tripled. (Those in Russia quadrupled.) African population growth was more modest, at 30 percent, but still extremely rapid by any prior standard. American populations increased ninefold. The global rate, finally, was over 110 percent. Only Pacific Oceania fell back, due to the final major impact of contact on virgin soil populations; but even here, vigorous growth resumed after 1850.

There were several causes of this unprecedented increase. Prior population growth, particularly in Europe and China, played a vital role: There were more potential parents available, so increased numbers of children almost inevitably resulted from trends already in place by 1750 or 1800. Surges in the Americas reflected the end of the virgin soil epidemics, which freed populations to enjoy highly fertile agricultural lands, with resultant high birthrates. Whites in the British colonies of North America married earlier than their European counterparts and had more children, seen as vital sources of labor. Massive immigration added to the growth in the colonies. African increases reflect the end of the slave trade and the clear impact of adoption of American foods, particularly corn.

Population growth, particularly where it was most concentrated, inevitably pushed to new patterns of migration, as in earlier historical periods. African migration now virtually ceased, with the international slave trade curtailed early in the 19th century (except for considerable, if traditional, sale to the Middle East). European migrations accelerated, however,

	-400	-200	10 C.E.	200	400	500	600	700	800	900	1000	1100	1200
China	19	40	70	60	25	32	49	44	56	48	56	83	124
South Asia	30	55	46	45	32	33	37	50	43	38	40	48	69
Middle East	42	52	47	46	45	41	32	25	29	33	33	28	27
Japan	1	1	2	2	4	5	5	4	4	4	4	5	7
Rest of Asia	3	4	5	5	7	8	11	12	14	16	19	24	31
Europe	19	25	31	44	36	30	22	22	25	28	30	35	49
Former Soviet Union	13	14	12	13	12	11	11	10	10	11	13	15	17
North Africa	10	14	14	16	13	11	7	6	9	8	9	8	8
Sub-Saharan Africa	7	9	12	14	18	20	17	15	16	20	30	30	40
North America	1	2	2	2	2	2	2	2	2	2	2	2	3
Latin America	7	8	10	9	11	13	14	15	15	13	16	19	23
Oceania	1	1	1	1	1	1	1	1	1	1	1	2	2
World Total	153	225	252	257	206	207	208	206	224	222	253	299	400

	1250	1300	1340	1400	1500	1600	1700	1750	1800	1850	1900	1950	1970
China	112	83	70	70	84	110	150	220	330	435	415	558	774
South Asia	83	100	101	74	95	145	175	165	180	216	290	431	667
Middle East	22	21	22	19	23	30	30	28	28	31	38	75	118
Japan	9	10	10	9	10	11	25	26	25	30	45	84	104
Rest of Asia	31	29	29	29	33	42	53	61	68	78	115	245	386
Europe	57	70	74	52	67	89	95	111	146	209	295	395	462
Former Soviet Union	14	16	16	13	17	22	30	35	49	79	127	180	243
North Africa	9	8	9	8	9	9	10	10	10	12	43	52	87
Sub-Saharan Africa	49	60	71	60	78	104	97	94	92	90	95	167	266
North America	3	3	11	4	4.5	3	2	3	5	25	90	166	228
Latin America	30	36	38	42	53	10	10	15	19	34	75	164	283
Oceania	2	2	2	2	3	3	3	3	2	2	6	13	19
World Total	421	438	453	382	476.5	578	680	771	954	1241	1634	2530	3637

Population Growth in the Major Regions, 400 B.C.E. to 1970 C.E. Adapted from Jean-Noel Biraben, "Essai sur l'évolution du nombre des hommes," *Population* 34 (1979): 13–25; Massimo Livi-Bacci, *A Concise History of World Population*, 2nd ed. (Malden, MA: Blackwell, 1997); William M. Denevan, ed., *The Native Population of the Americas in 1492* (Madison: University of Wisconsin Press, 1976).

and they were joined by new levels of Asian migration as well. Asian migration added to the global relocations of peoples that had begun in the early modern period, though specific patterns differed from European streams because of different immigrant attitudes and, particularly, new efforts at racial restriction.

Two other developments were particularly novel, though they both involved European populations (or European immigrants to places such as the United States) primarily at this point. First, medical and public health interventions began to add to population growth potential, particularly in urban areas. Second, the sheer level of expansion prompted new attention to growth as a problem, both socially and within family contexts, and to new methods of population control. These two innovations were particularly associated with the Industrial Revolution.

European Patterns

Because of industrialization, but also because of a vast increase in agricultural output, without which industrialization would have been impossible, West Europeans by the latter half of the 19th century enjoyed higher standards of living and longer, healthier lives than most of the world's peoples. European populations increased enormously, colonizing and populating three continents in addition to Europe, as well as part of the tip of South Africa and miscellaneous islands around the world. This vast population increase drastically altered the ethnic and cultural distribution of the world's peoples. The change also ushered in what some scholars call the *demographic transition*, a shift from high to low mortality but also from high to low fertility. The latter effect in Western society, visible by the end of the 19th century in a limitation of family size, resulted from reactions to high population growth and mechanization alike, in a new effort to assert control over the demographic forces that had been unleashed during the early modern centuries.

In Europe as a whole, population rose from 188 million in 1800 to 400 million in 1900. The continued expansion was quite general. Certain regions, even whole countries, experienced an unusually rapid rise. Britain and Germany approximately tripled their population during the 19th century, after an even faster rate of increase in the late 18th century. France barely doubled its population between 1700 and 1900. Obviously, differences in degree must be noted. Distinctions in date are equally important. The population boom in West and Central Europe was most intense between 1750 and 1850. The factors promoting this boom touched eastern and southern Europe in a more limited way, and it was the period after 1850 that saw the most significant increase in these regions, with the spread of Western techniques of midwifery and vaccination playing a leading role. Some areas, such as Italy and the Balkans, even increased their rate of growth after 1870. By 1900, virtually every area of Europe had contributed to the tremendous surge of population, but each major region was at a different stage of demographic change.

Improvements in food supply continued trends that had started in the late 17th century. New lands were put under cultivation, while the use of crops of American origin, particularly the potato, continued to expand. Setbacks did occur. Regional agricultural failures were the most common cause of economic recessions until 1850, and they could lead to localized famines as well. A major potato blight in 1846–1847 led to the deaths of several million persons in Ireland and the emigration of many more, and Ireland never recovered the population levels the potato had sustained to that point. Bad grain harvests at the same time led to increased hardship throughout much of Europe.

After 1850, however, the expansion of foods more regularly kept pace with population growth, though the poorer classes remained malnourished. Two developments were crucial. First, the application of science and new technology to agriculture increased. Led by German universities, increasing research was devoted to improving seeds, developing chemical fertilizers, and advancing livestock. After 1861, with the development of land-grant universities in the United States that had huge agricultural programs, American agronomic research added to this mix. Mechanization included the use of horse-drawn harvesters and seed drills, many developed initially in the United States. It also included mechanical cream separators and other food-processing devices that improved supply. The second development involved industrially based transportation. With trains and steam shipping, it became possible to move foods to needy regions within western Europe quickly. Famine (as opposed to malnutrition) became a thing of the past. Many West European countries, headed by Britain, began also to import increasing amounts of food, not only from eastern Europe, a traditional source, but also from the Americas and Australia–New Zealand. Steam shipping, which improved speed and capacity, as well as new procedures for canning and refrigerating foods (particularly after 1870), was fundamental to these developments.

Europe's population growth included one additional innovation by the 19th century: It combined with rapid urbanization. More and more West Europeans moved from countryside to city, and big cities (both capitals, such as Paris, and industrial centers such as Manchester and Düsseldorf) grew most rapidly of all. By 1850, over half of all the people in England lived in cities, a first in human history. In one sense, this pattern seems inevitable: Growing numbers of people pressed available resources on the land, even when farm work was combined with a bit of manufacturing, so people crowded into cities seeking work or other resources. Traditionally, however, death rates in cities surpassed those in the countryside by a large margin; cities had maintained population size only through steady in-migration. Thus rapid urbanization should have reduced overall population growth, but by the middle of the 19th century this was no longer the case. Urban death rates remained high, particularly in the lower-class slums, but they began to decline rapidly. The greater reliability of food supplies was a factor here. Even more important were the gains in urban sanitation, as well as measures such as inspection of housing. Reformers, including enlightened doctors, began to study the causes of high death rates and to urge remediation. Even before the discovery of germs, beliefs that disease spread by "miasmas" prompted attention to sewers and open garbage; Edwin Chadwick led an exemplary urban crusade for underground sewers in England in the 1830s. Gradually, public health provisions began to cut into customary urban mortality rates. By 1900, in some parts of western Europe, life expectancy in the cities began to surpass that of the rural areas. Industrial societies had figured out ways to combine large and growing cities with population growth—a development that would soon spread to other parts of the world.

Public health measures early on were particularly directed at epidemic disease. New levels of contacts with southern Asia, particularly India, brought major cholera epidemics—a disease with which Europeans had no experience. Vulnerability was increased by polluted urban water supplies. In one epidemic in the 1830s (which ultimately reached the United States), Paris grave diggers fled, letting bodies pile up in the streets, and English mobs attacked hospitals. Other epidemics hit in 1848 and 1852–1854. Medical reaction then began to be effective, in the form of improved sanitation and water supply measures. By the 1880s, only Russia, the Mediterranean, and a few southern United States cities remained susceptible. By this point, understanding of the germ theory led not only to sanitary controls but also to new advice about protecting the purity of infant foods and the importance of sterile procedures in childbirth and in hospitals. Europe and the

United States did not become disease-free—tuberculosis was a major problem, for example—but mortality rates began to decline rapidly, particularly in urban areas. Rapid changes in death-rate patterns began to surpass shifts in food supply as a source of population growth in the industrial regions.

The unprecedented increase in population, combined with urbanization, was the most important feature of demographic change, but it was not the only one. In the century and a half after 1780, Europe sent 40 million people to the two Americas, Australia, Asiatic Russia, and other areas. Emigration was one of the clearest expressions of the turmoil that increasing population brought to European society. In the first generations of demographic rise, economic opportunities failed to keep pace with the population. Emigration was most intense when population grew most rapidly, and it tended to decline once industrialization developed sufficiently to absorb most of the increase. Britain and Ireland supplied most of the emigrants at first, reflecting the intensity of population pressure in the two islands. In the Irish case this was tragically amplified by the huge potato famine, caused by plant disease, in 1846–1847. The agricultural crisis of the 1840s convinced many German peasants that the land could no longer support them, and a wave of German emigration ensued. Eastern and southern Europe provided most of their emigrants at the end of the 19th century. By 1914, 17 million people had emigrated from Britain and Ireland, 4 million from Austria-Hungary, 2.5 million from Russia, and 10 million from Italy. Only a few countries, such as France, largely escaped the movement. Between 1846 and 1932, Britain and Ireland sent out 18 million migrants; Spain and Portugal, 6.5 million; Italy, 11 million; Poland and Russia, 2.9 million.

Europe's population explosion thus continued—indeed, redefined—the rebalancing of peoples among key regions of the world that the Columbian exchange had begun. European immigration fueled the rapid westward expansion of the United States, and a bit later the same pattern emerged in Canada. It provided new peoples for Latin America, particularly in Argentina, Uruguay, Chile, and, to an extent, Brazil, among other things replacing the previous stream of African slaves. Argentina and Uruguay alone received 7.1 million European immigrants. From the 1780s on, the European migration populated Australia, pushing back the Aborigines, who were also decimated by disease. In most of these regions, in effect, Europe exported itself, creating new societies strongly European in people and culture. Smaller, though significant, European enclaves also entered southern Africa, Algeria, and a few other regions, where they long served as powerful minorities.

Recipients of European Migration: Rebalancing the Peoples of the World
(estimates for 1846–1932, in millions)

United States	34.2
Argentina and Uruguay	7.1
Canada	5.2
Brazil	4.4
Australia and New Zealand	3.5
Cuba	.9

Asian Patterns

Asian population growth rates were slower than those of Europe, but they operated from a much higher initial base and generated ever more concentrated numbers. The resultant levels could cause massive hardship and unrest, with peasants pressed against the limits of available land supply. Many scholars believe that the sheer burden and expense of dealing with larger populations restricted Chinese flexibility in the 19th century, limiting resources available for economic initiatives.

Japanese populations began to increase rapidly after the 1860s, because of the importation of agricultural methods from the West as well as government encouragement to more intensive rice growing. Agricultural research figured high on the agendas of expanding Japanese universities. Japan was also quick to adopt urban public health measures, of the sort pioneered in western Europe. The result was an end to the long period of relative population stability in the islands. New populations provided labor for industrialization. They also helped spur Japanese imperialism.

Asian population growth inevitably prompted new patterns of migration, though the numbers involved were lower than those of Europe, if only because major receiving territories lay in European hands. Significant numbers of Chinese and Japanese immigrated to Pacific island territories and also to European agricultural holdings and mining regions in Southeast Asia. It was Chinese immigrants, for example, who provided the labor for the growing tin mines of 19th-century Malaysia—mines that were responding to rising European demand for raw materials. By the 1860s, tens of thousands of Chinese immigrants were involved, often through contract labor. Large numbers of Asians also immigrated to the western United States and to the Pacific areas of Latin America. They were sometimes specifically recruited, for example, by American railroad builders. A number of patterns of indenture developed, for instance, Indian workers being moved to various British colonies, including territories in Africa and in the Caribbean.

Asian migration was often restricted by racist reactions. Australian and United States policies limited entry. Asian movement was also limited by intense cultural attachments to the native land—which included efforts to send bodies back for burial after death. Another problem, common in other immigration histories, involved disproportionate recruitment of males, which for a time limited marriage and reproduction opportunities. Nevertheless, substantial and durable Asian minorities did develop in a number of new areas in addition to more familiar centers, such as the southeast, in Asia itself. And the flow to Southeast Asia was itself substantial, particularly from China.

Gaining precise figures on the Asian migrations is difficult because some immigration occurred illegally, after restrictive laws were passed in places such as Canada, Australia, and the United States, and also because there were high rates of return to Asia. Overall levels did not match the European outflow, but they were high enough to establish the significant immigrant minorities in many parts of the world. During the 1890s, for example, 190,000 Indians emigrated outside Asia, often as part of indentured labor contracts and especially to the Caribbean. Overall, between 1846 and 1933, 1,194,000 Indians emigrated. In the same period, 518,000 Japanese emigrated; 246,000 left during the 1890s alone. By the early 20th century there were about 22,000 Japanese in Canada and 111,000 in the United States (plus another 44,000 in Hawaii). Chinese figures were higher still, reflecting the greater population pressure. In the 1870s, before restrictive laws and when railroad companies were actively recruiting, more than 100,000 Chinese came to the United States. Prior to that, in the 1850s and 1860s, more than 5,000 a year were indentured to Cuba, operating under long-term labor contracts. By 1922, 8 million Chinese were living abroad.

The largest numbers were in Thailand (1.5 million), Indonesia (2.8 million), and Malaya (with half a million). But 62,000 were in the United States, with another 24,000 in Hawaii; 45,000 were in Peru; and 43,000 were in Canada.

Birth Control and the Demographic Transition

While the population themes of the long 19th century involved unprecedented growth and resultant pressures, including migration, a final reaction emerged in western Europe and in the United States, Canada, and Australia during the period. Important in these societies at the time, it would have still wider consequences later on. A growing number of people began to reduce the number of children they had, below any levels that had been common for large populations before.

Birth control was not a new human phenomenon. Families that practice no restraint whatsoever—marrying by puberty and continuing maximum, procreative sexual activity throughout the years until menopause—will average 16 to 18 children. (This is called the Hutterite formula, named for a religious group in Canada that did precisely this for some generations in the 19th and early 20th centuries.) No large society has ever maintained these levels. By marrying after puberty, limiting conception by prolonging breast-feeding, and aborting or practicing infanticide, agricultural societies usually kept births to half the maximum or a bit less. And some people, from very early civilization, also attempted artificial birth control by using animal bladders as condoms or by introducing potions or magic formulas to avoid unwanted pregnancies (though none of these methods was very reliable).

By the 19th century, however, this common set of restraints was not enough. While infant deaths remained high, improvements in food allowed more children to survive, which added pressure to family life. More important still, the economic utility of children shifted. Beginning with the middle classes and spreading gradually to workers, and more gradually still to rural families, children's labor began to decline in utility. Machines replaced many children; laws, though only slowly enforced, restricted their work. At the same time, new adult expectations and, again, new laws began to press for greater school attendance, and this not only restricted work but also cost money for appropriate clothing and supplies. Children began to turn from assets to financial liabilities, and as families realized this, they reacted by seeking new limitations on births.

Specific dates for the changes vary. The United States, which had higher-than-average birthrates in the colonial period because of ample space and labor needs, began to cut birthrates in the 1790s. France, increasingly a nation of peasant landholders, did likewise, to protect property against too-numerous heirs. Britain and Germany chimed in a bit later. Generally, the middle classes led the way, because they first cut back on using their children for work and also had high expectations about the education or property they owed the children they begot. But some worker groups sought to protect themselves early on through new birth control, as did American farm owners. By the late 19th century, many voluntary groups, including labor organizations, pushed for lower birthrates in order to protect living standards and (sometimes) the health of mothers. Some of these groups were called Malthusians, the name derived from the views of a late-18th-century British moralist and economist, Thomas Malthus, who had warned that the poor tended to reproduce faster than their means allowed because of rampant sexual appetites, thus assuring perpetual poverty. Thanks to various pressures, by 1900 birthrates in the industrial countries, though somewhat varied, were dropping to an average of three to four children per family, in some cases less than half of what had prevailed a century before.

Most of the new birthrate reduction was initially accomplished through sexual abstinence, for reliable artificial methods were lacking, unknown, or disapproved by the moral standards of the time. As late as the 1890s, American middle-class families went through prolonged periods of sexual abstinence when they absolutely could not risk a child. But abortions spread as well, particularly among urban workers, even though new laws and moral codes were directed against them. In the 1890s, as many as 25 percent of Berlin working-class wives had had at least one abortion. Gradually, also, knowledge of new devices, particularly condoms and diaphragms (known as pessaries in the 19th century), spread as well. These devices became far cheaper and more reliable with the vulcanization of rubber in the 1830s, though use spread slowly because of hesitations about facilitating purely recreational sex.

A development as novel but also as private as the new levels of birth control inevitably sparks historical debate. Literally millions of ordinary people changed their habits, and so the course of population history. Some historians have argued that women took the lead, eager to protect their own health and to enhance the care available to children who were born. In some cases, women may have concealed the use of birth-control devices from their husbands (particularly diaphragms, or pessaries). Women in the American South seem to have argued on the basis of the pain and danger of childbirth. With a new emphasis on marital love, these arguments appealed to husbands in a way that had not been the case in the 18th century (when men tended to dismiss women's suffering more casually). There is ample evidence that more education for women correlated with higher rates of birth control, by whatever method. Class differences figure into the equation as well. Middle-class people cut birthrates in part to be sure of providing adequate education and job or marriage support for the children they did have. Recently, Wally Seccombe has argued that working-class people cut their birthrates simply because surviving in an urban economy was so difficult, given low wages and frequent periods of unemployment. Here, then, similar actions occurred for somewhat different reasons. Did families begin to value children more and cut birthrates as a means of doing better by each child, or did this relationship work the other way around? How did lower birthrates affect family life? One historian has argued that many European men around 1900 were profoundly disoriented by the new restrictions on this traditional proof of masculinity, maybe to the point of seeking other demonstrations of virility, such as war. By 1900 also, many children were growing up with few or no siblings around them, which changed the experience of childhood dramatically—making it more lonely and individualized, among other things. The ramifications of the new population regime are still being analyzed, and the findings relate to developments elsewhere in the world after 1900.

Birthrate reduction was accompanied, particularly in the forty years after 1880s, by a rapid reduction of infant and child mortality throughout the industrialized regions. Many families found their attachment to individual children growing precisely because the sheer numbers of children declined. They were eager to reduce traditional infant death levels. At the same time, many governments, worried about birthrate declines particularly for military reasons—the size of future armies seemed jeopardized—pressed for lower death rates as well, as did many doctors and humanitarians. The introduction after the discovery of germs of more sterile procedures in deliveries, in addition to general improvements in living standards and sanitation, did the trick. By 1920, over nine children of ten born would live to adulthood in western Europe and the United States, an unprecedented figure. Not only contagious diseases but also traditional infant killers such as diarrhea were cut back through improved sanitation (water quality was particularly important), parental attention, and medical care.

The combination of birthrate reduction and child-death reduction added up to a major demographic transition in the Western world, producing a population pattern different from that of all past societies. Average life expectancy at birth zoomed forward. Populations grew older on average, since even though far fewer children were being born, more were living into later adulthood. The transition was not easy, quite apart from the sexual restraints often required. Many parents worried that they were doing something wrong by innovating—men questioned their manhood, women their devotion to mothering. Societies where birthrates fell fastest, such as France, were consumed with a national anxiety about military decline in the face of more populous neighbors, such as Germany. Western leaders generally began to note the relative drop in European populations, particularly compared to the rapidly expanding Asian societies—the source of dire warnings about the "Yellow Peril" around 1900. In fact, Western populations still expanded for a while, on the strength of previous gains that had increased the number of available parents; but there was no question, by 1900, that Western populations were now the slowest-growing in the world.

Conclusion

The modern population story was hardly over in 1914. World War I confirmed key portions of the modern framework: Societies could now "afford" massive death rates in war, given the size of populations overall. While wartime deaths caused disruption and cultural shock for the European belligerents, prewar population levels were quickly recovered. And, though there was an important international influenza outbreak right after World War I, there were no huge disease consequences of the war itself; public health procedures and medical care, applied to armies, meant that most dying resulted from combat, not from the epidemics that once had accompanied armies on the move.

At the end of the long 19th century, however, in the world as a whole, it was public health and the continued expansion of food production, not the Western demographic transition, that set the stage for the immediate future. With populations in many areas already rising, further innovation merely increased the potential for explosive growth. The result, examined in chapter 22, became one of the major themes of the 20th century, and one of the century's major challenges to the world's future.

CHAPTER 19

STATE AND CULTURE IN THE CENTURY OF IMPERIALISM

Trends of strengthening and rationalizing the state, already prominent in the early modern period, continued in 19th-century western Europe. The result became something of a model for other societies, for the results, in sheer power terms, were obvious. Reformers in many regions tried to copy European bureaucratic and military organization and even prosaic developments such as modern tax collection. There was also wide interest in the expansion of functions of the European state, particularly its growing responsibilities for mass and elite education and for public health. Limited forays into state-sponsored welfare won less international attention at this point.

Use of the West as model does not mean that political uniformity gained ground. Some societies sought or were capable of selective imitation at best, because of lesser resources and different political traditions. Furthermore, the West itself sent some mixed signals; for along with government growth and new secular functions, Western societies also grappled with high levels of political unrest—which a number of other countries, bent on preserving order, hoped to avoid. Western nations experimented with a number of changes in government form, beginning with the French Revolution and its promotion of elected parliaments and a suggestion of outright (male) democracy. The need to redefine both the structure and function of government was heightened by the Industrial Revolution, but a clear new Western model did not emerge until after the 1860s. By this point, both political protest and government growth had led to important new relationships between state and society, and again, the results won international attention.

Developments in the cultural realm were important as well. In Europe, the long 19th century was in many ways a time of consolidation, as ideas about science and political theory gained wider hold. New directions arose in art, involving experimentation with more radical, less traditional styles. Cultural change was more dramatic in societies that sought to copy the West without necessarily seeking to become Western. Elites in India developed important new beliefs, including nationalism. Japan experienced a major cultural upheaval as part of its reform process. At the end of the century, missionary activity in Africa began to affect traditional religious patterns. No single formula covers the cultural developments of the period, both because reactions to the Western example varied and because the West itself sent out various cultural impulses, from missionary Christianity to highly secular consumerism and science. The growth of international contact and the need to come to grips with Western power, including its cultural roots if these could be determined, formed the basic framework.

Revolution and Consolidation

The diverse trends in Western government were brought together most clearly in the French Revolution of 1789, then in the further political innovations encouraged by the Industrial Revolution. Developments between 1789 and 1914 in effect defined stage two in the creation of the modern West European state. The French Revolution resulted from a variety of political and social grievances, spurred by the further spread of new ideas about citizen rights and the responsibility of the state to the well-being of its people. Revolutionaries created a parliament and constitution, ultimately abolishing the monarchy (and executing the king), while at one point spreading the vote to all adult males. They also continued the expansion of state power. Government support for mass education was discussed, though not implemented, but the government did continue a process of setting up schools for advanced technical training. Pressed by foreign attack, the revolutionary regime also instituted the principle of universal (male) military conscription, a huge expansion of the state's claims—and of its effective military force. Rationalization of regional administration through the creation of nontraditional units designed to displace local loyalties furthered an older process. Representatives (prefects) from the central government administered these new units. Finally, creating the first national anthems and national flags, the French Revolution promoted the idea of nationalism—intense national loyalty—directed to the state. Not all the achievements of the French Revolution persisted—monarchs returned after 1815, for another 33 years—but the basic patterns set a model for France and for other European and non-European nations. Prussia, for example, eagerly took up the idea of mass military conscription. Japan later would copy the prefect system and the idea of centralized coordination of education.

Throughout western Europe, including even liberal England, the Industrial Revolution also promoted a series of political changes by generating new needs and new discontents but also new levels of government revenue. The most obvious result of the rise of cities and new social classes was a growing level of political protest. Middle-class elements, increasingly successful economically, sought political representation. Reform movements and outright revolutions brought the vote to the middle class in places such as Britain, France, and Belgium by the 1830s. Working-class elements pressed for the vote as well. Democratic male suffrage spread in the United States during the 1820s (excluding slaves), then won out in France in 1848 and in Germany by the 1860s. Parliaments spread not only in Europe but in settler societies such as Canada and Australia. By the end of the 19th century, most Western countries had parliaments and constitutions, and most had democratic voting systems. Women were pressing for the vote as well and began to win political rights around 1900 in some American states, in Australia, and in Scandinavia.

Changes in political structure were matched by expansion of state functions. All Western governments grew during the 19th century, save, briefly, the government of Norway. This was even true in the United States, though the federal government remained fairly weak by European standards. Most governments reduced their defense of an established church, becoming more purely secular. Regulation of work increased because of industrial pressures. Beginning in the 1830s, many states limited child labor and also the working hours of women. A class of professional factory inspectors emerged as part of a growing bureaucracy. Led by Germany in the 1880s, governments also began to provide some social insurance against accidents, illness, and old age. Police forces expanded; a new force in Britain, created in the 1820s, not only opposed crime but also sought to regulate popular leisure habits. Record keeping proliferated: All governments began to conduct regular censuses while also requiring citizens to obtain birth, marriage, and death certificates from state offices.

The creation of state-run mass education was a huge innovation, providing massive new contact between governments and ordinary people. Most governments expanded school systems by the 1830s and then, by the 1860s (earlier in a few cases, such as Massachusetts), began requiring attendance. Insisting on special attention to the national history and literature, governments promoted loyalty as well as basic skills through the new systems. Public health constituted another major category of state activity, as regulation of housing, food supplies, and other areas was combined with massive programs of sewer construction, swamp drainage, and required inoculations. Most governments also took responsibility for developing other infrastructures, such as railroads, either building the systems directly or using government funding and legal authority to encourage private efforts. The United States, for example, gave huge chunks of public land to promote railway development, albeit by private companies.

By the end of the 19th century, European governments were conducting an unprecedented range of activities, relying on large bureaucracies. New civil-service procedures promoted specialized training of government officials and appointment by merit rather than through privilege of birth. At the same time, revenues expanded as new taxes, such as income taxes, were introduced to support the modern state.

Pressures of European Imperialism

During the 19th century, the example of the West European state became increasingly compelling. Successful military actions against China, Russia, and parts of the Ottoman Empire made it clear that European governments had achieved a new level of power. Most states had to seek at least an upgrading of their military organization, and many attempted wider reforms as well. At the same time, however, entrenched interests coupled with Western interference often limited successful political change.

Many governments imported European advisers, particularly in the second half of the century. China employed Europeans to help upgrade the system of tariff collection. Ottoman emperors used Germans to guide the reorganization of the military. Other changes included dismantling some older systems: The Ottomans, for example, abolished the Janissary corps in the interests of a more effective military force. Many governments also expanded their functions. Russia abolished serfdom in 1861 and then had to create a new system of local government to replace the old landlord system. Local government bodies, the *zemstvos*, were often active in improving road systems and setting up schools and public health facilities. The army along with the state expanded educational efforts, gradually increasing the pool of literate recruits. Many Latin American governments, after an initial period of uncertainty following independence in the early 19th century, became active in developing modern ports and rail systems and in beginning a commitment to public education. Colonial administrations also expanded: Britain, for example, took more direct responsibility for governing India, creating a rail system from the 1850s onward, introducing public health regulations, and attempting some changes in law.

At the same time, most political change was also limited. Efforts at reform by the Ottoman government failed to create a really new political system. Various sultans introduced new constitutions, but these had little impact. Even military reorganization, though significant, failed to prevent continued territorial loss. Changes in China were even more haphazard. Many bureaucrats resisted the idea of technological change, treating engineers with contempt, as social inferiors. At the end of the 1890s, a new young emperor did order military reforms, railroad building, and extension of education, but the widow of the previous emperor seized power and executed several leaders of the reform movement, backing the Boxer Rebellion against Western influence until it was put down by a small European-American military force. Even in Russia, where Western influence ran stronger, the army remained inefficient, the gap between often-corrupt officers and peasant recruits a serious impediment to effective operation.

In sum, interest in political change increased steadily around the world during the 19th century. It resulted in a variety of reform efforts, some expansions of government activity (as in public health and railroad building), even a series of constitutions and parliaments, usually with limited powers. Effective new political models remained elusive, however, and a more coherent pattern of change in state-society relations emerged only after 1900.

Japan was a vital exception. Beset by Western military and economic interference after 1853, the Japanese installed a new government system in 1868, under an emperor known as Meiji, or the "Enlightened One." Japanese leaders abolished feudalism and created a new ruling class that mixed some former samurai and new big-business men. Ultimately a new constitution established a parliament, though principal power remained with the executive branch. Government functions expanded rapidly, along with reorganization of military and other state organizations. New public health systems promoted rapid population expansion. A law of 1872 decreed universal, state-sponsored education for all, which was achieved amazingly quickly, by the 1890s. The powerful new ministry of industry supported economic development, including railroad building, running model heavy industrial operations directly. Use of Western advisers was tempered by an active, state-sponsored nationalism that included praise for traditions of group loyalty, over foreign individualism, and a revival of Shinto religious practices. Here was a distinctive but successful version of political change, establishing a host of new contacts between the state and ordinary people, including the promotion of a complex mixture of old and new cultural values.

New Forms of Cultural Exchange

Cultural influence from the West spread and penetrated more broadly in the 19th century than it had during the early modern centuries, as Western confidence in its scientific and political values grew and as Western power became inescapable. By this point, dealing with Western influence became the leading cultural issue in world history, though responses continued to vary widely. New technologies sped culture contact, while missionary and educational activities emanating from Europe expanded, in colonies and in other areas alike. Science and religion were not the only cultural sectors involved. Imitating Western sports, for example, shifted value systems as well as recreational patterns. Japan was playing American baseball by the 1890s. The first Buenos Aires soccer club, copied from local British residents, was founded in 1867, and a network of teams fanned out nationwide by the 1890s. An Argentine soccer-playing style developed that featured more individual heroics than did the team-minded British form—a case of sports syncretism.

This was not a period of fundamental cultural change in the West, if only because new beliefs had spread so widely during the early modern centuries. Science continued to develop. Charles Darwin's theory of evolution was a monument in biology that also challenged some traditional religious beliefs about creation. Physics and chemistry saw basic advances as well. Social-scientific work expanded, in sociology, economics, and new forms of history, while statistical inquiries gained ground steadily. New attention to psychology and the human unconscious at the end of the century suggested some novel directions for inquiry, away from the simplest beliefs in human rationality. Political theories branched out from Enlightenment ideas, particularly under the banner of liberalism. Socialism pressed further, and Marxist socialism, especially, emphasized historical processes and class warfare that would lead to a final working-class revolutionary victory; the ultimate goal was a classless, stateless society, almost an ideal Enlightenment-style utopia, but the references to violence and struggle were new. Nationalism also gained great attention. Nationalists might also urge liberal or social goals, but their priority was advancement of a collective identity, usually with an independent state to match. Western artists, finally, first under the banner of Romanticism and then, after 1848, in more abstract movements, sought a dynamic set of styles that would express movement and, often, defiance against an increasingly materialistic, scientific world. Western art was strongly influenced by awareness of styles from other societies, notably Africa and East Asia—an important case of cultural exchange in reverse of the current power balance.

With all these developments, the cultural models the West offered to the rest of the world were diverse, sometimes confusing. While Christianity declined in western Europe (less so in the United States) as both an intellectual force and a popular belief system, it ironically expanded its efforts abroad, sometimes bringing other Western ideas, including beliefs in scientific medicine or new ideas about women and children, in its wake.

Conversions to Christianity in several regions accelerated. This became a major trend in parts of Africa by 1900, and also in Korea. Even in China, some 100,000 persons had converted by 1900. All these changes also involved access to Western languages, new forms of education, and novel ideas about medicine and science. Beliefs about women were also

横濱海通圖
之岸濱

Cultural Adaptation in Japan. These European-style buildings were constructed in Yokohama after 1870, to house public schools, banks, and business firms that sprang up in the
wake of the region's flourishing silk industry. What remained "Japanese" about this section
of the city? Did the architecture combine any Japanese artistic conventions? How did the
functions of the buildings make imitation particularly logical? What other kinds of building might continue in a more traditional vein? From Yokohama Archives of History.
Reprinted by permission.

prone to change—Chinese Christians were among the leading opponents of foot binding. Religion aside, growing numbers of Asians and
Africans were educated in the United States and Europe—including
Mohandas Gandhi, from India, who began legal training in London in
1888.

Japan, as it was forced by Western military pressure to abandon iso-
lationism from 1852 onward, embraced aspects of Western culture more
extensively. Reformers visited the West and concluded that Japan needed
to emphasize Western-style science and mathematics instead of pure
Confucianism. Five thousand Western teachers were imported for the
expanding public schools during the 1870s, and training in English and
German grew rapidly. Crazes for Western styles, including clothing, and
habits such as toothbrushing spread rapidly among urban Japanese.
With all this, Japanese culture was not abandoned. From the emperor
on down, great emphasis was placed on maintaining group solidarity

and loyalty, and the revival of Shintoism combined with nationalism in generating extensive national discipline. An 1881 memorandum for teachers emphasized the importance of "loyalty to the Imperial House, love of country, filial piety toward parents, respect for superiors." By the 1880s, the government banned foreign books on morality.

Everywhere, in fact, individuals and larger groups tried to balance some seemingly inescapable imitations of Western culture, particularly in science, with efforts to maintain identity. Muslim reformers such as Jamal al-Afghani in Egypt (1839–1897) urged the importance of Islam but also argued for more rationalism and free inquiry. The Qur'an could be reinterpreted, not treated as an enslaving authority. In this vein, new schools arose combining religion with greater individualism, science, and modern history. At the same time, many intellectuals also attacked the West, urging the superiority of regional cultural traditions. In Russia, conservative Slavic writers blasted Western individualism, materialism, and lack of spirituality: Russian values were better. In Africa, a West Indian–born journalist, Edward Blyden, who had been denied university admission in the United States because of his race, argued for the advantages of African culture, including a strong sense of family and community as against Western exploitation and loneliness. In many areas, violent protests against Western intrusions urged a return to older values, such as Hinduism and Confucianism.

In this cultural ferment, nationalism, which had originated as a political value system in Europe during the 18th century, proved a widely popular compromise. Nationalists urged new, secular loyalties, instead of more traditional local or purely religious identities, to what they claimed was a common cultural unit. They usually argued for certain reforms, such as greater attention to science and Western medicine, to improve national strength. But they also insisted on the validity and superiority of regional beliefs and styles, in reaction against Western intrusion. Both traditionalists and innovators could join hands under a nationalist banner—just as, under nationalism, the West could be both imitated and opposed. Small wonder that strong nationalist intellectual movements emerged during the 19th century in Latin America, Russia, the Arab world, the Turkish part of the Ottoman Empire, India, China, and Japan—with sub-Saharan Africa soon to follow.

Nationalism embodied the complexity of cultural exchange during the 19th century. It was a common cultural impulse, yet it continued to differentiate specific areas. It reflected the need for new beliefs yet the equal need to retain older values and styles. Cultural change was becoming one of the leading sources of innovation in world history, yet the desire to use culture to hold the line against change, to preserve familiar identities, was a vital force in its own right.

Conclusion

Culture—people's basic beliefs and attitudes—served complex functions in the long 19th century. It was often a vital agent of change. Enough Europeans changed their minds about witches and magic in the 18th century to drive out traditional practices, including witchcraft trials, or at least to force them underground. The shifts toward science in Japanese education after 1872 brought huge changes to how people thought and the skills they had. Even nationalism brought new ideas about governments and ethnic cohesion, sometimes inventing traditions—such as Japanese emperor worship—that had not existed in the same form before. Yet culture was also used as a bulwark against change or as a cherished identity amid other shifts that could not be avoided. Thus many societies closed off to outside influence at key points or used customary ideas to provide identities. Here, finally, was a rich opportunity for syncretism, as groups in virtually all civilizations sought to blend old and new ways of understanding the world around them.

The complex combination of cultural change and continuity related closely to political developments. Expanding governments often sponsored cultural activities, and with mass education, the effort to shape popular beliefs extended widely. For established governments, promoting the new loyalty of nationalism was a vital component by the 19th century. Japan used nationalism heavily, along with a revival of Shintoism and emperor worship, as a control against excessive change. But new ideas could also put pressure on governments. Novel beliefs about justice and the possibility of redefining the state directly contributed to the revolutionary upsurge throughout western Europe and the Americas in the period 1776–1848. Ideas about political change, along with implications of the growing interest in science, then spread more widely. They could inspire reformist leaders in Japan or the Young Turk army officers in the Ottoman Empire. They could rouse nationalist protest in India or demands for political representation and social change in Russia. The old world was unmade, in political and cultural terms, by 1914, though the new one had not yet been clarified.

CHAPTER 20

GENDER STRUCTURES, 1750–1914

Many historians view what is often termed the "long" 19th century as the low point for women around the world, with new opportunities for men—gaining an education, earning vast amounts of money through trade or industry, traveling to new areas, choosing their own political leaders—remaining inaccessible to women because of legal restrictions or traditional norms. They note that during this period women were both held back by old and new institutions and left back as the gap between their experiences and those of the men from their area and social class widened. Women in many parts of the world remained secluded in their homes, and those not secluded were encouraged to make the home the center of their lives, a "haven in the heartless world" of industrialism and business.

This view can be supported with evidence from many cultures, but it can also be criticized in two significant ways: First, in many parts of the world, and for some groups in every part of the world, racial, caste, *casta*, or class structures determined people's experiences more than gender structures did, with both women and men living in a state of what has been described as an "equality of misery." This misery was compounded by the very developments that provided opportunities for some men, such as imperialism and industrialism; thus most men as well as women were left back. Second, opportunities for men were achieved through the breakdown of existing political, intellectual, and economic systems. Though this was often accompanied by a reinforcement of traditional gender structures to serve as a counterweight to change, eventually stark differences between men's opportunities and women's no longer made economic, intellectual, or political sense to many people. Thus, along with secluding and domesticating women, the 19th century saw the beginning throughout the world of movements for women's education, legal equality, and political rights.

Political Revolutions and the Gendering of Citizenship

During the political and intellectual ferment that led to the democratic political revolutions in North America, France, and Latin America, educated people debated new ideas about justice, equality, and freedom and discussed what qualities would be required for citizenship in states in which citizens had an actual voice in making political decisions. Women as well as men were involved in these discussions, in cities ranging from Paris (France) to San Juan (Puerto Rico) to Caracas (Venezuela), hosting meetings in their homes where political grievances were aired and plans for reforms mapped out. Less elite women were also important actors in these movements. In France, poor women marched from Paris to the king's palace at Versailles to demand that the king sign a new constitution, signed petitions, formed clubs calling for further political changes, and, along with men, carried weapons in armed protest marches through the streets of Paris. In what became the United States, women raised money for the Revolutionary War, refused to buy British goods, and took oaths not to marry men who were loyalists. In the Latin American movements for independence, women served as spies, carried weapons and supplies, and cared for the wounded in field hospitals; a few dressed as men in order to engage in combat.

Despite these efforts, all the new constitutional states that emerged limited citizenship rights to men and began to include the word *male* when passing laws regarding political rights. In France, women's political clubs were banned and women were barred from political meetings; voting rights were restricted to men. After the establishment of the United States under the Constitution, voting rights were restricted to white men with a certain amount of property. Gradually during the 19th century, almost all white men gained the right to vote; and after the Civil War, black men—at least in theory—did as well, leaving women, along with children, criminals, and the mentally ill, among the disenfranchised. In Latin America, the constitutions of the new states did not allow women to vote, hold political office, be witnesses in court, or be guardians over minors (including their own children). These gender restrictions could also be found in countries that broadened political rights more slowly, rather than through a revolution. In Japan, the Meiji Constitution of 1889 forbade women from voting, attending political meetings, or joining political parties. In Great Britain, property requirements for male voters were lessened throughout the 19th century so that almost all men could vote, though no woman could. In all these regions, civil law codes were enacted that further heightened gender distinctions: According to these codes, married women—which included the vast majority of adult women—were generally not allowed to sign contracts, buy or sell, maintain bank accounts, or keep their own wages; in some areas, such as Japan, they were denied existence as legal persons.

Though there were a few voices to the contrary, this exclusion of women from active citizenship was generally supported by the men who were the strongest advocates of political rights for men. Thomas Jefferson, for example, commented: "Were our state a pure democracy, there would still be excluded from our deliberation women, who, to prevent the deprivation of morals and ambiguity of issues, should not mix promiscuously in gatherings of men." The revolutionaries in France—with a few exceptions—were just as horrified as their monarchist counterparts at the actions of women during the revolution and argued that women's exclusion from political rights and limitation to domestic issues were matters set not by tradition or custom but by unchangeable Nature. One French official noted, "Is it to men that nature has confided domestic cares? Has she given us breasts to feed our children?" In his opinion, and that of most of his corevolutionaries, women's political actions would not only create problems in the household, as women neglected their husbands and children, but lead to an overturning of the entire order of society. Lopping off the head of a monarch paled by comparison and was, in any case, a matter among individuals destined "by Nature" to be active members of the body politic.

Industrialization and the Gendering of Work

In chapter 16, we noted the ways in which religious ideology and new organizations of production, such as craft and journeymen's guilds, worked together to define women's proper role as "helpmeet" to men in both the household and the workplace. The notion that women worked primarily as helpers also shaped the way in which the Industrial Revolution developed. Women were often the first to be hired as factories opened, particularly in cloth production, because their work was seen as less valuable and they could be hired more cheaply; tasks that were regarded as highly skilled or supervisory were reserved for men. Certain industries that developed slightly later, such as steel, also came to be regarded as "men's work," so that the industrial labor market was segmented by gender both within factories and across industries. When industries became more mechanized, so that fewer skills were needed—a process known as "deskilling"—women often replaced men as workers and wages went down, a process that can be traced in shoemaking, weaving, and secretarial work.

Factories brought new forms of work discipline in which overseers replaced parents as supervisors of production, machines concentrated in large numbers determined the pace of work, production was split into many small stages, and work was not easily combined with domestic or agricultural tasks. All of these changes made it difficult for adult women to combine factory work with their family responsibilities, so that factory work became the province of men; younger, unmarried women; and children.

Though the work women did in factories was often very similar to that done in household workshops, it was also more visible, and it thus became a topic of public discussion in the 19th century. Politicians and social commentators debated the propriety of young women working alongside or being supervised by men who were not their relatives, a debate fueled by instances of rape and sexual exploitation in the factories. Intermixing of the sexes at the workplace was described as leading to "immorality," hasty marriages, and increased illegitimacy, and female factory workers were often charged with having dubious sexual morals. Such fears led to further segmentation of the labor market by gender, as women—or their families—chose sex-segregated workplaces, which were viewed as more "respectable." Such gender segmentation was advantageous to employers, as it increased the competition for jobs, which further lowered women's wages; concerns about respectability also sharply limited the employment options for middle-class women and kept wages low in the few jobs regarded as appropriate, such as teaching.

Sex-segregated workplaces could go only so far in controlling morality, however, and an even better solution, in the minds of many commentators, was for women to avoid paid employment entirely. Middle-class authors, male and female, extolled the virtues of women remaining home to care for their husbands and children, arguing that motherhood and not wage labor was women's "natural" calling and a full-time occupation. In Japan, women were urged to stay in the home to become "good wives, wise mothers," and in Latin America they were advised to concentrate their efforts on family issues. Economic as well as moral concerns played a role in these debates, for male workers also opposed women in the factories because their lower wages drove all wages down. In Great Britain, union membership was often specifically limited to men, and in all industrializing areas, women made up a much smaller share of union membership than they did of the workforce, though they often participated with men in strikes, demonstrations, and protests for better conditions, even if they were not themselves union members.

The labor organizations that developed in the 19th century often argued in favor of a "family wage," that is, wages high enough to allow married male workers to support their families, so that their wives could concentrate on domestic tasks and not work outside the home. Both full-time motherhood and a family wage were only a ideals, of course, because in actuality, most working-class families survived only by the labor of both spouses and the older children. Older daughters—and less often, sons—often gave part of their wages to their parents even when they lived apart from them, and married women worked in poorly paid domestic service, took in boarders or laundry, or did piecework at home in order to make ends meet. These activities rarely showed up in the new statistical measures, such as gross national product, that governments devised in the 19th century, because they were defined as "housekeeping" and thus not really work.

The overall patterns of gender and work in industrializing societies were obviously complex. Women's labor was vital in the factories, particularly in initial decades, even amid a rhetoric of domesticity. But women's participation in the West European labor force did tend to decline over the first industrial period. This was also true in Japan after 1920. Household demands, pressure from male workers (including unions), and legislation that restricted women's work hours (but not men's), through some mix of humanitarian and other motives, all worked in this direction. Even so, more urban women worked than was recognized in formal tallies. But most middle-class women, and many married women generally in the cities, were not part of the official labor force. Domestic service, not factory work, was the most important urban occupation for working-class women, until the rise of white-collar opportunities at the century's end. These trends would continue into the early part of the 20th century, except when briefly disrupted by wars. One result, in many cases, was increasing female dependence on marriage for the greatest economic security.

Areas of the world that provided raw materials for industrialization also saw increasing gender divisions in work. During the 19th century, commercial agriculture for export began in many parts of Africa, accompanied in the 1880s by mining. Both activities employed many more men than women, with men leaving their villages for years at a time to grow cocoa, build railroads, or mine diamonds. Women continued the subsistence agriculture, though some of them also migrated to growing cities, where they supported themselves by petty trade, brewing, and prostitution. In Latin America as well, men frequently migrated to large plantations, cities, or other countries in search of paid labor, leaving women to engage in unpaid agricultural work and to care for children and the elderly; thus the matrifocal family patterns that had begun under slavery often continued after it was outlawed in the 19th century. Poor women could never follow the ideals of female seclusion and modesty—often termed *marianismo*, after the Virgin Mary, the mother of Jesus—prescribed for Latin American women; because they could rarely support their families, poor men were also unable to live up to the corresponding male ideal of *machismo*.

Intellectual Revolutions and the Gendering of the Self

As we have seen, gender distinctions in the state and the workplace were shaped by ideologies and ideals of masculinity and femininity, as well as by political and economic factors. These ideologies also shaped the ways in which people regarded themselves and others, with racial and ethnic distinctions—of paramount importance in the imperial world of the 19th century—understood in highly gendered terms. Particularly in the minds of the middle- and upper-class Europeans who ran Europe's colonies, all aspects of the self—mind, body, soul—were permeated by gender. New fields of knowledge such as psychology and anthropology often gave professionals and officials new languages to describe and discuss gender distinctions, both in Europe and in its colonies.

Some historians, most prominently Thomas Laqueur, argue that in the 18th and 19th centuries, people in Europe and North America increasingly saw the two sexes as totally different from each other, rather than viewing women as simply inferior men, as the Aristotelian tradition had maintained. They term this the *two-sex model*, as opposed to the one-sex model, and note that every aspect of human life came to be regarded as shaped by gender. This occurred at the same time that physicians and scientists began exploring the reasons for differences among humans, and not surprisingly, it shaped the results of their experiments and measurements. Male brains were discovered to be larger than female brains, and male bones to be stronger. When it was pointed out that female brains were actually larger in proportion to body size, female brains were determined to be more childlike, for children's brains are proportionately larger still. Such measurements were also applied to ethnic and racial differences, and it was "proven" that various groups had smaller brains or other markers of inferiority. Émile Durkheim, often referred to as the "father of sociology," linked racial and gender measurements by noting that "although the average cranium of Parisian men ranks among the greatest known crania, the average of Parisian women ranks among the smallest observed, even below the crania of the Chinese, and hardly above those of the women of New Caledonia." Such dichotomous crania were, in Durkheim's view, a sign of French superiority, for they marked the greatest gender distinctions.

Other historians disagree with Laqueur's chronology, pointing out that ideas about gender polarities go back to the ancient Greeks in the West and are part of the intellectual structures of many other cultures, such as Taoism and Confucianism in China and the traditions of a number of indigenous North American peoples. In some of these cases, the polarities led not to hierarchy but to a strong emphasis on gender complementarity; in more of them, however, it led to an emphasis on male superiority, as positive qualities such as reason, bravery, creativity, and loyalty were associated with men. This was why education and artistic training in many cultures was limited to men, and female artists, scientists, and intellectuals were often praised as having somehow transcended their sex. (The first woman was admitted as a full member of the Royal Society of London, the leading European scientific society, only in 1945.) Learned women were also often criticized, however, for having lost their female honor by contact with male realms. An 18th-century shogun in Japan commented, "To cultivate women's skills would be harmful," and a common Chinese saying noted, "She who is unskilled in arts and literature is a virtuous woman."

There is little dispute that gender and other types of differences were increasingly the subject of scientific scrutiny in the 19th century. By the latter part of the century, this scrutiny began to extend to sexual behavior as well. In 1886 the German physician and neurologist Richard von Krafft-Ebing published *Psychopathia sexualis*, a study of what he regarded as deviant sexual behavior, and slightly later the Austrian psychiatrist Sigmund Freud developed the idea that human behavior is shaped to a great extent by unresolved sexual conflicts that begin in infancy; these sexual conflicts are gendered, with girls suffering primarily from penis envy (the recognition that they are lacking something their brothers have) and boys from an Oedipus complex (the desire to kill their fathers so that they can possess their mothers). Freud's ideas were vigorously attacked, sometimes by his former associates, but they had a wide impact in fields far beyond psychology, such as literature, art, and education.

These scientific and medical studies of sexual attitudes and behavior led to two, somewhat contradictory ideas about sexuality. On the one hand, one's choice of sexual partners was increasingly regarded as a reflection of a permanent orientation toward homosexuality or heterosexuality, what came to be termed *sexual identity*. On the other hand, homosexuality and other types of "deviant" sexuality, such as nymphomania, were defined as physical or psychological illnesses, which could be cured through drugs, surgery, or psychoanalysis. By the 19th century, sexual offenders were no longer executed, but they might be imprisoned in mental hospitals and forced to undergo unwanted treatments. Popular and learned books advised readers about how to achieve a "healthy" sex life, and efforts were made to prevent sexual deviance as well as cure it. In Great Britain and the British Empire, the Contagious Diseases Acts passed in the 1860s led to the rounding up and examination of prostitutes and women simply suspected of prostitution, in an effort to prevent venereal disease. (Their male sexual partners were not arrested or examined.) A British soldier in Kenya, Robert

Baden-Powell, founded the Boy Scouts in 1908 explicitly to teach English boys what he regarded as the right sort of manly virtues and to keep them from masturbation, effeminacy, and homosexuality.

It is not surprising that Sir Baden-Powell (he was made a British peer because of his work with the Boy Scouts) spent most of his career in the British colonies in India and Africa, for it was in colonial areas that gendered ideas about difference were thrown into their sharpest relief. European officials, merchants, and missionaries brought with them notions of appropriate male and female dress and behavior that differed substantially from those held by indigenous peoples. They often viewed women's less restrictive dress in tropical areas as a sign of sexual looseness, men's lack of facial hair or trousers as a sign of effeminacy, and any marital pattern other than permanent monogamy as a sign of inferiority. The fact that European men initially vastly outnumbered European women throughout the colonial world resulted in frequent sexual relations between white men and indigenous women (and men), which were interpreted by Europeans as further signs of moral depravity (on the part of the indigenous people) and by the local culture often as temporary marriage. Such relationships became less common once more white women were available as marital partners, and European communities became more worried about mixed-race children and what they termed *racial survival*. Racial boundaries slowly hardened as race, along with sexual orientation, became a matter of identity of importance both to individuals and to governments, the latter using racial identity as a means of determining access to education, jobs, housing, voting rights, and other privileges. Racial distinctions can be maintained in the long run only by regulating sexual behavior, and laws were passed in nearly all multiracial areas (including the United States) that prohibited interracial marriage and other types of sexual relationships.

Racial identity was used by colonial governments to enhance white privilege, and it remained important in the nationalist movements that opposed European colonization in the late 19th and early 20th centuries. Part of creating and affirming a national identity was handling what was called "the woman question," determining what the legal and social status of women would be. Colonial rulers, especially the British, often regarded customs that were harmful to women, such as child marriage and *sati* (the immolation of a widow on her husband's funeral pyre) in India and clitoridectomy (the removal of a girl's clitoris) in Kenya, as clear signs of the backwardness and barbarity of indigenous cultures and of their need for outside rule. Nationalist reformers thus had to balance traditional customs and religious practices with their desires to appear modern enough to govern themselves. Few 19th-century Indian nationalist leaders, for example, defended sati, but a number continued to urge substantial female seclusion and educational segregation as part of Hindu tradition.

Reactions and Response: Women's Movements around the World

The woman question was not simply a colonial matter in the 19th century but emerged to some degree in almost every country of the world. The social problems created by industrialism, combined with the rhetoric of political equality that grew out of the 18th-century revolutions and with reactions against colonialism, led many people in the 19th century to call for major social and political changes. Socialist and communist groups urged revolution and other dramatic measures to overthrow existing political and economic systems; nationalists worked for the end of imperial rule; social reformers called for the end of slavery, the expansion of education, improvements in prisons and mental institutions, and an increase in public assistance to children, the elderly, and the poor.

Both middle- and working-class women joined reform organizations, political parties, labor unions, and socialist groups throughout the world, finding, to their dismay, that women's needs and issues were often perceived as unimportant by the largely male leadership. This led in many countries to the founding of separate women's groups, which called for education for women, more equitable marriage and divorce laws, temperance, protection for women workers, women's rights to own property, and sometimes even women's right to vote.

Access to education was one of the principal aims of many women's groups throughout the world. By the 19th century, most countries in Europe and North America were providing some free public education for both boys and girls, for the merits of basic literacy and numeracy had become clear to political leaders. Secondary and advanced education for women was still controversial, however, with arguments against it now couched in terms of biology instead of morality: Using her brain too much would cause a woman to faint or her uterus to shrivel. Reformers countered these arguments by stressing that education would make women better mothers, enabling them to improve the lives of their families and children. Such arguments, combined with the practical need for female teachers and nurses and with steady pressure by individual women, gradually led to more opportunities, with most European and many North and South American universities opening their doors to women in the late 19th and early 20th centuries, though often with restrictions on what women could study and a quota sharply limiting their numbers.

Calls for the education of women and girls in areas of the world in which women were secluded, such as India and China, were less successful, and female literacy remained low; in India, for example, the 1901 census listed the literacy rate among women in any language to be 0.7 percent. Male literacy was also very low in these areas, for education was limited to a small elite; many schools were run by Christian missionaries, and parents hesitated to send their children, as they feared they would convert. Such fears were well founded, for 19th-century missionaries saw education as a way both to "civilize" and to "Christianize" the people among whom they worked. In the United States, their efforts extended to Native Americans and sometimes involved force; as various tribes were forced off their lands and settled on reservations, officials and missionaries often removed children from their homes and sent them to boarding schools, thus disrupting family life completely.

Along with education, reformers and revolutionaries began to work for women's greater legal, economic, and political rights. Reformers in India urged an end to sati, female infanticide, and the prohibition of widow remarriage; those in Europe worked for women's rights to own property and control their own wages; those in the United States worked for temperance and dress reform; those in Latin America sought improvements in working conditions and a restructuring of the civil codes that limited women's economic rights. By the middle of the 19th century, groups specifically devoted to women's political rights began to be established in many countries of the world and to communicate with one another in what became an international feminist movement; international meetings included ones held in Washington, D.C., in 1888 and in Buenos Aires in 1910. The tactics and philosophies of women's rights groups varied from country to country: Those in England emphasized women's rights as individuals and ultimately turned to militant moves, such as hunger strikes and other types of civil disobedience, whereas in most other countries such groups stressed women's duties as citizens and used more moderate tactics, such as petition drives and letters of protest. In many countries, women used, rather than disputed, widespread notions of women's domesticity and motherhood; women, they argued, needed the vote to assure the well-being of their families and children and would clean up corrupt politics in the same way that they cleaned up their households. Suffragists were initially ridiculed and attacked physically, but their efforts, combined with international events such as World War I, led to a gradual extension of suffrage to women. Women first were allowed to vote in national elections in New Zealand in 1893 and in Finland in 1906. Suffrage rights were granted in the United States and many European countries right after World War I and in Latin America, the Philippines, India, China, Japan, and the rest of Europe (except Switzerland) in the 1930s and 1940s. Women were allowed to vote on an equal basis with men in most of the constitutions of African and Asian states set up after World War II and are now prohibited from voting only in a few countries of the Middle East.

Conclusion

The seclusion and domestication of women was such a prominent theme in advice literature, moral and political treatises, sermons, and law codes during the long 19th century that historians often used to describe this as a period during which the public sphere of politics and work became increasingly male, while the private sphere of home and family became increasingly female.

Though this gendered public/private dichotomy is certainly evident, it is increasingly clear that this is not the whole story. In most parts of the world hereditary rulership continued, with the women in ruling families still playing an important role in politics; even the women in the *harim* of the Ottoman sultan, some of the most secluded women in the world, were often powerful influences on court politics and imperial policies. In areas where political and nationalist revolutions established democratic governments, women were denied formal political rights, but this very exclusion sparked an international movement for women's rights, which often used the notion of women's responsibility for home and family as the very reason that women should have an equal voice with men. As first Europe and then other parts of the world industrialized, women and children formed a significant share of the factory workers in many areas, favored by industrialists because they would work more cheaply than men—a wage structure justified by the fact that women were "supposed" to be in the home. In the slave economies of the Americas and Africa, male slaves, apart from a few advisers to African rulers, had no political role, while the work of female slaves was never limited to the household. In the late 19th century, even as Japanese women were instructed to become "good wives, wise mothers," they were also recruited so heavily for factory work that 62 percent of the factory labor force in Japan in 1909 was female, their silk products earning the foreign exchange that made Japanese industrialism possible. Thus notions about public man and private woman shaped political and economic developments, but they described an ideal, not the reality of the increasingly industrial and colonial world.

CHAPTER 21

WORK AND LEISURE AMID INDUSTRIALIZATION AND IMPERIALISM

The greatest theme of the long 19th century was industrialization and the subsequent changes in work patterns. During this period, however, only a minority of civilizations underwent the process of industrialization. The first was western Europe, in the late 18th and early 19th centuries, with North America (the United States and Canada) following a few decades later. Only in the last decades of the 19th century did Japan and Russia join in the small group of countries that had substantial industry. In these countries, the introduction of factory work transformed how people lived and spent their leisure time. Initially, industrialization caused ever greater misery in the factories, though at the end of the 19th century, some of the benefits of increasing wealth in the industrialized sectors of the world trickled down to the workers in terms of living standards—though not necessarily in their basic work conditions.

Industrialization also had a substantial effect on virtually every other section of the world. The nonindustrialized part of the world focused more than ever on the production of raw materials for sale to the industrial powers. Also, the wealth and technological edge that the industrial powers had over those that had not undergone industrialization meant that, in some cases, they were able to determine economic (and thus labor) conditions more fully than ever before. This process was especially noticeable at the end of the 19th century, when western Europe, the United States, Japan, and Russia competed for colonies and spheres of influence in those regions too weak to withstand the might of the new technologies. Finally, population growth tended to reduce the value of labor in many regions, making it easier to cut pay and press for higher output.

Industrialization, along with changes in culture and in population patterns, produced one other vital effect on work: the end of most major systems of slavery and serfdom. Here was a truly historic development, after the long service of these two systems of coercive labor. It is important to deal with the causes and effects of this development.

Finally, industrialization altered leisure, though particularly, at this point, in the industrial societies themselves. Changes there set the stage for wider international patterns. And the results were not entirely predictable: leisure activities decreased initially, but in the later phases of industrialization increased.

The Impact of Industrialization

Industrialization was a complex process that consisted of many components. Three of these are important for the discussion of labor systems in world history. One is the specialization of labor, giving each individual a specific task that can be done quickly and efficiently before passing on the product to the next individual for the next task. The second is the use of machines in the production of goods. Machines proved much faster, more powerful, and more efficient than humans or animals, who could not generate the sustained operation, the amount of force, or the accuracy of the new steam-driven engines. Finally, industrial work moved out of the home and household area. We have seen that this development had a major impact on women's relationship to labor during the long 19th century. It also placed strain on men, now separated from their families for lengthy periods of time. Children, though sometimes able to work near relatives in the early days of the factories, also found their work-family relationship redefined, and here the ultimate solution was to pull children out of the labor force altogether.

These three developments had huge implications. Growing specialization meant that most workers did not see a finished product. Their skill levels declined. While skilled workers remained essential, the typical factory hand was semiskilled. He or she required a few months of training to attain peak efficiency but, by the same token, could be relatively easily replaced. Job security and a sense of purpose in work both declined. Introduction of new technology had significant effects, beginning simply with priorities: Machines became more important than ordinary workers to the production process. A French manufacturer in the 1830s regularly decorated the week's most productive machine with a garland of flowers; he offered nothing to the workers involved, and the symbolism was telling. Work became organized around technological requirements—and these frequently changed because of recurrent improvements and a demand for faster production. Workers in the 1890s thus complained about the passing of good old days, a few decades before, when machines were smaller and operated more slowly. Finally, the gap between family and work meant that workers, already subjected to laboring in larger settings than they were accustomed to, had to deal with strangers. While camaraderie might develop, the social atmosphere of work was growing less familiar.

Industrialization did not take shape overnight, and its gradual unfolding may have helped some workers to adapt. In textiles, initially one of the key sectors to be mechanized, a process called proto-industrialization developed in the 17th to 18th centuries. In Europe and elsewhere, some manufacturing had long been accomplished by rural workers using fairly simple equipment (such as hand looms and spindles) in their homes. Merchants brought raw materials and orders for goods, then picked up (and paid for) the work when it was completed. The system was called domestic manufacturing, or the *putting-out system*. With proto-industrialization, these operations simply expanded and intensified. Far more workers came to be involved, particularly when population growth began to reduce the availability of agricultural land. Operations became somewhat more specialized, with a specific focus on spinning thread, weaving cloth, or carding wool. Most important, proto-industrialization gave workers increasing experience in wage work and in working for someone else—a profit-minded someone else, based outside the village community. This was not industrial work (in the sense of technology or strangeness), but it was a foretaste.

A few factories arose as well before new machines existed. In the Spanish colonies, Indians in Mexico and the Andes were forced (as debt peons or to pay their royal labor tax) to work in textile factories called *obrajes*, where hundreds of people produced rough wool or cotton cloth for sale elsewhere in the colonies. Likewise, in India throughout the 18th century, fine cotton cloth was produced not only in households but, at times, in factory-like settings. Aside from cases where individuals could force laborers into factories, however, as in the colonial setting of Spanish America, most textile manufacturing remained a household activity because it was a strategy for peasants to supplement their income, derived mainly from the crops they produced. The organizers of the textile trade were unable to make people leave their homes to work elsewhere.

The initial move toward working permanently in places other than home came about in western Europe, and only when changes in rural production and urban migration as a result of overpopulation in the countryside created a class of people who had lost access to land and had only their labor to sell in order to provide for their livelihood. As Europe's population almost doubled in the 18th century, the need for alternative jobs, off the land, became desperate, leading to a willingness to accept unfamiliar work settings. The change in rural production occurred first in England and then spread to much of the rest of western Europe. In England, wealthy individuals began to fence off their land and purchase common lands from the villages, in a development called the enclosure movement. As fewer owners controlled more land, many villagers lost access to farm ownership. Many could not even work the land as occasional laborers or renters, since the new owners turned much of the land to sheep and cattle ranching, a much less labor-intensive activity than farming. Thus numerous villagers had no place to go other than the cities, where some began to work in factories. Clearly, the transformations in the western European countryside are essential for explaining the rise of industrialization.

Factories became even more profitable after inventors in western Europe devised steam engines to power the looms and other machines. The harnessing of steam began in the mid–18th century and accelerated in the 19th. Not only was a consistent source of power suddenly available, but because the engines were large and bulky and required fuel—coal—that was expensive to ship, workers had to go where the machines were located, rather than working at home. Using steam-powered machinery also had vast implications for the way in which work was performed. For one thing, the new machinery could work day and night, without rest and regardless of season. Human beings had to accommodate themselves to machines, working throughout the year, without regard to the agricultural rhythms they were used to. Rather than having a period of intense work (such as sowing and harvesting) followed by periods when less work was required, suddenly people had to work at a constant pace, without letup. Timing became important as well; because the machines could work day and night, people were required to work in shifts and were expected to be at the factory at precise times to relieve their comrades. Factory whistles and other clocks became important, delineating precise time periods in ways that previously had been unnecessary. Precision also became much more important in working; time became a valuable commodity by which one's labor (and compensation) would be measured. Schools began to mirror these changes as well, preparing children to become good workers by a system of bells and precise time periods for classes, just as on the factory floor. Indeed, this aspect of schooling continues to this day.

Besides new pressures of time and place and the impact of strangeness and specialization, workers faced new and intimate forms of supervision. Precisely because the new work patterns were unfamiliar and, to many, unpleasant, employers quickly devised detailed shop rules designed to keep workers to the task. Tardiness, taking naps, wandering around, singing, and chatting all were banned, and with them, many features of traditional work. Foremen were employed to monitor the work. Most workers would spend their lives doing work as other people arranged it, with scant possibility, and often scant interest, in rising to positions of more independent authority.

The new work forms inevitably had diverse impacts. Some workers liked them. A few skilled workers took great pleasure in the powerful machines they tended. Some women—for instance, many farm girls who came into New England factories in the 1820s—found the work less unpleasant than they had expected. For them, opportunities to get away from home and socialize with many other women provided new outlets; and since most did not intend to work for a lifetime but rather to save money to return to the countryside and marriage later on, this, too, may have cushioned the adjustment. Other workers suffered. Many former artisans found the contrast between their careful skills and traditions and the nature of factory work simply appalling. Loss of control and loss of a sense of artistry were common laments. Some craft work remained, but it was increasingly organized along industrial lines; furniture making, for example, became more rushed and standardized, less artistic, even before a factory system arose. Older workers also suffered: Machines required strength and an openness to innovation, and many older workers seemed to lack these qualities, or at least, so 19th-century employers believed. As a result, pay and job security declined with age, greatly adding to problems of old-age poverty. Ultimately, but really only in the 20th century, this issue would be addressed with the rise of formal retirement systems, which by definition separated old age from most work (a solution being rethought as the 20th century ends).

For almost all workers, labor conditions in 19th-century factories throughout western Europe were very poor in the beginning of industrialization. Many people who had arrived from the countryside had few resources and thus were at the mercy of factory owners. Factory floors could be dark, dank, and unhealthy places, with smoke and unsafe equipment threatening the lives of the workers. Laborers were expected to work at least 12-hour days, 6 days of the week for subsistence wages. Women and children worked as well as men, though receiving much lower wages. Charles Dickens, who grew up during the early period of industrialization in England, described these conditions vividly in his novels. Only later in the 19th century, as machines became more efficient and workers organized in labor unions, did conditions begin to improve somewhat.

Many early workers responded to work conditions with agonized protest. Luddism, which first arose in England between 1810 and 1820, was a movement that brought some workers into direct conflict with new machines, which they tried to tear down, hoping to return to older labor conditions. (The movement was named for an apparently mythical leader, Ned Ludd.) Direct protest against the new work systems failed, however. Many individual workers tried to slow things down, to change jobs frequently, or, in the first generation, simply to quit and go back to rural life; these recourses may have alleviated tensions somewhat. With time, workers became more accustomed to industrial styles of work. These styles did not improve in terms of skill levels or personal control, but they no longer seemed unfamiliar. At the same time, pressures in many respects intensified. By the late 19th century, the machines were bigger and faster and the supervision was more intense. Headed by the United States, companies began to hire industrial engineers to figure out how to prevent workers from wasting motions. And the work system now applied not just to factories but to construction sites and offices, as new technologies such as loading cranes and typewriters were devised. Small wonder that workers around 1900 could still lament their fate, as did the British operative who complained, "We are driven like dumb cattle in our folly, until the flesh is off our bones, and the marrow out of them. It seems to me that we are living to work, not working to live."

The imposition of industrial work systems was conditioned, finally, by the development of an explicit work ethic in the middle classes of Europe and the United States. This ethic argued that work was the highest form of activity a person could engage in. Life should, indeed, be organized around it. Early work ethic statements included Benjamin Franklin's injunction "Early to bed, early to rise." They included stories about how poor people rose to great wealth because of hard work. Some middle-class people internalized this new work culture, laboring long and hard, disliking such distractions as vacations. Others talked the talk, even if they walked more slowly. Most factory and office workers did not fully accept this work ethic because it made no sense according to their traditions or their new lives. But the ethic made it easy to condemn people who wished to work less hard. (It could also be turned against middle-class women, sometime condemned for idleness.)

The advent of machines, a crucial step for full industrialization, was first confined to western Europe and, slightly later, North America. Why didn't other regions of the world begin to use machines as the Europeans were doing, given that many regions had taken the first step of specialization already? First, machinery, at least initially, did not represent a great advantage compared to extremely cheap labor available outside western Europe. Building machinery was not easy to do; most regions of the world had neither the expertise to build machines with the necessary precision nor the capital to import them (and hire the engineers to keep them working). This was the case in Mexico, where the government established a textile industry in the 1830s but was unable to keep the steam engines and the looms in working order. In other regions of the world, western European officials favored their own manufacturing industries over that of their colonies. In India, English factories helped wipe out the thriving textile-manufacturing sector; hundreds of thousands of rural manufacturing workers, including many women, were thrown out of jobs in the decades around 1800. Even when cotton-cloth factories began to spring up in Bombay in the 1850s, the British provided favorable treatment to Lancashire cloths at the expense of Indian manufactures. Indian factories thrived in Bengal only in the second half of the 19th century, where they produced jute rope and bag cloth, an industry for which there was no competition in the British Isles. By the end of the long 19th century, only Japan and Russia outside the West were able to begin the wrenching process of industrialization, thus undergoing many of the same transformations in labor patterns as Europe and North America had already experienced.

Nevertheless, despite its regional concentration, industrialization affected workers in vast regions of the world, even outside the industrialized areas. Industrially enhanced European economic domination meant the immiseration of a large number of people throughout the world. The world economy quickened as a result of industrialization, providing greater resources to export-oriented elites in places such as Latin America and Africa, who became wealthy as a result of the export of raw materials to the industrializing North Atlantic. These elites in nonindustrialized regions were able to create plantation economies and mining enclaves, using strategies such as debt peonage to force workers to toil for low wages. This was the case in most of Latin America, where in Peru labor contractors went to the highlands to recruit poor Indians by buying them drinks and clothes and then requiring them to work off their debts in the sugar plantations on the coast. Once on the coast, the natives had to purchase all their goods from the plantation owners and could be kept in debt and thus prevented from leaving the plantation. Labor demand rose so high that, in the mid–19th century, Peruvian planters hired Chinese workers, often kidnapped from taverns in the coastal ports of China. The term *shanghaied* arose from this practice. Slavery in the cotton plantations of the southern United States thrived as the demand for raw materials exploded in the textile mills of western Europe and the northeastern United States. Slaves worked in the coffee fields of Brazil and in the sugar plantations in the Caribbean, feeding the newly prosperous tastes of western Europe.

Pressures on slaves and other coerced workers were combined with halting efforts to get them to work faster. Plantation owners in the American South, for example, were aware of factory systems, and they thought that tougher supervision might increase the pace of work and so production. Similar efforts arose in Latin America and on the serf estates of Eastern Europe. It was hard, however, to do too much to change this kind of work, because there were few incentives. This limitation, in turn, helps explain why, in a century of hard-driving work, literally coerced labor of the traditional sort diminished in popularity.

The End of Slavery and Serfdom

Between the 1790s and 1892, slavery was abolished throughout the Americas. Between 1789 and the 1860s, serfdom was abolished throughout eastern Europe. The American Revolution prompted some northern states to abolish slavery. Haitian slaves rose against their system in 1798 and cast it out. England spearheaded a movement to ban trans-Atlantic slave trading early in the 19th century, and some Latin American countries, such as Mexico, ended slavery as part of their independence movements. The United States fully ended slavery only with the Civil War, and the large system in Brazil was dismantled only in the 1880s. Serfdom collapsed in part through the French Revolution, while the revolutions of 1848 ended the system in Central Europe. Russia's great serf emancipation occurred in 1861.

By 1900, some slavery still existed in the Middle East and Africa. In Africa, ironically, slavery had increased during the early 19th century, as landowners responded to the end of the trans-Atlantic slave trade by organizing the production of vegetable oils and other goods for export, using coerced labor in the process. But European imperialists worked against African slavery, and the system was in decline by 1900.

Industrialization in the long run caused slavery (though not somewhat less coercive systems, such as debt peonage) to disappear as an important labor system. Although at first the growing prosperity of western Europe intensified slave systems, in the end, slavery proved incompatible with industrialization. There were a number of reasons for this incompatibility. For one thing, complex machinery and slavery did not mix. Slaves had no incentive to work fast; poor maintenance and outright sabotage of machinery were in the slave's best interest, since doing so would halt work. A free labor force could not afford to ruin machinery, as not being able to work meant not being able to feed their families. In a larger sense, slavery was also doomed to disappear in regions colonized by the western European powers, since slaves consumed very little compared to free laborers; thus regions with many slaves presented poor markets for European goods. A moral element came into play as well, as western Europeans began to feel abhorrence at treating people as chattel because of the new humanitarian ideals of the Enlightenment.

Historians have vigorously debated the reasons for the increasingly successful attack on slavery. Some argue that Western humanitarians raised the cry against slavery to distract from harsh conditions in their own industrial factories and to convince workers that whatever their complaints, the lot of slaves was far worse. Others take the humanitarian impulse at face value; they note that new Christian movements, such as Methodism in 18th-century England and American Quakerism, along with the ideals of the Enlightenment provided new arguments against holding people as property. Probably some combination of impulses was involved. But it should also be remembered that the attacks on slavery took place in a context of rapidly expanding populations, which produced a growing number of workers, including immigrant workers, willing to take on hard labor simply in order to survive. In this context, and amid changes in work demands associated with commercial and industrial production, slavery became less necessary and less effective. And while the result was a vital step in human freedom, it did not always improve the quality of work.

The consequences of the end of slave systems were, inevitably, complex. Some freed workers found it hard to get jobs. People of African origin in the United States and Brazil, once liberated from slavery, often had to struggle to find land or work, for with rare exceptions, nothing was offered. Racist attitudes (even in more tolerant Brazil) often relegated black workers to the lowest employment category, last hired and first fired. Immigrants from eastern and southern Europe were preferred, and the urban skills of many black workers actually declined in the later 19th century. Former serfs in Russia were free, but not quite, as continuing obligations tied many of them to the land until they paid off their former landlords. Change there was, in sum, but its glories were tarnished. Finally, new systems of coercion, though less complete than slavery, flourished. Company stores could keep workers in debt, unable to leave—a common ploy in Latin America and the southern United States. Children could be bought—an ingredient in Japanese industrialization early on. Indentures tied many Asian immigrants in Southeast Asia, at least for periods of time. Contract labor worked on sugar and pineapple plantations in Hawaii or sugar estates in British Guinea in Latin America. A typical contract bound an Indian or Chinese worker to 10 years of service, at set pay and hours (12 hours a day, 6 days a week for field workers). Workers could go home in five years if they paid their own way. Needless to say, work conditions were rigorous, while company-supplied housing and health care provided scant reward. Even in the 20th century, efforts to force immigrant workers to accept abysmal conditions by seizing their passports and preventing their contact with the outside world—a system installed by some United States clothing companies on American-controlled Pacific islands—remind us that coercion is not completely dead.

Still, the main story of the 19th century is the historic replacement of most coercion with wage labor. And the main question about the century, in work terms, involves assessment of how much better wage labor was, in the conditions imposed by factories.

Regulation and Protest

Toward the end of the modern period, governments began to crack down on abusive labor practices in industry. In western Europe and North America, states began to regulate the work of women and children, though, as we have seen, this action had various motives and consequences. Workers organized into labor unions and sometimes won the right to better working conditions, higher pay, and shorter hours. In many industrialized countries, political parties sprang up to address workers' rights on the national level. This was the case with the Social Democratic Party in Germany, the biggest of all in western Europe, as well as with socialist and communist parties in other parts of the world. Repression of these movements was common, but workers nevertheless were able to gain some benefits, if only because the government wanted to co-opt workers before radical movements could gain popularity.

By this point, most protests did not address basic industrial work systems. Unions and strikers did not try to make work more interesting or to decrease the pace (except through a reduction of the amount of time spent at work) or to slow up technological innovation. The main focus of protest was instrumental: It accepted that workers did not control job conditions, while asking for better pay and shorter hours. Work should become an instrument for a better life off the job. This was not a traditional attitude, but it made sense in context, and it did begin to create some adjustments that made the industrial scene more palatable.

Leisure Activities

Leisure activities remained much the same throughout the world during this period, except where industrialization transformed society. In western Europe, many changes in leisure patterns actually antedated industrialization, as discussed in chapter 17. Around the middle of the 18th century, with industrialization in its infancy, western European society had already begun to become more individualistic, in ways that presaged the change in labor patterns. Beginning in the 1750s, for example, cooks began to produce recipe books to cook meals for families rather than for large gatherings, such as feasts and community festivals. This mirrored a trend, reinforced by industrialization, of spending more time with the nuclear family and making that, rather than the whole community, the primary group with which to spend one's leisure time.

Industrialization's first leisure impact was to reduce traditional forms still further. In western Europe, as we have seen, industrialists actively attacked customary patterns of mixing recreation with work; new factories tried to ban singing, chatting, napping, as well as drinking on the job. Work rules, requiring daily attendance on pain of fines, also cut into the network of community festivals, viewed by industrialists as a waste of precious time and money and potentially a seedbed of unrest. Leisure lost ground outside the West as well. Estate owners in Africa and Latin America in the late 19th century also sought greater discipline over leisure, including festivals and drinking, and while they were not entirely successful, older patterns did recede.

At least in the industrial societies themselves, the first decades of industrialization typically worsened the quality of leisure life, even as work conditions tightened. Festivals declined, not just because of official opposition (though about half the time of the new British police force went into controlling leisure activities) but also because festivals amid urban strangers difficult to organize. Informal recreations mixed with work declined. Japanese artisans, long famous for extensive time off and elaborate recreational pursuits, were prodded into greater discipline around 1900. What was left? Many workers used Sunday afternoons to stroll with their families, often into the countryside. Tavern drinking went up. Small bars dotted working-class neighborhoods, at one point with one bar per 25 families in Belgian cities (the world's leader at the time). Drinking establishments provided escape but also, perhaps more important, companionship. Efforts to control drinking through temperance movements and, sometimes, legislation did not manage to bring this leisure outlet down. Sexual activity, at least for men, became a more important recreational outlet as well.

With traditional leisure largely killed, and with important but limited additional options, the situation was ripe for the second stage of leisure innovation under industrialization. New leisure forms proliferated in western Europe and the United States, particularly after about 1850, in which spectatorship and consumption of professional performances played a greater role. Sports were redefined, for players and viewers alike, and took on new attributes directly related to industrial work.

Industrialization changed athletic activities in many ways. For the first time, statistics and other accurate measures were used not just to determine winners and losers but as an essential part of the game itself. Baseball and football, which emerged in the United States, illustrate this trend. Baseball fans' delight in the arcane statistics of various players, such as batting averages and numbers of strikeouts, is a reflection of industrialization's greater emphasis on accuracy and statistics. Football developed similar facets as it emerged, from the 1860s onward, with players moving with predetermined military precision (at least, that is the ideal), progressing toward the goal line. Players in both sports (and many others that became popular in the late 19th century) now played in uniforms and became largely indistinguishable from one another other, apart from the numbers painted on their clothes. People liked to see or participate in sports that reflected their environment, which by this time was more regimented and uniform than it had been ever before. In many ways, leisure patterns reflected the new societies as much as they offered an alternative to the industrial setting.

The adoption of baseball in Japan is a good example of this phenomenon. Sailors from U.S. warships introduced the sport soon after Commodore Matthew Perry's opening of Japanese harbors to foreign trade. The Japanese adopted baseball as part of the cultural package of the West during the Meiji reforms, when the country reorganized in a sustained effort to catch up to the West. Although baseball would lose some popularity in Japan in the 1930s, as nationalists railed against Western influences, after World War II, baseball's popularity surged again, constituting Japan's leading sport. The precision and the statistical nature of the game appealed to Japanese sensibilities just as in the United States, but the emphasis on ritual and politeness during the games—in contrast to American ritualistic arguments with umpires—showed continued cultural differences between Japan and the West.

Leisure activities became more explicit in industrialized countries; the idea of set, daily times for leisure as opposed to work was a modern one. In agricultural societies, there had been little concept of vacations; after all, agrarian rhythms basically determined when people could relax or celebrate important times of the year. With industrialization, seasons became much less relevant for changing the intensity of work; machines didn't care whether it was summer or winter. First white-collar workers and then, increasingly, blue-collar workers, as the latter gained some benefits toward the end of the 19th century, could schedule time off to spend with their families. Vacations and the tourism industry began to emerge in embryonic forms, especially for the new middle class. New transportation technologies, such as railroads, were crucial in this regard. People could travel relatively comfortably and quickly from their town or city to another one in ways never possible before. Families went away from their homes to the shore or to medicinal springs in order to spend some time, scheduled many months in advance, to relax. To be sure, going elsewhere was still a luxury confined largely to the upper classes and to the rapidly increasing middle sectors; only in the 20th century did Western society spread enough of its wealth to the working classes to allow them to go far from home as well. But workers in Britain did take day excursions to beaches by the 1880s, where they often relaxed—fully dressed, for they did not know how to swim. Amusement parks, another marriage of technology and leisure, emerged in the United States, providing diversion for the masses.

In the West, and to a lesser extent elsewhere, leisure activities were decoupled more and more from religious events. Carnival in Catholic countries—the frolicking before the austerity of Lent—and other religious events still described some key holidays. But vacations and amusement parks had little to do with religion or community festivals. Civic events, especially after the French Revolution in 1789, became more prominent, celebrating the important dates of nations that tried to use elaborate ceremonies to develop a sense of pride in citizenship, as well as to educate their population in the symbols and duties of the new nation-state. Bastille Day in France and Independence Day in the United States were exemplary in this regard, joining leisure activities with civic functions such as parades and speeches. This pattern was not, of course, unprecedented; classical societies had tried the same approach to leisure.

The rise of modern leisure was not uncomplicated. Many middle-class observers and government officials were appalled at mass taste. They objected to excessive drinking, rowdiness, and bawdiness. The creation of public parks raised bitter disputes between "respectable" people and the working class (including immigrants in the United States). There were also battles over popular theater. Music hall or vaudeville entertainment spread widely in European and American cities. It initially involved crude humor, sexual innuendo, and social satire, along with raucous audiences. By the 1880s middle-class people, eager for more leisure excitement in their own lives, began to attend these shows—"slumming," the practice was called. In response, the shows toned down, an interesting compromise. When the popular theater tradition merged with early motion pictures around 1900, another compromise was struck. Movies might maintain some popular themes, but audiences must be quiet. (Initially, working-class audiences had maintained their traditions of boisterousness.) So movies became a quintessential modern leisure form: sold to people by commercial companies and requiring passive, silent spectatorship. The system worked: As with spectator sports, the popularity of movies and popular theater soared. Finally, as an additional sop to respectability, highbrow entertainments, such as operas and Shakespearean plays, became places for the elites alone, in contrast to their more varied popular roots. Here, respectable people could enjoy fancy dress and elaborate manners without compromise, and ordinary people would come to regard the performances as irrelevant and boring.

Transformations in leisure patterns were most important in the West during this period, though they often diffused elsewhere through the vast colonial empire western Europe had created by the 19th century. While this chapter has emphasized these changes, it is important to keep in mind that during the modern period in much of the rest of the world, things remained pretty much the same. In places such as China, Africa, the Middle East, and Latin America, people survived on farming, with its inevitable periods of low activity followed by more intense work. Time away from work continued to be marked by community festivals, and religion loomed large in these celebrations. Sports were largely participatory, with leisure activities generally little changed from the postclassical period. Only at the end of the 19th century did European-style sports begin to spread rapidly to other areas, backed by the prestige of Western culture and the active urging of European businessmen and administrators throughout the world. As with work, though more slowly, international leisure currents were beginning to take shape.

EPILOGUE

Most world historians argue that the Industrial Revolution should be compared with the advent of agriculture, in shifting the basic framework of human existence. Even in its first century and a half, industrialization created unprecedented military weapons. It spurred the growth of European cities to embrace, in some cases, over half the total population–another historical first. It redefined key problems of government but also gave states new means to contact and compel (or solicit) ordinary people.

Yet the long 19th century was just a beginning, and it is not surprising that tremendous diversity persisted. Industrialization enhanced international economic gaps, between the minority of societies able to engage the process fully and the majority that were increasingly exploited and intimidated by the industrial elite. Even population patterns diverged, as industrialization brought new incentives to reduce birthrates in some areas while creating new means to reduce traditional mortality levels, and so increase population growth, in many others. Industrialization divided men and women in new ways. Some of these divisions proved temporary, suggesting that people initially used gender identities to react to change but, as industrial life became more familiar, later eased their efforts. Men, displaced from traditional forms of work or ownership, compensated in some instances by asserting new superiorities over women. Some of the new divisions proved surprisingly durable, such as the idealization of the female-headed home in several societies. Even leisure patterns divided, at least for a time, not only between industrial and agricultural societies but also between self-consciously respectable people and others. Here, too, developments in the 20th century reduced some of these initial diversities.

Industrialization brought many new problems. The widespread routinization of work was one. Factory life involved increasingly repetitious, fast-paced jobs: By the later 19th century, complaints about nervous stress began to enter the cultures of industrial societies, where they have remained ever since. But work on agricultural estates, under managers eager to maximize production for export, changed as well. The abolition of slavery was a momentous step; fewer workers could be easily driven to an early death. But the lifelong quality of labor probably deteriorated for many other groups.

Yet there were countercurrents. It was ideas of human dignity that helped bring an end to most forced slavery in the 19th century, though they had less impact on the newer forms of labor discipline. Governments began to develop a tentative new sense of responsibility for general welfare. New beliefs and novel cultural contacts promoted some changes in the conditions for women. Feminist movements emerged. As it entered its reform period after 1868, Japan rejected what it saw as an excessive deference to women in the West, but it extended mass education to women as well as men after 1872. The spread of new leisure forms, such as modern sports, also provided new interests and excitement. Here, too, growing cultural contacts in the 19th century allowed access to leisure innovations in many different societies. Finally, though hesitantly, people in some societies sought to gain new control over their lives by unprecedented limitations on family size, in the demographic transition that first began in the West. And other dynamic ideas surfaced: Nationalism, spreading in the 19th century, was a new focus for loyalty that touched base with real or imagined values from a region's past. This proved a vital recourse for leaders and reformers in Asia and Africa.

Whether the new loyalties, the new policies, and the new diversions provided an adequate replacement for what was being lost in community ties and in the capacity to regulate one's own work was a vital question on the eve of the 20th century; it remains a vital question for the world's peoples today. On the heels of many decades of rapid, fundamental change, it was difficult to evaluate the overall results in terms of how people were able to live their lives and establish personal meanings and community identities.

FOR FURTHER READING

POPULATION/BIOLOGY

A. J. Coale and S. C. Watkins, *The Decline of Fertility in Europe* (1986).
Warren Dean, *With Broadaxe and Firebrand: The Destruction of the Brazilian Atlantic Forest* (1995).
John Gillis, Louise Tilly, and David Levine, eds., *The European Experience of Declining Fertility, 1850–1970: The Quiet Revolution* (1992).
Kenneth Kiple, ed., *The Cambridge World History of Human Disease* (1993).
Thomas McKeown, *The Modern Rise of Population* (1976).
Michael Piore, *Birds of Passage: Migrant Labor and Industrial Society* (1979).
Wally Seccombe, *Weathering the Storm: Working-Class Families from the Industrial Revolution to the Fertility Decline* (1993).
E. A. Wrigley, *Population and History* (1989).

CULTURE

Catherine L. Albanese, *America, Religious and Religion* (1992).
W. G. Beasley, *Japan Encounters the Barbarians: Japanese Travelers in Europe and America* (1993).
Jeffrey Brooks, *When Russia Learned to Read: Literacy and Popular Culture* (1987).
V. Harvey Graff, *The Legacies of Literacy* (1982).
Maria Jansen and G. Rozman, *Japanese Transition from Tokugawa to Meiji* (1986).
Peter Stearns, *Battleground of Desire: The Struggle for Self-Control in Modern America* (1999).
———, ed., *The Other Side of Western Civilization* (1999).
Michael Stephens, *Japan and Education* (1991).
P. J. Vatikiotis, *The History of Modern Egypt: From Muhammad Ali to Mubarak* (1991).
Siegfried Wichman, *Japonisme: The Japanese Influence on Western Art in the Nineteenth and Twentieth Centuries* (1981).
Rosalind Williams, *Dream Worlds: Mass Consumption in Late Nineteenth-Century France* (1982).

STATE AND SOCIETY

S. A. M. Adshead, *China in World History* (1988).

C. A. Bayly, *Indian Society and the Making of the British Empire* (1988).

Susan Bayly, *Caste, Society and Politics in India from the Eighteenth Century to the Modern Age* (1999).

Kenneth Pomeranz, *The Making of a Hinterland: State, Society, and Economy in Inland North China, 1853–1937* (1993).

J. Mark Ramseyer and Frances M. Rosenbluth, *The Politics of Oligarchy: Institutional Choice in Imperial Japan* (1995).

Evelyn S. Rawski, *The Last Emperors: A Social History of Qing Imperial Institutions* (1998).

T. Skidmore and P. Smith, *Modern Latin America* (1984).

Charles Tilly, *The Contentious French: Four Centuries of Popular Struggle* (1989).

GENDER

Harriet B. Applewhite and Darline Gay Levy, eds., *Women and Politics in the Age of the Democratic Revolution* (1993).

Caroline Daley and Melanie Nolan, eds., *Suffrage and Beyond: International Feminist Perspectives* (1994).

John D'Emilio and Estelle B. Freedman, *Intimate Matters: A History of Sexuality in America* (1997).

David Barry Gaspar and Darlene Clark Hine, *More than Chattel: Black Women and Slavery in the Americas* (1996).

Nikki R. Keddie and Beth Baron, eds., *Women in Middle Eastern History: Shifting Boundaries in Sex and Gender* (1991).

Thomas Lacqueur, *Making Sex: Body and Gender from the Greeks to Freud* (1990).

Anne McClintock, *Imperial Leather: Race, Gender and Sexuality in the Colonial Contest* (1995).

Sonya Rose, *Limited Livelihoods: Gender and Class in Nineteenth-Century England* (1995).

LABOR AND LEISURE

William Baker, *Sports in the Western World* (1982).

David B. Davis, *The Problem of Slavery in the Age of Revolution* (1975).

Seymour Drescher, *Capitalism and Antislavery* (1988).

Andrew Gordon, *The Evolution of Labor Relations in Japan* (1985).

Patrick Joyce, *Work, Society, and Politics: The Culture of the Factory in Later Victorian England* (1980).

Jürgen Kocka, *White Collar Workers in America, 1890–1940: Social-Political History in International Perspective* (1980).

Peter Kolchin, *Unfree Labor: American Slavery and Russian Serfdom* (1987).

Richard D. Mandell, *Sport: A Cultural History* (1984).

Roy Rosenzweig, *Eight Hours for What We Will: Workers and Leisure in an Industrial City* (1983).

Peter Stearns and Herrick Chapman, *European Society in Upheaval* (1991).

James Walvin, *Leisure and Society, 1830–1950* (1998).

PART VI

The Contemporary Period, 1914–

Highlights. Several fundamental developments differentiated the 20th century from the modern period that had preceded it. First, rapid population increase and massive urban growth through most of the world altered the structure of human existence and placed new demands on the environment. Second, the pace and intensity of international contacts accelerated, due in part to revolutionary developments in transportation and communication. Third, the world economy was partially redefined. Because of rapid industrialization in East Asia and considerable manufacturing growth in other parts of the world, the old disparity between an industrial West and raw-materials-producing regions was modified, though economic inequalities remained important. Fourth, after five centuries of growing Western international dominance, the world balance of power was revised. The West remained an important civilization, but it no longer had an overwhelming military advantage, as armament elsewhere, as well as the success of other kinds of warfare, such as guerrilla tactics, modified its lead. Decolonization began to strip away earlier Western holdings, creating a host of new nations—many of them, such as India, quite powerful. Finally, the new period was marked by political and cultural changes. Few of the political systems that existed in 1900 survived to the 1990s; most monarchies and empires were toppled, sometimes through revolution. Culturally, world religions were challenged by the spread of science and secular belief systems, though patterns of change remained complex as religions survived or revived in several major areas.

Key Developments. The 20th century divides into three subperiods. The first is 1914–1945, ushered in by World War I, a devastating battle among European powers on a global stage, with Britain, France, and Russia opposing Germany and its allies. Germany lost, setting the stage for massive resentments. More important, the war damaged the European economy while raising new hopes for independence in other parts of the world. It also triggered a major, communist revolution in Russia. The decades after World War I were marked by major tensions and a massive, worldwide economic depression. Anti-colonial nationalism spread and began to win promises of independence, particularly in the Middle East, where the Ottoman Empire had ended but European countries had gained governing rights. Latin American states, reacting to the depression, won greater control over their economies, reducing, though not eliminating, Western and United States influence and beginning to promote a larger manufacturing sector. Revolution in China, launched before World War I, ended the traditional imperial system. Japan's industrialization accelerated, and the nation launched new attacks on neighbors, including China—a process that ultimately led to World War II in the Pacific. Germany, under an unprecedented fascist dictatorship, rearmed and provoked renewed war in Europe, abetted by West European and American hesitancy. Even more than World War I, this struggle took on international dimensions, involving key parts of Africa and much of Asia as well as the Pacific.

The end of World War II ushered in the 20th century's second subperiod. Europe, drained by battle, managed a surprising revival, accelerating economic growth and embracing democratic political forms more uniformly. But the West's international hold loosened. From 1946 onward, colonies were abandoned, sometimes peacefully, sometimes with brief struggle. Asia came first in this decolonization process, then Africa and remaining parts of the Caribbean. Most new nations attempted democracy but then fell back to some form of authoritarianism, though democratic India was a key exception. Along with decolonization and new nation formation, the postwar period was dominated by the global struggle between the Soviet Union—as the revolutionary Russian Empire was termed—and its satellites in Eastern Europe on the one hand and an alliance between the United States and Western Europe on the other. The rapid spread of atomic weapons, first introduced in World War II, added dire prospects to this international rivalry. But this was a cold war, and only a few regional conflicts actually broke out, mainly involving the United States in Asian battles. The cold war umbrella helped many societies promote their own

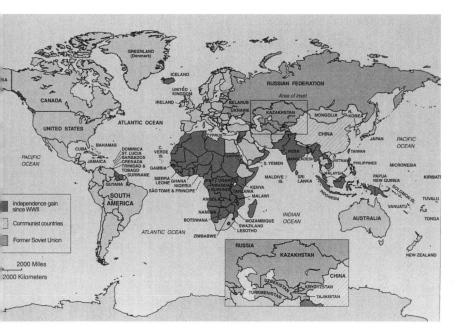

Global Relationships at the End of the 1990s. From Peter N. Stearns, *World History in Brief: Major Patterns of Change and Continuity*, 3rd ed. Copyright 1999 by Addison-Wesley Educational Publishers Inc. Reprinted by permission.

independence, courted by both the Soviet and Western powers, and even advance their economies. By the 1960s, Mexico, Brazil, Turkey, and several other countries were expanding their manufacturing sector, while South Korea, Taiwan, and other Pacific Rim countries were engaged in full industrialization.

The cold war ended around 1989. The Soviet Union had overextended itself in the arms race, leading to domestic economic collapse amid massive environmental pollution. Reformers led a peaceful overthrow of the communist system and abandoned the struggle with the United States. The Soviet Union itself disbanded into smaller republics, though Russia retained great size and strength. Democracies spread through most of Eastern Europe, and also in Latin America, where they replaced a common pattern of authoritarian rule. A few communist systems survived, notably that of China, but here, too, market economic principles were introduced, along with a stubborn effort to prevent political liberalization.

Through most of the 20th century, rapid population growth was spurred by improvements in public health systems. A few industrial areas had cut their birthrates, and after the 1970s, the rate of population expansion began to slow worldwide. But the additional billions of people remained a major force for change. Cities grew, often concentrating poverty; centers in Asia and Latin America surpassed Western urban concentrations in size. New migration patterns brought millions of Asians, Africans, and Latin Americans to Western Europe and the United States.

Novel patterns of international contact showed in many ways. Multinational companies, based in the West or the Pacific Rim, set up production and sales operations literally worldwide. Cultural dissemination brought products such as American television, fast foods, and recreational facilities and clothing to all corners of the globe. Communism and nationalism, along with Western science and consumer values, competed actively with older religions, though religion remained a lively force in the Middle East, India, and Latin America, while Christianity and Islam gained ground in sub-Saharan Africa. Political changes featured a replacement of traditional monarchies and colonial systems with one of three newer forms:

First, communist revolutions took hold in societies with strong-state traditions, such as China and Russia, where massive social attacks against old cultural systems and the landed elite seemed essential preconditions for change and for justice. China, for example, attempted a more liberal revolution after first unseating the empire in 1911, but the communist forces of Mao Tse-tung finally won a long struggle in 1949. The second modern system, the authoritarian regime—whether one-man, one-party, or military rule—was the most common pattern in new nations in the Middle East, Southeast Asia, and Africa, where political order seemed essential. They were also common in Latin America and in parts of Europe at key points in the century. Finally, democracy spread from its base in the West to India, Japan, and then many other parts of the world, especially in the 1980s and 1990s.

The new period in world history could not be fully defined at the end of the 20th century. Some observers, for example, predicted a full triumph for democracy and Western consumer culture. Others pointed to the revival of different traditions in Confucian and in Muslim areas. Another issue involved world balance of power: Some anticipated a century or more dominated by East Asia, but others wondered why any single civilization area should take over the position the West and, before it, Islam had once held. On a related point: Would some coherent kind of international rivalry take over from the now-defunct cold war? Population growth was slowing, but existing momentum promised additional billions to the world ranks, and this, along with mounting industrial growth in such places as China and Latin America, raised obvious questions about environmental degradation and resource exhaustion. A few decades into a new period, questions were normal; the shape of world history had not quickly emerged in previous transitions either. But for a future just around the corner, even predictable questions seemed particularly tantalizing.

VI. Contemporary

1903   United States–backed revolt in Panama; independence from Colombia
1904–1905 Russo-Japanese War
1905   Revolution in Russia; peasant reforms and Duma
1910   Annexation of Korea by Japan; first use of assembly-line production in the United States
1910–1917 Mexican Revolution
1911   Chinese Revolution, fall of the last (Q'ing) dynasty; occupation of Morocco by France; takeover of Tripoli (present-day Libya) by Italy
1912–1913 Two Balkan wars
1914–1918 World War I
1915ff.   Rise of Arab nationalism, encouraged during World War I
1917   Russian Revolution, abolition of the czarist regime, Bolshevik victory; promulgation of Balfour Declaration, promising Jewish homeland in Palestine
1918   Collapse of the Ottoman Empire
1918–1919 End of German Empire, Habsburg Empire
1919   Paris Peace Conference (Versailles), founding of League of Nations; British colonial reforms in India, limited representative government; first meeting of Pan-African Congress, rise of African nationalism

1919–1939	Period of U.S. isolationism
1920s	Rise of fascism
1920	Beginning of Mohandas Gandhi's nonviolent movement in India
1921	Vladimir Lenin's New Economic Policy promulgated; formation of Chinese communist movement
1923ff.	Independent Turkey created by Ataturk, beginning of modernization drive; rise of independent Persia under Shah Riza Khan
1927	Joseph Stalin in full power; beginning of collectivization of agriculture in the Soviet Union
1929–1939	Worldwide economic depression
1930s	Import substitution experiments in Latin America; Hollywood in United States becomes dominant movie-producing location
1930	First Soccer World Cup played in Uruguay
1931	Japanese invasion of Manchuria
1933–1944	Nazi regime in Germany
1934	"Long March" led by Mao Tse-tung in China
1937	New Japanese attack on China
1937–1938	"Great Purge" conducted by Stalin
1939–1945	World War II
1940ff.	Rise of women in industrial labor force; Japanese invasion of Southeast Asia
1941	Pearl Harbor attacked
1945	Atomic bomb dropped on Japan; United Nations established
1945–1948	Soviet takeover of Eastern Europe
1947ff.	Cold war begun between United States and Soviet Union; decolonization, rise of new nations
1948	Full control of South African government gained by Afrikaners' independence from Britain and extension of apartheid

1949   Communist victory in China; formation of
        NATO
1950s   India, China engage in import-substitution
        industrialization; television becomes domi-
        nant entertainment media
1950–1962   Completion of independence of Arab states
1954   End of French war against Vietnamese na-
        tionalists and communists; independence
        and division of Vietnam
1955   First meeting of nonaligned nations; forma-
        tion of Warsaw Pact
1956   China's "Great Leap Forward" industrial-
        ization attempt; Hungarian revolt and its
        suppression
1956, 1967, 1973   Israeli-Arab wars
1957   Sputnik, the first artificial satellite, launched
        by Soviet Union, beginning the "space age"
1957–1980   Independence to most of black Africa
1958   Founding of the European Economic Com-
        munity (Common Market)
1959–1960   Fidel Castro's revolution in Cuba
1960s   Mao's Cultural Revolution
1960sff.   Independence achieved by most West Indies
        territories
1963   Beginning of authoritarian rule under Ferdi-
        nand Marcos in Philippines; military coup in
        Indonesia
1967–1970   Nigerian civil war
1968   Revolt in Czechoslovakia and its repression;
        widespread student protests in United States
        and Western Europe
1970s   Mexico, Central America, and "Asian
        Tigers"—South Korea, Taiwan, Malaysia,
        Thailand—industrialize through assembly
        plants; rise of Muslim fundamentalism in the
        Middle East; introduction of the microchip

	computer; gradual reduction of birthrate in most parts of the world
1971	Revolt in Pakistan; creation of independent Bangladesh
1973	End of Vietnam War
1973–1979	Increase in world energy prices promoted by OPEC
1976	Death of Mao; more pragmatic regime in China
1977	Egyptian-Israeli peace
1979	Iranian Revolution
1980s	Personal computers introduced on massive scale for business, pleasure
1980ff.	New democratic current in Latin America
1981ff.	Iran-Iraq War
1986	Fall of Marcos regime in the Philippines
1989–1991	Collapse of Soviet Union; new regimes in Eastern Europe, Central Asia; end of cold war
1990s	Internet becomes prominent; spread of some democratic regimes in Africa
1994	Nelson Mandela elected president of South Africa
1996	Mexico City becomes world's largest city
1999	World population tops 6 billion

CHAPTER 22

THE POPULATION EXPLOSION OF THE
20th CENTURY

The huge world population growth of the 19th century proved a pale fore-shadowing of the massive surge of the 20th century. Correspondingly, the seemingly unending proliferation of the human species was one of the key developments—many would argue, *the* key development—in 20th-century world history.

Between 1900 and approximately 2000, world population surged from 1.6 billion people to 6.2 billion—it quadrupled. Every region participated, but as always in human history, there were important differentials. The Asian populations rose at only slightly more than the overall world rate, while the Americas and particularly Africa strongly surpassed the rate; the African population grew more than sixfold. The European population, in contrast, rose less than 90 percent. One obvious result was a significant rebalancing among major regions. European peoples had outnumbered both Africans and Americans in 1900 but were noticeably overmatched by the century's end. One result of this development, fundamentally a familiar one, was another shift in migration patterns, as people from newly crowded regions sought less populous and/or wealthier alternatives.

Still, the main point is massive growth. Even Europe's increase, if modest by the unprecedented standards of the century, was considerable in historical terms. Never before had the human capacity for sustained reproduction of the species been so abundantly demonstrated. The outcome was yet another redefinition of the human relationship to physical nature, in which the use of natural resources and the alterations of the environment in order to gain space and food outstripped anything that had happened before.

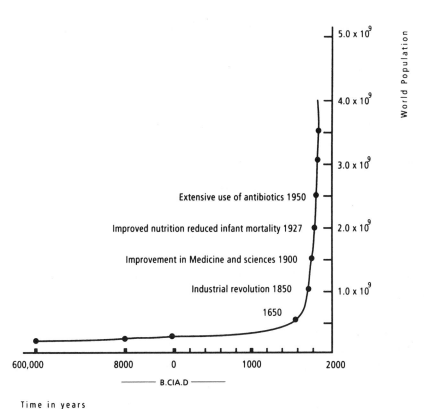

A Classic World Population Graph. It shows almost vertical growth since 1950.

Despite the magnitude of the population change and its consequences, the causes behind it were not terribly complex. The 20th-century explosion was prepared by the massive increase that had preceded, which provided a larger breeding pool. This was enhanced by a further decrease in the mortality rate worldwide. Despite acute problems with health in many societies, death was pushed back almost everywhere. Even less frequently than in the 19th century were there major epidemics that would serve recurrently to control the new levels of population vitality; this historic restraint was dramatically lowered. At the same time as people found the motives or available methods to cut back customary birthrates, these moves were inadequate to address the steady increase in the number of parents and the reduction of mortality levels. Finally, food supplies, often hard pressed, overall kept pace—otherwise the death rate would have recovered its sting.

Not surprisingly, by the second half of the 20th century, world population levels were seen as a critical problem—by individual governments, by many experts, and, ultimately, by international organizations such as the United Nations. Efforts to cut back on growth now became a vital part of population history.

Causes of Change

Just as the rate of 20th-century population growth exceeded all past precedent, so the causes added vital new ingredients to the process of populating the earth. The most important component involved public health measures, broadly construed. These involved attacks on disease-carrying insects, through draining swamps and the use of pesticides; increasingly widespread inoculations, particularly against childhood diseases and smallpox; information campaigns to encourage the boiling of water, particularly in the preparation of foods for children; and programs to control sewage and other contaminants, which operated with particular impact in the growing cities of the world. Public health measures by no means eliminated disease, and mortality rates continued to vary depending on climate and levels of prosperity. But life expectancy at birth went up almost everywhere, and it continued to rise fairly steadily throughout the century, generating more people and, as always, more potential parents. The reduction of the rates of child deaths almost literally reversed all historical precedent, with dramatic effects. Population growth rates easily overcame a continued regional incidence of epidemics and famines (but worldwide disease surges did decline), as well as the bloody wars and genocides that dotted the century.

The new public health regime, which, broadly speaking, extended measures that had already been developing in Western Europe and the United States, took hold by the late 19th century. One of the first "Western" features copied by the Japanese government after its reform era began in 1868, for example, was the urban public health system, which, in turn, generated an unprecedented period of Japanese population growth that supported both Japanese industrialization—by providing available workers—and often desperate efforts at imperial expansion. Colonial administrations—for instance, in Africa—began to install public health measures, if only to help protect European enclaves. Increasingly, governments of all sorts began to take greater responsibility for health, as a humanitarian matter and also as the basis for expanding populations useful for economic and military purposes. With the formation of the League of Nations and later the United Nations, international agencies also placed public health high on their agenda.

India, one of the key centers of rapid population growth, provides an example of the process. (While growth continued in China, it was far less rapid and dramatic than the new surge in other parts of Asia.) India had been wracked by disease in the 19th century, with recurrent regional epidemics. Increasing international contacts under British rule did not produce virgin soil epidemics, for India had long participated in global trade; but traditional disease rates remained high. The annual mortality rate reached 50 deaths per 1,000 inhabitants by around 1900. Even in the decade 1911–1920, the rate held at 48.6. But then it dropped to 36.3 in 1921–1930, 31.2 in 1931–1940, 27.4 in 1941–1950, and by 1970 the figure was 15.3 per 1,000 inhabitants. In other words, the mortality rate had plummeted by over 300 percent. The same pattern applied to infant mortality: Here, the rate was 212 deaths per 1,000 births between 1911 and 1920 but only 113 in 1966–1970.

Medical and sanitary intervention provides the leading explanation of change. New types of smallpox vaccinations had been introduced as early as 1802 and gradually won impact. Mass immunization and chemical spraying also later combined to push back cholera and malaria. By the mid–20th century, in fact, some experts were claiming that medical technology was providing the capacity for reducing mortality without improvements in food or living standards. As a result, the population could become larger without rising above meager subsistence.

More dependable food supplies were essential to support these changes, and some authorities argue that these were more important than public health measures in promoting the Indian population upheaval in the first place. New farming methods included a rapid expansion of irrigated agriculture, from the late 19th century onward, as well as use of the rail system to carry foodstuffs to areas suffering from localized bad harvests.

Severe famines in India ended after 1908 (except for a recurrence in 1943–1944 in Bengal), and the diseases most associated with famine, smallpox and cholera, receded accordingly.

Whatever the precise combination of public health measures and food supply, developments were striking. Deaths from smallpox per decade fell by 700 percent between 1868 and 1943 (though periodic outbreaks remained possible; Indian health conditions could still raise traditional concerns). Annual vaccinations, at 4.5 million per year in the 1870s, rose steadily amid growing government pressure, reaching 40 million by 1950. Cholera, which still caused 4 million deaths per decade in the late 19th century, dropped to about 70,000 deaths in the 1970s, due to gradual progress in inoculation and, in the cities, sewage treatments.

Sub-Saharan Africa was another new center of population growth in the 20th century, again despite huge continuing problems with disease and food supply. African growth rates by the end of the 20th century, indeed, were the highest in the world. And the average pace of expansion has been striking. Again, there is debate about precise causation, in this case between those who point to some general improvements in socioeconomic conditions (despite massive poverty) and those who emphasize public health.

The most obvious gains in African health as European colonies spread were for whites: Use of quinine against malaria was a case in point. Sewage treatment was installed in white sections of cities. Contacts with Europeans and the use of migrant African labor in the mines, in addition to deteriorations in the food supply, actually caused an increase in mortality around 1900, with new epidemics of sleeping sickness and other diseases. Racial segregation arose in part to protect the health of whites, given beliefs in the hygienic inferiority of the Africans. Gradually, however, there was spillover in public health measures to Africans themselves. Sulfa drugs began to be used in the 1920s, with marked success against yaws, an endemic disease in many parts of Africa. Colonial administrations also directed considerable efforts against sleeping sickness from the 1920s onward, with medical inspections, quarantines, and other measures. And of course, smallpox was attacked, while chemicals successfully reduced the insect carriers of malaria. As in India, these developments generated important questions. Ill health and dire poverty remained, now compatible with rapidly growing population size. Was there any real improvement in health, more broadly understood? Pressure on food supplies was tremendous. Recurrent droughts in the north and east, as well as a tendency to overplant, which reduced soil fertility and spread desertlike conditions below the Sahara, led to devastating regional famines in such places as Sudan and Ethiopia. Newly independent African governments often lacked the funds fully to maintain public health programs. Yet for all the agonizing problems, the population surge continued in the subcontinent as a whole.

Impacts of Population Growth

The huge surge of world population had a number of vital results. The new numbers of people pressed food supplies. On the whole, it seems clear that 20th-century population advance was not primarily caused by new foods—in contrast to earlier periods, where the opening up of new regions or the exchange of foods helps explain major breakthroughs. But changes in food supply were vital concomitants of the population surge, for otherwise famine and nutrition-related diseases would have shut down the trend. Population explosion also prompted relocation between countryside and city, in ways somewhat different from the urbanization patterns of the previous century. Finally, the explosion generated new migration patterns—a quite traditional result, but this time with major implications for world history and the world's future.

Agriculture

Against many expectations, and often dire predictions, world food production on the whole kept pace with population growth—which means that agriculture was itself revolutionized. Foods were inequitably distributed within and among countries, and regional famines and severe malnutrition among the poor persisted. Overall, however, the application of additional fertilizers, new seed types, and pesticides to agriculture steadily increased output in established leaders, such as the United States and Canada. Food exports from these areas expanded as well. Many European countries raised their output, as peasants became more commercially minded and more knowledgeable about machinery and scientific farming. France, with farming supported by government subsidies, became a grain exporter once again. But the big advances were in the population gainers themselves. India was able to feed its new numbers (though often badly) throughout most of the century. Imports were needed only in the 1960s. Application of more scientific methods to agriculture in places like India ultimately became known as the *green revolution*, a term coined in the 1960s to describe the transfer of agricultural technology from industrial countries to peasant societies. Agricultural experts particularly developed higher-yielding seeds of rice and wheat, capable of responding to the application of fertilizers with dramatic increases in productivity. Some of the crops were also more easily machine-harvested and were less vulnerable than their predecessors to weather changes or wind damage. Wheat-seed studies began in Mexico, supported by the Rockefeller Foundation. The center later worked also on corn improvement. The International Rice Research Institute was set up in the Philippines by American foundations, in conjunction with the Philippine government. Here, a key result was a so-called miracle rice, IR-8, and associated rice-growing technology. Centers of this sort trained experts from other parts of Asia and Latin America (and, to a lesser degree, Africa), with major effects on grain production in India, Pakistan, Malaysia, and Turkey. There were drawbacks: The new seeds increased vulnerability to new pests and diseases, in part because only a few seed types were now used. (Some peasants, however, sensibly mixed the new seeds with some of more traditional varieties, which reduced the problem somewhat). Fertilizer costs often rose, which limited the new techniques because such massive amounts of chemicals were required. Nevertheless, world food production advanced massively.

The problem of famine continued to surface, particularly in individual regions or in the aftermath of disruptions caused by war or civil strife. Poor nutritional levels were an even more widespread issue. And many experts continued to worry about food supplies for the future. Progressive attacks on forest areas in such places as Brazil and Africa constituted a traditional response to growing food needs. More marginal lands were brought under cultivation; forest acreage shrank annually, particularly in tropical regions, which reduced ecological variety and affected global climate. Thus both old and new agricultural responses to the dramatic increase in food needs created problems of their own, while significant hunger remained.

Urbanization

In many areas of the world—most strikingly, in the Middle East, Africa and Latin America—massive population growth put huge pressure on land resources. Peasants found that there was insufficient land to go around, while new methods of agriculture allowed higher food production levels with relatively fewer workers. A key result was growing rural misery. In many areas, population pressures on the land spurred massive peasant protests, a recurrent element in 20th-century revolutions and other risings, in Mexico, the Andes region, China, and elsewhere.

Urbanization was another key recourse. As population surged in 19th-century Europe, many people flocked to cities seeking jobs. On the whole, the growth of factory industry provided these jobs, so that urbanization closely correlated not just with population growth but with industrialization. Urbanization in the 20th century, particularly in less industrial, so-called Third World* areas, was rather different. Here the excess rural population pressed into the cities without a corresponding increase in urban jobs. Migration to cities tripled in the less industrial areas between 1925 and 1950, outstripping overall population growth. People were seeking in the cities not only jobs but potential welfare or charity assistance, as well as better living conditions, such as safe water.

Cities grew massively as urban centers in Mexico and China, for instance, began to surpass the size of established industrial or commercial cities in Western Europe, the United States, and Japan. In Latin America and the Middle East, urban populations outnumbered rural ones by the later 20th century, well in advance of full industrialization. African cities rose to encompass from 4 to 20 percent of the population early in the century to a third or higher by the 1980s. Urban growth in India and China

---

* The term *Third World* was originally coined in the cold war, to mark nations such as India and Egypt that did not want to take sides between the West and the Soviet bloc. Most of these nations were poor and nonindustrialized, and the term has shifted to emphasize these features. The term is misleading in that so-called Third World countries range from places with substantial manufacturing sectors, such as Mexico, to places where poverty is much more pervasive and industry almost nonexistent. But the term continues to designate a large number of countries different from the "industrial world" by measurements such as per capita income, life expectancy, and education level.

was slower—26 percent of the Indian population was urban in 1985, though, given massive overall growth, this meant huge and rapidly expanding cities. Brazil, 46 percent urban in 1960, was 73 percent urban by 1985, and countries such as Egypt showed similar trends. Urban misery increased as a result of this migration and growth pattern. Sprawling shanty towns surrounded Third World cities, with people living in corrogated huts amid dreadful poverty. In Mexico City, the world's largest by 1996, 30,000 people scavanged for food and clothing in garbage dumps. Crime rates increased. Begging levels soared in China after the strict controls were removed after 1978. Yet three of four urban migrants gained in the process. They were far more likely to have access to purified water and electricity in cities than in rural areas. They received better medical attention. Key measures that had been introduced to control disease, in other words, helped make even impoverished urban sectors viable. Urban residents also earned more money; newcomers to cities in Brazil earned three to five times what their rural counterparts could make. Yet, precisely because of these successes and steady overall population growth, the pressures continued, despite efforts by some governments, such as Indonesia, to slow the tide. Levels of urban pollution caused by traffic, congestion, and energy use mounted dangerously. Urbanization highlighted some of the fragile balances that the population explosion was creating.

Immigration

Changes in population differentials obviously redefined the world's migration patterns. Europeans stopped emigrating in large numbers by the 1920s, though there was a brief renewed surge after the dislocations of World War II. Migration from Asia had already solidified during the 19th century, as excess peoples coupled with the urgent recruitment of foreign labor brought Indians to South Africa and some of the Pacific Islands, Chinese and Japanese to the Americas. Asian outflows continued to be substantial through the 20th century. Large numbers of Chinese continued to move into Southeast Asia, serving as a key merchant group in such places as Thailand. Under British colonial rule, many Indians moved to eastern and southern Africa before World War II and also to the Caribbean. Filipinos as well as other Asians moved to islands in the Pacific. After World War II, Asian migrants included large numbers of West Asians—mostly Muslims, from Turkey and the Arab world—as well as numerous North Africans to Western Europe and the United States. Also new was substantial migration from sub-Saharan Africa and, particularly, from parts of Latin America and the Caribbean. Finally, key destinations of migrants after World War II included not only the United States, Canada, and Australia but also Europe and, to a very modest degree, Japan. The flow was obvious: Migrants from high-growth areas sought space in regions with lower birthrates and greater prosperity. The pressures involved were enormous, as high levels of illegal immigration combined with legal transfers often eagerly supported by employers interested in cheap labor.

Key transfers went from former colonies to industrial host nations. Thus Britain gained many people from Pakistan, India, and the West Indies, and France many migrants from Algeria. As European economic growth soared in the 1960s, many countries deliberately invited immigrants, who in Germany were euphemistically referred to as "guest workers." Sources of immigration to the United States shifted from Europe to parts of Asia, including the Philippines and Korea, and Central America. Muslims became the most rapidly growing religious minority. Levels of immigration to the United States after the 1950s were higher than ever before in the nation's history.

Population shifts of this sort inevitably caused dislocation. Most immigrants were shunted into the worst-paying, least-stable jobs. Many industrial countries periodically tried to limit entry or even to send some "guests" back home. Racial prejudice intensified amid visible cultural differences and competition for jobs, and there were many violent attacks on immigrants in the United States, Britain, Germany, and elsewhere. Difficulties were compounded by the fact that most immigrant populations maintained a higher birthrate than that of the host country and so expanded their population share in this manner as well. In Germany in the 1970s, for example, immigrants constituted only 7 percent of the total population but accounted for 15 percent of all births. The same pattern held among people of Latin American origin in the United States. Yet the immigrants did provide valuable labor. Many adjusted quickly, and some were able to take advantage of new educational opportunities. Their birthrates declined amid industrial conditions as well, though they remained higher than the national averages in the recipient areas. Here were additional legacies of the world population explosion.

Limiting Population Growth: The Push toward Demographic Transition

The 20th century created a new world problem: overpopulation, or its threat. Specific regions had faced overpopulation in previous times. China recurrently had generated populations larger than its food capacity at the time; famine and disease then had cut size back. European populations had exceeded agricultural resources by the end of the classical period, which generated compensations, including the European family system, designed to hold the birthrate down a bit. But overpopulation at the world level was a new issue. It reflected the massive growth. It also reflected growing intolerance, among officials and ordinary people alike, for the normal mechanisms of population restraint. Leaders in various political systems believed that renewed disease or food shortages would harm their societies and suggest an inhumane or backward system.

Western experts took the lead in urging population restraint. Many demographers and economists sincerely believed that contemporary levels of growth threatened to overwhelm basic resources and generate levels of pollution that would permanently limit global potential. Books with titles such as *The Population Bomb* won wide attention by the 1960s. Experts and popularizers alike argued that contemporary growth assured poverty and ill health, for while the new populations might survive, they could not attain prosperity. Indeed, many claimed, population excess retarded economic innovations. Third World societies had to devote so many resources simply to keeping people alive that they lacked capital and energy to institute a full-blown industrial revolution. There was debate here. Some observers noted a certain amount of racial anxiety in these population arguments: People in largely "white" societies could not fail to note that their birthrates were being outpaced by those of people of color. Yet many leaders in Asia and Latin America came to accept the basic need for population restraint. While the most eye-catching "population bomb" arguments receded after the 1970s, as it became apparent that food supplies were keeping up with people, various international organizations, including the United Nations, pushed for population restraint; so did environmental groups, and also feminists eager to make sure that women gained a greater voice in family-planning decisions.

But the turn to a demographic transition was slow. Some political leaders resisted the new arguments, maintaining more traditional views that population growth was a sign of a healthy political and economic system. China's revolutionary leader Mao Tse-tung in the 1960s rejected population-control arguments as a Western ploy to limit Asian strength; more people would spur China's economic and military power. Various Mexican leaders at times pushed aside population limitation goals. Fascist leaders in Europe, bent on military strength, also tried to promote birthrate increases, praising traditional fertility and urging women to concentrate on motherhood. Major religious groups hesitated as well: The Catholic Church firmly resisted artificial birth control and abortion, on grounds that sexuality for pleasure alone was sinful and that human souls should not be lost. Many practicing Catholics disagreed—most American Catholics rejected the church position, at least on birth control, by the 1950s—but the arguments had influence, particularly at the policy level. Muslim leaders also argued against birth control, and regions that were strongly Muslim maintained some of the world's highest birthrates by the end of the 20th century. The United States government, pressed by Christian groups, usually resisted international promotion of birth control, and debates over the issue, including abortion, fueled major political divisions within the country.

Strong resistance also resulted from ingrained popular habits and values, sometimes enhanced by religion. New types of birth control could affect basic sexual practices. They exposed people to unfamiliar medical procedures. They challenged beliefs about gender roles and family. Even when new goals were espoused, people sometimes were ignorant of effective methods or unable to afford them. Many people depended on large numbers of children to provide labor—child labor continued to be a vital factor in many Third World economies, both reflecting and causing high birthrates. Families in India looked to surviving sons as a source of support in parents' later age; it often seemed prudent to have large families, simply to make sure that at least one adult son would be available later on.

Chinese tradition even more strongly valued sons as a sign of family and maternal success. Cultural and familial economic systems eventually yielded to growing evidence that more children were surviving, to the family's detriment; but they yielded slowly, amid confusion and controversy. Government efforts to promote population controls were often resisted or evaded in this context.

It had taken at least a century for Western societies to react to population explosion with new birth-control strategies, even when successful industrial revolutions facilitated change. Much of the rest of the world displayed a similar lag in the 20th century. This was unsurprising, but it had enormous consequences as the population train continued to barrel ahead until the century's final decades.

Population in Industrial Societies

Headed chronologically by Western Europe and the United States, where key changes had occurred in the 1800s, most industrial societies developed a fairly standard demographic pattern during the 20th century. Families generally kept average birthrates down to near-replacement levels, with about two children per unit. At times, indeed, rates dipped below replacement levels: That is, without immigration, the societies involved would have begun to shrink. This was true in France by the 1930s, then in Italy, Greece, and some other European countries, as well as Japan, by the 1990s. Growing numbers of families decided that too many children made life in an industrial economy too difficult, by jeopardizing living standards and imposing child-care problems now that work was separate from the home. Expectations about what each child should have rose as well: People increasingly thought in terms of consumer items and more advanced education for children, and these goals were most readily achieved through lower birthrates. The historic shift to more women's work involvement, from the 1950s onward, also figured in throughout the Western world. (The interaction between women and population patterns is discussed more fully in chapter 20.)

Motives and commitments for novel forms of birth control predated the 20th century in Western Europe and the United States. (Efforts to control births by means of medicines and abortions were, of course, not new;

what was new was the array of methods and the levels of control now sought.) Advancing industrialization helped spread the "modern" pattern to additional areas, particularly in southern Europe, that had previously maintained higher growth levels. The trend was facilitated by growing use of artificial devices. Middle-class families in the United States were routinely using diaphragms by the 1930s, prescribed by doctors and now quite respectable, if not openly discussed. Lower-class families were more hesitant, particularly because of various prejudices against restricting male sexuality and reproduction. Generally in industrial demography, poorer families had more children than middle-class families—a reverse of the pattern common in preindustrial centuries, when peasants had carefully limited family size through late marriage and birth spacing. But lower-class use of new devices spread as well. The advent of contraceptive pills in the 1960s also facilitated birth control, which now increasingly spread to people engaging in sex before or outside of marriage. Increasingly, in the 20th century, the distinction between sex for pleasure and sex for conception gained ground, and a growing number of births were carefully planned. By the 1970s it was estimated that fewer than 20 percent of all births in the United States were unintended.

Demographic transitions—that is, dramatic reductions in traditional birthrates—also spread to other industrial societies, for the same basic reasons as in the West. The separation of work from home, the decline of child labor and the rise of education, and the growing commitment to securing living standards prompted a growing effort to restrict birthrates. The birthrate issue was intensely debated in the Soviet Union during the 1920s, and laws restricting the dissemination of birth-control information and abortions were greatly eased. In the Soviet Union and in other communist societies after World War II, such as Romania, many families sought to keep their rates low, amid pressures on urban housing and a desire to devote more attention to the care and education of individual children. High rates of employment for married women added to the mix. In this region, abortion loomed larger as a birth-control method than in the West, in part because of the cost and, often, the poor quality of artificial devices. But the net result was a demographic system quite similar to that of the West by the second half of the 20th century: small families, particularly in the urban areas.

Japan converted to this pattern with a vengeance after World War II. Here, both birth-control devices and abortions were widely used. After decades of promoting birthrates as part of Japan's military ambitions, the government now shifted to a vigorous campaign to promote demographic stability in what was a very populous island nation. Even though the numbers of married women in the labor force were comparatively low, the desire to protect living standards and to lavish attention on individual children pushed in the familiar direction. Methods in Japan reflected the role of government policy: A number of people were sterilized, to guard against birth defects or to protect health. Abortion rose even more rapidly, from 9 abortions per 100 births in 1947, to 57 by 1953, to 80 by 1957. And the birthrate, correspondingly, began to plunge below Western levels.

The demography of industrial societies thus increasingly settled into a common pattern. Low birthrates were combined with high survival rates for children born. Life expectancy at birth soared. By the late 20th century, a child born in most industrial societies could expect to live into his or her 70s. (Female life expectancy normally surpassed the male's at this point, in part because of the concomitant reduction of deaths in childbirth; but a few areas, such as Scandinavia, displayed only a small gender gap.) Medical improvements also began to affect adults. The introduction of sulfa drugs, and then penicillin in the second quarter of the century, dramatically reduced adult deaths from respiratory disease. Improvements in living conditions, including better diet and work safety, fed this trend. Additional medicines after World War II, including pharmaceuticals that controlled blood pressure, spurred further gains. Increasingly, adults were living into their 80s and 90s in industrial societies. (Adults in their 80s were the most rapidly growing age group in the United States at the end of the 20th century.)

Improved public health—including a growing range of inoculations—and medical care had further consequences in the industrial societies. The causes of death were revolutionized, as part of the process of pushing death back. Rather than epidemics and endemic disease, accidents and the deteriorations of age became the most common killers (headed by heart disease and cancer). Attitudes toward death changed: Most people now died in hospitals, rather than at home; contact with death diminished, and some observers claimed that the whole subject of death became taboo in the industrial world. Age structures shifted dramatically. Industrial societies began to have a declining percentage of young people, a growing percentage of elderly. The importance of the old, in politics, for example, increased. Most industrial societies, both in the West and in Japan, pushed for formal retirement policies during the 20th century as a means of assuring adequate jobs for the young. But this meant that the growing percentage of old people had to be supported by a more slowly growing working population. By 1990 in Japan, fewer than three people were working for every person retired, and this pattern was spreading to the West as well. (Some Japanese officials, in fact, began to advocate higher birthrates to compensate for aging; Western countries, accepting more young immigrants, did not make this turn.) Here was another sign of the redefinition of key social issues that resulted from the revolutionary demography of the industrial world.

Standard industrial patterns continued to permit some anomalies and differentiations. In the late 1940s, most Western nations experienced an unexpected birthrate increase—the baby boom. Reacting to a decade of depression and war, many families sought a slightly higher number of children, and postwar economic prosperity facilitated the shift. The baby boom peaked in the late 1950s and then receded, as stricter birthrate limitations returned amid criticisms of population expansion and the new patterns of women's work. But the effect, in terms of population growth, had been considerable. After the baby boom, many Western societies experienced a surge of premarital teenage pregnancies, even as overall birthrates plummeted, which caused and reflected important social and generational divisions. This issue particularly affected the United States, which was unwilling to promote birth-control devices among adolescents; European nations and Japan reacted with less controversy and had markedly lower teenage pregnancy rates as a result.

Demographic patterns in Russia posed a more striking exception to the common trends by the 1980s. Low birthrates persisted. As in many industrial societies, there were internal differentials: Birthrates in Muslim regions were much higher than among ethnic Russians, which occasioned concern for the future among some leaders. But with declining living standards associated with the Soviet economic collapse, two unusual developments occurred: First, infant death rates began to rise; second, adult life expectancy also began to drop, in part because of increased alcoholism. More generally, high levels of environmental pollution began seriously to affect both infant and adult health in a number of regions. Russian mortality levels rose far more than the norm in industrial societies, surpassing a number of Third World areas, even as birthrates remained low.

Exceptions and differentials were significant, but the emergence of a dramatic new industrial population pattern was more significant still. The controls over natural constraints on population growth possible in the 20th century, as a result of food supply and attacks on disease, now led to new levels of control over conception, most commonly through a separation of recreational sexuality and birthrates. The results in terms of aging, family size, even attitudes toward sex itself were striking and would clearly have further repercussions in the future.

Demography in Developing Societies: Trends and Contrasts

Outside the established industrial societies, three patterns predominated in the 20th century. First, obviously, population growth was quite high. Mortality rates declined more rapidly than birthrates. Second, there was nevertheless a gradual decline in birthrates, and this accelerated in the final decades of the century as many societies, even though not yet fully industrialized, clearly achieved the demographic transition. Finally, great diversity prevailed. Trends operated at various speeds; regional policies and cultures differed sharply.

India and China form an important contrast, showing the significance of differentials; the contrast is of obvious global significance because of the huge size of the two populations. Communist revolutionaries initially scorned population issues. In 1949, Mao declared, "China's vast population should be viewed as a positive asset. Even if it should multiply many times, it will be fully able to resolve the problems created by this growth." Nevertheless, increasing realization of the rate of expansion prompted some halting measures. Systematic attention developed only after 1971, however. At this point, the government began to require later marriage (23 to 25 years of age for women); 4-year intervals between the first and second child; and, by 1977, no more than two children per family. In 1979 the limit was reduced to one child per couple, with exceptions for special situations, including families in border areas. Government officials were responsible for monitoring the requirements in each province. Couples were required to meet with local group leaders to determine who was authorized to have a child the following year, while benefits rewarded families that lived up to the commitments and penalties, including wage cuts, applied to families that disobeyed. Widely distributed birth-control devices, including the IUD (intrauterine device, available since the 1960s), undergirded this process, along with extensive sterilization. (Sterilization, mainly through tubal ligation but also through vasectomies, had great advantages in reliability and cost, compared to birth-control devices.) Abortions were also common, free, and did not require the husband's consent.

These draconian measures, which built on China's long tradition of a strong state, had clear effects, though enforcement was not uniform. By the 1990s, total fertility stood at 1.9 children per family, which was more than 60 percent below 1950s levels. At the same time, Chinese industrialization had advanced, which added to the context for birth control, and average health had improved, with an 8-year increase in average life expectancy. To be sure, there were reports of unintended consequences, particularly a return to female infanticide in some rural regions as couples sought to assure the birth of a son while adhering to government limits. But China seemed to have reached a situation in which, by about 2020, population levels would stabilize (at approximately 1.2 billion people). Continued increase in the interim simply reflected the higher number of potential parents as a result of previous growth; the actual reproduction rate was stationary. China also began to display other symptoms of the demographic transition, including the growth of older age groups as a percentage of the total.

India, with stronger religions and a much weaker government tradition, changed more slowly. While the Indian economy evolved, with considerable manufacturing growth, there was no industrial breakthrough comparable to post-1978 China; this sluggishness reflected the burden of more rapid population growth, but it also limited the motives for families to change their birth policies, since children could still be seen as assets in a predominantly preindustrial economy.

Birthrates did decline in India in the second half of the 20th century, but only by a third—half of China's result. Government policies called for reductions from 1952 onward, and family-planning centers were set up, but the outcomes were modest. In 1970, only 14 percent of all Indian women, mainly urban and upper-class, were using birth control (primarily sterilization, after a desired number of children had been achieved). In 1976, the government of Indira Gandhi tried to speed up the program, calling for mandatory sterilization after the birth of a third child. But the policies were not enforced, and they prompted violent protests that toppled the government in 1977 elections. The government pulled back, though still calling for increased investments in family planning and pressuring for use of the IUD and sterilization. But the IUD triggered objections, because medical officials who could insert it properly were lacking and because exaggerated reports spread about the dangers of the device to health. The government did not authorize oral contraceptives. By the 1990s, 40 percent of all Indian women were currently using contraception (two-thirds of them had been sterilized), and the fertility rate had dropped to 3.4 children per family. While Indian population growth would clearly continue far longer than China's (India was expected to surpass China as the world's most populous country around the year 2000), many observers believed that the trends were now pointing to stabilization toward the middle of the 21st century.

Birthrate reductions in Latin America were more dramatic than in India, though without the unusual government intrusions that China had adopted. Rural and urban clinics pressed women to use birth-control measures by the 1960s and 1970s. Barriers were obvious: Catholic priests argued against use of the pill, while many men, in a highly macho culture that stressed sexual controls over women, feared that birth control would allow women to engage in sexual activity with other men. Some women stopped going to church and hid pills from their husbands to counter these problems. The motivation seemed clear: As one Mexican woman put it, "I told you we were very poor when I was a child. We were six children, and my father didn't earn much. That is why I want just two or three children. I don't want my children to grow up like me—without an education. . . . I want them to be independent and proud of themselves." By the 1990s, fertility rates in Latin America as a whole stood at about 2.2 children per family, and key societies such as Brazil and Mexico had clearly made the turn to demographic transition. As in China, population growth would continue still for about two generations, but an end seemed ultimately in sight. And, despite variety and hesitation, this was the predominant international pattern. By the final decades of the 20th century, over 85 percent of all the world's governments backed new types of family planning. Popular opinion was shifting, if slowly—with women often in the lead—toward insistence on smaller families, though methods of achieving this goal varied. Here was one of the historic changes of 20th-century world history, leading to predictions of a return to global population stabilization soon after the mid–21st century on the basis of widespread family limitation, low death rates, and redistribution of the overall age structure.

Yet, for all the change, huge numbers of unwanted children persisted in 2000, the legacy of the earlier population surge. Children were often killed and abused in Latin America and South Asia; they served in workforces and armies in parts of Asia and Africa. They died from untended diseases and even from growing use of infant foods sold by Western companies and prepared without adequate sterilization. Sick, overworked, often uneducated children formed another legacy for the world's future.

Prospects and Anxieties: After a Century of Population Upheaval

By the end of the 20th century, world population was still increasing by the total size of the United States population every two years. The tremendous shift in global population during the 20th century, the overturning of so many of the traditional controls on growth, inevitably occasioned worried comment. Even though the rate of increase was measurably slowing, the anticipation of over a half century more of residual expansion, simply on the strength of current momentum, made some authorities wonder if stabilization would come too late. Even current population size, some argued, might be impossible to sustain.

Concerns involved the tensions associated with contemporary migration patterns. Many recipient societies began to limit the number of immigrants, particularly from the most populous areas, in an effort to preserve jobs and space for their own inhabitants. Racial bias also entered in strongly. Tensions over immigration policies were severe, and the situation could worsen in future. The simple fact was that even comparatively open spaces of the sort that had continued to buffer population growth even in the 19th century no longer existed. Would conflict over differing levels of population pressure worsen in future? How would societies that were failing to reproduce themselves—such as Italy—and rapidly aging deal with labor needs and the pressure of migrants from other areas? Japan, for one, had already staked a high-tech course, leading the world in the introduction of robots and other forms of automated production and allowing entry to only a small number of immigrants for the more menial jobs.

Food supply caused anxiety. There was no question that improvements in agricultural productivity had confounded some pessimistic predictions issued as recently as the 1970s. But could expansion be maintained? In some regions of Africa, pressures to increase production had already severely reduced soil quality. Were other regions overgrowing? The heavy use of pesticides was another issue: Many societies routinely used pesticides already banned in places such as the United States as dangerous to human health. At the same time, agricultural research continued, and genetic engineering might usher in still further productivity gains (or, some worried, new kinds of health problems). The most serious issue involved the continued poor nutrition of large segments of the world population, which did not heighten death rates but did open the quality of life to serious question.

Some experts also pointed to the dangers of a return of new forms of epidemic disease. Here the argument highlighted the extent to which patterns in recent centuries were unusual in human history, along with a fear that growing contact heightened possibilities for contagion. The reduction of tropical forests forced insects and animals into new contact with people, and new strains of contagious disease might result. Sporadic outbreaks of fatal viruses such as ebola, though quickly confined by quarantine, might foreshadow wider problems. Further, remedies such as antibiotics were being so widely used that bacteria were evolving to adjust, weakening the potency of the medicines. The great 20th-century biological achievement, the reduction of classic fatal contagions, might be called into question.

For a time, the outbreak of the AIDS epidemic confirmed for many the fears of a resumption of an international plague cycle. AIDS, or acquired immune deficiency syndrome, is a degenerative disease of the major organ systems, including the immune system and the central nervous system, resulting from a virus. Caused initially by contacts between monkeys and humans in Africa, it is transmitted among humans by exchange of blood or tissue. The disease was first recognized in 1981, though infections, which often take considerable time to manifest themselves, had begun earlier. The disease seems to have spread from Africa, with incidence in almost every nation. Disease rates remained highest in East Africa, where migrant labor patterns encouraged use of multiple sexual partners, and where government capacities to regulate and educate remained limited. But AIDS spread rapidly to the Caribbean, the Americas, Europe, and, to a lesser extent, Asia. (Asian contacts with some of the key infection areas were more limited, and in some areas, sexual habits were more closely restricted by family and community controls.) By the late 1980s, tremendous fears arose about potential worldwide mortality. In fact, however, aside from East Africa and a few parts of Latin America, disease incidence stabilized. The virus was fragile, perishing quickly without contact, and this helped limit the epidemic. Further, governments in many areas embarked on safe-sex education programs, promoting the use of condoms, which had clear effects. Massive medical research programs bore some fruit in the industrial countries, though while the disease might be slowed, there was as yet no cure (and people in poorer regions had no access to the latest treatments). The disease remained serious, with an estimated 14 million people infected throughout the world by 1995. But, despite initial fears and analogies, this was not a modern version of the Black Death. Still, the experience of a novel contagion pointed to other, possibly more severe problems in future.

Population size and growth related directly to concerns about global pollution. Land clearance for agriculture expansion changed chemical balances, contributing to global warming. Growing energy use, to accommodate expanding industrialization and population increase alike, directly heightened chemical pollution. Third World cities frequently experienced devastating smogs—called the "Yellow Dragon" in China, which, because of population size and industrial growth, moved into second position behind the United States as a contributor to chemical pollutions worldwide. The impact of severe pollution on human health and mortality was already visible in the scarred landscapes of the former Soviet Union and some of its erstwhile East European allies. Human beings had already modified the environment in previous eras, expanding desert regions by intensive agriculture and marring other areas through chemicals used in manufacturing. Key societies had already declined because of environmental deterioration, as it reduced the capacity for agriculture and directly affected human health. Now, some observers warned that the potential for catastrophe was outstripping anything previously experienced.

The sheer level of biological change that defined the 20th century inevitably raised questions. What had happened was reasonably clear, despite the defiance of historical patterns. But what the human surge portended for the future was decidedly murky, as people sought to adjust to new levels of crowding and as some of the responses, such as new types of birth control, raised tensions of their own.

CHAPTER 23

UPHEAVALS IN POLITICS AND CULTURE

The 20th century witnessed immense political and cultural changes, in virtually every society. Almost all the colonial regimes, monarchies, and empires dominant in 1900 were gone by 2000. Several societies experienced numerous changes in basic regime during the century. Few societies, also, maintained the same basic cultural patterns that existed in 1900: Key traditional religions were challenged, and even successful religious counterthrusts involved major innovations. Artistic expressions shifted widely with the spread of international styles and "modern art."

Relationships between the world's population explosion and the pattern of cultural and political change are not obscure. Population pressure helps explain recurrent revolution. More generally, governments assumed new functions in public health but then also had to take on the task of population control. Urbanization and migration helped shake up established belief systems. We have seen also that different patterns of cultural change related to decisions about birth control; new beliefs could be part of family or community response to the population surge.

The challenge is not to note major change in politics and culture but to determine basic directions and impacts. While most societies rethought the state, they did not come to the same conclusions. Democracy, communism, and authoritarianism (including fascism) competed for political allegiance, with varying success depending on the traditions and current conditions of each major civilization. Almost everywhere, political institutions had to contend with massive population growth that put pressure on resources and fueled new discontents. In culture, while consumerism and science gained ground widely, new religious affiliations also spread in some places, and nationalist and Marxist cultural frameworks loomed large as well. Diversity amid basic change is an obvious 20th-century feature.

How do new beliefs and styles and new state forms affect ordinary people? In politics, growing government power to compel made the state at the end of the 20th century more important, in wider reaches of life, than it was in 1900. This pattern is true no matter what the form of government. New cultural values encouraged basic new behaviors, such as birth control and a higher valuation of consumer acquisitions. They also launched, for many people, an ongoing debate about what choice or combination of values is most appropriate. Tension, even conflict, over cultural change was an important feature of 20th-century life, and the process continued as the 21st century began.

The State: Basic Patterns of Outreach

Political change through events such as revolutions, decolonization, and the collapse of East European communism recurrently claimed center stage in the 20th century. Amid great variety, what are the underlying directions and impacts?

The steady expansion of the state is a key phenomenon. This was particularly pronounced in communist or fascist regimes, but it applies to other systems as well. Bureaucracies and government functions grew steadily during the 20th century. World War I provided a basic lesson in how much governments could take over. To further the war effort, European states rationed goods, allocated labor, and undertook massive, mind-numbing propaganda. The Russian communist state, after the 1917 revolution, deliberately imitated some of these extensions of state power.

Responding to rapid urbanization, expansion in literacy, advancement in communications technology, and people's political participation through votes, governments became extensive social and economic regulators as well as providers of security and comfort for the people (in order to perform their traditional task of maintaining order and retaining popular support). There were several turning points in the development of world states and societies during this period, even after World War I and the Russian Revolution: the economic depression initiated in 1929 and the subsequent rise of new fascist and communist regimes, the cold war between the Soviet Union and United States, the decolonization process, and the emergence of new states, as well as the post–cold war era. Each development had worldwide impact, but the effects varied in different countries.

Functional expansions of state power applied to a number of areas. Government role in education steadily increased with the expansion of state systems. Countries in Africa and South Asia began to construct systems of mass education, while more industrialized areas, such as the United States and Japan, expanded the length of schooling into secondary and tertiary levels. Governments took on additional economic functions and public health roles. Even colonial administrations, in places such as Africa during the first half of the century, sketched these developments, which would be continued in most states after colonial controls were removed. Most governments also expanded police forces and peacetime armies; with decolonization, military spending soared in many states in Asia, and the military functions of the United States and Russia intensified massively during the cold war.

A number of societies also created what was called the welfare state, initially in response to the 1930s depression. Welfare states took responsibility for using tax revenue to protect minimal material conditions for those who were sick, elderly, or unemployed. State-sponsored insurance, pensions, and national health systems developed. The systems were most extensive in advanced industrial countries, for they were quite expensive, but communist regimes also introduced sweeping welfare provisions (including even state-sponsored vacations for workers), and other societies incorporated at least some new welfare activities. Here was a massive redefinition of government's role in human life. In the United States, the establishment of the Social Security system in the 1940s led older people to shift their expectations for support from family to state by the 1950s. New ideas and growing international competition led to attacks on the welfare state by the 1980s, and some programs were scaled back; but nowhere, at the end of the 1990s, had government responsibilities been massively reduced.

The growth of governments made bureaucratic employment a growing category of the labor force, on a worldwide basis. Increased tax revenues were sought not simply as a function of economic growth but through new systems such as the personal income tax or, by the 1970s, more sweeping sales or "value-added" taxes. Here, too, government expansion had direct contact with ordinary people's lives, and rueful comments about tax levels became a staple part of humor and, sometimes, political protest.

Regional Patterns

The most striking innovations in political form that occurred in the 20th century involved the rise of what some scholars called totalitarian states— states that sought to eliminate all internal political competition and to gain a wide range of control over economic and cultural as well as political life. In retrospect, it is realized that totalitarian states, though fearsome, did not destroy everything from their past; many pockets of quiet resistance and traditional outlook remained. In fact, there is debate over the whole totalitarian concept, which may be a cold war relic. The Soviet Union had strong police and propaganda powers, but it did not manage to destroy religion, and it was quite sensitive to aspects of worker opinion, seen as vital to preserve support. Nazi Germany did not seize control over the whole economy or even over private landed estates. So-called totalitarian governments, in other words, either did not or could not achieve total dominance. But such states did wield unprecedented power, and they did generate important social and cultural changes while eliminating most effective opposition.

Adolf Hitler's Germany was the leading example of fascist totalitarianism. From his accession to power in 1933, Hitler progressively eliminated independent trade unions and political parties. He curtailed the power of Protestant churches and intimidated Catholic officials. He set up elaborate youth and women's groups to attract active mass loyalty, and he unhesitatingly utilized political police and extensive concentration camps, initially filled primarily with potential opponents. Hitler's state frequently cooperated with profit-seeking employers, but it bent production to military uses and also set up new state-run enterprises such as the modern highway system, designed to promote employment as well as to facilitate military transport. State-run propaganda was omnipresent, blinding many Germans to the terror and militarism fostered by the state. This was a government, finally, that was unseated only by loss in World War II.

The communist state in Russia was a second totalitarian model, particularly after Joseph Stalin took the helm in the late 1920s. Extensive propaganda and political police tried to assure popular loyalty, or at least acquiescent fear. Cultural efforts included systematic attacks on many religions, as well as promotion of new, Socialist-realist artistic styles designed to glorify the communist cause. The government also supported scientific research but suppressed findings that might call communist ideology into question; Darwinian evolution, for example, was attacked because it might undermine belief in rational progress, as opposed to random survival of the fittest. The most important extension of state power occurred in the economy. Stalin replaced peasant ownership with collective farms, killing and exiling millions of resisters. In industry, state planning replaced free-market operations in allocating supplies and determining prices. State-run five-year plans managed to further rapid industrialization, though the same system left major gaps (for example, in transportation facilities) and frequent bottlenecks in supply. The state aimed to control all resources and their disposition. The Soviet system was spread to East-Central Europe in the wake of Russia's victories in World War II.

China also adopted a communist state. Here, as in Russia and Germany, was a country that already possessed a strong-state tradition, that was now revolutionized in the wake of new pressures and the quest for more rapid economic change. China had undergone a democratic revolution in 1910, but the new regime was not successful in administering the whole country. Japanese attacks, leading up to World War II in Asia, exacerbated the chaos. Communist forces gained ground from the late 1920s onward, then won state control outright by 1949. As in Russia, the party monopolized power, controlling both government and army and banning political opposition. Economic policies varied, but the state ran many large industries and monopolized basic economic planning.

Totalitarianism was not the only innovative political form, though it attracted many followers in various parts of the world because of its strength, its capacity for promoting economic change, and its apparent success in defying Western democracies. Authoritarian regimes arose in many regions. In Latin America, one-party or strongman rule succeeded in creating unprecedentedly active and effective governments during the 1930s, in part in response to the economic woes brought by worldwide depression. In 1933, Lázaro Cárdenas became president of Mexico, where one political party predominated, and launched a series of government-sponsored reforms. He extended education, displacing church control, and redistributed considerable amounts of land to the peasants. He also nationalized all foreign-owned oil fields, setting up an effective state monopoly, and tried to promote a more active pattern of economic growth. In Brazil in the 1930s a strongman ruler, Getúlio Vargas, used the government to initiate firmer controls over imported manufactured goods, seeking to support national industries instead, in a policy known as "import substitution." Vargas also sponsored Brazil's first modern steel industry, which in a few decades would be capable of exports even to the United States. In general, more active Latin American governments under authoritarian rule helped win an improved competitive position in the world economy, though many weaknesses remained. The same governments frequently brutalized potential opponents, sponsoring widespread political arrests and torture.

The small states of East Asia formed another center of authoritarianism after the defeat of Japan in World War II. Governments in Taiwan, South Korea, and Singapore maintained internal stability, limiting opposition. Using Confucian traditions of deference and group loyalty, the same governments actively promoted economic growth. Taiwan's government sponsored land reforms and built up domestic industry through extensive tariff protection and economic assistance. The rapid spread of effective education furthered this program, facilitating technological change.

Authoritarian regimes also developed in Africa and the Middle East after decolonization. Here, new nations struggled to find competent political leadership and overall political acceptance, amid boundaries that had often been created by European colonialists with no reference to customary political allegiances and units. Most African states passed under military dictatorship, seen as necessary to preserve fragile unity. In Ghana, the first new state, an initially democratic leader, Kwame Nkrumah, soon jailed his political opponents and outlawed all parties save his own. His goal was a one-party state, capable of arousing the kind of loyalty that would hold the nation together as well as maintain his personal power. Inept economic management foiled Nkrumah, whose government was soon replaced by military leadership in what became a familiar African pattern.

During much of the 20th century, democratic regimes with freedom for political competition maintained strongholds in only a few key areas. These included parts of Western Europe as well as the United States, Canada, Australia, and New Zealand. They also included the independent nation of India, freed from British control in 1947, and Japan, after its own experiment with authoritarian rule ended in defeat in World War II. Democratic systems themselves changed, picking up additional functions of general economic planning and the responsibilities of the welfare state.

Debates over the nature of the state took a new turn in the 1970s and 1980s, with an international growth of democracy a key beneficiary. Western economic success served as a good advertisement for this political system. In the 1970s and 1980s, most Latin American countries produced democratic regimes and also scaled back state activities in the economy. More free-market operations seemed imperative for economic growth, and Western nations, headed by the United States, actively supported this conversion. The collapse of the Soviet Union from 1985 onward led to another surge in democratic growth. The new Soviet leader, Mikhail Gorbachev, concluded that the totalitarian system was incapable of reversing a growing economic deterioration; a combination of greater political freedom and more free-market economic operations was essential. Political changes of this sort spread through most of East-Central Europe. Meanwhile, several East Asian countries converted to greater democracy, and during the 1990s, 20 African nations moved to reestablish democratic systems as well, headed by South Africa and, more tentatively, Nigeria. In the West itself, particularly the United States and Britain, the 1980s saw the election of conservative leaders who sought to push back welfare expenditures; debate over the role as well as the form of government was widespread.

The democratic current was not unopposed. China loosened state control of the economy in 1978, allowing more private business, but maintained tight political constraints. Many Middle Eastern countries resisted democracy, sometimes in the name of one-party rule, sometimes in the name of the new surge of Muslim fundamentalism. Key African countries prevented democracy. Moreover, by the end of the 1990s, as economic problems mounted in East Asia, another set of leaders began to resist the constant Western pressure to limit government involvement in the economy, arguing that a single economic policy could not extend around the world. The government of Malaysia was particularly vigorous in insisting on the need for state economic controls. Political diversity and debate continued, as they had throughout the 20th century. It was not clear how far democracy would extend or whether the new debate over state economic and welfare roles would significantly modify the long-term process of government growth. Even in the West, the late 1990s saw a new division between conservative American politics, bent on trimming welfare activities, and a new wave of reformist socialism in Western Europe, insistent on government responsibilities to the poor.

Another important development, picking up steam in the later 20th century, involved the government role taken on by international organizations. The basic movement dated from the 1860s, when various European countries banded together to set agreements about international mail delivery and shipping rights. The formation of the League of Nations after World War I brought wider efforts to use international discussion to influence national policies; for example, the International Labor Office worked to improve conditions on the job. International coordination accelerated after World War II. The creation of the United Nations allowed new opportunities for international debate, and occasionally debate led to action, against states that were viewed as aggressors or in the interests of reducing internal civil war. The International Monetary Fund and the World Bank were designed to assist the reconstruction of postwar Europe. Later, they became major lending agencies for developing nations, offering loans in return for domestic reform measures, including reduced government spending and more open markets. These agencies, in sum, applied powerful pressure to alter internal policies in the interest of receiving outside aid; they operated according to market economic models dear to experts in the West, particularly the United States. The World Trade Organization (founded in 1947 as the General Agreement on Tariffs and Trade; the name was changed in 1995) intervened with national governments to impose trade rules in the interests of global capitalism. With the 1990s, a series of international conferences also sought to regulate internal environmental policies. Industrial areas such as Japan and the United States had to agree to cut back pollution, though whether real initiatives would result remained to be seen.

In addition to international government operations, regional coalitions developed. In the 1950s, key European states set up the Common Market (ultimately called the European Union, as it expanded to more and more members). This group began primarily as a tariff-cutting operation, but it soon set up a regional government, with powers to regulate internal economic policies, currency values, even court systems. By the 1990s, European nations operated in a complex web of national and international government systems. Other regional arrangements were more modest. Nineteen Arab states joined to form the Arab League in 1945, in order to facilitate mutual defense and economic cooperation. Oil-producing states formed a group in 1960, the Organization of Petroleum Exporting Countries (OPEC), which managed to achieve greater independence from the control of Western oil corporations and buyers. The Organization of African Unity (first formed in 1963) managed to send troops to quell internal warfare in some member states. The North American Free Trade Agreement (NAFTA) was essentially a tariff-cutting group, though it imposed some rules about labor and environmental policy.

In an age when international economic forces became steadily more important, when huge multinational corporations spanned the globe—often with greater powers and resources than many national states—the adequacy of the nation-state system of government was increasingly questioned. But the balance between international or regional institutions and national states remained tense, as feelings of national pride and identity remained strong. Further, few supranational governments had any direct contact with the democratic process. (The European Union had an elected parliament, but most of its policies were determined by administrative experts not explicitly responsible to any voting group.) Here, too, was an open question for the future.

Culture and Contacts: An Explosion of Change and Resistance

The 20th century was one of the great periods of cultural change in world history, comparable in many ways to the early postclassical period, when the world religions spread widely at the expense of customary polytheism. Harder to define, contemporary cultural change nevertheless rivaled the redefinitions of the state in importance and in impact on daily life. Few people by the late 1990s maintained the same value system that their great-grandparents had adhered to a hundred years earlier, and many groups went through one or more genuine conversion experiences to new clusters of beliefs and styles. Because cultural change was so rapid, resistance also developed in the name of older patterns—though even these usually involved important innovation, often including a decline of traditional tolerance.

A number of forces, operating through much of the century, pushed for change. New economic structures, migrations, and the growth of cities pulled many people away from familiar contexts, making old beliefs seem less relevant. A host of political leaders and commercial outlets pushed for new commitments to the nation, to a revolutionary ideology, or to the values associated with mass consumerism. Agents of this sort served as missionaries for new ideas. The spread of formal systems of education provided yet another means of reaching people in the name of new values such as nationalism or a commitment to modern science.

International contacts played a key role in cultural change. New technologies speeded acquaintance with beliefs elsewhere in the world. By the late 20th century, over a quarter of the world's population might watch the same show on TV (such as World Cup soccer) at the same time—an unprecedented experience. Export, mainly from the West, of popular movies and shows, as well as consumer outlets such as fast-food restaurants, offered another link. Travel was vital. Individual students would come to Western Europe, the United States, and Russia, usually for technical training, and might also learn Marxism or nationalism or consumerism or modern art, to take back home. Larger migrations of workers—for example, Turkish workers to Western Europe after World War II—provided another source of new ideas, as they kept in contact with friends back home. Tourism, particularly from the West and Japan, could bring awareness of new styles and gender values to ordinary people in resort areas. By the same token, reactions against cultural change often included efforts to limit international contact, in the name of threatened local styles and beliefs.

New Cultural Systems

Two new belief patterns spread widely, affecting virtually every society to some extent and winning cultural dominance in some. Marxist socialism was one system. Marxism began as a political philosophy in Western Europe in the 19th century. It argued that history could be interpreted through the battle between social classes for control of the means of production. Government and culture, by this theory, were shaped by this battle. In a capitalist society, the working class, or proletariat, grew and became more miserable; violent revolution was the inevitable result. After a transitional period, society under workers' control would operate amid substantial equality and full freedom; the state and all forms of compulsion would wither away. Marxism also involved a firm commitment to a belief in science and to technological advance, as well as a vigorous hostility to religion, "the opiate of the masses." Marxism made gains among many intellectuals and workers in Western Europe by 1900, though it was stronger in some places (e.g., Germany and France) than others (e.g., England and Scandinavia). By the 1890s, Marxist doctrines won many converts in Russia, setting up the victory of Marxist organizations and beliefs in the revolution of 1917. Marxism also persuaded important revolutionary leaders in China and Vietnam, often after their direct experience as students or workers in Europe. Revolutions in these societies, as in Russia, brought governments that worked to impose Marxism on the whole population, attacking established religions—and in China, Confucianism—and promoting a new, Socialist-realist style of art that was also partly copied from Russia. Communist styles were held up as superior to decadent Western artistic taste. Important conversions also occurred in parts of Latin America, in India, and in Africa, though only a minority was attracted in these cases. Marxism made least headway in societies where one or more major religions were firmly established, as in the United States, the Middle East, and much of Southeast Asia. Its hold declined after the collapse of the Soviet system in 1989, though it remained a vital force in China, Vietnam, North Korea, and Cuba and among minorities in key parts of Europe.

The second modern belief system was more diffuse, but it also spread from Western Europe and the United States. A composite value system, sometimes called *cosmopolitan liberalism*, gained ground from the 19th century onward. This involved a commitment to improvements in living standards and an interest in consumer acquisition; growing interest in sexual expression was often included as well. Strong beliefs in the value of science, including the central role of science in dealing with health problems, were also central. Cosmopolitan liberals might have a variety of specific political beliefs, ranging from conservatism to moderate socialism, but they did defend democracy, certain individual freedoms (including freedom of religion), and the importance of tolerance of diversity. The system also was marked by a strong commitment to education. Some people used this value system to defend capitalism and individualism, but here there were gradations. Many Japanese, for example, particularly after World War II, adopted strong consumer interests—including a fascination with huge department stores—and certainly demonstrated a faith in science but nevertheless remained highly group oriented. The United States remained at an extreme in its defense of the capitalist system per se.

Both Marxists and cosmopolitan liberals were predominantly secular in orientation, though they might retain some moderate religious interests. The commitment to science was matched by a faith in some kind of progress in human life—though definitions of progress differed between the two belief systems.

Cosmopolitan liberalism spread widely with the outpouring of consumer goods and commercial entertainments, often from the West. Hollywood was enshrined as the international film capital from the 1920s onward. Urban Africans, also as early as the 1920s, often preferred commitment to new consumer acquisitions, to sexual freedoms, and to an urban lifestyle over traditional communal attachments. Secular leaders in the Middle East such as the new head of independent Turkey in the 1920s, Kemal Ataturk, defended the importance of science and a secular state over traditional religion. By the 1970s, the attraction of Western popular music and consumer styles such as blue jeans spread to Russia and other parts of Eastern Europe, particularly among young people, modifying attachments to Marxism. Various facets of Western popular culture spread around the globe. Rock music concerts occurred in Asia and Africa as well as Europe and the Americas. Fast-food outlets spread widely, amid great fanfare along with adjustments to local foods—such as vegetarian McDonald's offerings in India. The enticement of change, along with appeals to international standards as measures of modern sophistication, was widespread. New, unconventional styles in painting and architecture, often called "modern" or "international" art, also spread from centers in the West. Many Latin Americans participated strongly in these artistic currents, as did Japanese, Israelis, and others.

Shared popular culture meant that Israeli and American teenagers could readily talk (in English) about the same movie and rock stars, based on hours of ardent viewing of MTV and consumption of fan magazines. It meant that Japanese youth regularly and knowledgeably voted on their favorite Western popular musicians, and that even markedly American music styles such as country-and-western won Japanese aficionados. It meant that celebration of All Souls' Day in Mexico—a very important traditional religious holiday in Latin American Catholicism—began to pick up the trappings of American Halloween, complete with costumes and trick-or-treating. It meant that successful businessmen from the Pacific Rim increasingly sought access to golf courses—a sign of relaxed affluence in the West—even though population density made the construction of such courses extremely expensive and particularly damaging to the environment. Shared popular culture meant that when communist China began to accept more foreign contact and more private economic initiatives after 1978, a vital though unexpected result was the growing popularity of Western-style romance, including public kissing, among young courting couples in Chinese cities. Examples multiplied as the century wore on, but earlier cases can be cited as well. Peasants in East Africa who managed to profit from export agriculture by the 1940s, even as more of their fellows suffered from the pressure to abandon traditional subsistence farming, eagerly defined their new standard of living in essentially Western terms, with an imported car and reproductions of popular Western paintings in their homes. Even more widespread than English, an international symbolic language was developing based on Western-style popular and consumer culture.

Nationalism

The spread of new beliefs included growing conversions to nationalism. Here, however, cultural change was usually wedded to some explicit defense of older values—a combination that might make nationalism particularly popular amid the challenge of international cultural influences. Nationalists urged loyalty to a particular cultural unit, as they defined it, and also sought independence and strength for the national state. Specific formulas varied. Indian nationalists, led by Mohandas Gandhi, sometimes attacked Western materialism and individualism. They praised many aspects of the Hindu tradition, though in the name of national unity they attacked the caste system and urged harmony with Muslims. In other words, they mixed tradition with important new social values, and while distinguishing India from the West, they accepted political concepts such as democracy. Most African nationalists had less to do with religion: Polytheism was associated with tribal divisions, whereas newer religions, notably Christianity, were hard to defend as part of the specific national tradition. Insisting on the need to end Western imperialism, nationalists urged some use of Western science and technology while praising African values such as family harmony. Some Middle Eastern nationalists were also secular—as in the case of Turkey—whereas others associated more closely with Islam.

Nationalism spread widely in the 20th century. The Japanese government continued to encourage nationalism as part of a culture of intense loyalty and group consciousness, though the loss of World War II reduced the religious components; emperor worship, for example, was ended. The Soviet Union, though as a Marxist state officially hostile to nationalism in favor of international proletarian loyalty, in fact tapped into Russian nationalist fervor, particularly under the somewhat isolationist regime of Joseph Stalin. Authoritarian leaders from the fascists in Europe to Juan Perón in Argentina trumpeted nationalist values.

While nationalism could ease the tension between new, international cultural influences and more customary beliefs and styles, it was not a panacea—partly because nationalism itself was a new loyalty. Many rural groups were not particularly touched by nationalism, maintaining older local and religious allegiances. A gap often opened between rural and urban cultures, and also between elites and ordinary people—the former more likely to be in active contact with one or more of the newer belief systems and affected by international influences. New cultural divisions and tensions opened up almost inevitably in a period of great change.

Religion

In this context, particularly from the 1970s onward, a number of religious revivals occurred, seeking to increase religious fervor and to return to real or imagined religious ideals as an alternative to secular beliefs and foreign contacts. These religious movements were not purely traditional; they involved new political claims, such as asking for new levels of government defense of religious goals. They used modern media, including broadcasting. They were often less tolerant of minorities than had traditionally been the case.

Religious revival was particularly striking in the Middle East. Adherents who were often called Islamic fundamentalists particularly attacked Western consumerist influence. (They were also hostile to Marxism, but this was a lesser cultural and political factor in the region.) They abhorred revealing clothing and the passion for material acquisition; they were appalled by changes in the status of women. Symbols such as Hollywood films and Western-style vacation resorts drew demonstrations of wrath. The Islamic revival sought governments that would defend Muslim law and a popular return to basic religious rules and goals. Nationalism was not attacked directly, but secular nationalists were held to be inadequate; religion, not the nation, should come first. Somewhat similar movements spread in India, with a Hindu fundamentalist current that utilized more elements of Indian nationalism, however, while seeking a state that would promote the religion both against the Islamic minority and against Western-style secularism. Christian fundamentalists, particularly in the United States, similarly sought to place religion first, as against undue commitments to science, changes in gender roles, and rampant consumerism and sexual hedonism. Protestant fundamentalist missionaries also made some headway in Eastern Europe, after the collapse of communism, and in Latin America, where in countries such as Brazil this form of fundamentalism became the most rapidly growing cultural movement by the later 20th century.

Cultural change in the century as a whole was clearly marked by great diversity as well as intensity. Many new divisions and internal cultural conflicts opened up, and the role of international influences was vigorously disputed even as, for the most part, contacts increased. Whether or not world cultures would ultimately move toward greater homogeneity and whether the disputes would cool through the triumph of revived religion or a fuller commitment to secular values were unclear. World historians continue to debate appropriate models. Some, such as Theodore von Laue, talk of international Westernization, with the whole world exposed to Western-derived standards in politics, gender relations, and consumer culture. Others, however, point to the strength of adapted culture traditions. Samuel Huntington, a political scientist, paints a post–cold war period divided among key cultural traditions, which he assumes will become increasingly mutually hostile: Western values will define one region, but Islam another and Neo-Confucianism yet a third. Analysis of the cultural trends of the past century provides evidence for both approaches.

Syncretism and Identity

Many groups, as in the past, navigated cultural change in part through various kinds of syncretic combinations. Religious syncretism continued, taking some striking new forms. In the 1920s, a religious leader in Brazil, Zelio de Moraes, opened a center near Rio de Janeireo. Guided by his spirit, he drew on a combination of Brazilian Indian, Afro-Brazilian (from former slaves), and European influences, setting up a new faith called Umbanda. Strongly emphasizing trance states and religious excitement, Umbanda grew steadily into the later 20th century. Elements from earlier coastal Indians showed in the highlighting of visionaries and ritual healers, who helped the faithful maintain communication with spiritual powers; these elements had survived into the Catholicism the native populations had accepted during the 16th and 17th centuries, despite priestly efforts to expunge them. African ingredients involved certain kinds of processions, which had been incorporated into parades commemorating saints when slaves were converted to Catholicism, and also various religious dances. They also included African beliefs in a hierarchy of spiritual forces under a creator god. European influences included not only Catholicism but also a pseudo-scientific doctrine devised in the 19th century by a French thinker, Allan Kardec (who himself incorporated Hindu beliefs, as well as the new evolutionary theory propounded by Charles Darwin). Kardec had postulated a complex spiritual hierarchy ranging from striving human souls to noncorporeal spirits to Jesus and on to God. Kardecist groups had formed in Brazil from the 1870s onward, using spirit mediums to encourage spiritual growth and also charity for the poor. Estimates by the 1970s suggested that up to a third of all Brazilians were participating in this spiritual amalgam at least occasionally.

Elsewhere in the world, many Americans combined elements of more traditional religion with ardent consumerism and considerable nationalism. Italian Marxists, devoted to this political culture, nevertheless might continue to have their children baptized in church—just in case. Africans were often torn between a desire to attain new goals, such as improved standards of living or greater education for women, and older values. Thus women might argue for the importance of nationalism, birth control, and more equal schooling—new cultural impulses on the whole—at the same time urging that these should be devoted to rebuilding a strong, protective family; in other words, new means to achieve more traditional values.

Syncretism in the 20th century most commonly applied to secular cultural systems, where Western influences merged with more customary values. Japan, already a successful cultural amalgamator, had new recourses to syncretism after World War II. American occupation after the war was bent on Westernizing as many facets of Japanese culture as possible, on grounds that this would prevent a resurgence of Japanese militarism and would also promote greater social justice. Thus Japan's giant firms were broken up, at least in principle, while women were given new rights. Japan accepted some of this new Western influence during the postwar decades. Military exercises, for example, were dropped from school programs. Mass cultural institutions such as baseball gained new currency, while a Disney amusement park outside Tokyo proved widely popular. Articulate Japanese conservatives were outraged at the further loss of national identity. The writer Yukio Mishima, for example, though enjoying many Western contacts and interests, came to hate what he saw as a bastardized Japan. In 1968 he founded a private army devoted to restoring Japanese ideals, and he ultimately performed a ritual suicide in 1970. He wrote: "I came to wish to sacrifice myself for this old beautiful tradition of Japan, which is disappearing very quickly day by day."

Yet, overall, Japan continued to adapt Western messages, rather than accepting or rejecting them outright. A craze for television game shows, copied from the United States, was quickly given a distinctive twist: In the Japanese versions, losing contestants were elaborately shamed, subjected to ridicule to highlight their failure to live up to group norms. In group-oriented Japan, shame was an important disciplinary tool, reminding people that violation of collective standards resulted in harsh exclusions—in contrast to the West, which, being more individualistic and more concerned with supporting self-esteem, had increasingly abandoned shaming in institutional practice. Thus apparent cultural imitation in fact served as a vehicle for enforcing distinctive norms.

Education was another area of ongoing amalgamation. The Japanese on the whole welcomed American-sponsored reforms that opened greater educational access. When American occupation ended, conservatives pressed to reserve high educational slots for more privileged groups, but their move failed. But the Japanese did restore centralized control of textbook selection and curriculum, reducing teacher initiatives. And they urged renewed attention to distinctive moral education. In 1966 the Ministry of Education issued a paper condemning "egotistic and Epicurean attitudes" and calling for "the cultivation of ethical consciousness." Group ideals were seen as essential to counter Western-style individualism and also undue materialism; devotion to the common good should remedy what the ministry termed a "spiritual hollowness." And Japan still emphasized different kinds of gender distinctions, a looser division between government and private business, and a higher rate of personal savings, as opposed to sheer consumerism. The postwar constitution even enshrined a special devotion to the elderly as a national obligation—again, recasting a traditional, in this case Confucian, cultural theme. Japan's culture—largely secular, undeniably open to Western fads and influences—retained its own flavor in many domains.

Important cases of syncretism involved remedies for ill health. Taiwan, open to growing Western influence, offered examples: A young man suffers from weakness, lack of concentration, and a chronic ulcer. A Western diagnosis labels his problem sexual neurosis, which is not uncommon in the 1970s among young Taiwanese men. The young man himself worries about nocturnal emissions and frequent masturbation, concerned that he is losing his vital essence, or *ch'i*. His mother, taking up the family responsibility for health, guides him to a variety of practi-

20th-Century Mass Culture. Movie poster from India's thriving film industry (featuring the actor Shashi Kapoor in the film *Deewangee*). Is this simply a marriage of a new entertainment technology with Indian cultural traditions? What other influences are suggested? Reprinted by permission Jehangir Gazdar/Woodfin Camp and Associates.

tioners. Western-style doctors repeat the psychiatric diagnosis, perhaps a bit more vaguely, and recommend tranquilizers. Traditional Chinese-style doctors claim the problem is physical, lodged in the kidneys, and offer some customary medicines that do little good. The mother and son also go to a Taoist temple, appealing to the healer, or *tangki*. The healer emerges with chants, locked in a trance in which he believes the god of the temple speaks through him. He briefly offers his diagnosis: The ghost of an unknown young girl is pursuing the man. The remedy would be further chants and the burning of spirit money. The mother is not fully satisfied, among other things because the whole ritual lasted only ten minutes; but the son seems relieved, at least for the moment. The continuing blend of Western and traditional recourses allowed many Taiwanese to maintain some parallel beliefs about what causes illness or promotes remedy. The result of this combination may not have brought full satisfaction, but it certainly provided an important cultural detour around any single commitment.

Some of the most important and subtle examples of cultural blending occurred in the sphere of popular culture. Here, on the surface, Western styles often seemed to triumph without dilution. In fact, however—just as with the Argentinean twists on British soccer in the 19th century—imitation almost always combined with more distinctive cultural content. Comic books, for example, spread to Mexico from the United States beginning in 1934; they depended on some of the same advances in printing and some of the same halting developments in expanding literacy. And the United States strips were imported directly, simply translated into Spanish; Tarzan and Superman were two cases in point. Yet Mexican content, both customary and novel, quickly infused the genre. Imported strips were often made smaller, to highlight the local products. Mexican comic-book figures corresponded to local standards of beauty rather than to United States norms; they integrated other facets of popular culture, such as bullfighting, along with scenes from Spanish and Mexican history; they embraced different, often less starkly realistic design features; and they included explicit support for Mexican nationalism. Thus one series was advertised through such comments as "He was no vulgar bandit, he shared with the poor who live under the lash of vile capitalism" or "It is the story of a noble, audacious, and very Mexican man who struggles against injustice, aiding the social class he came from"—clear references to the rhetoric of the Mexican Revolution of the early 20th century. Gender standards were distinctive, with great latitude for masculine exploits and conquests. At the same time, emphasis on kinship and community ties was greater than in materials north of the border, for Mexican readers at mid-century wanted their comics to reflect aspects of real life. Relatedly, reader responses were more widely used in Mexican than in United States versions to establish plot lines; romantic stories developed more widely, in appeals to a female audience. The comics were also longer than those in the United States, which made sense to readers accustomed to prolonged oral stories. Religious themes were far more prominent, even though the Catholic Church condemned the comic-book craze in Mexico as sinful.

Comic-book publishers were sensitive to criticisms that they operated in the shadow of the United States. Often explicit notes established that "this is an ORIGINAL magazine, made by Mexican writers, artists, and technicians for Latin America." Mexican heroes might be pitted against United States characters such as the "Invincible Jack Superman of Indianapolis"—with the gringo characters losing every time. Geographical settings and praise for local food helped establish the national character—the *mexicanidad*—of the comics. So did treatment of currently important themes, such as the migration of people from peasant villages to urban settings and the demands of modern technology. The result, clearly, was a hybrid product, influenced not just by the United States in form and technology, but infused with explicit Mexican nationalism and regional symbols and values. One key result of adaptation was a distinctive popularity: By the 1950s, 34 percent of all Mexicans read comic books with some regularity, a far larger percentage of people than in the United States. Clearly, though initially borrowed, comic books came for a time to fill a different cultural space in the Mexican setting, precisely because they could blend additional ingredients.

Combinations might not be sufficient, however, to prevent some real concern about cultural identity. African writers, mainly educated in Western-style school systems and writing in English or French, lamented the loss of traditional village and religious cultures. But at the same time, they could not bring themselves to advocate a return to customary ways of treating women or dealing with children, because their commitment to newer standards made the old culture, however appealing in its integrity, too outdated and embarrassing. Many Latin American and Japanese intellectuals took up the identity theme, wondering how, amid rapid cultural change and international influence, people could place themselves in a coherent cultural package. And while identity issues may have been particularly pressing on writers and theorists, they bothered ordinary people as well, who were unsure when or how to commit to older ways of doing things, given the pressure to respond to new signals.

Conclusion

Massive conflicts over political and cultural systems and serious changes in the functions of governments and in the values many people cherished inevitably spilled over into other facets of social life in all the world's regions in the 20th century. Just as changes in structures, such as the spread of cities and new work settings, helped generate new demands on the state and challenges to older beliefs, so, too, political and cultural trends had substantial impacts on other behaviors. Cultural debates often focused on gender issues, for example, with communists and cosmopolitan liberals usually pushing for reductions of patriarchal systems, at least in principle, but with many nationalists hesitant and many religious revival leaders opposed. Governments often sought direct intervention into population patterns, trying to promote new kinds of birth control and working to limit customary levels of disease and death. Political and cultural pressures did not always generate desired results, but they entered seriously into the ways in which many people conducted their daily lives. Examining the results of cultural and political shifts and conflicts provides a crucial entry point into topics as personal as family life and how children were raised in societies throughout the world.

CHAPTER 24

GENDER STRUCTURES, 1920–2000

The tremendous political, demographic, and economic changes of the 20th century shaped all areas of gender structures for many people of the world. Family relationships, the gender division of labor, and women's access to political rights and education were often quite different at the end of the century than they had been at the beginning, but change was not uniform or unidirectional. For members of political and economic elites throughout the world, international connections became increasingly common and swift, so that their ideas of the proper roles and possibilities for men and women generally grew more similar and more egalitarian. This often split them from middle- and lower-class people in their own countries, for whom changes in the gender order proceeded at a slower pace and were often vigorously opposed. Even for people with little personal contact with cultures other than their own, however, the internationalization of business, popular culture, and communications and entertainment media brought familiarity with a variety of gender structures. These alternative structures were regarded with everything from admiration and emulation to horror and disgust, with individuals and groups responding by migrating, changing laws and norms, establishing or abolishing institutions and agencies, and pressuring governments for a faster or slower rate of change.

Families

Explosive population growth in the 20th century was accompanied by the development of effective birth-control techniques, and as we have seen, families first in wealthier, industrialized countries and later elsewhere limited their number of children. Most industrialized countries developed systems of social support so that people did not have to rely on their children in old age; in parts of Europe, North America, Japan, and Australia, by the mid-1950s people no longer viewed having children as necessary for the family's or their own economic survival but rather as a matter of choice. In these wealthier countries, reliable methods of contraception such as the birth-control pill were affordable to most people and increasingly viewed as culturally acceptable. Laws restricting the dissemination of birth-control information and devices were generally lifted by the 1960s (though not everywhere), and by the 1980s, disputes about reproductive control revolved largely around moral issues relating to abortion and medically assisted reproductive techniques such as in vitro fertilization, surrogate motherhood, and genetic testing.

Elsewhere, access to birth control was slower in coming and directly shaped by government policies. In Germany, Italy, and Japan in the 1930s, birth control was prohibited, and large families were rewarded among groups judged to be desirable; those judged undesirable were sterilized or executed. (Sterilization of "undesirables" also occurred in the United States from the 1930s to at least the 1970s.) In the Soviet Union right after World War II, the government encouraged population growth by limiting access to all contraception; even after the desire for more people abated, birth-control pills never became widely available, so that abortion became the standard means of birth control for most women, a practice that continued in post-Soviet Russia.

In other parts of the world, governments actively intervened to limit population, as we have seen: In India, Puerto Rico, and elsewhere, the government encouraged or condoned widespread sterilization, while in China, in policies introduced after 1978, families who had more than one child were penalized by fines and the loss of access to opportunities. (Sterilization was the most common form of birth control worldwide by 1990, and all forms of birth control together had lowered fertility rates from 4.97 births per woman in 1950 to 3.38 in 1990, with Italy seeing the lowest rate [1.3] and Rwanda the highest [8.5].) Though governments that introduced strict population policies tried to minimize gender differences in their effects, the value put on male children was still higher than that on female children, which led in some countries to selective female infanticide, abortion of female fetuses, and better care and nutrition for infant boys.

Coercive government measures provoked strong resistance in some areas from both religious and women's organizations, and toward the end of the century, aid agencies recognized that a more effective means of decreasing the birthrate was to increase the level of basic and technical education for girls and women while providing small loans for sewing machines, farm flocks, or even cellular phones, so that women could gain economic independence. Both lower birthrates and education for girls were opposed in some parts of the world for much of the 20th century by traditional and colonial authorities, for they regarded women's proper role as tied to the household. Because of this, girls' education lagged behind boys' in many parts of the world; in 1975, for example, 88 percent of women in Africa were illiterate, as compared with 66 percent of men, and comparable figures for the entire world were estimated at 44 percent illiteracy among women and 30 percent among men. This gap narrowed in the last quarter of the century, however, as school attendance rates for girls worldwide grew closer to those of boys, particularly at the primary levels. (Estimates from UNESCO for 1980 found that 80 percent of boys worldwide, ages 6 to 11, were registered in school, compared with 68 percent of girls.)

Families in many parts of the world not only saw first more and then fewer births in the 20th century than they had previously, they also changed shape and became more varied. Though marital patterns in many parts of Africa remained polygynous, urban marriages were increasingly likely to be monogamous, both because of cultural influences such as Christianity and because of economic change. In terms of actual family life in Africa, men's migration from villages to cities and mines throughout much of the century meant that women and children often lived by themselves, while men lived in dormitories or other housing close to their work. Not surprisingly, this led to an increase in prostitution in urban areas, particularly as there were few wage-labor jobs for women in the cities, who otherwise supported themselves by trading or brewing beer. Increased mobility meant a weakening of African kinship and lineage ties, with older men having less power over both younger men and women than they did earlier; this allowed for greater independence in such matters as choice of spouse or job but also left individuals, especially women, more vulnerable because they did not have a lineage to support them economically or emotionally.

A similar living pattern, though under much different economic circumstances, developed in post–World War II Japan, tied in some ways to earlier Japanese traditions. Japanese companies favored male workers, expecting them to work very long hours and to socialize together after work, sometimes in the company of female hostesses called geishas. Women were expected to work only until they had children and then to devote themselves to their children. Thus, like many men in Africa, men in Japan rarely saw their wives and had little role in the upbringing of their children, though almost all of them continued to marry, for marriage remained a central part of Japanese culture and was expected by Japanese companies.

In Japan, China, and the Arab world, more than 95 percent of people continued to marry at some point in their lives, but in other parts of the world, the 20th century saw a dramatic decline in marriage rates. In the Caribbean, male mobility and the lack of good jobs for either women or men meant that many people did not marry until quite late in life or never married at all. As we saw in chapter 16, households were matrifocal, with a woman and her children living together and men joining the household on a more temporary basis. Matrifocal households could also be found among African Americans in the United States, while in both Western Europe and the United States, a growing number of couples lived together but did not marry; in 1995 in Germany there were ten times as many couples living together without marrying as there had been in 1972. Increasing divorce rates in developed countries—in the United States, the divorce rate in the 1990s was three times what it had been in the 1920s—and the social acceptability of remarriage after divorce meant that many families either were headed by a single parent or included the children of several different relationships. To this variety were added households in which children were raised by their grandparents, by gay or lesbian couples, by adoptive parents, and by unmarried individuals who had no intention of marrying. This variety of family forms was perceived by some observers as a social problem but showed little signs of changing in the 1990s.

Work Patterns

The 20th century saw dramatic alterations in the gender division of labor in many parts of the world, though these changes were not the same everywhere. In contrast to the situation in England, the United States, and Japan noted in chapter 20—where young women were the first to be hired as factories opened—the introduction of wage labor in agriculture, mining, and industry in other parts of the world in the 20th century provided jobs initially for boys and men. Men traveled to plantations, mines, and cities, leaving women responsible for producing food, largely through subsistence agriculture. Cash crops for export took the best land, so women were left with increasingly infertile land on which to support burgeoning populations. This problem was most acute in Africa, exacerbated by the fact that colonial governments and international development agencies assumed—based on Western practices—that men were the primary agricultural producers; they thus often sought to "modernize" agriculture by teaching men new methods of farming or processing crops, in cultures where these tasks had always been done by women. Only in the 1980s did the focus begin to shift somewhat to smaller-scale projects directed at women, such as small irrigation systems, improvements in stock-raising techniques, and credit associations.

In the last several decades, the composition of the industrial labor force in more recently industrialized countries shifted. By the 1980s, the most profitable industries were those in electronics, clothing, chemicals, and textiles, rather than heavier industries, and multinational corporations increasingly favored women—and in some areas, children—as workers. In the 1990s, perhaps as many as 80 percent of the workers in factories geared for world markets were young women. Particularly in East, Southeast, and South Asia, young women were as likely as young men to migrate to cities in search of work, though they were more likely to send the majority of their wages home to their families. This was not the case in the Muslim countries of the Middle East, however, which remained the area of the world in which women formed the smallest share of the paid labor force, generally between 2 and 10 percent. (Many of these were highly educated professionals, such as teachers and health care workers, trained to assist other women in sex-segregated settings.)

In the parts of the world that industrialized first, the 20th century saw swings in women's total participation in the paid labor force and, beginning in the 1980s, significant shifts in the gender balance in many occupations. During both world wars, through a combination of government propaganda campaigns, improved wages, and facilities such as child-care centers, women were encouraged to enter the paid labor force to replace men who were fighting; during World War II, for example, 40 percent of the workers in aircraft plants in the United States were women. After both wars, all special programs ended, and women were urged to concentrate on domesticity or simply were fired for being women; in the United States after World War II, the birthrate rose to the highest level in history in the postwar "baby boom." By the 1960s, this movement of women out of the paid labor force had reversed, and pressure to end both official and covert gender discrimination was slowly growing. Gradually during the 1970s–1990s, access to education and to jobs previously limited to men was opened to women in most industrialized countries, though most employed women continued to be concentrated in lower-paying service jobs (dubbed the "pink-collar ghetto"), so that women's average full-time earnings remained about two-thirds those of men in industrialized countries. (Sweden was the most egalitarian, with female wages about 90 percent of male wages in 1985, and Japan the least, with female wages about 43 percent of male wages, a situation that led many highly educated young Japanese women to leave Japan.)

Relying on statistics about the paid labor force for understanding gender divisions of labor in the 20th century is misleading for a number of reasons, however. Despite the spread of wage labor, in many parts of the world much work was still undertaken by families either completely outside the cash economy or with the proceeds reported as belonging to the (usually male) household head. Thus, in those same Middle Eastern countries that reported women's participation in the paid workforce as under 10 percent, half to three-quarters of the unpaid agricultural workers were women, but they were not counted as "working"—just as, in the 19th century, women who took in laundry or boarders were overlooked in the United States and Europe. In many parts of the world, women predominated in the "informal" or "underground" economy in rapidly expanding cities, selling commodities on a small scale and performing services such as laundering or watching children. Most of these transactions—and similar ones performed by men on an informal basis—were intentionally never recorded, so that the people who did them were not liable for taxes. They thus did not form part of official statistical measures but nonetheless represent the only way in which people survived. Such work "off the books" was also an important part of many European economies: Estimates from Italy suggest that the unrecorded exchange of goods and services probably equaled that of the official economy after World War II, and that women were especially likely to participate in this "black market" or "gray market" economy.

Evaluation of the gender division of labor must also take unpaid work within the household into account. Even in areas in which women made up more than half of the full-time labor force outside the household, such as the Soviet Union, women continued to do almost all the household tasks. In the Soviet Union and communist Eastern Europe, shortages in foodstuffs and in household goods such as soap meant that women had to spend hours each day (after their paid workday was done) standing in lines; because of this "second shift," women were not free to attend Communist Party meetings or to do extra work on the job that might earn them promotion. The time needed to obtain basic consumer goods was much shorter in Western Europe, so the second shift was less onerous there, but it was no less gender specific; in a 1995 survey in Germany, more than three-quarters of married men reported that they had never done the laundry, ironed, or washed a window.

Political and Legal Developments

During the first half of the 20th century, European colonial powers often attempted to impose their own views of proper gender relations on their far-flung colonies. Missionaries and governors established schools for girls that concentrated on domestic skills, teaching them to be good Christian wives for elite men; all technical training and most postprimary education was for boys. Women not attached to men, such as those who migrated to the cities, were viewed as a source of disorder, and colonial rulers joined with lineage elders in attempting to limit these women's independence by requiring new types of taxes, permits, or registration documents. Women often resisted these moves through protests and boycotts or joined with men in both local and national resistance movements against the colonial powers.

Resistance to colonialism swept Africa and Asia after World War II, and both women and men were active in all types of opposition, though men usually emerged as the official voices of the nationalist movements, and young men in particular formed the majority of all military units. (Two-thirds of the guerrillas in the Rhodesian war that ended in 1980, for example, were men under the age of 24.) Women participated in military actions (both independently and as members of guerrilla units), demonstrated for the relief of political prisoners, made speeches, and engaged in civil disobedience, boycotts, protests, and riots. In India, both women and men were imprisoned for participation in boycotts and other types of nonviolent protests against British rule in the 1930s. In the Algerian war against French rule (1954–1962), women smuggled information and bombs under their long clothing, and some were tortured or executed for their activities. In South Africa, both black and white women protested the imposition of apartheid and the forced relocation and dividing of African families.

Despite women's support of nationalist movements, and despite the support for women's issues expressed by some nationalist leaders, such as Julius Nyerere of Tanzania, women's access to formal political power continued to be limited in most postcolonial states of Africa and Asia. The few women who had high political positions were generally related to men with political power (often their daughters, such as Indira Gandhi, elected prime minister of India in 1966, and Benazir Bhutto, elected president of Pakistan in 1988), and women's concerns, such as more equitable marriage laws, were generally not a high government priority. Carmen Pereira, an independence leader who fought the Portuguese in Guinea-Bissau in the 1970s, recognized this tendency and noted that women were "fighting two colonialisms"—one of gender discrimination and one of nationalist struggle.

In some areas, the relationship between women's rights and nationalist opposition to Western political and cultural domination was the reverse of that envisioned by Pereira. Though young male nationalists were often successful at ending painful initiation rituals through which older men had held power over them, traditions that involved women were viewed positively. Opposition to the West was often described as a return to "tradition," which generally meant a greater emphasis on women's role within the household and restrictions on their education, dress, movements, and opportunities. Efforts to change marriage laws or to end practices such as female genital mutilation were denounced as Western imperialism, and women's modesty and sexual honor were linked with social stability and family loyalty. This linkage appealed to many women, particularly those who had gained little advantage from educational and economic changes, and women as well as men became exponents of "tradition."

In parts of the Islamic world, this emphasis on tradition was tied to a resurgence of religious fundamentalism and a return to Islamic law. The impact of Muslim fundamentalism on women's lives was most dramatic in the 1970s in Iran, when wearing the veil became compulsory for women, and in the 1990s in Afghanistan, when Taliban rebels closed all girls' schools and forbade women to work outside the home. As we saw in chapter 12, the links between Muslim ideas and restrictions on women are debated by scholars, but it is clear that legal distinctions based on gender continued to be very sharp in countries in which Muslim law (the *shari'a)* formed the basis of the legal system, such as Saudi Arabia and North Yemen. For example, while women could not divorce their husbands, men could divorce their wives simply by repudiating them with no explanation, a procedure that happened very frequently. (In some Arab countries, the number of divorces registered each year in the 1980s was nearly one-quarter of all marriages registered in the same year; men retained custody of the children in divorce.)

A similar disjuncture between theory and practice occurred in most communist countries during the 20th century. On the one hand, as in nationalist movements, women played a variety of roles in the communist revolutions in Russia, China, Cuba, and elsewhere, and Marxist ideology proclaimed that men and women were equal. Educational opportunities for women were vastly improved in communist countries, and women entered certain professions, such as medicine, in numbers far exceeding those in Western Europe or the United States. Women had equal rights in terms of property holding, marriage, divorce, and authority over their children, and they could be party members and officials. On the other hand, once blatant forms of oppression such as foot binding in China were ended, issues perceived as "women's issues," such as access to birth control and programs to end family violence, were not regarded as important. Almost all high political positions were held by men. The end of communism in the Soviet Union and Eastern Europe and the loosening of economic controls in China provided opportunities for some individuals, but these appear to have been shaped by existing gender structures. Men were more able to gain capital with which to make investments and develop new business enterprises; for many women, especially in Eastern Europe, the end of communism meant food shortages, an end to paid maternity leaves and government-supported day-care centers, increased street violence, and a huge growth in prostitution. Ultraconservative nationalist leaders in formerly communist countries often attributed social problems to women: Working women were held to be the cause of unemployment; complaining wives, the cause of family violence, male alcoholism, and divorce; selfish mothers, the cause of disaffected young people and gangs.

In most Western countries, the 20th century brought formal legal and political equality for men and women. The women's rights movement that began in the 19th century gained increasing adherents during the first part of the 20th century, and right after World War I, women in many Western countries, including England, the United States, and Belgium, were given the right to vote. This change was often explicitly linked to women's work for the war effort, as was the granting of women's suffrage in other European countries, such as France and Italy, during or after World War II. (Switzerland and Liechtenstein were the last European countries to give women the right to vote, in the 1970s, and the Scandinavian countries the first, in the decade preceding World War I.)

Women in South and Central America and in many other countries throughout the world also gained the vote during the 1930s to the 1950s, and throughout much of the world, women began to be elected to a few political offices and appointed to a few positions, such as judgeships. (In 1999, Kuwait was the only country that specifically limited voting to men. There were protests against this by women in Kuwait in the 1990s, because of women's active role in the Persian Gulf War. There were other countries that had no elected legislature, so that neither women nor men voted.) Though both supporters and opponents of women's suffrage expected women's voting patterns to differ sharply from those of men, in most elections they did not, and in some countries, such as Egypt, few women ac-

Feminism in the United States: Opening of the National Women's Conference in Houston in 1977. The torch had been brought by runners from Seneca Falls, New York, where the first women's rights conference had convened in 1848. Feminist author Betty Friedan is at the far right. From Linda Kerber and Jane De Hart, eds., *Women's America: Refocusing the Past* (New York: Oxford University Press, 1987). Reprinted by permission.

tually voted. After gaining suffrage, many women's groups turned their attention to other types of issues, such as educational, health, and legal reforms or world peace.

By the 1960s, women in many parts of the world were dissatisfied with the pace at which they were achieving political and legal equality, and a second-wave women's movement began, often termed the *women's liberation movement.* Women's groups pressured for an end to sex discrimination in hiring practices, pay rates, inheritance rights, and the granting of credit; they opened battered-women's shelters and rape crisis centers and pushed for abortion rights, day-care centers, university courses on women, and laws against sexual harrassment. International meetings discussing the status of women around the world were held under UN auspices in Mexico City (1975), Copenhagen (1980), Nairobi (1985), and Beijing (1995). By the early 1970s, advocates of rights for homosexuals had also mobilized, sponsoring demonstrations, political action campaigns, and various types of self-help organizations.

The reinvigorated feminist movement sparked conservative reactions in many countries, with arguments in both industrialized countries, such as Japan and the United States, and former colonies couched in terms of "tradition." Women's rights, it was argued, stood against "traditional family values" and had caused an increase in the divorce rate, the number of children born out of wedlock, family violence, and juvenile delinquency. Gay rights were even more dangerous. Such arguments were effective in stopping some legal changes—in the United States, for example, the Equal Rights Amendment was not ratified by enough states to become law, though Canada passed a similar measure in 1960 and Australia in 1984— but the movement toward greater egalitarianism in political participation, education, and employment continued. In the United States, the number of women in state legislatures quadrupled during the period 1970–1990, and the number of female lawyers and judges rose almost as much. Around the world in 1990, women held about 10 percent of the seats on national legislatures. Figures on university, seminary, and professional school attendance also showed increasing gender parity, as did participation (though not salaries) in the arts, science, the military, and athletics. In 1998, the International Olympic Committee—a body that had no female members until 1981—ruled that no new sport would be added unless it had both a men's and a women's division.

Conclusion

At the end of a century of tremendous change, it is very difficult to predict what will happen to gender structures in the coming decades. According to some measures, traditional gender arrangements, or those that are being promoted as traditional, are still firmly in place. A majority of people in India approve parent-controlled marriages. A majority of people in South America have negative views of women taking jobs outside the home. Private law that governs marriage, divorce, and inheritance has remained remarkably stable in many countries, despite sweeping political and economic changes. Nearly half the married women in West Africa live in marriages with at least one co-wife. Forced marriages continue in China and the Arab world, and dowry deaths (where husbands kill wives because of inadequate dowries) and female infanticide continue in India. In the industrialized world, occupations in which the majority of workers are women consistently pay less than occupations in which the majority of workers are men. In addition, there are trends not linked to traditional patterns that appear to be creating greater gender disparities. Poverty is becoming increasingly feminized, with the fastest-growing segment of the homeless population worldwide made up of mothers with children. Three-quarters of the world's refugees are women. The international sex trade is outpacing many other types of multinational business in levels of growth, despite the presence of sexually transmitted diseases such as AIDS among many of the world's sex workers. Economic crises and programs of debt restructuring in many countries have led to sharply decreased spending on health and education, which has a greater impact on women's lives than on men's.

Another complexity involves serious debate, outside Western Europe and the United States, about what path reform for women should take. A number of active women leaders, such as the scholar Ifi Amadiume in Nigeria, argue that Western measurements of liberation are undesirable. They contend that many traditions, such as cohesive families, protected women better than Western individualism does. They point to high levels of poverty and isolation among Western women, for example, in cases of divorce. They may want change in their own societies, but they do not necessarily accept a dominant "international feminist" model.

Apart from a few places such as Afghanistan, however, the possibilities for women at the end of the 20th century are far more similar to those of men than they were at the end of the nineteenth. In the industrialized world, though young women hesitate to call themselves feminists, many of the demands of the feminist movement are now accepted as self-evident, at least in theory: equal pay for equal work, access to education, legal equality for women and men. Throughout the world, local organizations are working toward an end to laws and practices that they regard as harmful to women and developing their own models of gender equity, many of which look different from the Western model. On a less lofty plane, though it is clear that postindustrial capitalism can coexist with many family forms, the preference of many multinational corporations for women as workers is provoking changes in hierarchical gender structures. Such changes will no doubt continue to be perceived in the 21st century by both women and men, as unsettling and as a sign of disorder; but it is hard to imagine a widespread return to laws and practices regarded as self-evident and natural just a century or even a half century ago, when maleness was a necessary attribute for diplomats, plumbers, soldiers, athletes, photographers, pilots, firefighters, and voters.

· CHAPTER 25 ·

LABOR AND LEISURE IN THE 20th CENTURY

The 20th century, especially the second half, represents a new era in the development of labor. Fundamental new trends included an explosive growth in service jobs and the transfer of manufacturing jobs from the oldest industrialized regions to what had remained, up to 1900, essentially agricultural civilizations. The pursuit of leisure changed ever more radically, with new forms of entertainment emerging and with the ever-growing commercialization of sports on a global scale. The changes were similar to those involving gender, and often interrelated.

The Spread of Industrial Work

For many work patterns, the first half of the 20th century can be seen as an extension of the late 19th century. Despite major political and military upheavals (in particular, World Wars I and II), working conditions changed little in this period, compared with the Industrial Revolution a century earlier. Western Europe and the United States continued to have the most manufacturing jobs, in both heavy industry and consumer goods, though other societies, such as Russia and Japan, were catching up. It is worth briefly comparing some of the most industrialized regions, specifically the West and the Soviet Union.

In the West, industrialization created contradictory trends in work performance. On the one hand, more machinery and new labor management methods made manual laborers work harder and faster than ever before. Factory owners invested in new machines, eventually replacing a large number of workers. Increasing mechanization enhanced the productivity of the remaining blue-collar workers.[*] The working experience changed as well; after about 1910, factories increasingly adopted the methods pioneered by Frederick W. Taylor, an American engineer. His studies analyzed the most efficient and fastest way to use human labor on the shop floor. This often meant extreme specialization of production, leading workers to perform the same task, such as welding a door on an automobile, over and over again throughout the workday. Since Taylor's methods implied little skill on part of the worker, many factory workers became interchangeable and lost whatever autonomy or need for special skills they might have possessed. Henry Ford introduced these methods in the early 20th century in his car-manufacturing plants, and eventually most factories in the West, as well as in the Soviet Union, adopted similar methods.

On the other hand, in the West workers eventually experienced a shortening of the workweek. Labor shortages that occurred during World War I gave new strength to labor unions, which were able to force employers to give their members eight-hour workweeks. In continental Western Europe, workers achieved this goal through pressuring for national legislation, rather than through industry-level strikes. In Great Britain and the United States, sporadic trade union success and, in the case of the United States, decentralized government meant that the adoption of the eight-hour workweek happened only in piecemeal fashion. Rising prosperity in the industrialized world and greater sensitivity to workers' needs—either because governments were afraid of the workers' revolutionary potential and thus tried to prevent trouble or because workers had a greater say in politics—provided for some redistribution of the great wealth accumulated by these societies.

Industrialization accelerated in Russia, though with much more state coercion than in the West. After the Russian Revolution in 1917, the new Soviet state built on patterns of industrialization that had begun in the late 19th century during the czarist regime. After 1928, Joseph Stalin reorganized the labor regime of the vast majority of Soviet citizens in Five-Year Plans that were designed to bring Russia up to the level of Western states. These plans included the urban areas as well as the countryside. In rural

---

[*] Blue-collar workers are those who work with their hands, such as factory workers; white-collar workers are those who work in offices and do administrative duties.

areas, Stalin led a campaign toward collectivization of agriculture, in which both small farms and large estates were consolidated into large, centrally managed collectives. Small farmers lost their independence, and when they resisted, as in the Ukraine, purges and outright famines in the 1930s destroyed opposition to these policies, at the cost of millions of lives. The state introduced new machinery that transformed the labor requirements of the countryside. Peasants worked just as hard as before (and perhaps harder), but now to produce for the state and its citizens, rather than marketing the goods for their own gain.

Industrialization in the communist era also changed labor in the urban areas. In certain aspects conditions improved, at least in the official legislation. Workers during the czarist period had worked up to 16 hours a day, but the Bolsheviks in 1918 decreed an eight-hour workday. In fact, labor discipline—such as coming to work on time and not drinking on the job— declined immediately after the revolution and well into the 1920s, largely because of the social and economic chaos of the period, where workers spent their "free" time hunting for scarce food. During the Stalinist era, Soviet authorities emphasized greater efficiency and productivity during the workday by rewarding those who produced more than their assigned quota. Workers who attempted to outdo their quotas were called Stakhanovites, after Alexei Stakhanov, who once dug fourteen times his quota in coal in a six-hour shift. This system did not work well in the long run, because inevitably there were bottlenecks (not everybody was able to work at the same pace), sometimes halting the whole production process for hours or days. After a period of enthusiasm for these types of labor practices, however, by the 1950s the Soviets also adopted principles of Taylorism to speed up manufacturing processes, putting factories largely on par with those in capitalist countries. As the previous chapter makes clear, however, a major difference between Soviet and Western labor systems was the much greater participation of women in the Soviet workforce.

Being of working-class origin was seen as an advantage in progressing up the Communist Party hierarchy. An elaborate social welfare system grew up, giving advantages to the working class and raising their standard of living by the 1950s to unprecedented levels. Despite often long lines, workers had access to all the basic necessities of life, with the exception of good housing. Progress made in industrializing the country came at a huge

"We Are Building Socialism." Posters were used to exhort greater production and further industrialization in Soviet Russia. From the Merrill C. Berman Collection. Reprinted by permission.

cost in terms of potential repression, as the secret police and other state security organisms brutally eliminated any vestiges of opposition. Even loyal party members lost their lives simply on the suspicion that they were disloyal to the regime.

Industrialization transformed the agricultural sector as well, and here the impact pushed beyond the world's industrial leaders. Machinery such as tractors, harvesters, and mechanical plows replaced oxen and human muscles. This trend began in the 19th century with devices such as primitive harvesters and tractors. Yet only in the 20th century did the mechanization of agriculture become important on a global scale, partly in response to the population explosion. Temperate-zone agriculture benefited the most; mechanization revolutionized the cultivation of wheat and other grain crops in North America, northern Europe, South America (in countries such as Argentina, Uruguay, and Chile), and Australia. Tropical crops were less affected by machines; sugarcane continued to be cut by hand, just as coffee beans had to be picked individually from the bushes. Machines nevertheless played some part in tropical agriculture: Factories took over sugar processing, leading to ever-larger plants. Overall, the trend toward mechanization in agriculture reduced human work in the countryside, leading to greater migration to the cities. Also, the use of expensive machines meant that corporations with considerable capital had an advantage over family farmers, who could not compete against the higher efficiencies of mechanized agriculture. Government policy in Western Europe and in North America generally favored the family farm, however, keeping the number of workers in agriculture artificially high (though falling) despite economic forces to the contrary.

A final work development emerged in the early 20th century, involving the rapid growth of the service sector. In all industrialized countries, a new group emerged during this period—the white-collar workers. These were bank employees, salesmen, and the administrative staffs for the new corporations, who worked in offices rather than in the factories or the fields. Their work rhythms were somewhat different from those of the blue-collar workers; undoubtedly, their work was less physically demanding or dangerous, and they could dress more respectably (indeed, they were required to). While white-collar workers tried hard to distinguish themselves from the manual laborers, however, many similarities existed. Both groups were tied to specific workday schedules, worked outside the home, and were closely supervised by management. Certain groups, such as secretaries, even received lower pay than their blue-collar fellow employees did. Efforts to speed the work pace were facilitated by devices such as typewriters and cash registers. White-collar workers usually thought of themselves as middle-class, and they were less likely to unionize than their blue-collar counterparts. But their work lives fit the larger industrial model.

Import-Substitution Industrialization after the Depression

The Great Depression, which began with the 1929 New York stock market crash and did not end until World War II, had a tremendous impact on labor conditions worldwide. For the first time, virtually the whole world was deeply affected by the decline of production in the industrialized countries of the West. Not only did men and women lose their jobs in the United States and in Western Europe, but available work in agricultural and mining regions declined as well with the shrinking of industrial markets. The drop in the price and demand for copper, for example, threw copper miners out of work both in Chile and in the Belgian Congo. Raw-materials producers were affected by the depression as much as, and at times even more than, the industrialized countries. Only the Soviet Union was largely untouched, as it had cut off economic ties with much of the rest of the world.

When world trade declined in the 1930s, those countries that had depended on the West for manufactured goods saw the need to produce their own whenever possible. This was the case with the more prosperous countries of Latin America, such as Brazil, Mexico, and Argentina, which had large consumer markets. Some industrialization had taken place in these countries previously, especially in the processing of raw materials for export, for instance, meatpacking in Argentina and making sacks for exporting coffee beans from Brazil. The types of jobs this activity produced were often dangerous and hours were long, though wages for manual labor in countries such as Argentina were higher than in Western Europe. Unionization lagged initially, but labor unrest was common, leading to major strikes from the early 20th century onward.

The working classes from these fledgling industries gained importance in the political sphere, and visionary politicians such as Getúlio Vargas of Brazil and Juan Perón of Argentina based their electoral strategies on appealing to them. Because of their base in the working class (without really threatening any of the other social groups), these new Latin American leaders were called *populists*. As a way of amplifying their working-class support and resolving the problem of acquiring goods previously manufactured in the industrial North Atlantic, many populist Latin American governments engaged in a policy of economic development called *import-substitution industrialization*. With the exception of Brazil, which skillfully played on United States fears about German economic penetration in order to obtain a huge American-sponsored steel mill, most of the growth occurred in light industry, such as textile manufacturing. As a result, the working class grew throughout most of Latin America, with labor unions receiving preferential treatment from governments as long as they supported the current populist administration. Living standards rose for the workers throughout the region, though at the expense of making the unions completely dependent on the populist leaders. This is only one part of the story; although the urban labor force was the fastest-growing and most dynamic sector, it is important to keep in mind that a majority of all Latin American workers until the late 20th century continued to perform the back-breaking work in the countryside, with few machines to help them.

Other regions were not able to duplicate Latin America's experience, since much of the rest of the world remained under the political hegemony of Western Europe. Africa, for example, had been carved up into various Western European colonies only in the late 19th century and was expected to contribute its raw materials to its masters. Male workers faced demanding conditions in the expanding mines, while many rural workers had to accept rigorous production quotas from estate supervisors, with little new technology to spur their efforts. India had developed some industry in the 19th century but was likewise hampered by its colonial status in the British Empire. China, which had led the world in economic innovations over many centuries, in the 1930s and 1940s could not overcome the devastation it was experiencing from the dual scourges of the Japanese invasion in the 1930s and various civil wars. Outside of Latin America, only in the Middle East, in countries such as Iran and Turkey, did import substitution policies take hold before World War II. Here, too, a growing minority of factory workers diversified the labor force.

Industrial Growth after World War II

As a result of the communist takeover in China in 1949 and the independence of India in 1947, both countries began to emphasize many of the import-substitution strategies tried earlier, with some success, in Latin America. Nevertheless, there were telling differences between the two societies. India established high tariff barriers for foreign goods and in the 1950s encouraged industrialization to cover domestic demand. As industries grew in India, the working class grew as well. India's industrialization drive did not eliminate social differences the civilization had developed in earlier centuries. Discrimination based on caste was abolished in the 1949 constitution, but workers tended to be from the lower castes, whereas managers and other white-collar workers came especially from the higher castes. Despite these problems, and in the midst of an overwhelmingly agrarian and peasant-based society, in the second half of the 20th century certain cities such as Bombay thrived as large industrial centers, with substantial working classes and an emerging professional middle class.

China's workers had a similar experience, though efforts to become essentially self-sufficient in industrial goods impacted on workers differently than in India. The Communists initially followed the Soviet model, especially in the countryside. As in Russia, the government consolidated landholdings into agricultural collectives, which were now supervised by state officials. Soon, however, China chose a different path of economic development. In the 1950s the principal leader of the Communist Revolution, Mao Tse-tung, proposed the Great Leap Forward to bring China into the industrial age within a short time span. Rather than building huge factories in cities, on the Soviet model, Mao proposed a more decentralized and rural approach. He encouraged peasants to build small foundries in their backyards, producing crude pig iron instead of big steel mills. The government mobilized the countryside, but by the 1960s it became clear that this scattered effort had fallen short. In 1965, Mao launched the Cultural Revolution, in part to cover his failings in the Great Leap Forward. Intellectuals, government workers, and all others who were considered anti-revolutionary were sent to the countryside to work in the communes. The amount of coerced labor went up considerably during this time, and the labor of common criminals and political prisoners constituted a hallmark of the communist labor system in China even at the end of the 20th century. China was able to build up an industrial base during this period, but at as high a cost, or perhaps higher, in human suffering as that in the Soviet Union a few decades earlier.

Globalization of Industry

Labor patterns underwent major changes on a global scale in the 1970s, changes that continue to affect us in the 21st century. The major transformation was the accelerated spread of factories to much of the rest of the world, away from the industrial core in the West and Japan. By the 1970s, many corporations were truly global enterprises in ways they had not been before. That is not to say that multinational corporations did not exist prior to the 1970s; indeed, many of the oldest multinationals, such as trading companies and banks, had their origins in the 19th century or even earlier. Rather, the reduction of trade barriers made it easy for corporations to establish factories where labor was the cheapest, without much consideration of national boundaries. This was possible as, slowly but surely, international trade pacts such as GATT (General Agreement on Tariffs and Trade—now the WTO or World Trade Organization) facilitated economic access between countries. This trend accelerated in the 1980s and 1990s with the disappearance of the Soviet bloc, producing a largely integrated world economic system with profound implications for work in both industrial and partially industrialized regions of the world.

The loosening of worldwide trade restrictions brought about the dispersal of factories throughout the world. At first textile manufacturing, an industry relatively easy to set up anywhere and with high labor costs, left the industrial core to countries previously not industrialized, where low wages predominated. Blue jeans, tennis shoes, toys, and shirts were assembled in countries such as Malaysia and Mexico, where a largely female workforce could be paid a fraction of wages standard in the United States, Japan, and Western Europe. Other basic industries, such as steel, began to leave the West. Steel production thrived in modern plants in low-cost

Brazil and Mexico, and companies there could easily underbid decrepit World War I–era steel plants in Pennsylvania or the British Midlands. By the 1980s, many complex products were not manufactured just in one country; rather, companies brought raw materials and parts from throughout the world to one location and then assembled whole products in factories with low labor costs, to be marketed in the highly industrialized world or elsewhere. This was the case with automobiles, in which an engine might be produced in Japan, though including pistons from Detroit, while the seats might be made in Malaysia, and the whole car assembled in a factory in northern Mexico.

The nature of work shifted in Western Europe and the United States as manufacturing in the old industrial core began to employ fewer people. The manufacturing that remained was highly capital intensive and specialized, with robots and other machines doing more and more of the physical labor. White-collar work, however, expanded. The service sector, ranging from flipping hamburgers at a McDonald's to providing medical care to a rapidly aging population in the Japan and the West, became by far the largest sector of the economy. In crucial areas, the spread of computers brought a quicker pace and greater regimentation to much white-collar work.

By the end of the 20th century, a new division of labor had occurred in the world economy. The original industrial economies exported their most labor-intensive industries (and often, their most polluting ones) to previously nonindustrialized regions of the world. The economies in the industrial core oriented themselves more toward controlling knowledge, through collection of royalties, holding patents, and doing research. Manufacturing jobs decreased, making it possible for uneducated workers to aspire only to low-paying service-sector jobs. For those fortunate enough to receive a good education by going to a university or technical institute, wages went up as they entered into white-collar professions such as engineering, medicine, management, teaching, and law. Less skilled white-collar workers hovered between the blue-collar and professional sectors. In turn, those areas that had lacked industries, such as Southeast Asia and some parts of Latin America, expanded their manufacturing sectors. In Latin America, these sectors included operations called *maquiladoras*, from the women who toiled at the assembly plants that dotted the desert towns along the border between the United States and Mexico. Most of the work in these new factories, run by Western or Japanese-based multinationals, involved assembly activity; it was relatively low-paying but still better than the wages available in the countryside. Unions and protest were vigorously opposed, with governments allying with employer interests. Standards of living rose in the cities but often at the expense of the quality of life, as some urban centers, such as Bangkok, Mexico City, and Shanghai, became so large and so polluted as to be virtually unmanageable. In many ways, these cities reproduced the 19th-century chaos that had occurred in cities in the West over the period of rapid growth during early industrialization, but on a much more massive level. While predominantly agricultural areas remained, the later 20th century saw the industrialization of work on a global scale.

Globalization's impact on work was supplemented by dramatic new technology, adding to new skill demands and job insecurity for many workers, particularly in the so-called advanced industrial societies. Some argued that the proliferation of the computer and information technology since the 1970s would revolutionize the workplace. Although some changes undoubtedly occurred, the hype surrounding the addition of computers had not, by the end of the 20th century, been matched in actual results. It is true that the highly industrialized world underwent extensive computerization, but while this expanded the technological gap between the West in particular and the rest of the world, the actual workday experience of most adults did not change significantly as a result of computer technology. In many ways, particularly for office workers, computers intensified the ever quicker pace and routinization of labor that had long been part of the industrialization process.

Sports and Technology: Changes in Leisure Patterns

Leisure patterns changed dramatically in the 20th century, more than in any other epoch in history. This was due to new technologies for leisure activities, the profound social revolutions of the 20th century (including urbanization), and the exaltation of sports and entertainment media on a global level. Leisure activities also became more secular, reflecting cultural change, with religious festivals continuing to lose importance. Two other factors were crucial: First, commercial companies and many governments sought to promote new leisure interests, in order to sell products and win loyalties. Second, changes in work left many people eager for excitement and escapism, though some analysts wonder if the leisure forms prevalent at the end of the 20th century really compensated for pervasive work routines.

The amount of formal leisure time expanded throughout the world in the 20th century. This trend was most marked in the old industrial regions. Factory and office workers throughout the world gained more recreational time than large numbers had enjoyed since before the advent of agriculture. After World War I, the concept of paid vacation time became standard, though the amount of the allocation varied considerably among civilizations. In the West, paid vacations expanded for all classes by the 1920s, though there were important differences among countries. Western European workers enjoyed much longer vacations by the mid–20th century than those in the United States did—four to five weeks instead of two. In Russia, the number of rest days was relatively small, and it decreased after the Bolshevik Revolution because the authorities recognized fewer religious holidays. In Japan, many office workers had the legal right to take between 6 and 20 days off but refused to do so, because it would look bad to their fellow workers.

Industrial technologies made their mark on leisure activities beyond the transportation technology that underwrote vacation travel in the West. Machines became an integral part of some diversions, for example, with the introduction of car races, in which drivers pitted machines against each other. At the beginning of the century, film technology had developed to such a point that it was possible to reproduce a whole play on celluloid, permanently etching and making this type of entertainment accessible to a wide audience, with little cost to the individual. Movie industries grew up beginning after 1910 in various parts of the world, including France, Germany, and Russia and, later, India. But the one with the greatest global impact centered in Hollywood, California, which soon managed to entice directors and actors from other parts of the world to work in the United States. Other technologies affected leisure patterns as well: Beginning in the 1920s, radio became a commercial hit, and it took off when the record industry made possible the reproduction of music. Television became widely available in the West by the 1950s, and by the 1970s it had developed into a technology that provided information, propaganda, and entertainment in all but the most isolated parts of the world. Much of television became dominated by programming produced in the United States; by 1974, for example, 90 percent of all television time in Thailand was devoted to American-generated programming.

All of these technologies that made possible the massive reproduction of sight and sound bound the world together in profound ways, but they also pulled it apart. On the one hand, people worldwide began to share certain entertainments, such as Hollywood movies that were seen in theaters around the globe or records, and later compact discs, that played youth music over sound machines and radio stations throughout the world. In fact, in the late 20th century, television viewing took the largest amount of time of any leisure activity in countries as diverse as Japan, the United States, Poland, and Brazil. By the 1960s, important sports events such as the Olympic Games and the World Cup soccer matches became shared experiences throughout the world through the medium of television. On the other hand, entering a darkened theater or listening at home to music had a profoundly atomizing effect. A new trend at the very end of the 20th century, the proliferation of computer games, individualized entertainment even more. Communal festivals lost importance. Certain sporting events in large stadiums still brought people together amid excited team loyalties, but the focus was generally on the athletes on the field, rather than on socializing, and most leisure interaction was limited to small groups of friends.

The consumption of music, which, through recordings, now did not require the physical presence of musicians, became mainly an individual activity, in which people could listen to their choice of music in the privacy of their homes. With the advent of rock and roll in the 1950s, music also began, for the first time, to divide generations along the lines of musical taste. In the West in particular, certain types of music were produced specifically for younger age groups, who gloried in the disapproval of parents and other adults. (Such popular music, however, mostly produced in the United States and Western Europe—especially England—in the second half of the 20th century, did not split people along generational lines to the same extent in the rest of the world.) The recording industry also made possible the reproduction of national or regional music, though only a few non-U.S. styles, such as reggae and salsa from the Caribbean, received consistent worldwide attention.

During the 20th century, Western sports diffused throughout the world. The trend began during the late 19th century but accelerated considerably in the twentieth. The most important initial promoter of sports was Great Britain, which, by the end of the 19th century, possessed the largest colonial empire the world had ever seen. Thus sports such as soccer, cricket, and rugby were introduced by the British colonizers, though natives were usually not allowed to play with the Europeans. Cricket found its way to India, the Caribbean, and Australia in this manner. By the 20th century, as a mark of modernization, many native elites had adopted these sports as their own, and diffusion toward the lower classes began. Even regions that remained outside of the direct control of the West, such as South America, adopted Western European games as a sign of their degree of civilization (as defined by Europeans) and made them their own. This was especially the case in Latin America, where Argentina fielded respectable rugby teams and boasted soccer clubs named Newell's Old Boys and River Plate, an homage to the British merchants who had introduced these games.

Thus it was less industrialization itself than a desire to adopt modern codes, as exemplified by European and North American customs, that accounted for the adoption of many sports outside their native countries. After all, labor patterns in the Caribbean, where baseball became a popular passion, were nowhere near the rhythms of work in steel-producing Pittsburgh in the United States. Even in the Caribbean, however, there the plantation economies had brought about greater regimentation than had existed before, without industrialization per se. And, as we have seen, urbanization worldwide proceeded rapidly, providing a context for new leisure patterns. Sports were a direct outlet for a few talented individuals, an absorbing spectacle for many more.

For the most dramatic feature of modern sports was the rise of spectatorship, first in the West and then, slowly, elsewhere in the world. To be sure, the ancient Romans had their circuses and chariot races, where many watched and few participated. Village wrestling matches and the famous cockfights of Southeast Asia had emphasized often enthusiastic spectatorship and gambling. But now the scale, availability, and importance of sports enthusiasms all increased, as the new word *fan*, short for *fanatic*, suggested in the United States around 1900. By the late 19th century, the organization of professional sports teams began a trend where much larger numbers of people merely watched the athletic performance of others than played themselves. New communications technologies such as newspapers and the telegraph, as well as rising literacy levels in the West, facilitated spectatorship. It was now easy to chart your team's progress in cities far away and to measure that of other teams as well. The advent of radio and then television, where one could follow a game played at the other end of a continent, accentuated this trend even among less literate populations.

As with movies, the United States took a considerable lead in sports professionalization and spectatorship, particularly after World War II. Basketball and, to a lesser extent, American football became more popular through television, the first as both a spectator and participant sport, the second mainly as a spectator pastime. The most important worldwide sport, however, remained soccer, a sport much less popular in the United States than in most other countries throughout the world. More spectators see the World Cup, in which national soccer teams throughout the globe compete against each other, than are drawn to any other event, including the Olympics.

Despite the international leisure trends that tend to make the world more similar, significant differences still exist across civilizations. A good example is India. The Indian film industry is the largest in the world, cranking out more (and longer) films a year than the United States. These remain very popular in the subcontinent, though they so far have had limited appeal in the rest of the world. Thus, the Indians have adopted the new medium, but without importing many ideas or themes from the West. Also, Indian society has not emphasized sports to the degree that is common in the rest of the world. A different mix of leisure pursuits thus continues to exist across societies.

Yet the dominant leisure patterns of the industrial societies continue to gain ground worldwide. The results are widely debated, on various levels. Members of elites question mass taste. This was a common theme in the West in the 1920s, when mass audiences began to dominate movie and radio fare, and it surfaced more widely after World War II. Nationalists decry commercial intrusions from the West. Scholarly debate rages: Some leisure historians, such as Foster Rhea Dulles in a classic work on American recreations, praise the rise of new games and media, noting the growing availability of free time and ostensible choice. Others disagree. Johann Huizinga, a Dutch historian, claimed in the 1930s that the play element was disappearing from leisure, as contemporary sports and games became too professional, serious, and organized. The result, in his judgment, was a narrowing of life and of creativity. More recent scholars, such as Christopher Lasch, writing about the United States, emphasize how much leisure is shallow, passive, and individualized, dulling spectators and inhibiting community cohesion without providing fulfillment. Yet is it possible to prove that activities such as television that clearly draw mass popularity are actually unsatisfying?

Conclusion

Similar basic forces reshaped both work and leisure in the 20th century. New global companies promoted factory work patterns in virtually every society, and also the new media fare—the commercialized films, TV shows, and even amusement parks. Technology underwrote changes in work, such as assembly lines and computerized office complexes, and also the products and infrastructure essential for mass leisure. Both work and leisure demonstrated a new fascination with speed and record setting, from production quotas to athletic prowess. But leisure was also supposed to compensate for tensions and inadequacies at work. Certainly, the enthusiasm for Western-generated leisure forms demonstrated a desire to innovate in leisure life. Yet questions about the results persisted: Were mass-produced, increasingly homogeneous, and vicarious leisure forms adequate, given the traditional expressive and community-building functions older forms of leisure had once served? Was vital regional diversity in leisure yielding to international commercial powerhouses, such as Disney? Efforts to promote different kinds of leisure standards—more participatory or more reflective of regional traditions—indicated an ongoing struggle to define what was, in fact, a very new set of human experiences in an increasingly industrial world.

EPILOGUE

Trends in 20th-century world history inevitably raise questions about where the world is heading. The future, obviously, will be shaped by the past, and particularly the recent past. Questions about ongoing trends are important, but answers that point toward the future must inevitably be tentative.

For example, the 20th century saw massive political upheavals; innovation was a fundamental theme. But decisions about what political system to adopt varied, shaped by each society's prior institutions and values and by the precise circumstances of the 20th century itself. Former colonies, for example, without recent political experience save in resistance, had different options from countries such as Japan and Russia. By the end of the 20th century, the surge of enthusiasm for democracy suggested unprecedented, though not universal, agreement on this political form—but few could be confident that this enthusiasm would persist indefinitely.

The 20th century had experienced unprecedented population growth, perhaps the most important single development of the age. By the century's end, however, the pace of growth was slowing, given widespread adoption of various new birth-control measures. Would this new trend persist, as most experts now suggested, producing world population stability by the mid-21st century? Would the world be able to absorb the new numbers generated before stabilization, in terms of resource availability, including food supply, and environmental quality? And what of ongoing disparities, as some parts of the world continued to expand far faster than others? Migration streams, legal or illegal, from crowded to less crowded areas were almost certain to continue; what was not clear was the level of tension that population disparities would bring. Another set of concerns involved possible new epidemic diseases. Levels of mortality from epidemics had declined sharply in world history, in some places by the 15th century, more generally in the 20th century. But new levels of crowding coupled with possible bacterial mutations in response to medicines raised the possibility of a resumption of higher death rates in the 21st century. Population issues, still fundamental to human history, thus raised a series of questions concerning the future.

One key issue in relating the world's past to its future, certainly not resolved as the world entered the 21st century, involved the balance between forces of homogenization and those of diversity. New levels of international contact were obvious. Due to growing commercial and cultural contacts, international travel, and communications technology, more people around the world shared interests than ever before. Popular icons such as Disney characters and World Cup soccer stars were far from trivial; they demonstrated widespread participation in the common consumer, sports-oriented culture. Pressures for the kinds of changes in women's rights and roles urged by Western reformers formed another example of homogenization. Most societies now allowed women to vote. Birthrate reductions reflected shared concerns by women in different regions, and they produced new opportunities for women as well, beyond family roles. Patterns of work became more similar as a growing portion of the world's population became urban, and as manufacturing spread beyond the highly industrial regions.

But differences, both new and old, loomed large as well, and many regions seemed eager to assert their particular identities. Disputes over cultural systems showed the limits to international homogenization. Among regions, but also within them, groups quarreled over the proper balance between religion and secularism: It would be hard to predict a definitive triumph from either cultural orientation in the new future. Women's conditions varied greatly, according to precise economic conditions and cultural context. While most women were gaining in the education area, the rates of change and the relationships to men's educational levels were hardly uniform. While work engagement was growing for women in some key societies, in others women seemed disproportionately relegated to traditional, rural occupations, sometimes losing ground when their opportunities were compared to men's. Work itself depended on very different levels of technology and industrialization. In many regions, the transition between agriculture and manufacturing work was just barely underway. In other areas, the big issues involved the decline of manufacturing employment in favor of service-sector, white-collar occupations, which had different educational requirements and different requirements for self-presentation than either factory or agricultural work.

The 20th century tossed up more questions for the world's future than answers. In one sense the statement is trite, true at any point in the world's past. But question marks multiply, given the host of novel developments the century has launched—developments whose future implications are particularly challenging. The world has never had so many people as the 20th century bequeathed. It has never had so many children live past infancy or such a large old-age sector. It has never had such high educational levels, particularly for women, or so much pressure for changes in the laws and ideas that apply to gender. It has never had so many people engaged in work other than agriculture, many of them living in cities of unprecedented size. It has never had so much technology and commercial attention applied to leisure and recreation. The innovation list is long, and reactions to it will enliven and bedevil the human panorama for decades to come.

FOR FURTHER READING

POPULATION/BIOLOGY

W. Alfonso, ed., *Population in an Interacting World* (1987).
J. Bongaarts, *The Fertility Impact of Family Planning Programs* (1993).
R. C. Chirimuuta and R. J. Chirimuuta, *AIDS, Africa and Racism* (1987).
Warren Dean, *With Broadaxe and Firebrand: The Destruction of the Brazilian Atlantic Forest* (1995).
Club of Rome, *Limits to Growth* (1972).
P. R. Ehrlich and A. E. Ehrlich, *The Population Explosion* (1990).
John Foster, *Economic History of the Environment* (1994).
Y. Hayami and V. W. Ruttan, *Population Growth and Agricultural Productivity* (1985).
S. Hecht and A. Cockburn, *The Fate of the Forest: Developers, Destroyers and Defenders of the Amazon* (1989).
Donald Hopsun, *Princes and Peasants: Smallpox in History* (1983).
Michelle McAlpen, *Subject to Famine: Food Crises and Economic Change in Western India* (1983).
N. Patrick Petrore and Ana Karina Galue-Peritore, *Biotechnology in Latin America* (1995).
Nicolás Sánchez-Albornoz, *The Population of Latin America: A History* (1974).
J. L. Simon, *Population Matters: People, Resources, Environment and Immigration* (1990).
B. L. Turner et al., *The Earth as Transformed by Human Action: Global and Regional Changes in the Biosphere over the Past 300 Years* (1990).
Ian Tyrrell, *True Gardens of the Gods: Californian-Australian Environmental Reform, 1860–1930* (1999).

CULTURE

Samuel Huntington et al., *The Clash of Civilizations and Remaking the World Order* (1996).
Gilles Kepel, *The Revenge of God: The Resurgence of Islam, Christianity, and Judaism in the Modern World* (1994).
M. Meisner, *Mao's China, and After: A History of the People's Republic* (1989).

Roland Penrose, *Picasso: His Life and Work* (1981).

Stephen Rees, *American Films Abroad: Hollywood's Domination of the World's Movie Screens from the 1890s to the Present* (1997).

Ronald Segal, *The Black Diaspora* (1995).

Theodore von Laue, *The World Revolution of Westernization* (1989).

STATE AND SOCIETY

Leroy A. Bennet, *International Organizations: Principles and Issues* (1988).

Thomas B. Gold, *State and Society in the Taiwan Miracle* (1986).

Kenneth Lieberthal, *Governing China: From Revolution through Reform* (1995).

Vincent Ostrom, *The Meaning of Democracy and the Vulnerability of Democracies: A Response to Tocqueville's Challenge* (1997).

Dmitri Volkogonov and Harold Shukman, *Autopsy of an Empire: The Seven Leaders Who Built the Soviet Regime* (1998).

GENDER

Ifi Amadiume, *Reinventing Africa: Matriarchy, Religion and Culture* (1997).

Rae Lesser Blumberg, ed., *Gender, Family and Economy: The Triple Overlap* (1990).

André Burguière et al., eds., *A History of the Family*, vol. 2: *The Impact of Modernity* (1996).

Lenor Masterson and Margaret Jolly, eds., *Sites of Desire, Economies of Pleasure: Sexualities in Asia and the Pacific* (1997).

Chandra Talpade Mohanty, Ann Russo, and Lourdes Torres, eds., *Third World Women and the Politics of Feminism* (1991).

Ruth Roach Pierson and Nupur Chaudhuri, eds., *Nation, Empire, Colony: Historicizing Gender and Race* (1998).

Claire Robertson and Iris Berger, *Women and Class in Africa* (1986).

Nancy Shoemaker, ed., *Negotiators of Change: Historical Perspectives on Native American Women* (1995).

Margery Wolf, *Revolution Postponed: Women in Contemporary China* (1985).

LABOR AND LEISURE

Charles Bergquist, *Labor in Latin America: Comparative Essays on Chile, Argentina, Venezuela, and Colombia* (1986).

Victor Bulmer-Thomas, *The Economic History of Latin America since Independence* (1994).

Allen Guttmann, *Sports Spectators* (1986).

David Lane, *Soviet Labour and the Ethic of Communism: Full Employment and the Labour Process in the USSR* (1987).

Christopher Lasch, *The Culture of Narcissism: American Life in an Age of Diminishing Expectations* (1979).

Alec Nove, *An Economic History of the USSR* (1969).

V. B. Singh, ed., *Economic History of India, 1857–1956* (1965).

Atsushi Ueda, ed., *The Electric Geisha: Exploring Japan's Popular Culture* (1994).

Kathryn Ward, ed., *Women Workers and Global Restructuring* (1990).

Peter Lionel Wickins, *Africa, 1880–1980: An Economic History* (2986).

INDEX

ABOUT THE AUTHORS

P A U L V . A D A M S , professor of history at Shippensburg University, has been teaching world and comparative history at freshman through graduate levels since 1985. His fields of research are historical demography and agrarian economic history in western Europe and Southeast Asia since the 17th century. He is also a practicing farmer in the northeastern United States and southern Philippines. In 1999–2000 he was a Fulbright Teaching Scholar at the University of San Carlos, Cebu City, and Far Eastern University, Manila, Philippines.

L I L Y H W A is an assistant professor teaching Chinese history and world civilizations at the University of St. Thomas at St. Paul, Minnesota. She has written articles on political ideas and government in imperial China and on Chinese women and has published many English translations of classical Chinese materials. Her current research is the political ideas and government of Emperor T'ai-tsung of the T'ang dynasty.

E R I C K D . L A N G E R is associate professor at Georgetown University. He has taught world history since 1986. His research interests concern primarily Latin American history, especially in the postindependence period.

P E T E R N . S T E A R N S is Provost of George Mason University. He has taught a freshman world history course for 15 years. His research specialty is social history, with emphasis recently on the history of emotions and body control. His book *Battleground of Desire: The Struggle for Self-Control in Modern America* appeared in 1999.

M E R R Y W I E S N E R - H A N K S is professor and chair of the Department of History at the University of Wisconsin–Milwaukee. She is the author or editor of 12 books, including *Christianity and Sexuality in the Early*

Modern World: Reforming Desire, Regulating Practice, Gender, Church and State in Early Modern Germany, Discovering the Western Past: A Look at the Evidence, Women and Gender in Early Modern Europe, and of over 40 articles on various aspects of women's lives and notions of gender in the early modern period.